BLOODY MONDAY

VOLUME 6

Ryou Ryumon
Art by Kouji Megumi

Translated by Mari Morimoto
Lettered by Karl Felton

KODANSHA
COMICS

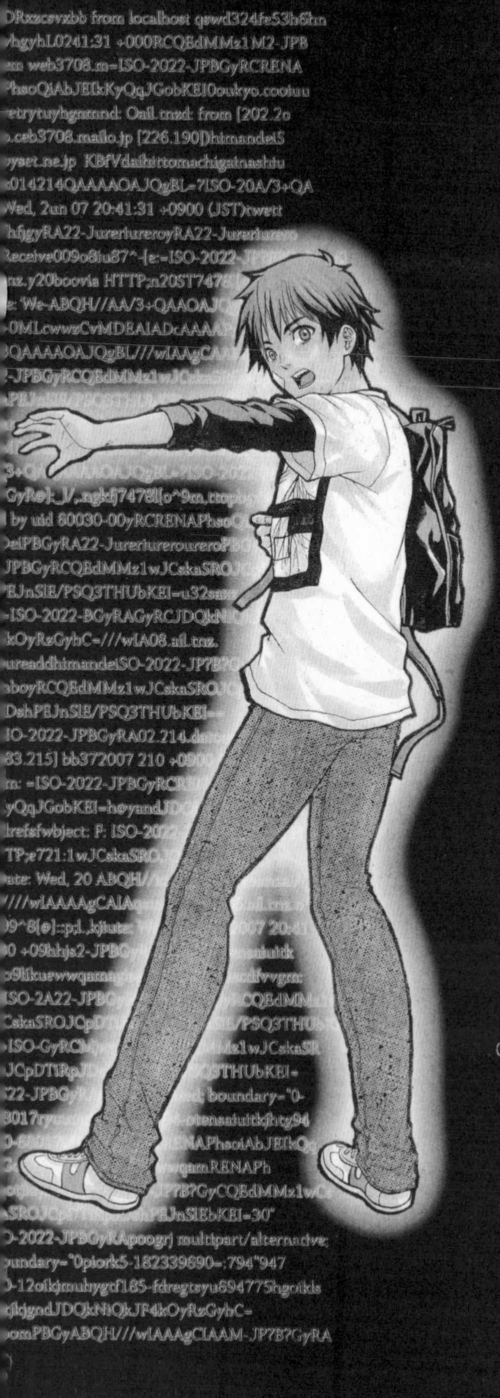

AUTHORS' NOTES

The iPhone is finally available in Japan. I'm already immensely curious how this not-just-for-work gadget will be used in this nation that posesses the world's most powerful high-speed mobile network. The brilliance of Apple's, or rather its CEO Steve Jobs' vision lies in his empathy with the human consumers that are using the machines. To aim for things that are user-friendly rather than pursue technological superiority--I think that philosophy is what Japan's mobile devices lack.

-RYUMON

Recently, more and more of the art supplies I use are no longer being manufactured. Is this part of the wave of digitalization... perhaps?... I'm a bit sad. [NOTE: Megumi's thoughts can be quite scattered.]

-MEGUMI

BLOODY MONDAY

VOLUME 6

Story by Ryou Ryumon
Art by Kouji Megumi

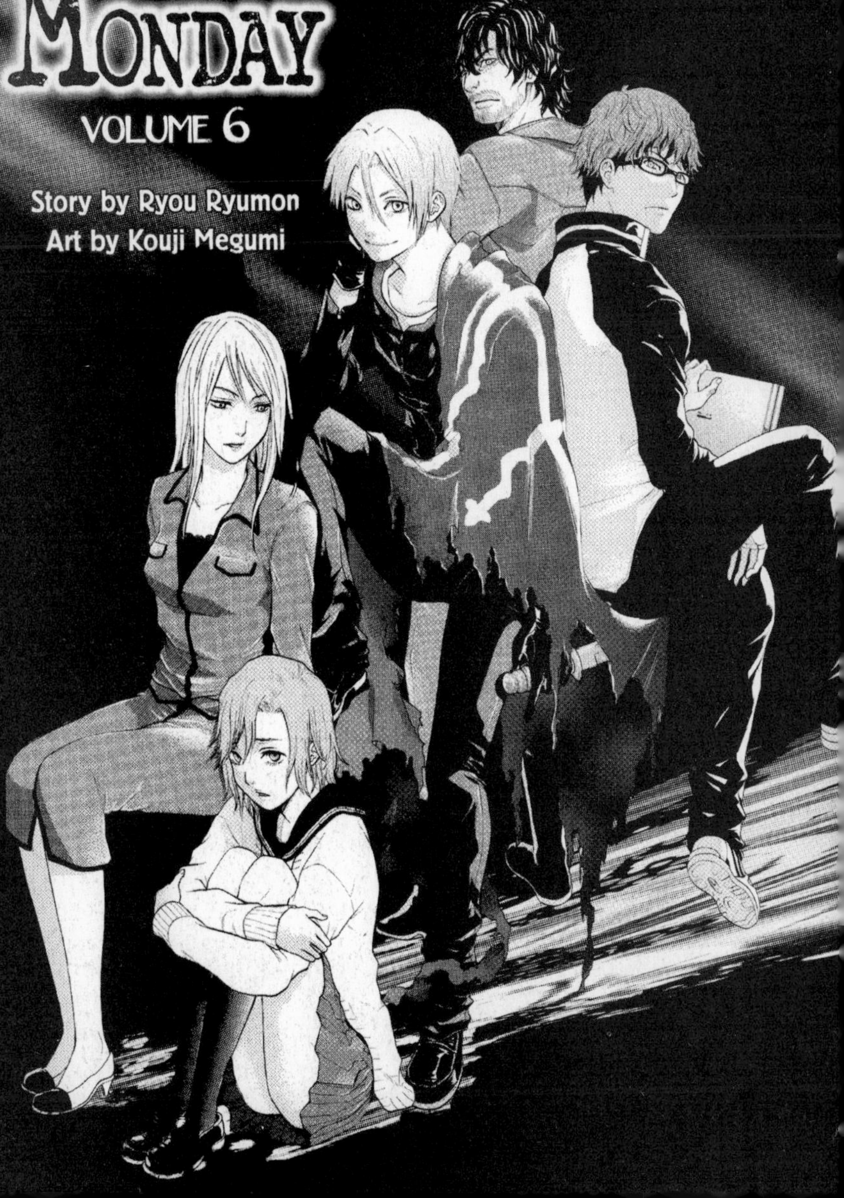

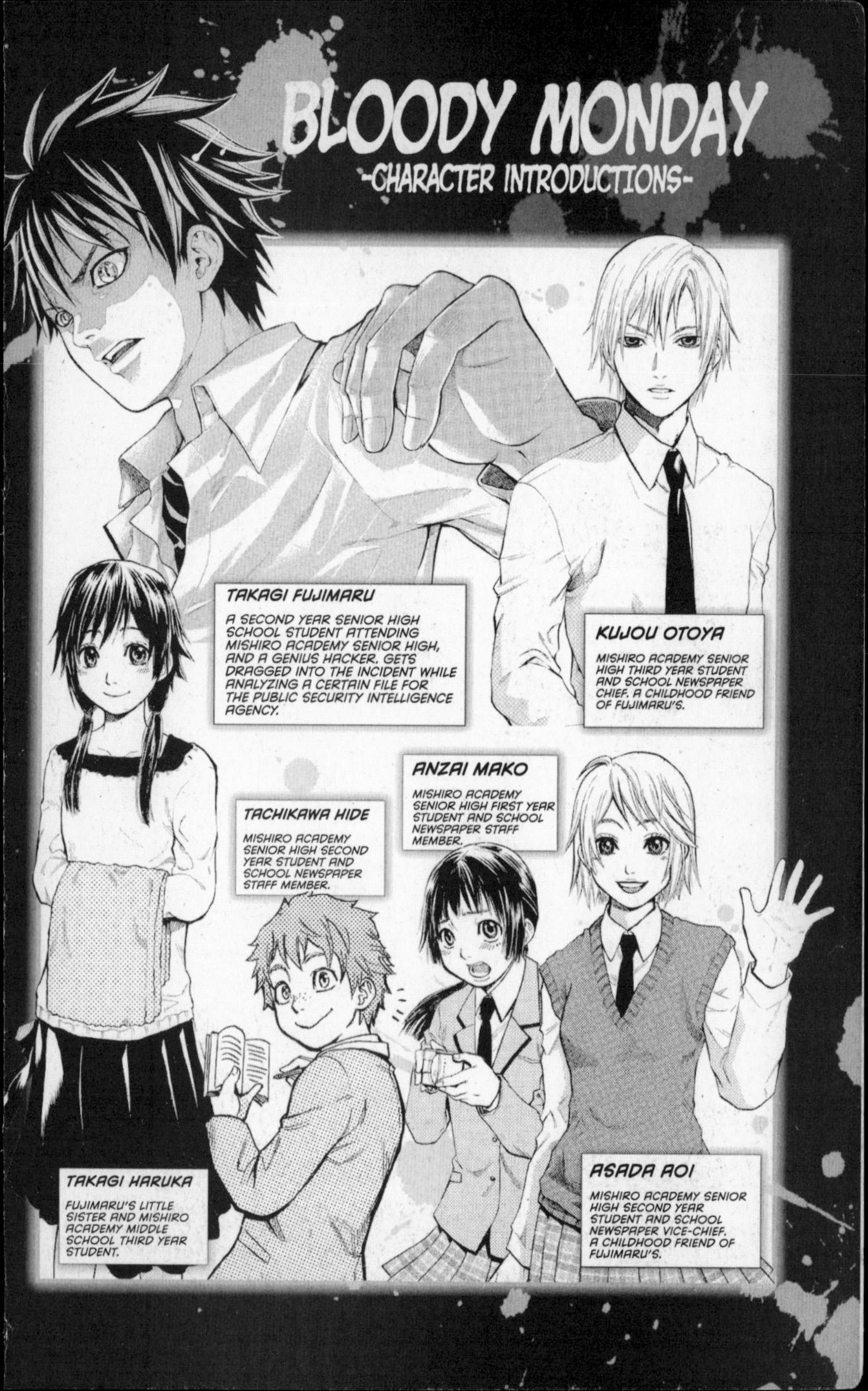
BLOODY MONDAY
-CHARACTER INTRODUCTIONS-
TAKAGI FUJIMARU
A SECOND YEAR SENIOR HIGH SCHOOL STUDENT ATTENDING MISHIRO ACADEMY SENIOR HIGH, AND A GENIUS HACKER. GETS DRAGGED INTO THE INCIDENT WHILE ANALYZING A CERTAIN FILE FOR THE PUBLIC SECURITY INTELLIGENCE AGENCY.
KUJOU OTOYA
MISHIRO ACADEMY SENIOR HIGH THIRD YEAR STUDENT AND SCHOOL NEWSPAPER CHIEF. A CHILDHOOD FRIEND OF FUJIMARU'S.
ANZAI MAKO
MISHIRO ACADEMY SENIOR HIGH FIRST YEAR STUDENT AND SCHOOL NEWSPAPER STAFF MEMBER.
TACHIKAWA HIDE
MISHIRO ACADEMY SENIOR HIGH SECOND YEAR STUDENT AND SCHOOL NEWSPAPER STAFF MEMBER.
ASADA AOI
MISHIRO ACADEMY SENIOR HIGH SECOND YEAR STUDENT AND SCHOOL NEWSPAPER VICE-CHIEF. A CHILDHOOD FRIEND OF FUJIMARU'S.
TAKAGI HARUKA
FUJIMARU'S LITTLE SISTER AND MISHIRO ACADEMY MIDDLE SCHOOL THIRD YEAR STUDENT.

J

AN OFFICER-LIKE ENTITY WITHIN THE TERRORIST ORGANIZATION.

K

THE MYSTERIOUS INDIVIDUAL WHO COMMANDS THE TERRORISTS.

ORIHARA MAYA

A TERRORIST WHO UNDERTAKES THE "BLOODY MONDAY" VIRUS PLOT UPON "K"'S ORDERS. SHE INFILTRATES MISHIRO ACADEMY IN THE GUISE OF AN INSTRUCTOR.

MUNAKATA HITOMI

AN OLD FRIEND OF RYUNOSUKE'S AND A RESEARCHER AT THE BIOCHEMICAL RESEARCH INSTITUTE.

THIRD-i

HOSHO SAYURI

MEMBER OF THIRD-i. SHE IS DISCOVERED TO BE A MEMBER OF THE TERRORIST ORGANIZATION, AND DIES.

KANO IKUMA

MEMBER OF THIRD-i. PART OF TEAM TAKAGI.

TAKAGI RYUNOSUKE

FUJIMARU'S FATHER AND DEPUTY CHIEF OF THE PUBLIC SECURITY INTELLIGENCE AGENCY, FIRST INTELLIGENCE DEPARTMENT, THIRD DIVISION (A.K.A. "THIRD-i"). WOUNDED, HAVING BEEN SHOT BY THE TERRORIST ORGANIZATION.

SAWAKITA MIKI

MEMBER OF THIRD-i.

MORIMI SATSUKI

MEMBER OF THIRD-i. INFECTED WITH A VIRUS ON THE B3 LEVEL OF THIRD-i.

YAJIMA YUGO

MEMBER OF THIRD-i. INFECTED WITH A VIRUS ON THE B3 LEVEL OF THIRD-i.

KIRISHIMA GORO

MEMBER OF THIRD-i. PART OF TEAM TAKAGI.

The Story So Far:

Fujimaru, caught up in a virus terrorist plot called "Bloody Monday" led by "K" and "J" from religious group, is now held in captivity by Maya.

He negotiated with Maya and managed to meet up with "J", hoping to capture him, but "J" outwitted Fujimaru at the end.

And then, "J" and his associates attempted to collect back the original chip of "Christmas Assassination", they sprayed a deadly virus "BLOODY-X" on the third basement level at "THIRD-i"!!

Contents

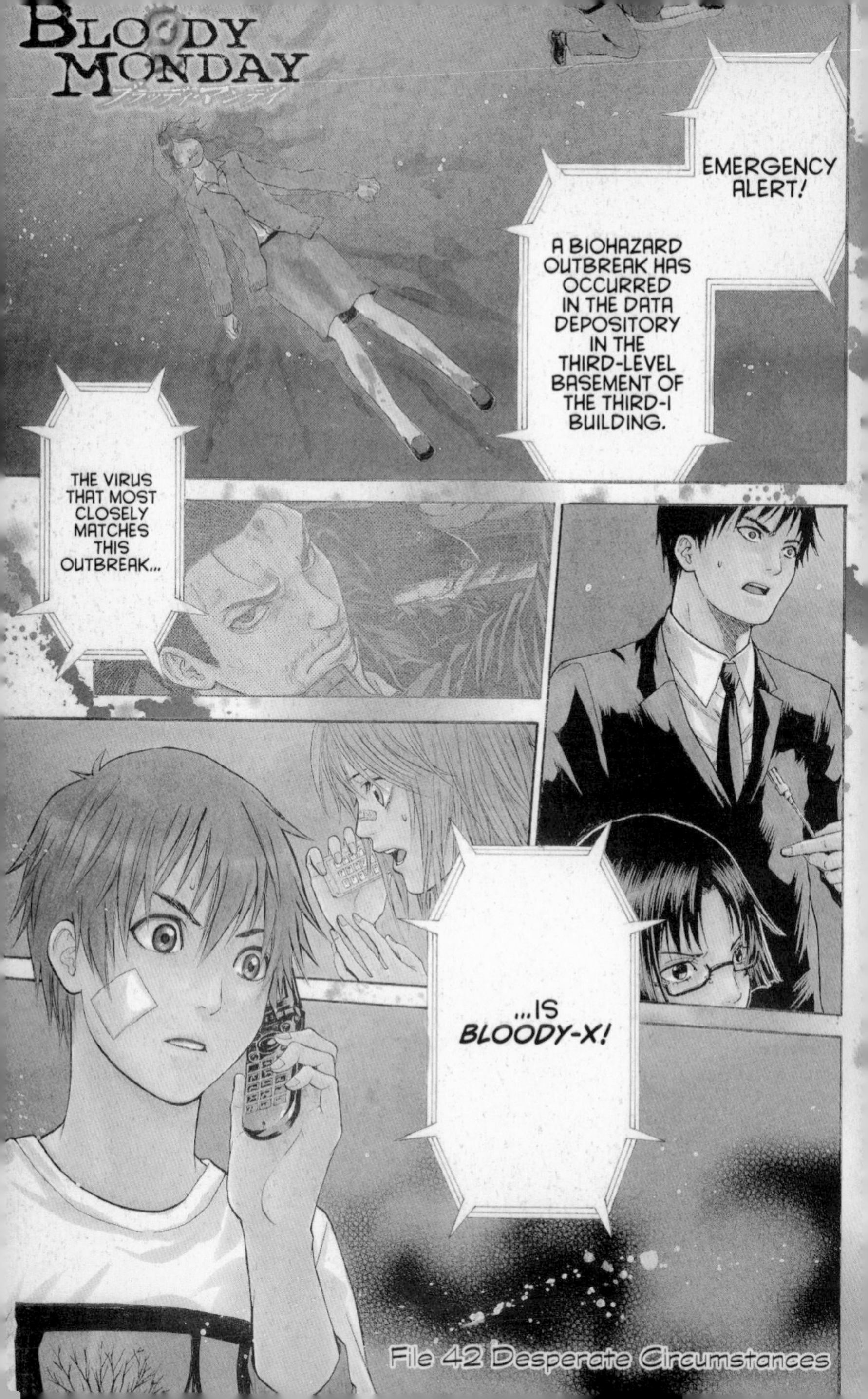
BLOODY MONDAY
ブラッディ・マンデイ
EMERGENCY ALERT!
A BIOHAZARD OUTBREAK HAS OCCURRED IN THE DATA DEPOSITORY IN THE THIRD-LEVEL BASEMENT OF THE THIRD-I BUILDING.
THE VIRUS THAT MOST CLOSELY MATCHES THIS OUTBREAK...
...IS *BLOODY-X!*
File 42 Desperate Circumstances

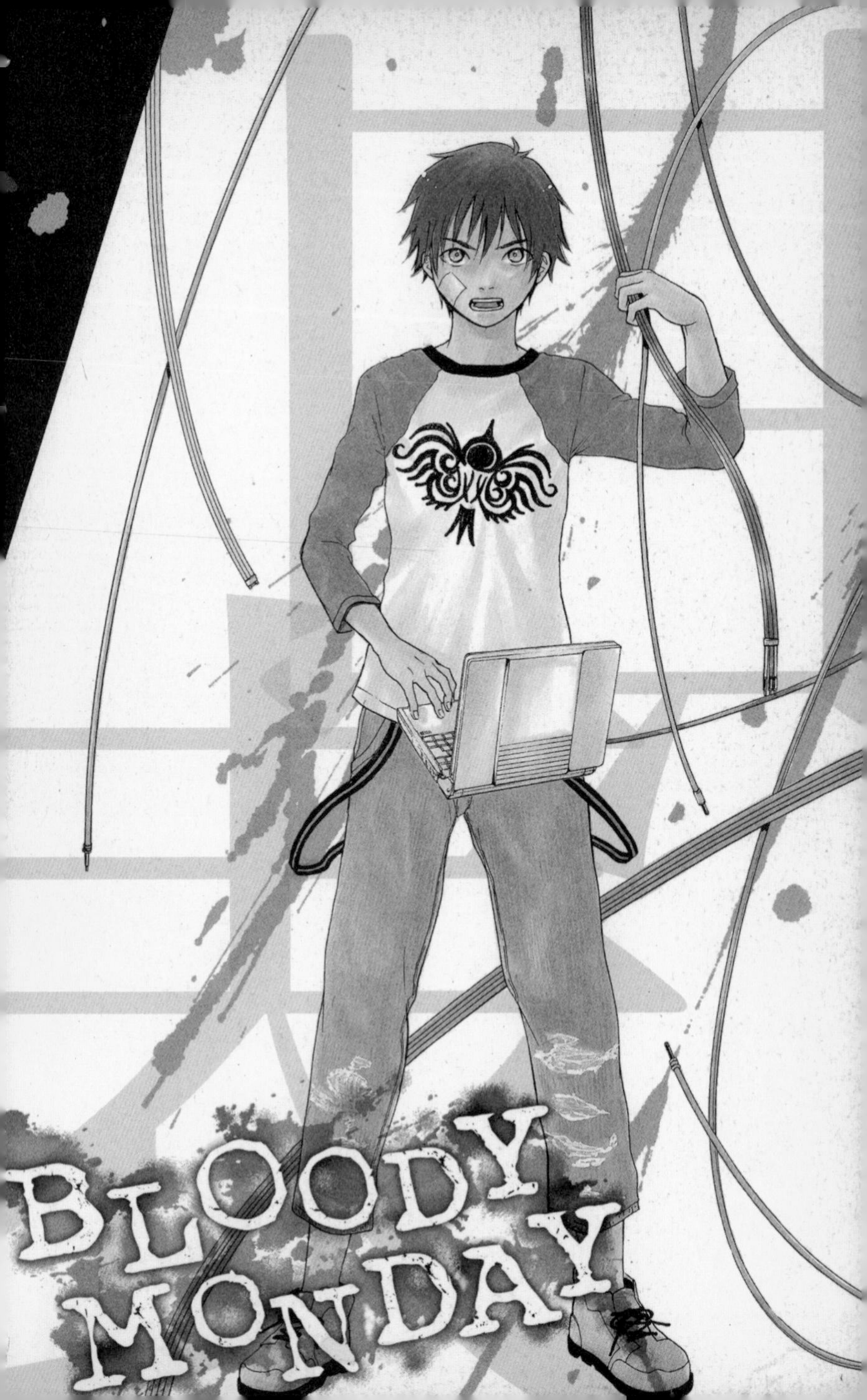
BLOODY
MONDAY

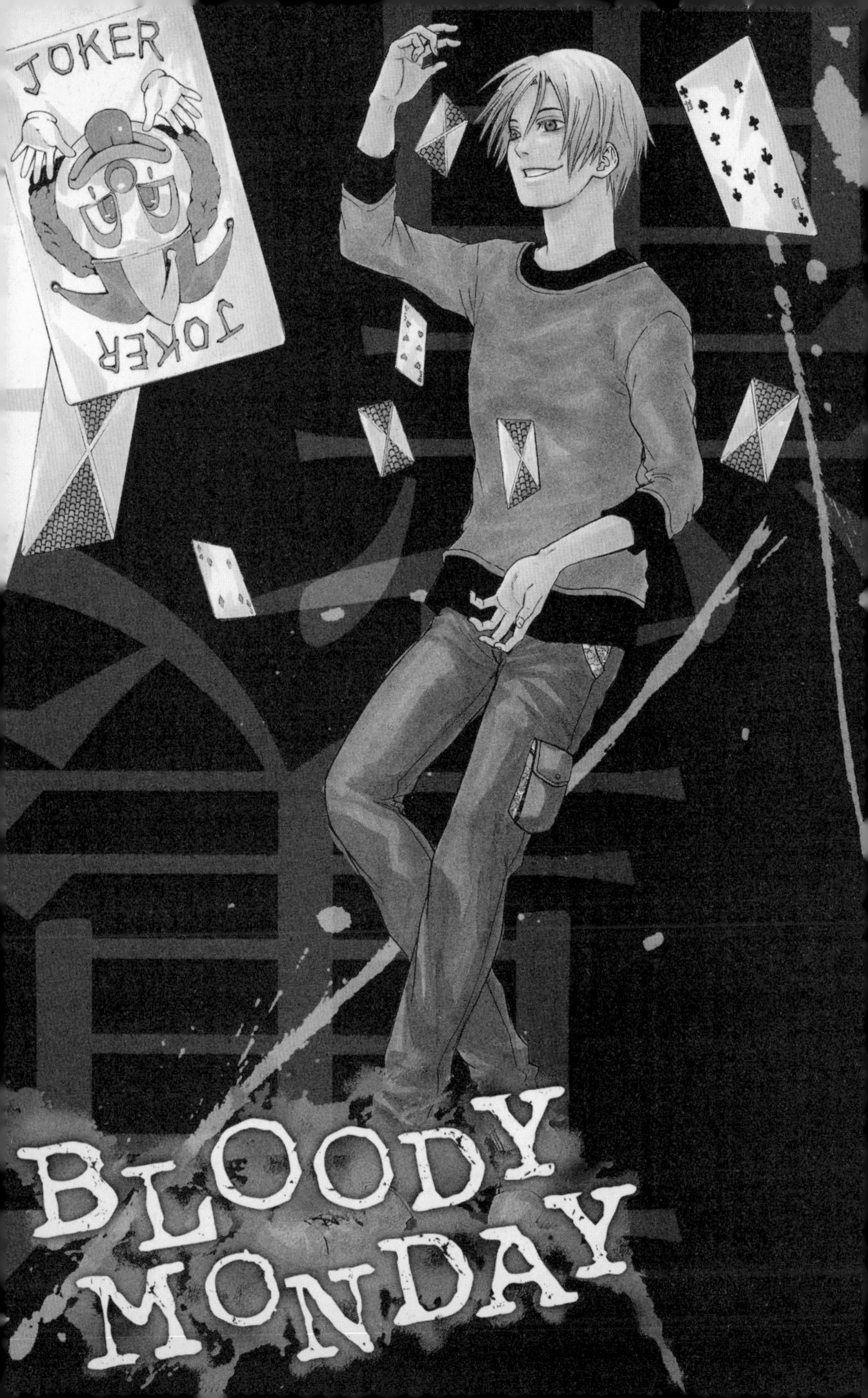
JOKER
JOKER
BLOODY
MONDAY

BLOODY MONDAY
– GLOSSARY OF TERMS · LIST 12 –

Upload P53
To transfer data saved on a client computer onto a host computer via the internet or other method. The inverse is called "download".

(Development) Code name P54
An alias or transient name used to refer to a product under development, mainly by the developing company (or individual). Oftentimes a different, official name is utilized when the product goes to market.

Spam mail P75
Junk e-mail. Electronic mail that is widely distributed to an unspecified large number of people, without their consent, for commercial purposes.

Transmission log P98
A record of data transmitted by a (particular) computer. Contains details such as the time and date stamp of the transmission or other computer operations.

Beta version P142
A test version of software, etc. that is still under development.

THE RECIPIENT ADDRESS HAD BEEN OBSCURED IN HIS TRANSMISSION LOG.

DID YOU LEARN ANYTHING?

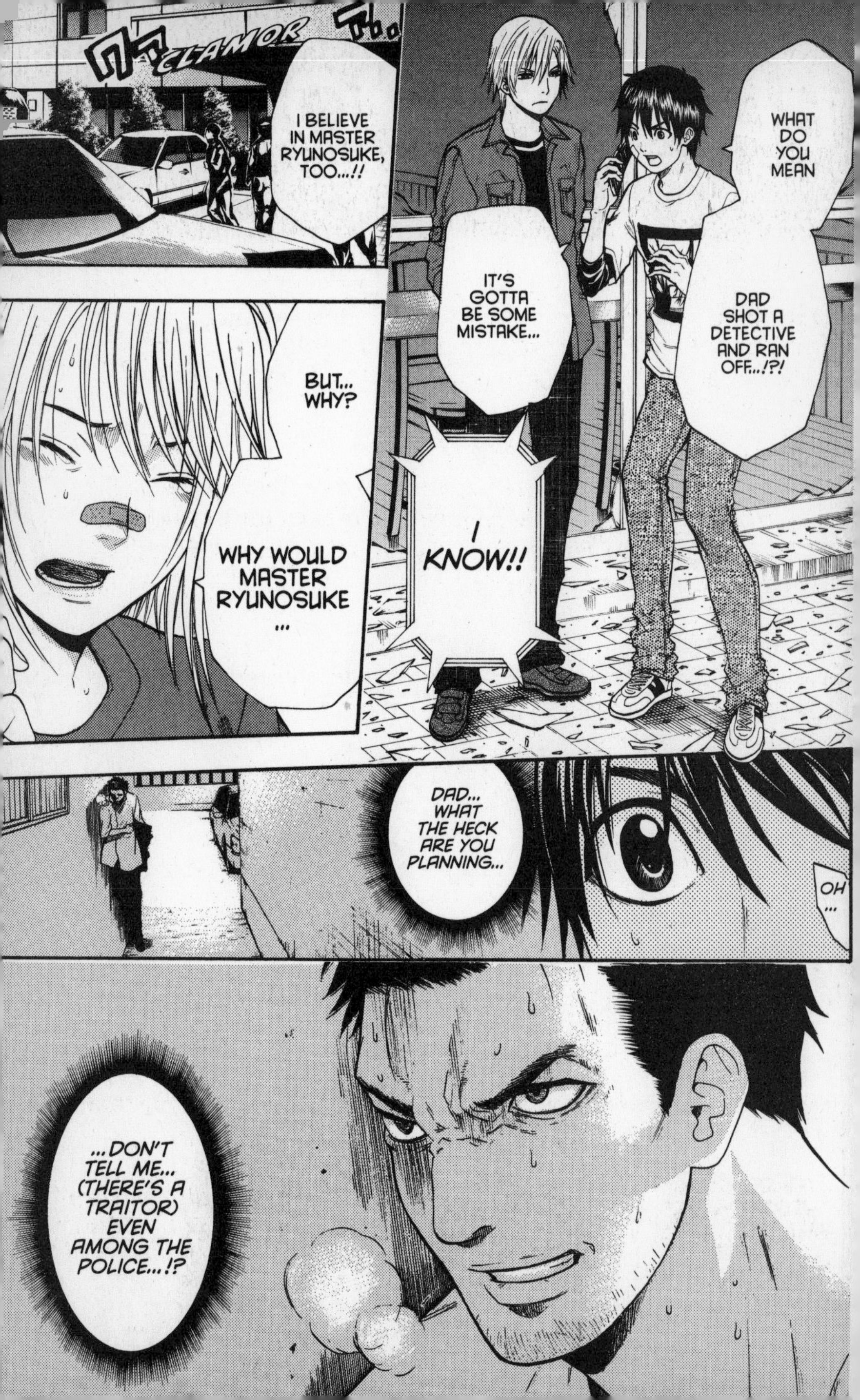
WHAT DO YOU MEAN
DAD SHOT A DETECTIVE AND RAN OFF...!?!
IT'S GOTTA BE SOME MISTAKE...
I KNOW!!
CLAMOR
I BELIEVE IN MASTER RYUNOSUKE, TOO...!!
BUT... WHY?
WHY WOULD MASTER RYUNOSUKE ...
OH ...
DAD... WHAT THE HECK ARE YOU PLANNING...
...DON'T TELL ME... (THERE'S A TRAITOR) EVEN AMONG THE POLICE...!?

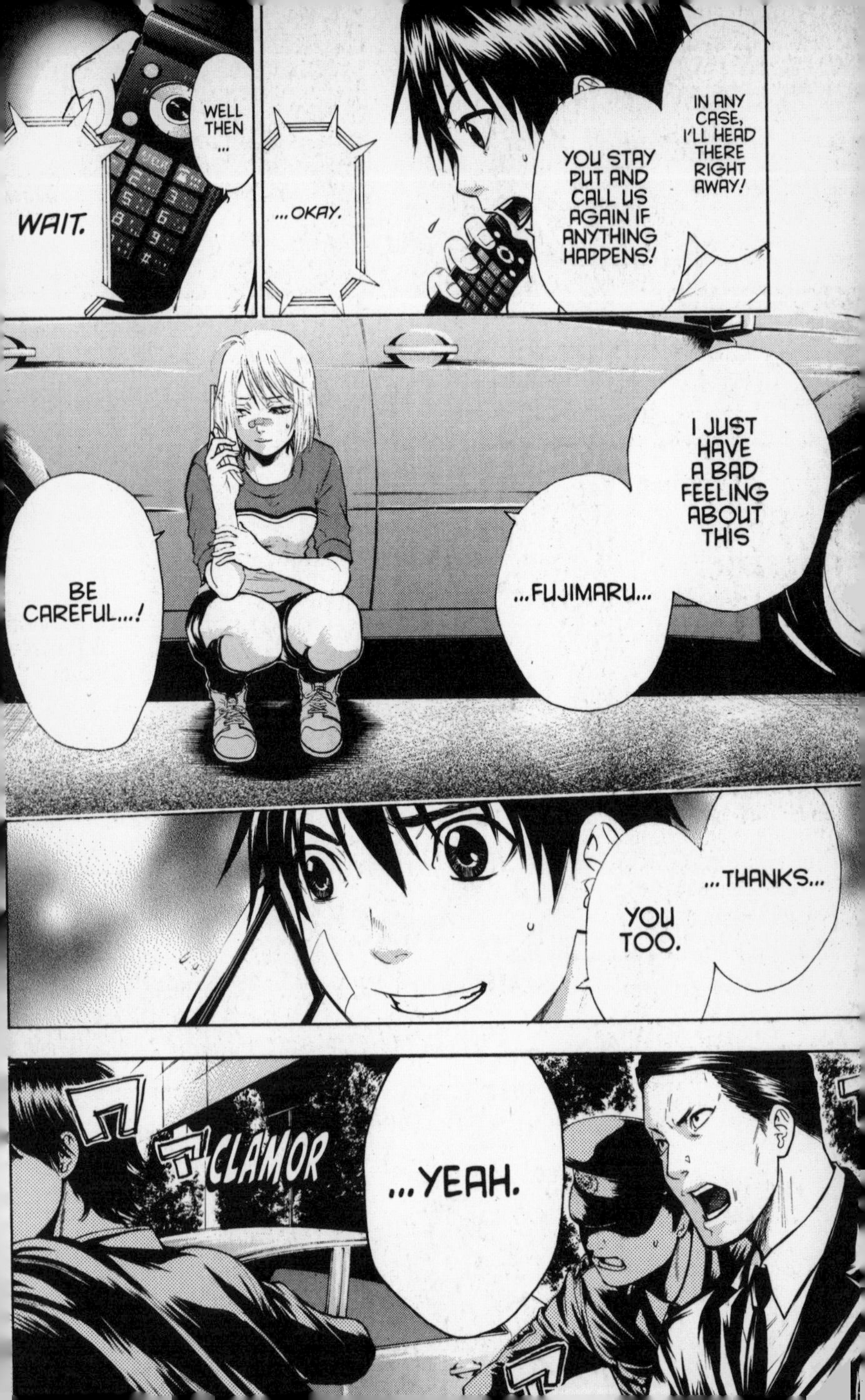
IN ANY CASE, I'LL HEAD THERE RIGHT AWAY!
YOU STAY PUT AND CALL US AGAIN IF ANYTHING HAPPENS!
...OKAY.
WELL THEN ...
WAIT.
I JUST HAVE A BAD FEELING ABOUT THIS
...FUJIMARU...
BE CAREFUL...!
...THANKS...
YOU TOO.
...YEAH.
CLAMOR

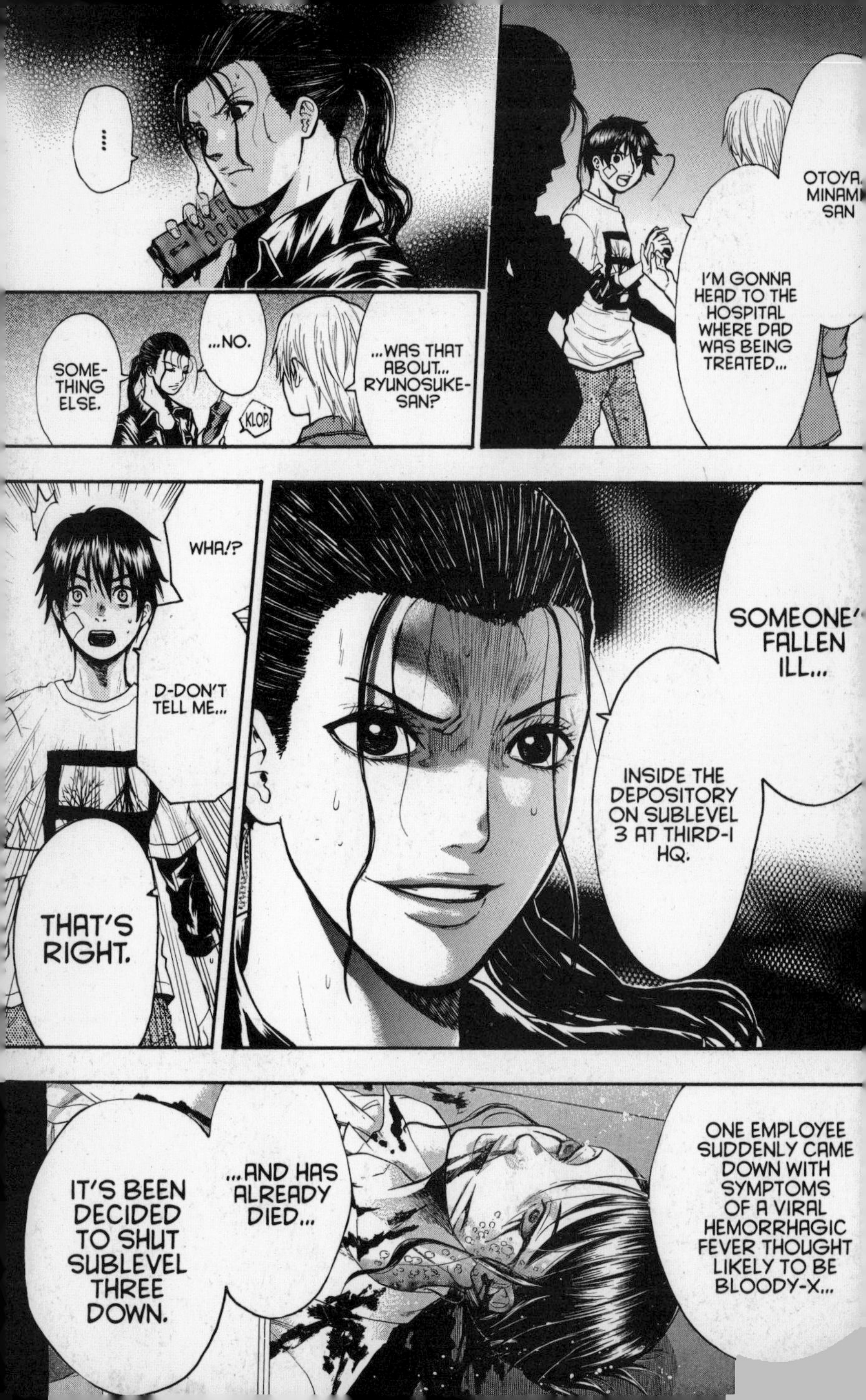
OTOYA, MINAMI SAN
I'M GONNA HEAD TO THE HOSPITAL WHERE DAD WAS BEING TREATED...
......
...WAS THAT ABOUT... RYUNOSUKE-SAN?
KLOP
...NO.
SOME-THING ELSE.
SOMEONE' FALLEN ILL...
INSIDE THE DEPOSITORY ON SUBLEVEL 3 AT THIRD-I HQ.
WHA!?
D-DON'T TELL ME...
THAT'S RIGHT.
ONE EMPLOYEE SUDDENLY CAME DOWN WITH SYMPTOMS OF A VIRAL HEMORRHAGIC FEVER THOUGHT LIKELY TO BE BLOODY-X...
...AND HAS ALREADY DIED...
IT'S BEEN DECIDED TO SHUT SUBLEVEL THREE DOWN.

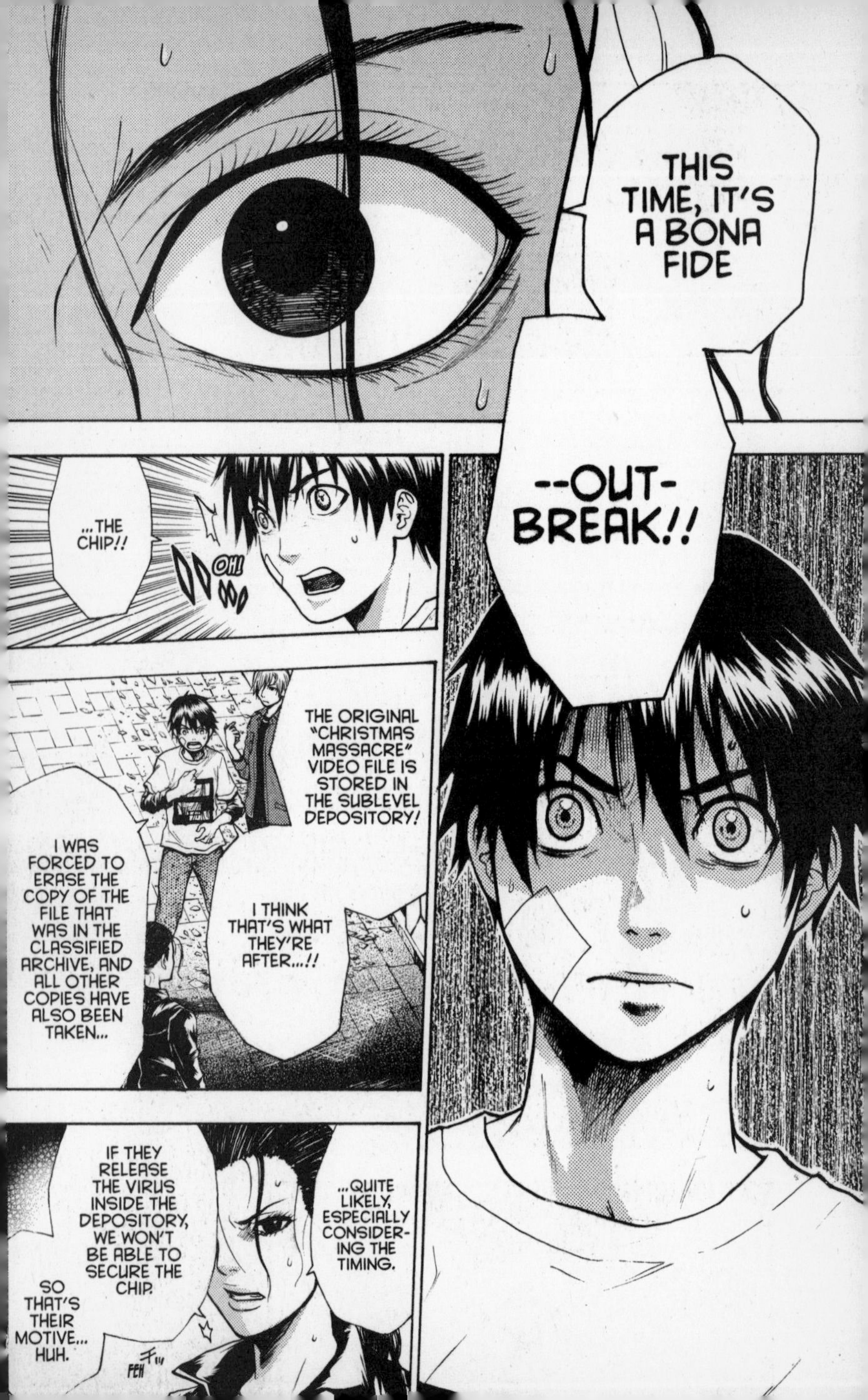
THIS TIME, IT'S A BONA FIDE
--OUT-BREAK!!
...THE CHIP!!
OH!
THE ORIGINAL "CHRISTMAS MASSACRE" VIDEO FILE IS STORED IN THE SUBLEVEL DEPOSITORY!
I THINK THAT'S WHAT THEY'RE AFTER...!!
I WAS FORCED TO ERASE THE COPY OF THE FILE THAT WAS IN THE CLASSIFIED ARCHIVE, AND ALL OTHER COPIES HAVE ALSO BEEN TAKEN...
IF THEY RELEASE THE VIRUS INSIDE THE DEPOSITORY, WE WON'T BE ABLE TO SECURE THE CHIP.
...QUITE LIKELY, ESPECIALLY CONSIDERING THE TIMING.
SO THAT'S THEIR MOTIVE... HUH.
FEH

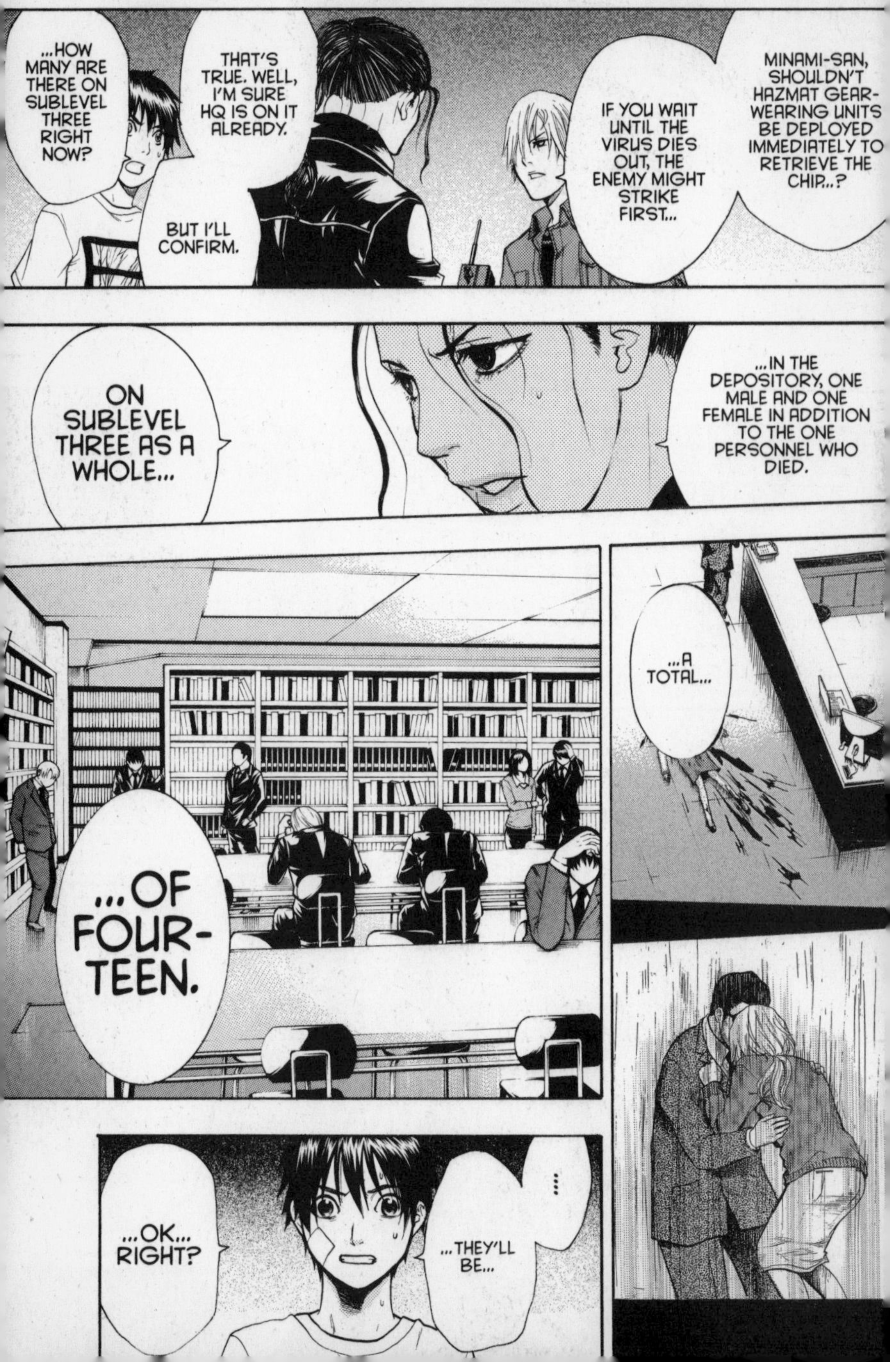
MINAMI-SAN, SHOULDN'T HAZMAT GEAR-WEARING UNITS BE DEPLOYED IMMEDIATELY TO RETRIEVE THE CHIP...?
IF YOU WAIT UNTIL THE VIRUS DIES OUT, THE ENEMY MIGHT STRIKE FIRST...
THAT'S TRUE. WELL, I'M SURE HQ IS ON IT ALREADY.
BUT I'LL CONFIRM.
...HOW MANY ARE THERE ON SUBLEVEL THREE RIGHT NOW?
...IN THE DEPOSITORY, ONE MALE AND ONE FEMALE IN ADDITION TO THE ONE PERSONNEL WHO DIED.
ON SUBLEVEL THREE AS A WHOLE...
...A TOTAL...
...OF FOUR-TEEN.
...
...THEY'LL BE...
...OK... RIGHT?

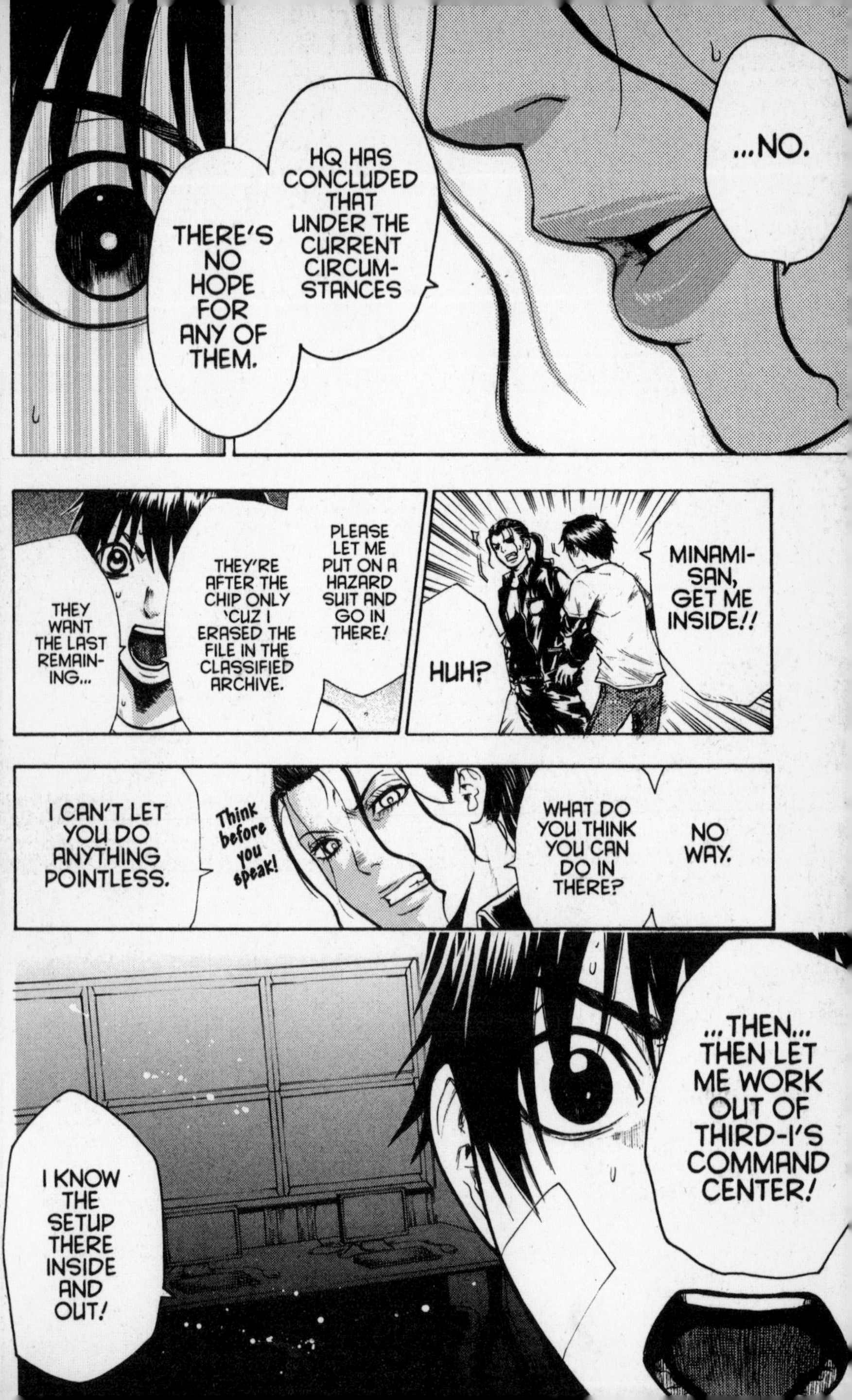
...NO.
HQ HAS CONCLUDED THAT UNDER THE CURRENT CIRCUMSTANCES
THERE'S NO HOPE FOR ANY OF THEM.
MINAMI-SAN, GET ME INSIDE!!
HUH?
PLEASE LET ME PUT ON A HAZARD SUIT AND GO IN THERE!
THEY'RE AFTER THE CHIP ONLY 'CUZ I ERASED THE FILE IN THE CLASSIFIED ARCHIVE.
THEY WANT THE LAST REMAINING...
NO WAY.
WHAT DO YOU THINK YOU CAN DO IN THERE?
Think before you speak!
I CAN'T LET YOU DO ANYTHING POINTLESS.
...THEN... THEN LET ME WORK OUT OF THIRD-I'S COMMAND CENTER!
I KNOW THE SETUP THERE INSIDE AND OUT!

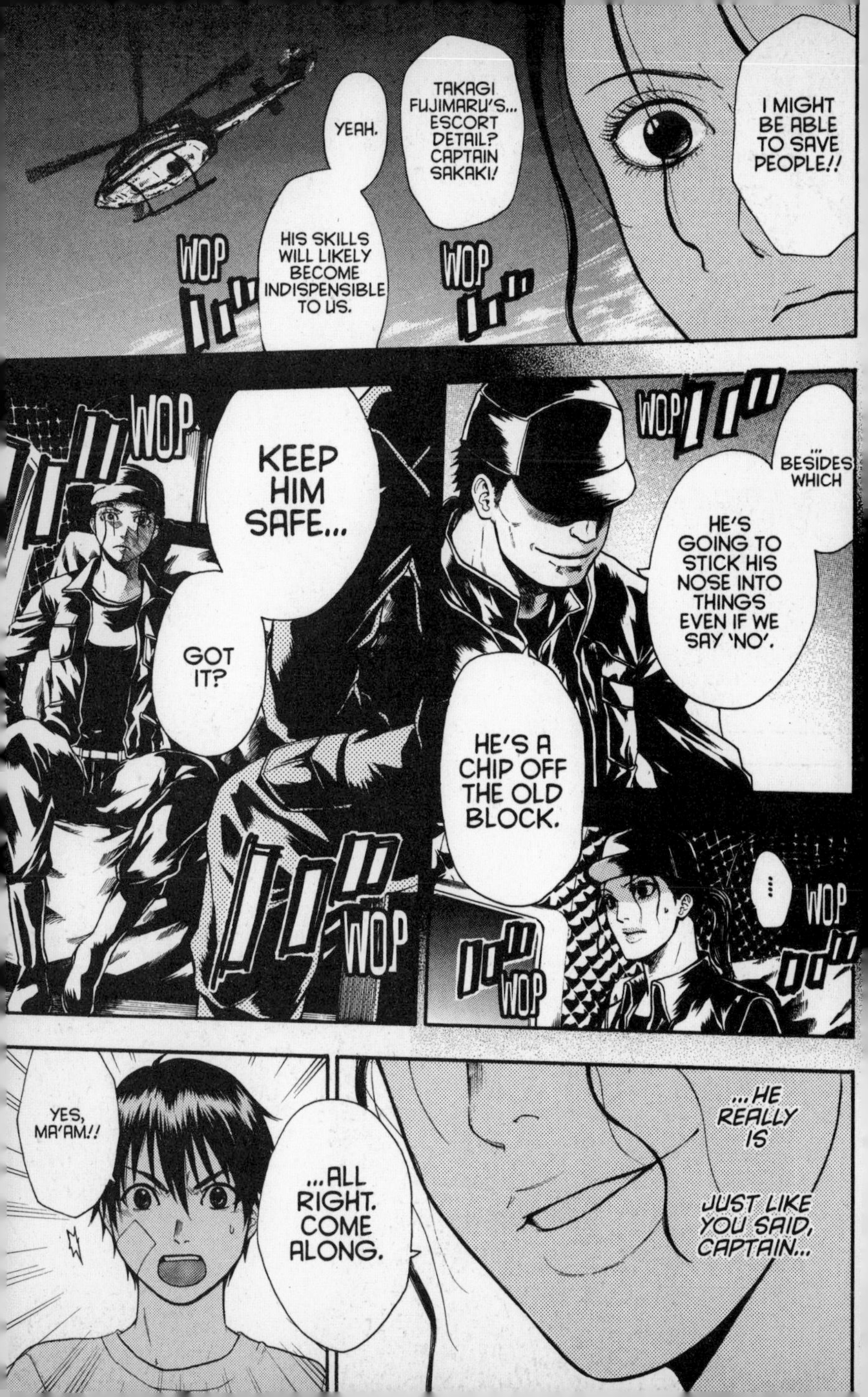
I MIGHT BE ABLE TO SAVE PEOPLE!!
TAKAGI FUJIMARU'S... ESCORT DETAIL? CAPTAIN SAKAKI!
YEAH.
WOP
HIS SKILLS WILL LIKELY BECOME INDISPENSIBLE TO US.
WOP
WOP
...BESIDES WHICH
HE'S GOING TO STICK HIS NOSE INTO THINGS EVEN IF WE SAY 'NO'.
HE'S A CHIP OFF THE OLD BLOCK.
...
WOP
WOP
WOP
KEEP HIM SAFE...
GOT IT?
WOP
...HE REALLY IS
JUST LIKE YOU SAID, CAPTAIN...
...ALL RIGHT. COME ALONG.
YES, MA'AM!!

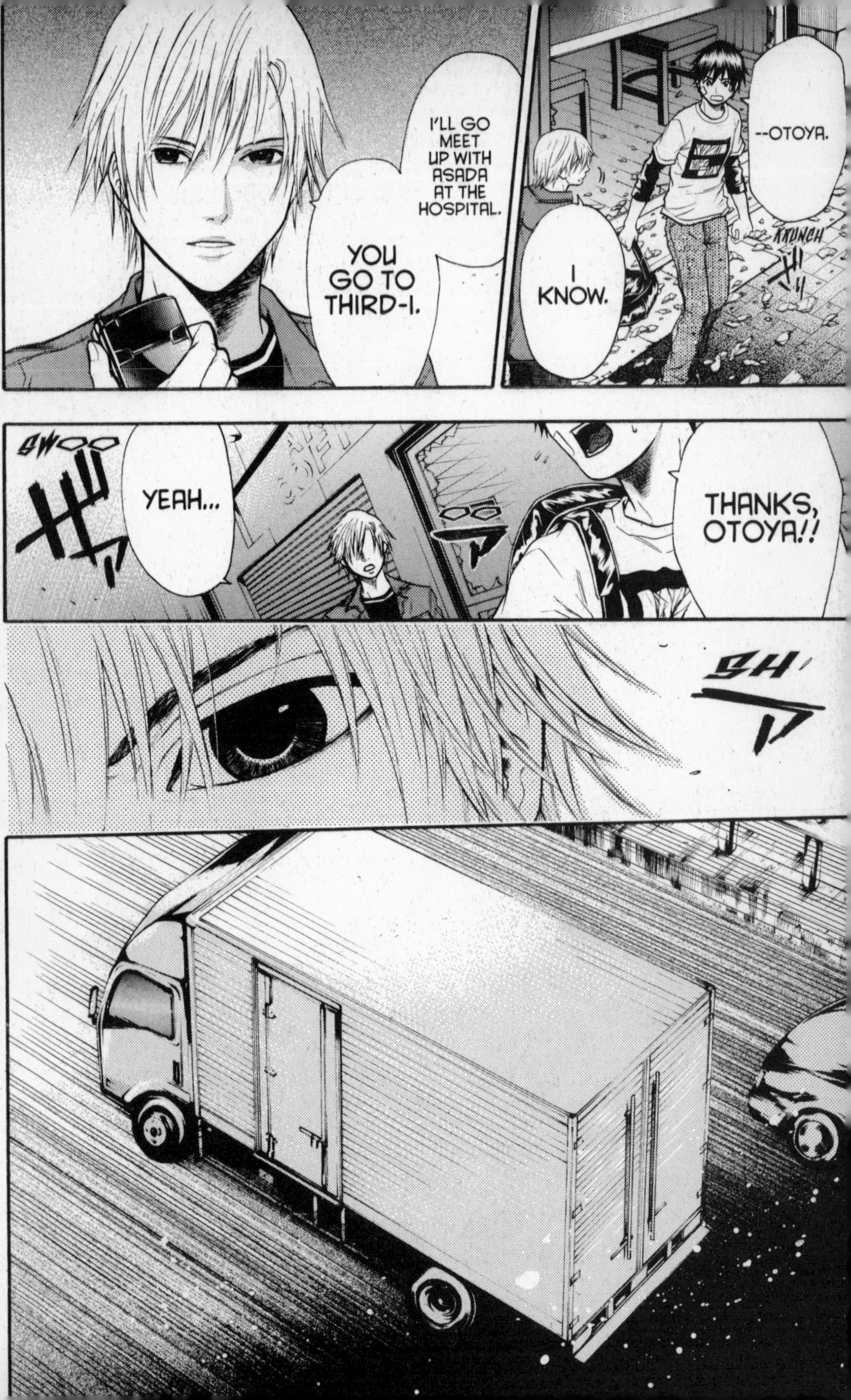
--OTOYA.
KRUNCH
I KNOW.
I'LL GO MEET UP WITH ASADA AT THE HOSPITAL.
YOU GO TO THIRD-I.
THANKS, OTOYA!!
YEAH...
SWOO
SH

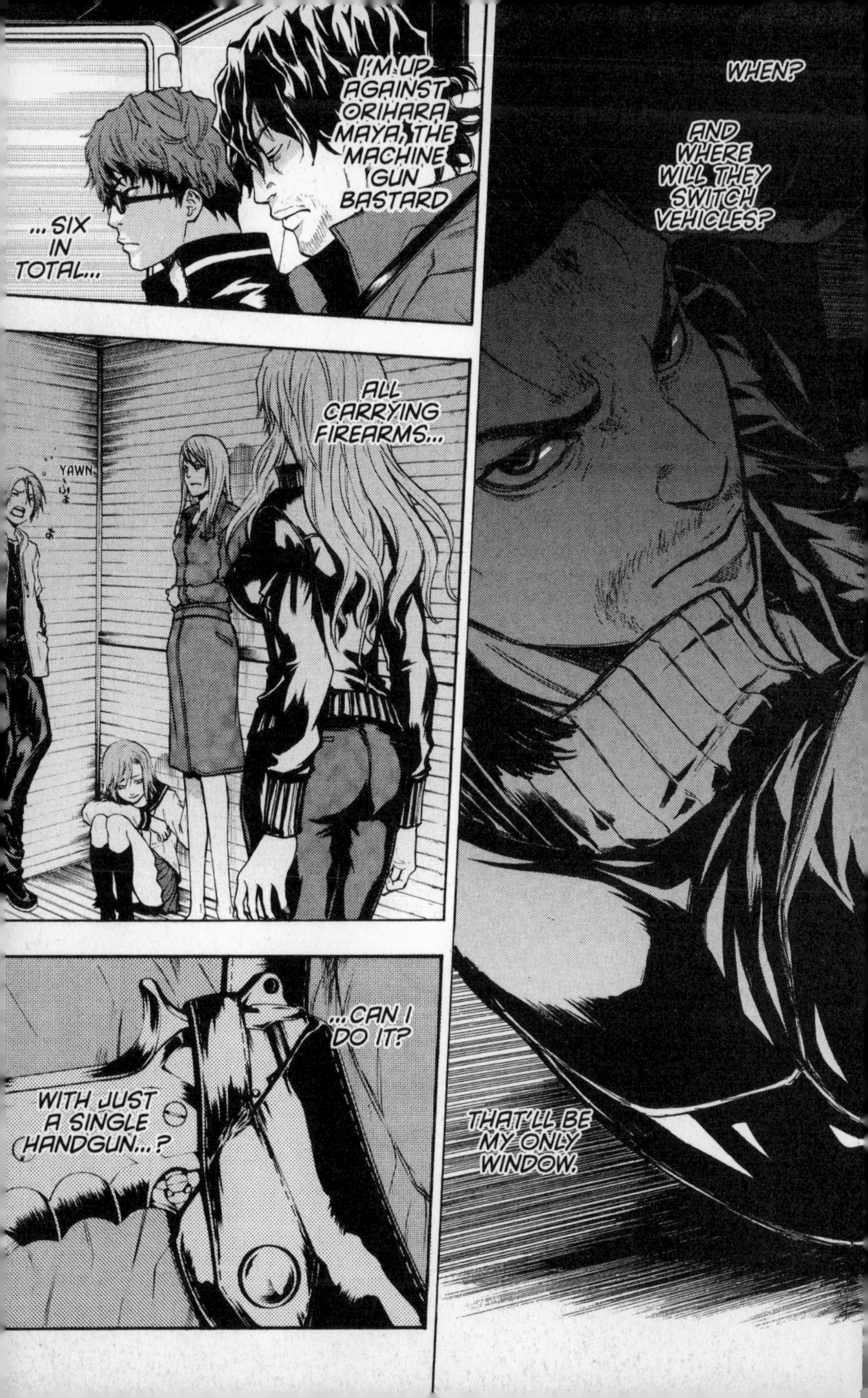
WHEN?
AND WHERE WILL THEY SWITCH VEHICLES?
THAT'LL BE MY ONLY WINDOW.
I'M UP AGAINST ORIHARA MAYA, THE MACHINE GUN BASTARD
...SIX IN TOTAL...
ALL CARRYING FIREARMS...
YAWN
...CAN I DO IT?
WITH JUST A SINGLE HANDGUN...?

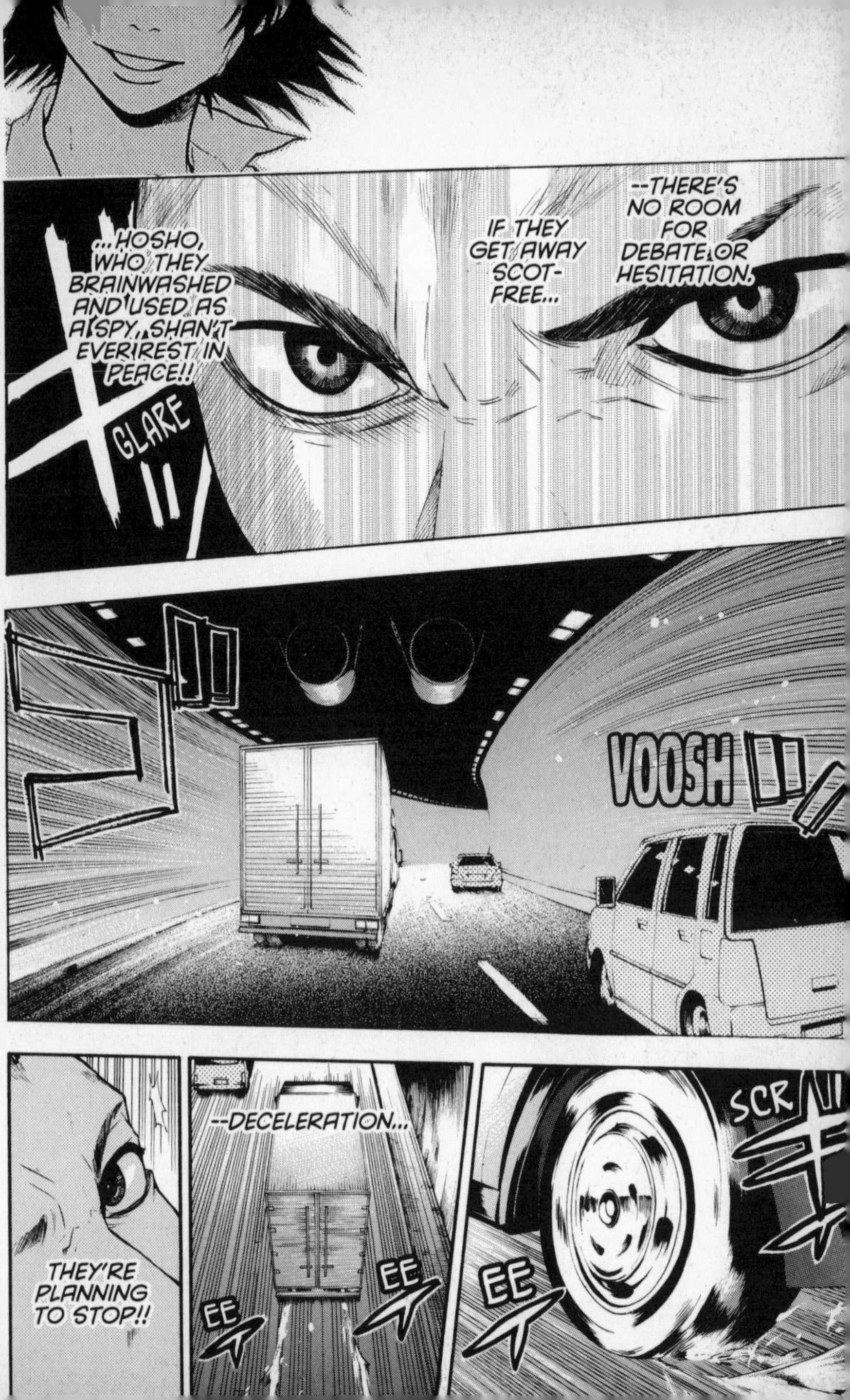
--THERE'S NO ROOM FOR DEBATE OR HESITATION.
IF THEY GET AWAY SCOT-FREE...
...HOSHO, WHO THEY BRAINWASHED AND USED AS A SPY, SHAN'T EVER REST IN PEACE!!
GLARE
VOOSH
SCR
EE
--DECELERATION...
EE
EE
THEY'RE PLANNING TO STOP!!

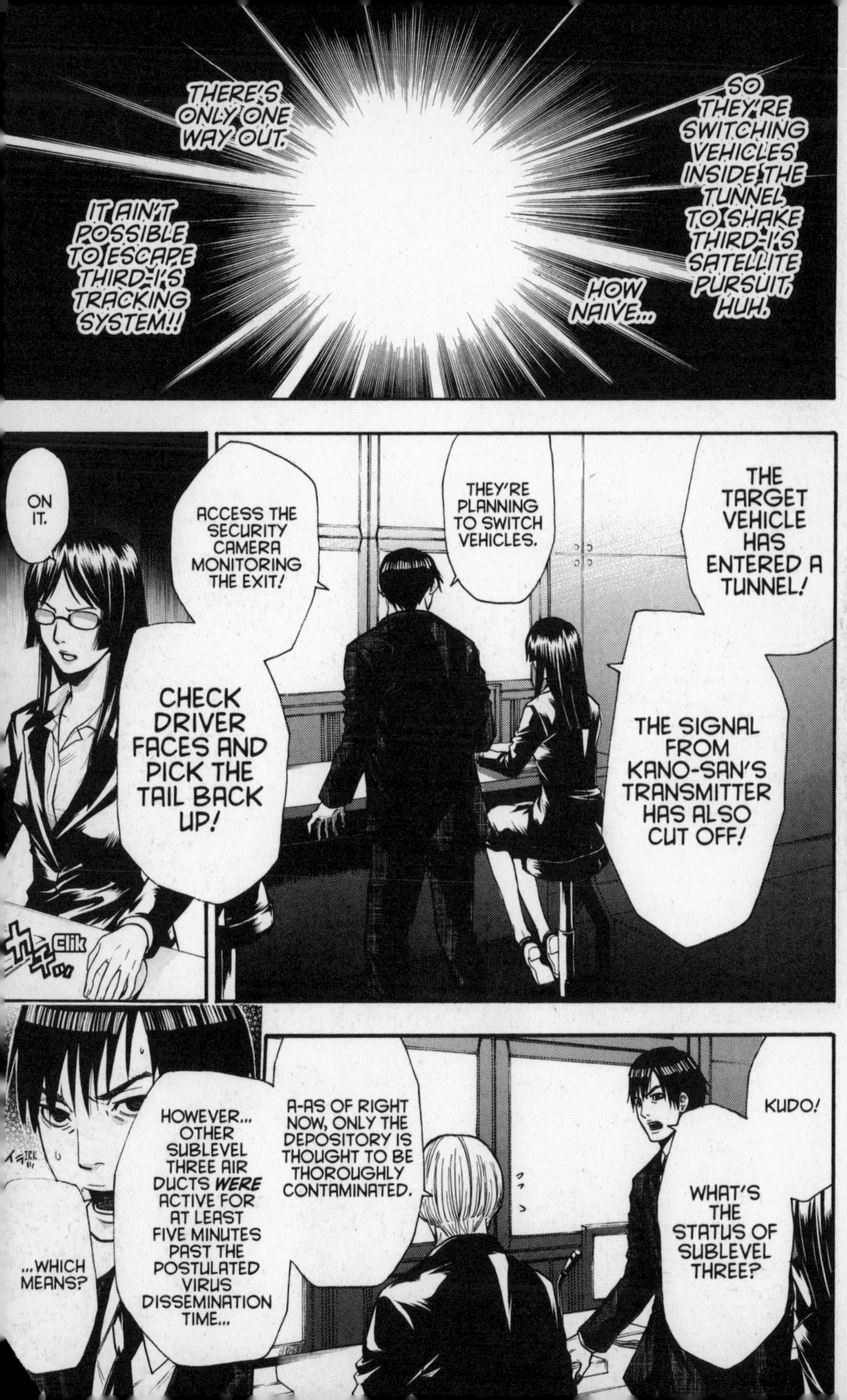
SO THEY'RE SWITCHING VEHICLES INSIDE THE TUNNEL TO SHAKE THIRD-I'S SATELLITE PURSUIT, HUH.
HOW NAIVE...
THERE'S ONLY ONE WAY OUT.
IT AIN'T POSSIBLE TO ESCAPE THIRD-I'S TRACKING SYSTEM!!
THE TARGET VEHICLE HAS ENTERED A TUNNEL!
THE SIGNAL FROM KANO-SAN'S TRANSMITTER HAS ALSO CUT OFF!
THEY'RE PLANNING TO SWITCH VEHICLES.
ACCESS THE SECURITY CAMERA MONITORING THE EXIT!
CHECK DRIVER FACES AND PICK THE TAIL BACK UP!
ON IT.
CLIK
KUDO!
WHAT'S THE STATUS OF SUBLEVEL THREE?
A-AS OF RIGHT NOW, ONLY THE DEPOSITORY IS THOUGHT TO BE THOROUGHLY CONTAMINATED.
HOWEVER... OTHER SUBLEVEL THREE AIR DUCTS *WERE* ACTIVE FOR AT LEAST FIVE MINUTES PAST THE POSTULATED VIRUS DISSEMINATION TIME...
IRK
...WHICH MEANS?

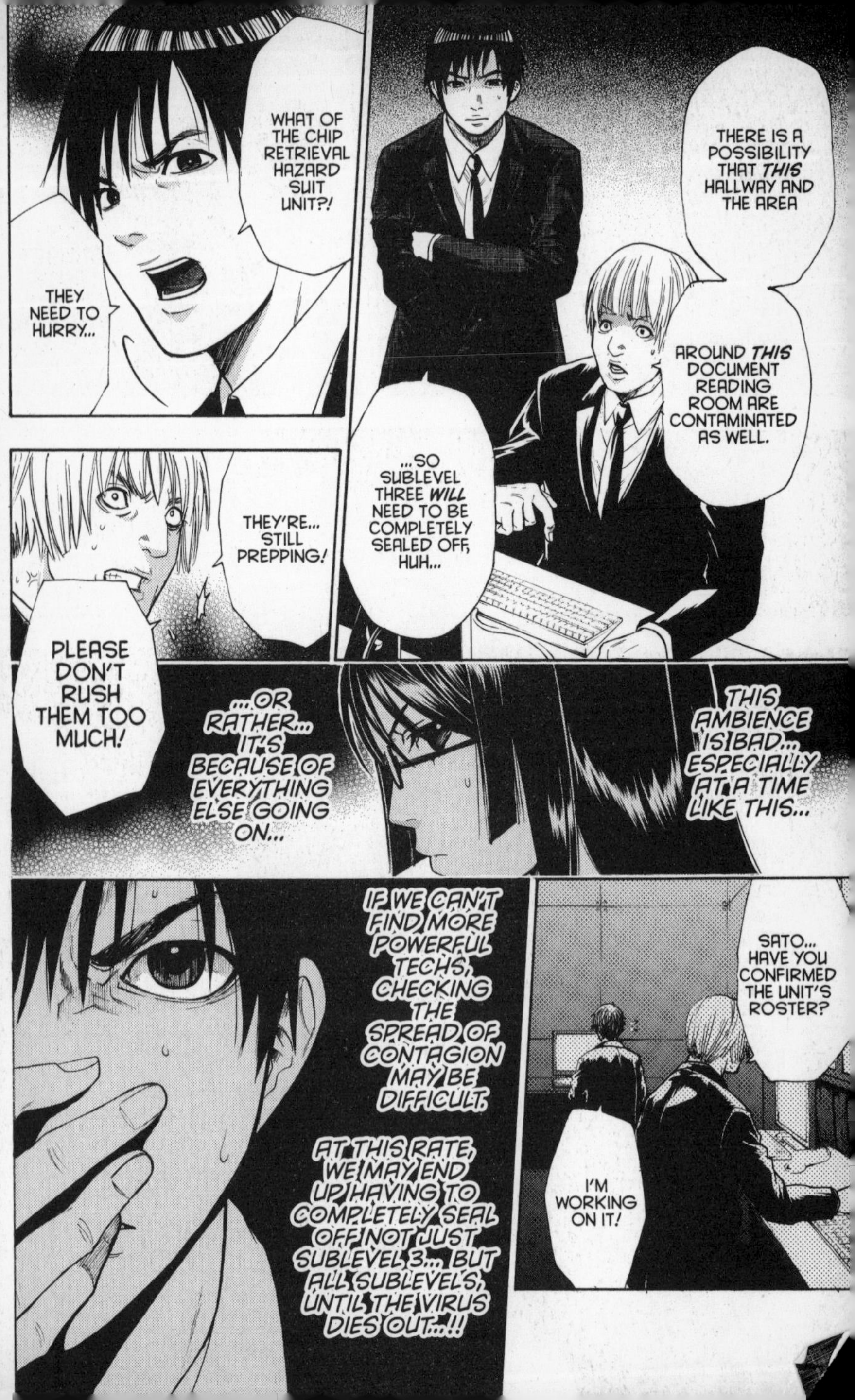
THERE IS A POSSIBILITY THAT *THIS* HALLWAY AND THE AREA
AROUND *THIS* DOCUMENT READING ROOM ARE CONTAMINATED AS WELL.
...SO SUBLEVEL THREE *WILL* NEED TO BE COMPLETELY SEALED OFF, HUH...
WHAT OF THE CHIP RETRIEVAL HAZARD SUIT UNIT?!
THEY NEED TO HURRY...
THEY'RE... STILL PREPPING!
PLEASE DON'T RUSH THEM TOO MUCH!
THIS AMBIENCE IS BAD... ESPECIALLY AT A TIME LIKE THIS...
...OR RATHER... IT'S BECAUSE OF EVERYTHING ELSE GOING ON...
SATO... HAVE YOU CONFIRMED THE UNIT'S ROSTER?
I'M WORKING ON IT!
IF WE CAN'T FIND MORE POWERFUL TECHS, CHECKING THE SPREAD OF CONTAGION MAY BE DIFFICULT.
AT THIS RATE, WE MAY END UP HAVING TO COMPLETELY SEAL OFF NOT JUST SUBLEVEL 3... BUT ALL SUBLEVELS, UNTIL THE VIRUS DIES OUT...!!

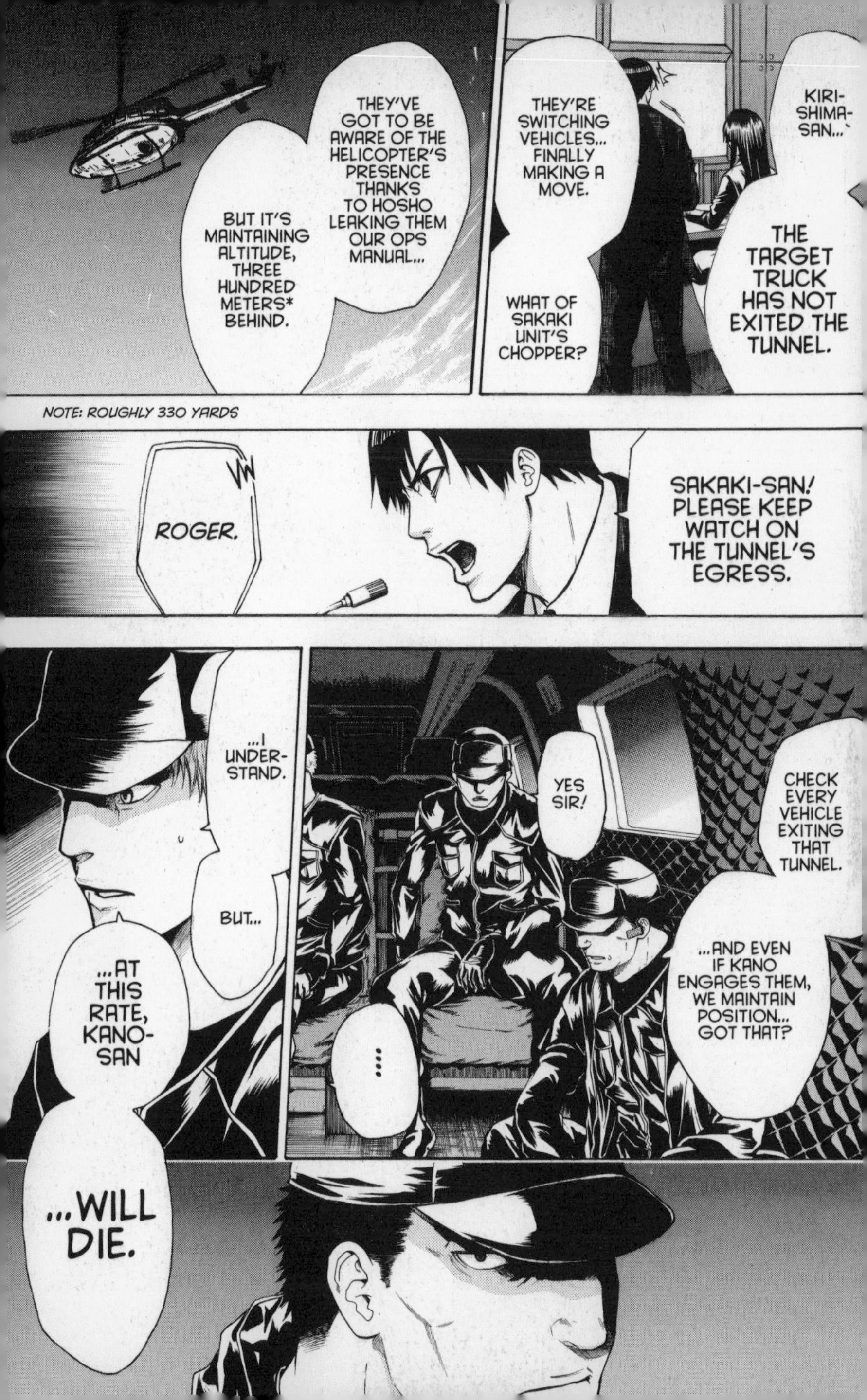
KIRI-SHIMA-SAN...
THE TARGET TRUCK HAS NOT EXITED THE TUNNEL.
THEY'RE SWITCHING VEHICLES... FINALLY MAKING A MOVE.
WHAT OF SAKAKI UNIT'S CHOPPER?
THEY'VE GOT TO BE AWARE OF THE HELICOPTER'S PRESENCE THANKS TO HOSHO LEAKING THEM OUR OPS MANUAL...
BUT IT'S MAINTAINING ALTITUDE, THREE HUNDRED METERS* BEHIND.
NOTE: ROUGHLY 330 YARDS
SAKAKI-SAN! PLEASE KEEP WATCH ON THE TUNNEL'S EGRESS.
ROGER.
CHECK EVERY VEHICLE EXITING THAT TUNNEL.
YES SIR!
...AND EVEN IF KANO ENGAGES THEM, WE MAINTAIN POSITION... GOT THAT?
....
...I UNDERSTAND.
BUT...
...AT THIS RATE, KANO-SAN
...WILL DIE.

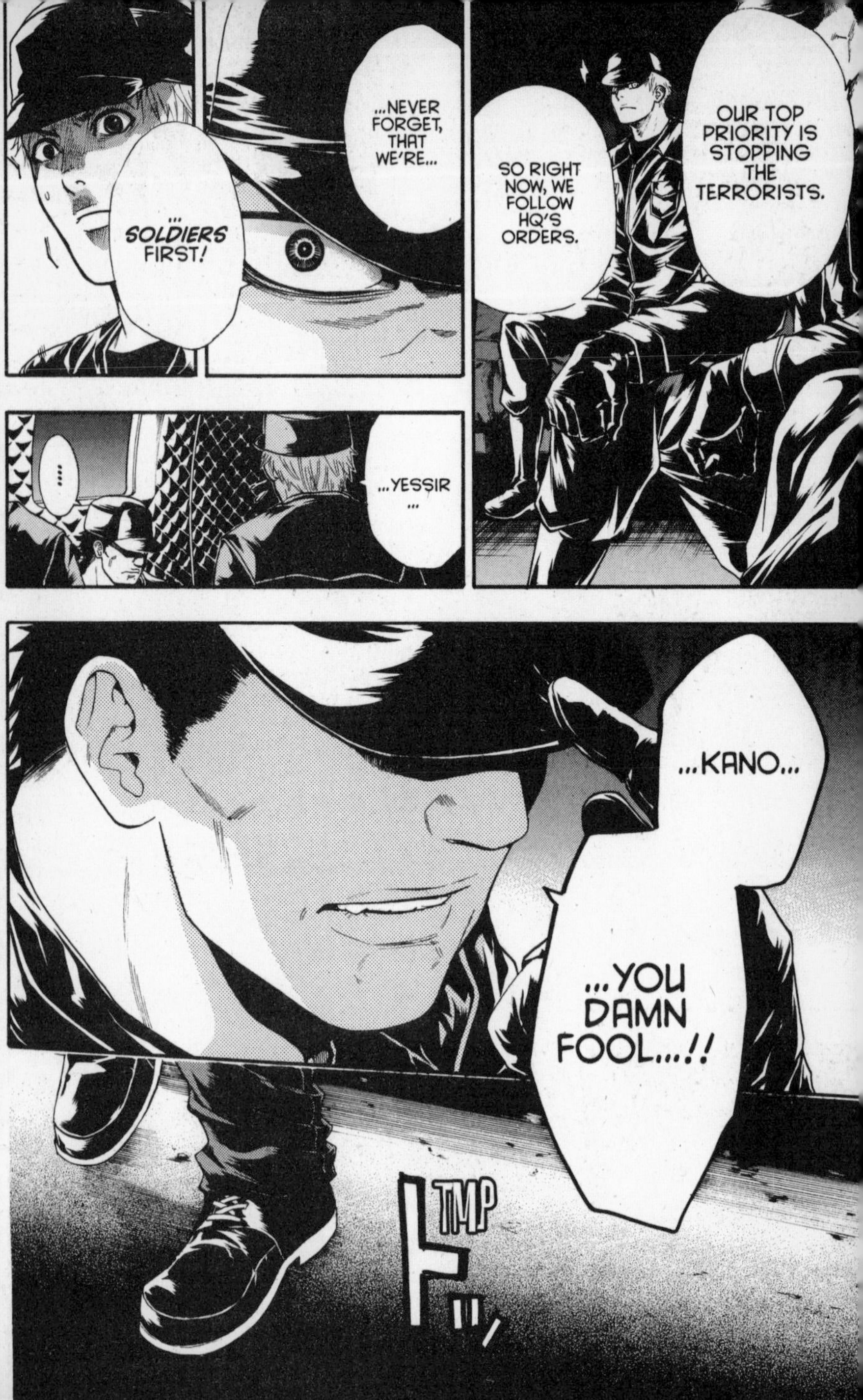

OUR TOP PRIORITY IS STOPPING THE TERRORISTS.
SO RIGHT NOW, WE FOLLOW HQ'S ORDERS.
...NEVER FORGET, THAT WE'RE...
...SOLDIERS FIRST!
...YESSIR...
....
...KANO...
...YOU DAMN FOOL...!!
TMP

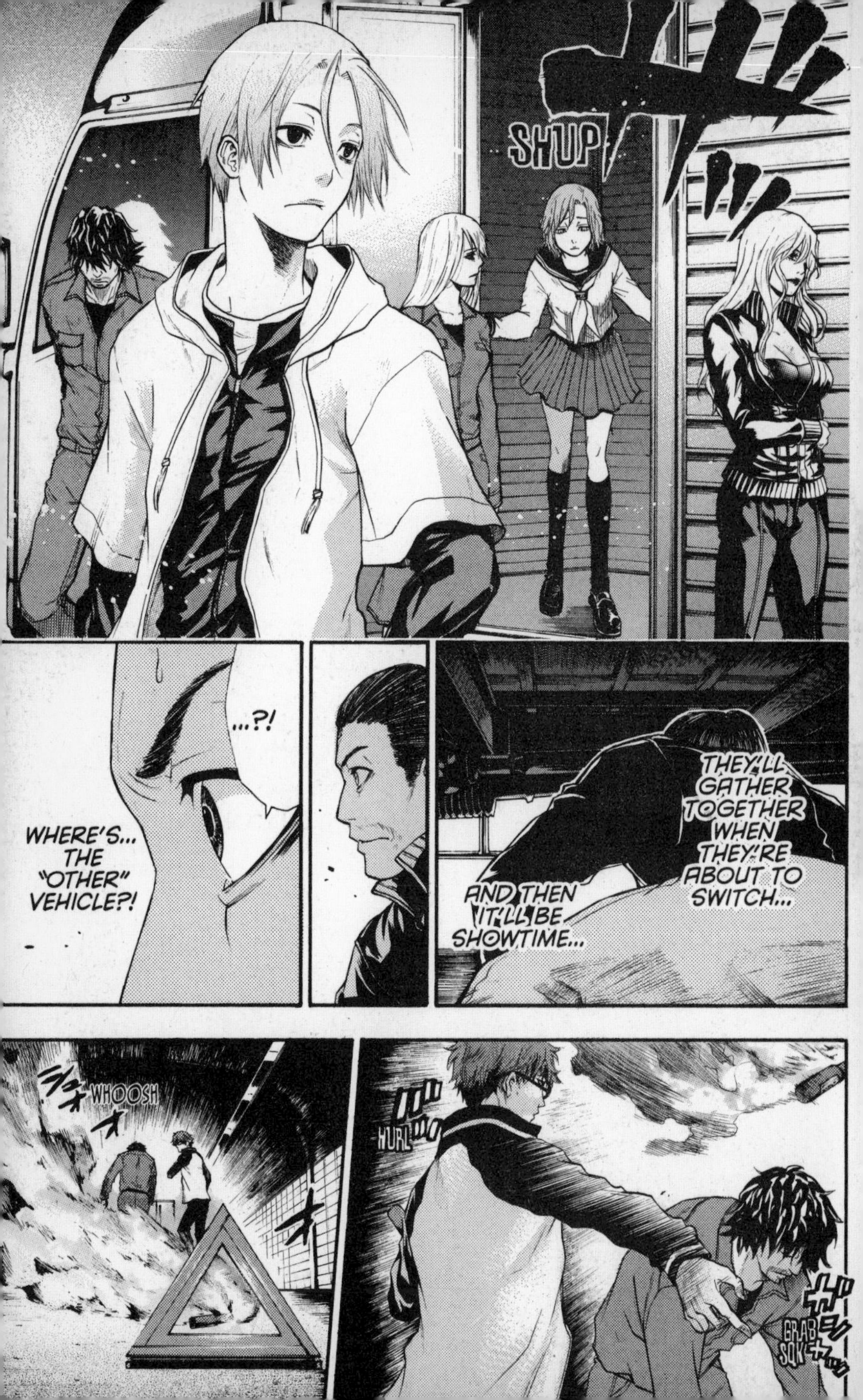
SHUP
THEY'LL GATHER TOGETHER WHEN THEY'RE ABOUT TO SWITCH...
AND THEN IT'LL BE SHOWTIME...
...?!
WHERE'S... THE "OTHER" VEHICLE?!
HURL
GRAB SQK
WHOOSH

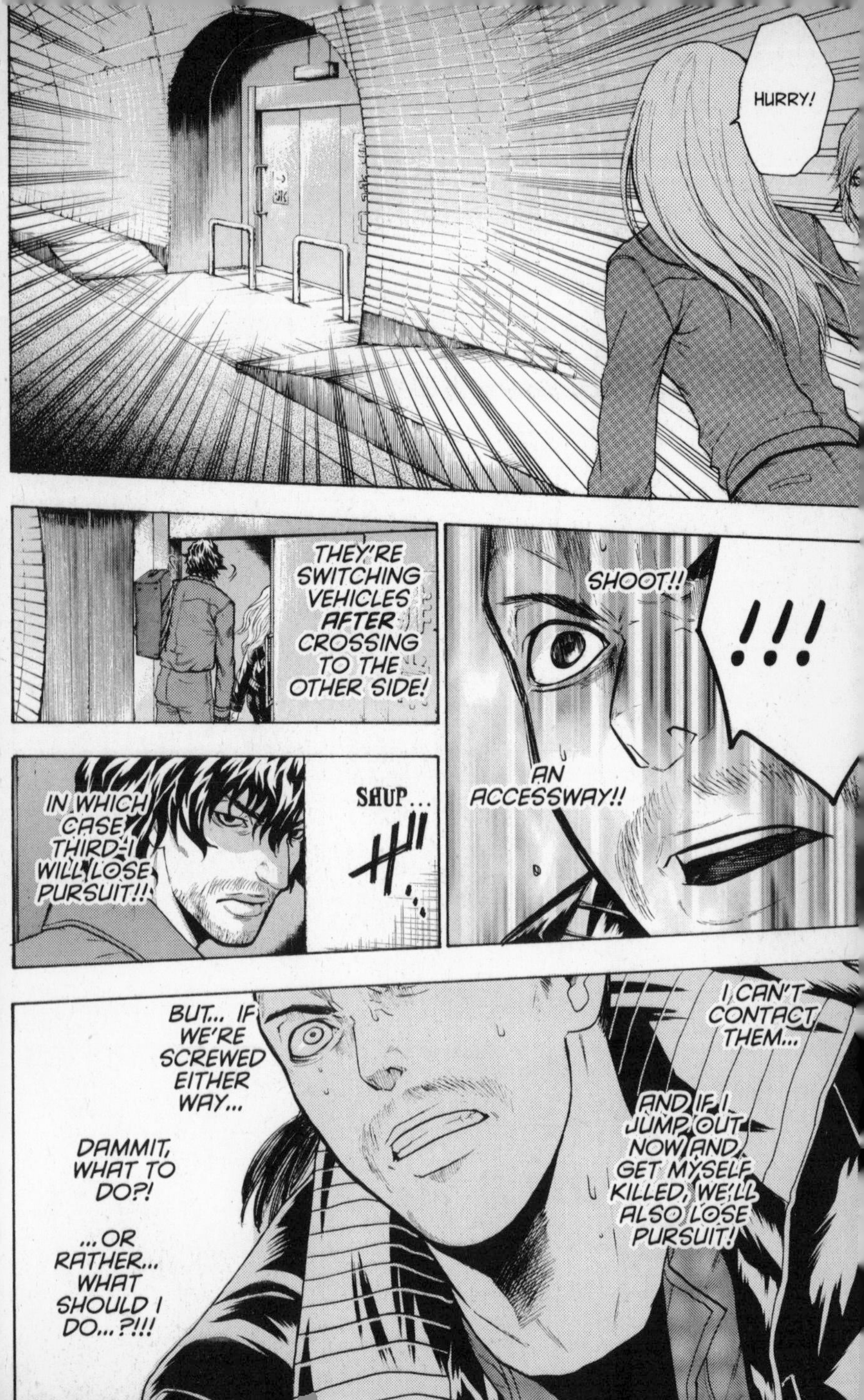
HURRY!
!!!
SHOOT!!
AN ACCESSWAY!!
THEY'RE SWITCHING VEHICLES AFTER CROSSING TO THE OTHER SIDE!
SHUP...
IN WHICH CASE THIRD-I WILL LOSE PURSUIT!!
I CAN'T CONTACT THEM...
AND IF I JUMP OUT NOW AND GET MYSELF KILLED, WE'LL ALSO LOSE PURSUIT!
BUT... IF WE'RE SCREWED EITHER WAY...
DAMMIT, WHAT TO DO?!
...OR RATHER... WHAT SHOULD I DO...?!!!

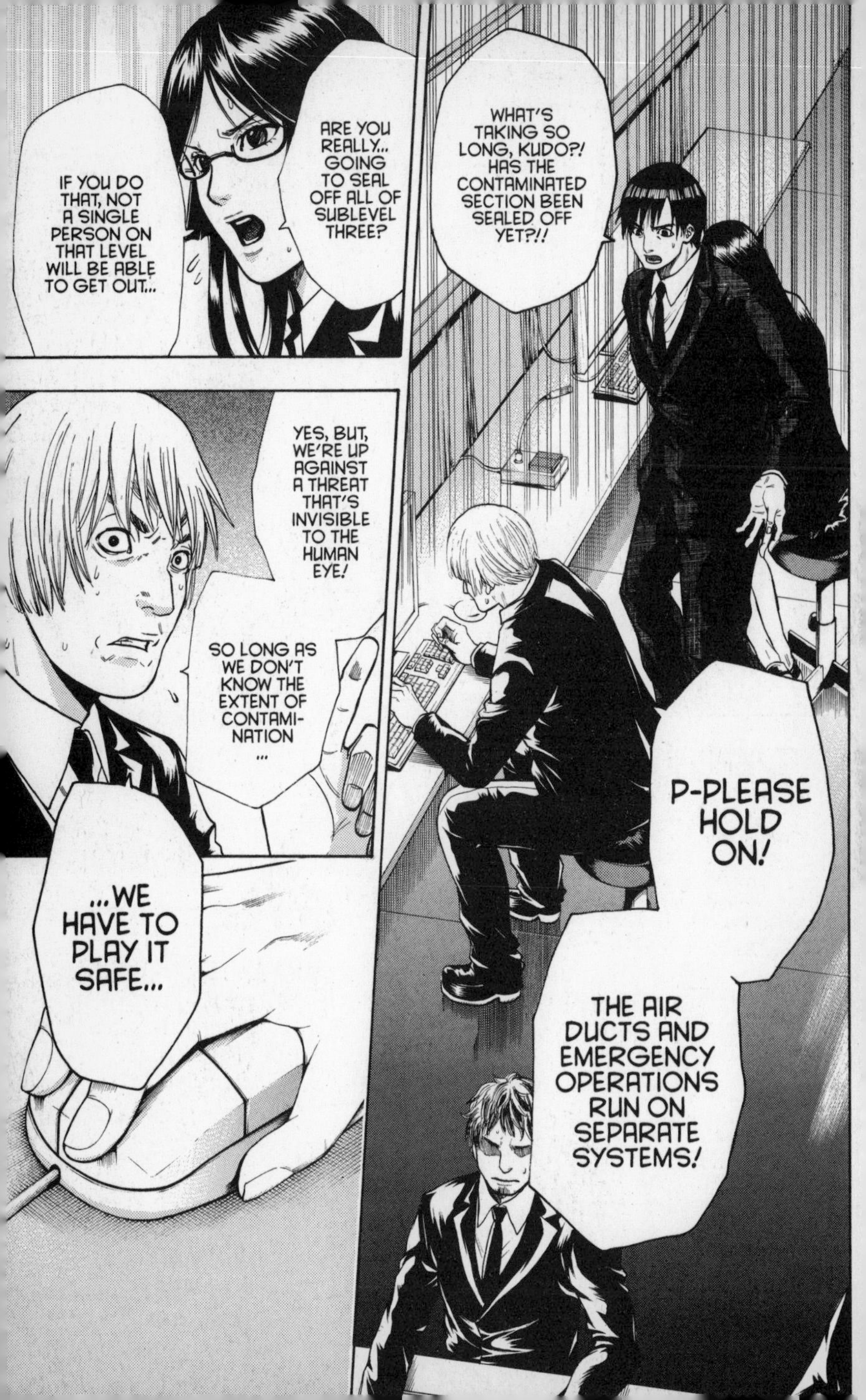
WHAT'S TAKING SO LONG, KUDO?! HAS THE CONTAMINATED SECTION BEEN SEALED OFF YET?!!
P-PLEASE HOLD ON!
THE AIR DUCTS AND EMERGENCY OPERATIONS RUN ON SEPARATE SYSTEMS!
ARE YOU REALLY... GOING TO SEAL OFF ALL OF SUBLEVEL THREE?
IF YOU DO THAT, NOT A SINGLE PERSON ON THAT LEVEL WILL BE ABLE TO GET OUT...
YES, BUT, WE'RE UP AGAINST A THREAT THAT'S INVISIBLE TO THE HUMAN EYE!
SO LONG AS WE DON'T KNOW THE EXTENT OF CONTAMINATION...
...WE HAVE TO PLAY IT SAFE...

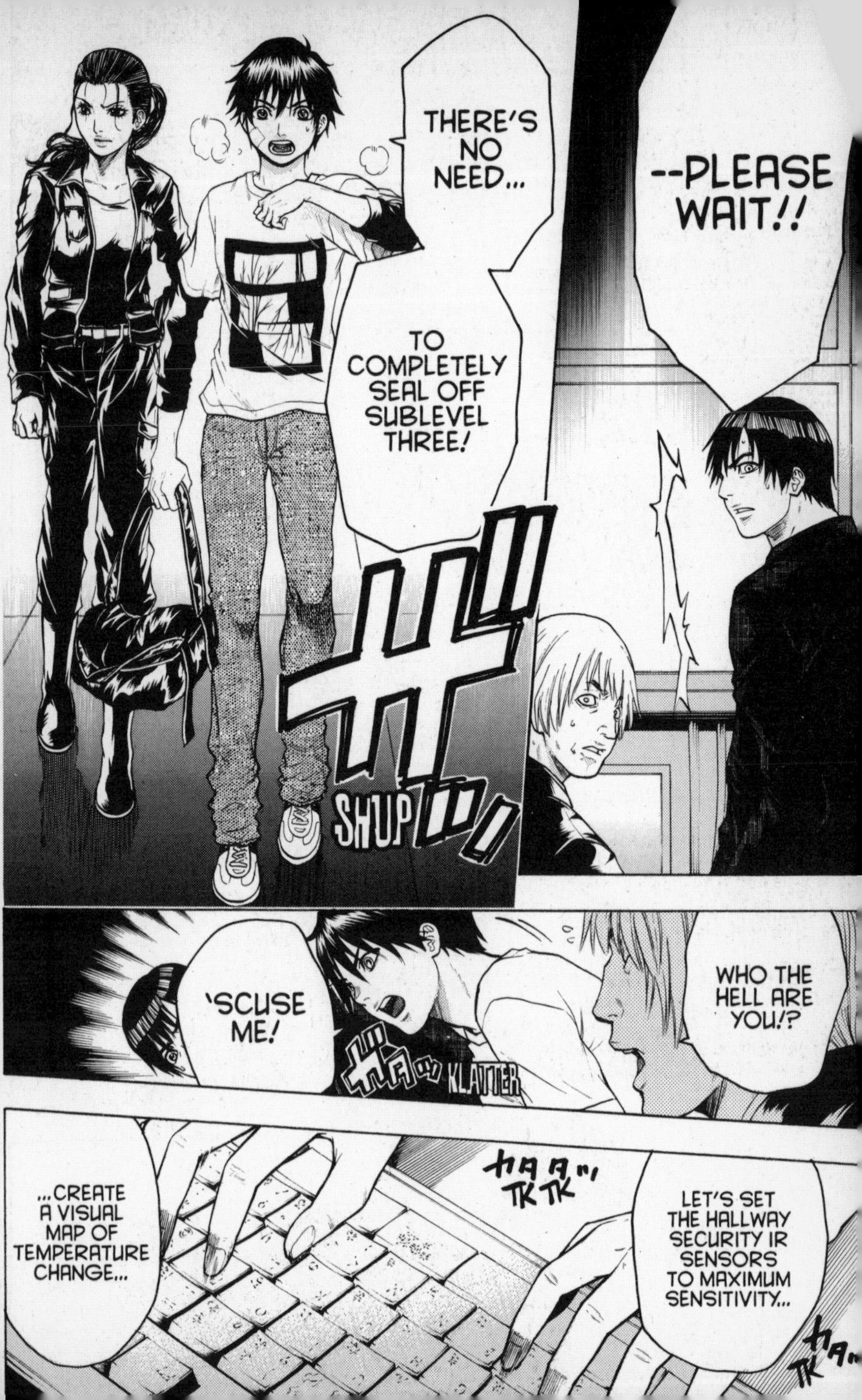
--PLEASE WAIT!!
THERE'S NO NEED...
TO COMPLETELY SEAL OFF SUBLEVEL THREE!
SHUP
WHO THE HELL ARE YOU!?
'SCUSE ME!
KLATTER
TK TK
LET'S SET THE HALLWAY SECURITY IR SENSORS TO MAXIMUM SENSITIVITY...
TK
...CREATE A VISUAL MAP OF TEMPERATURE CHANGE...

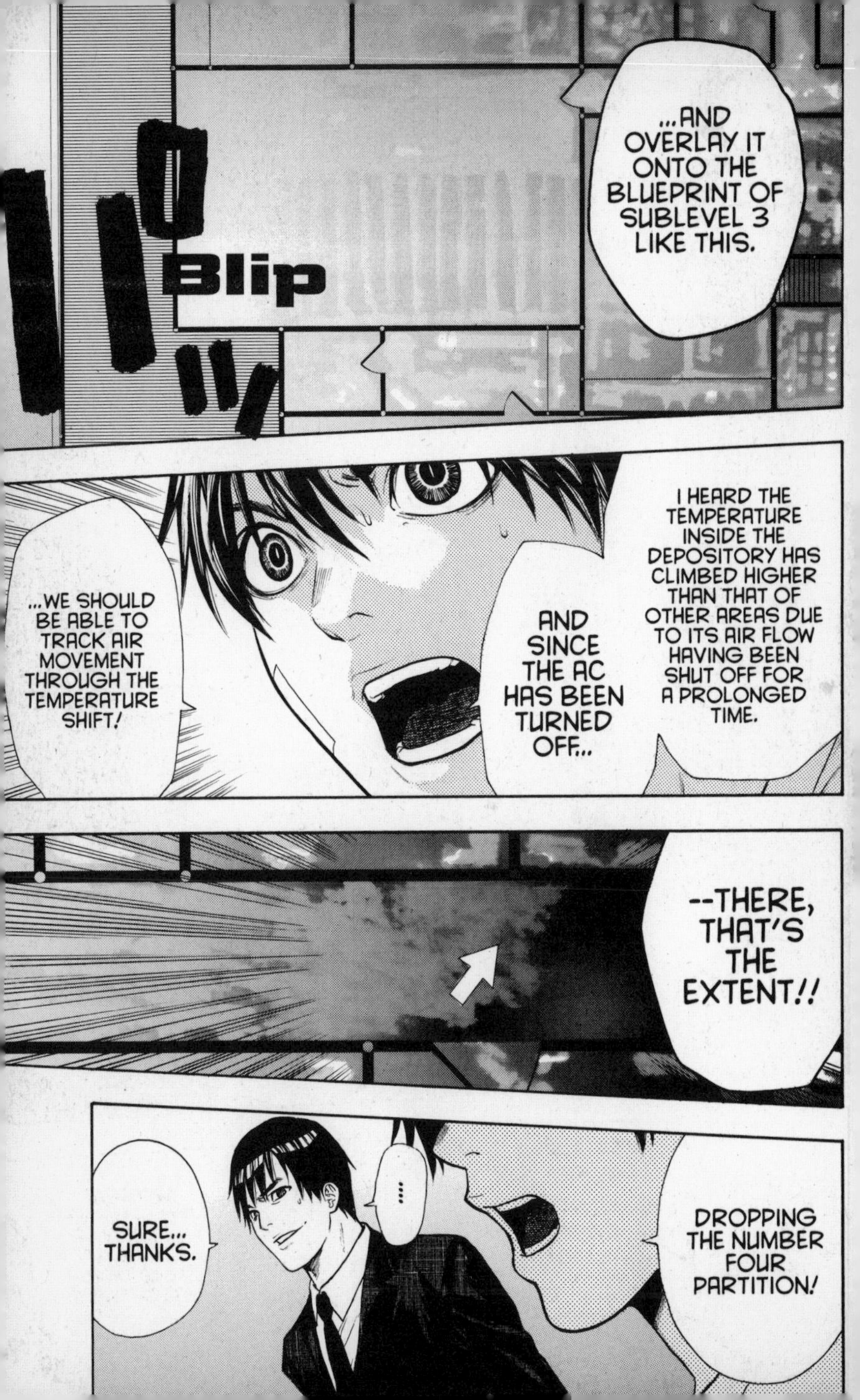
...AND OVERLAY IT ONTO THE BLUEPRINT OF SUBLEVEL 3 LIKE THIS.
Blip
I HEARD THE TEMPERATURE INSIDE THE DEPOSITORY HAS CLIMBED HIGHER THAN THAT OF OTHER AREAS DUE TO ITS AIR FLOW HAVING BEEN SHUT OFF FOR A PROLONGED TIME.
AND SINCE THE AC HAS BEEN TURNED OFF...
...WE SHOULD BE ABLE TO TRACK AIR MOVEMENT THROUGH THE TEMPERATURE SHIFT!
--THERE, THAT'S THE EXTENT!!
DROPPING THE NUMBER FOUR PARTITION!
....
SURE... THANKS.

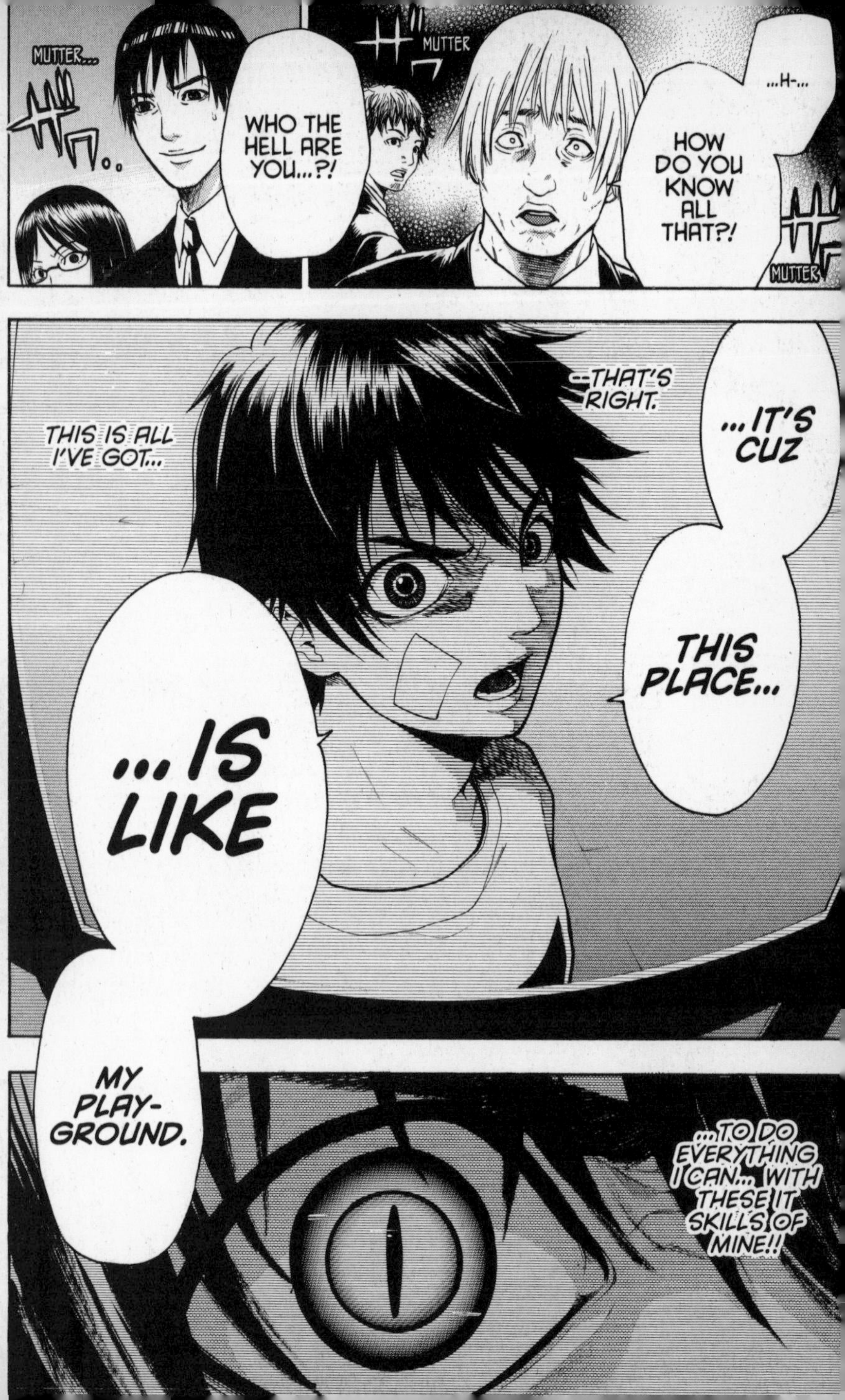

...H-...
MUTTER
HOW DO YOU KNOW ALL THAT?!
MUTTER
WHO THE HELL ARE YOU...?!
MUTTER...
...IT'S CUZ
--THAT'S RIGHT.
THIS PLACE...
THIS IS ALL I'VE GOT...
...IS LIKE
MY PLAY-GROUND.
...TO DO EVERYTHING I CAN... WITH THESE IT SKILLS OF MINE!!

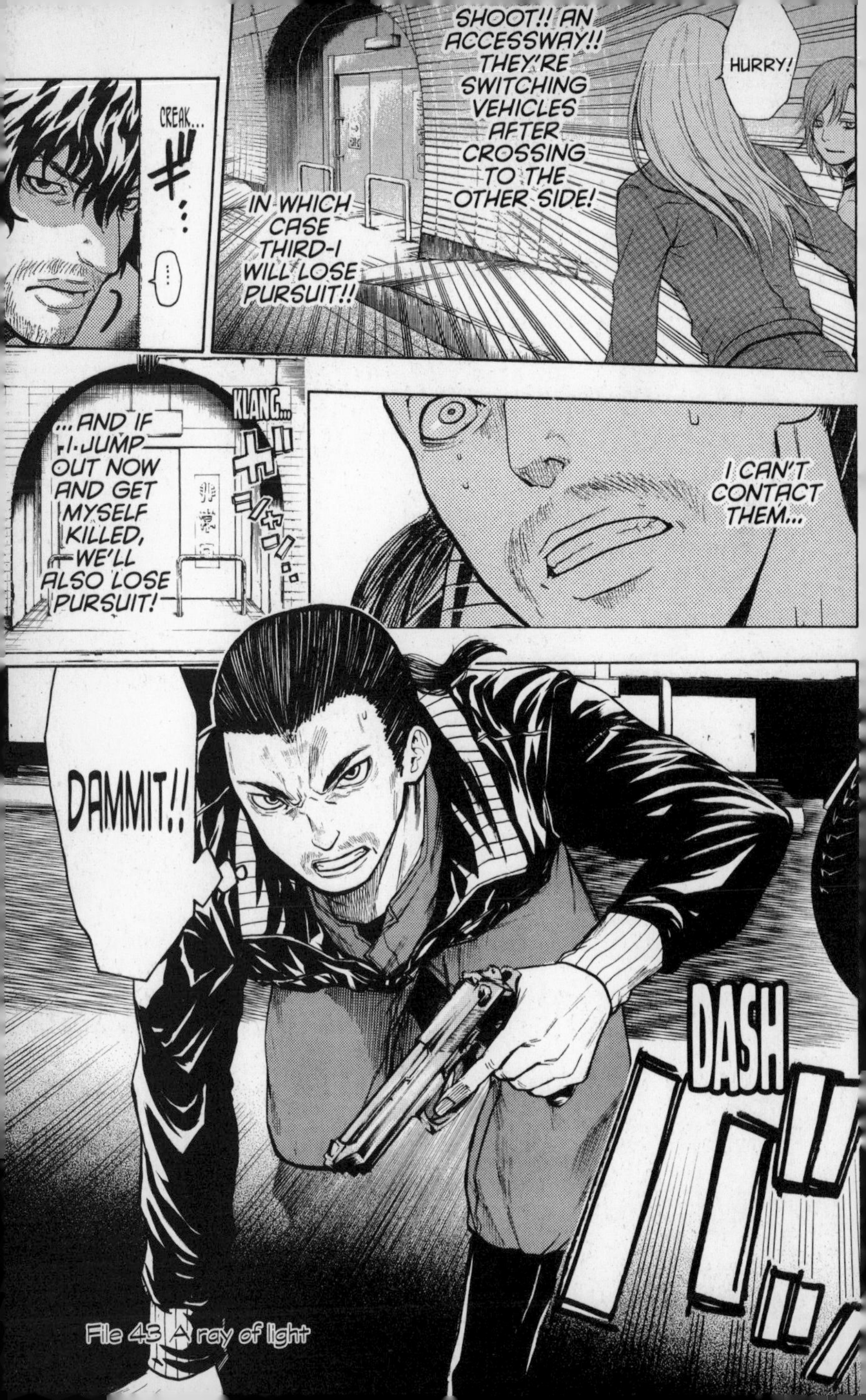
HURRY!
SHOOT!! AN ACCESSWAY!! THEY'RE SWITCHING VEHICLES AFTER CROSSING TO THE OTHER SIDE!
IN WHICH CASE THIRD-I WILL LOSE PURSUIT!!
CREAK...
...
I CAN'T CONTACT THEM...
KLANG...
...AND IF I JUMP OUT NOW AND GET MYSELF KILLED, WE'LL ALSO LOSE PURSUIT!
DASH
DAMMIT!!
File 43 A ray of light

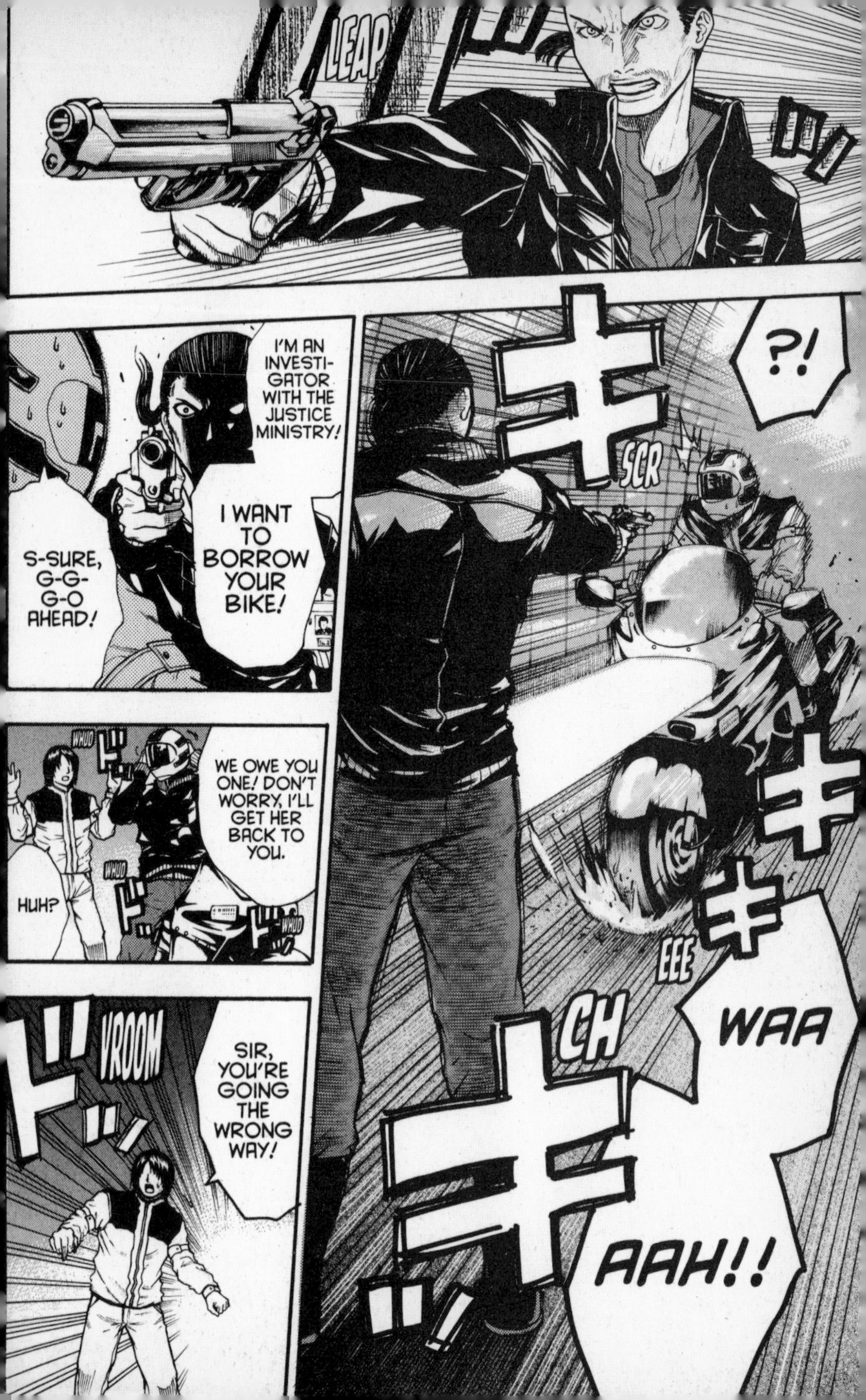
LEAP
?!
SCR
EEE
CH
WAA
AAH!!
I'M AN INVESTIGATOR WITH THE JUSTICE MINISTRY!
I WANT TO BORROW YOUR BIKE!
S-SURE, G-G-G-O AHEAD!
WHUD
WE OWE YOU ONE! DON'T WORRY, I'LL GET HER BACK TO YOU.
WHUD
WHUD
HUH?
VROOM
SIR, YOU'RE GOING THE WRONG WAY!

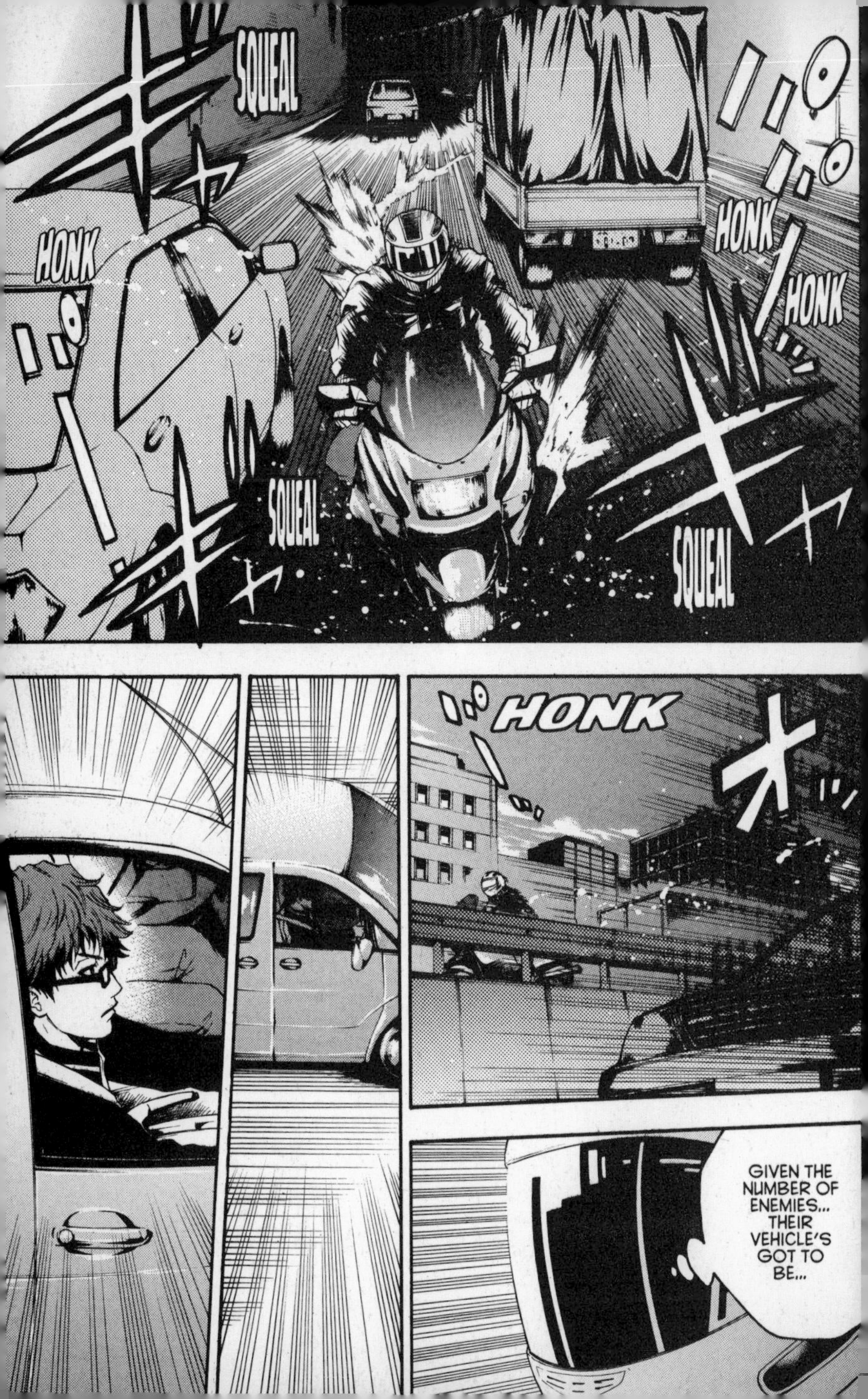
HONK
HONK
SQUEAL
HONK
SQUEAL
SQUEAL
HONK
GIVEN THE NUMBER OF ENEMIES... THEIR VEHICLE'S GOT TO BE...

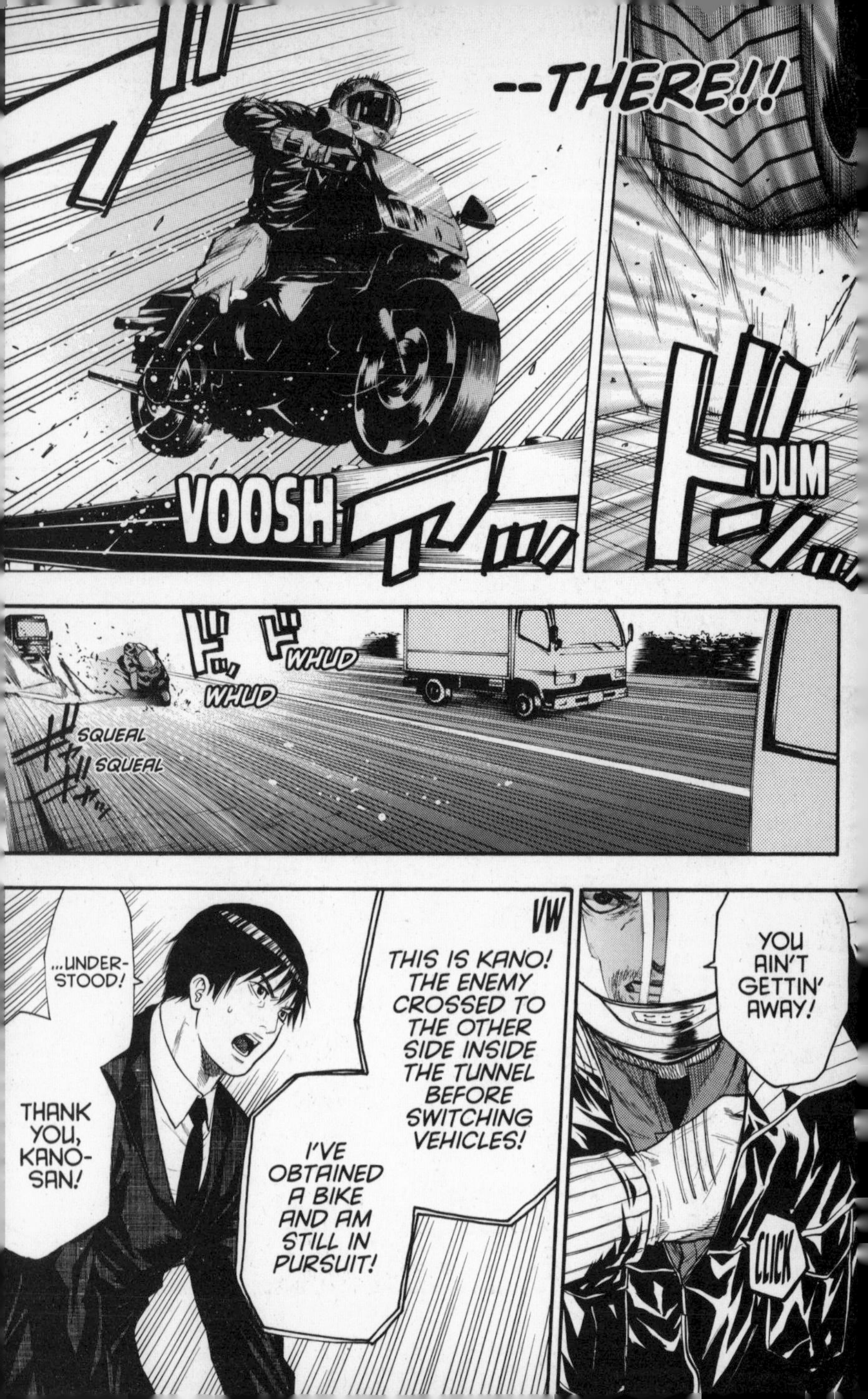
--THERE!!
DUM
VOOSH
WHUD
WHUD
SQUEAL
SQUEAL
VW
YOU AIN'T GETTIN' AWAY!
CLICK
THIS IS KANO! THE ENEMY CROSSED TO THE OTHER SIDE INSIDE THE TUNNEL BEFORE SWITCHING VEHICLES!
I'VE OBTAINED A BIKE AND AM STILL IN PURSUIT!
...UNDER-STOOD!
THANK YOU, KANO-SAN!

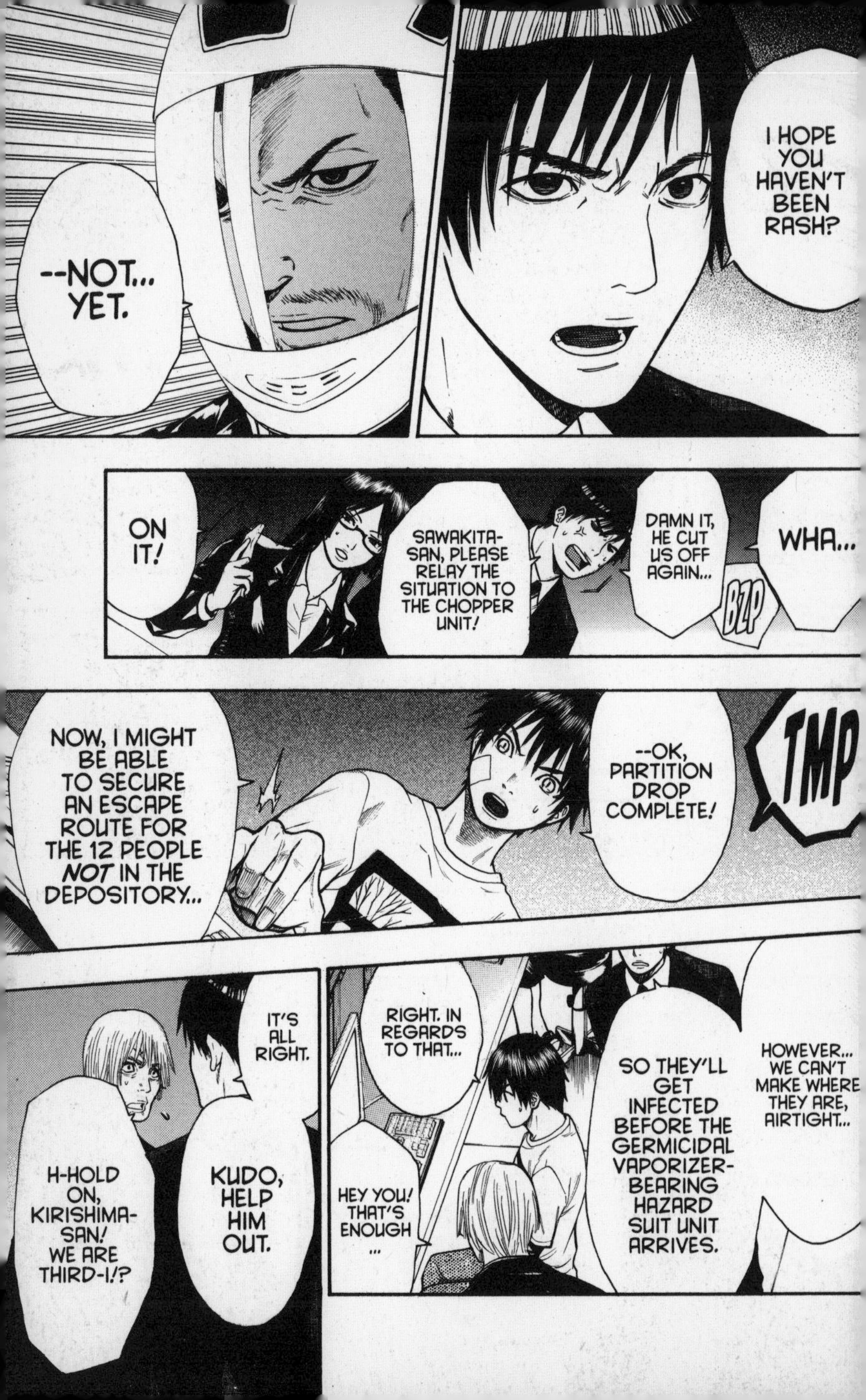
I HOPE YOU HAVEN'T BEEN RASH?
--NOT... YET.
WHA...
BZP
DAMN IT, HE CUT US OFF AGAIN...
SAWAKITA-SAN, PLEASE RELAY THE SITUATION TO THE CHOPPER UNIT!
ON IT!
TMP
--OK, PARTITION DROP COMPLETE!
NOW, I MIGHT BE ABLE TO SECURE AN ESCAPE ROUTE FOR THE 12 PEOPLE *NOT* IN THE DEPOSITORY...
HOWEVER... WE CAN'T MAKE WHERE THEY ARE, AIRTIGHT...
SO THEY'LL GET INFECTED BEFORE THE GERMICIDAL VAPORIZER-BEARING HAZARD SUIT UNIT ARRIVES.
RIGHT. IN REGARDS TO THAT...
HEY YOU! THAT'S ENOUGH ...
IT'S ALL RIGHT.
KUDO, HELP HIM OUT.
H-HOLD ON, KIRISHIMA-SAN! WE ARE THIRD-I!?

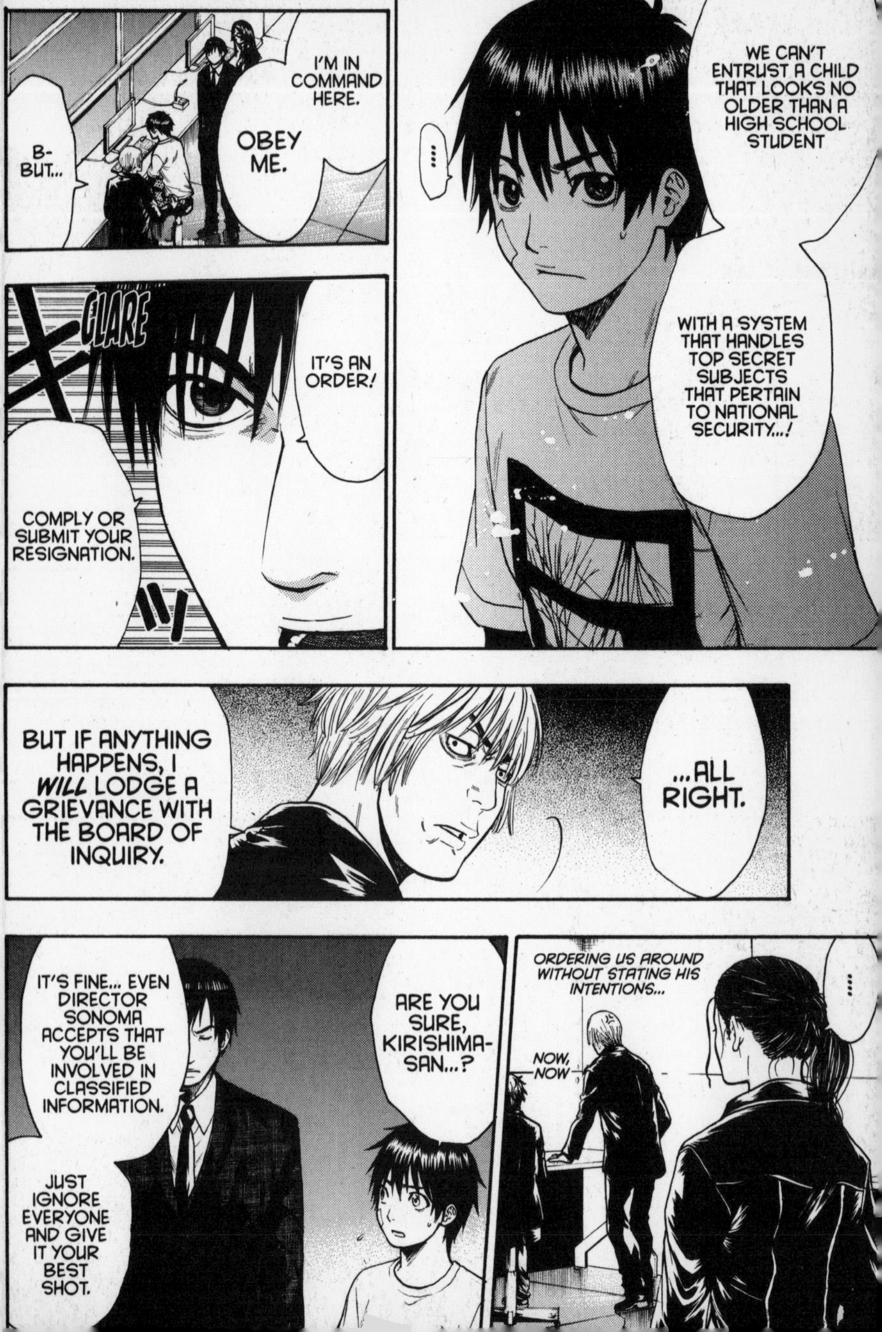

WE CAN'T ENTRUST A CHILD THAT LOOKS NO OLDER THAN A HIGH SCHOOL STUDENT
WITH A SYSTEM THAT HANDLES TOP SECRET SUBJECTS THAT PERTAIN TO NATIONAL SECURITY...!
....
I'M IN COMMAND HERE.
OBEY ME.
B-BUT...
GLARE
IT'S AN ORDER!
COMPLY OR SUBMIT YOUR RESIGNATION.
...ALL RIGHT.
BUT IF ANYTHING HAPPENS, I *WILL* LODGE A GRIEVANCE WITH THE BOARD OF INQUIRY.
....
ORDERING US AROUND WITHOUT STATING HIS INTENTIONS...
NOW, NOW
ARE YOU SURE, KIRISHIMA-SAN...?
IT'S FINE... EVEN DIRECTOR SONOMA ACCEPTS THAT YOU'LL BE INVOLVED IN CLASSIFIED INFORMATION.
JUST IGNORE EVERYONE AND GIVE IT YOUR BEST SHOT.

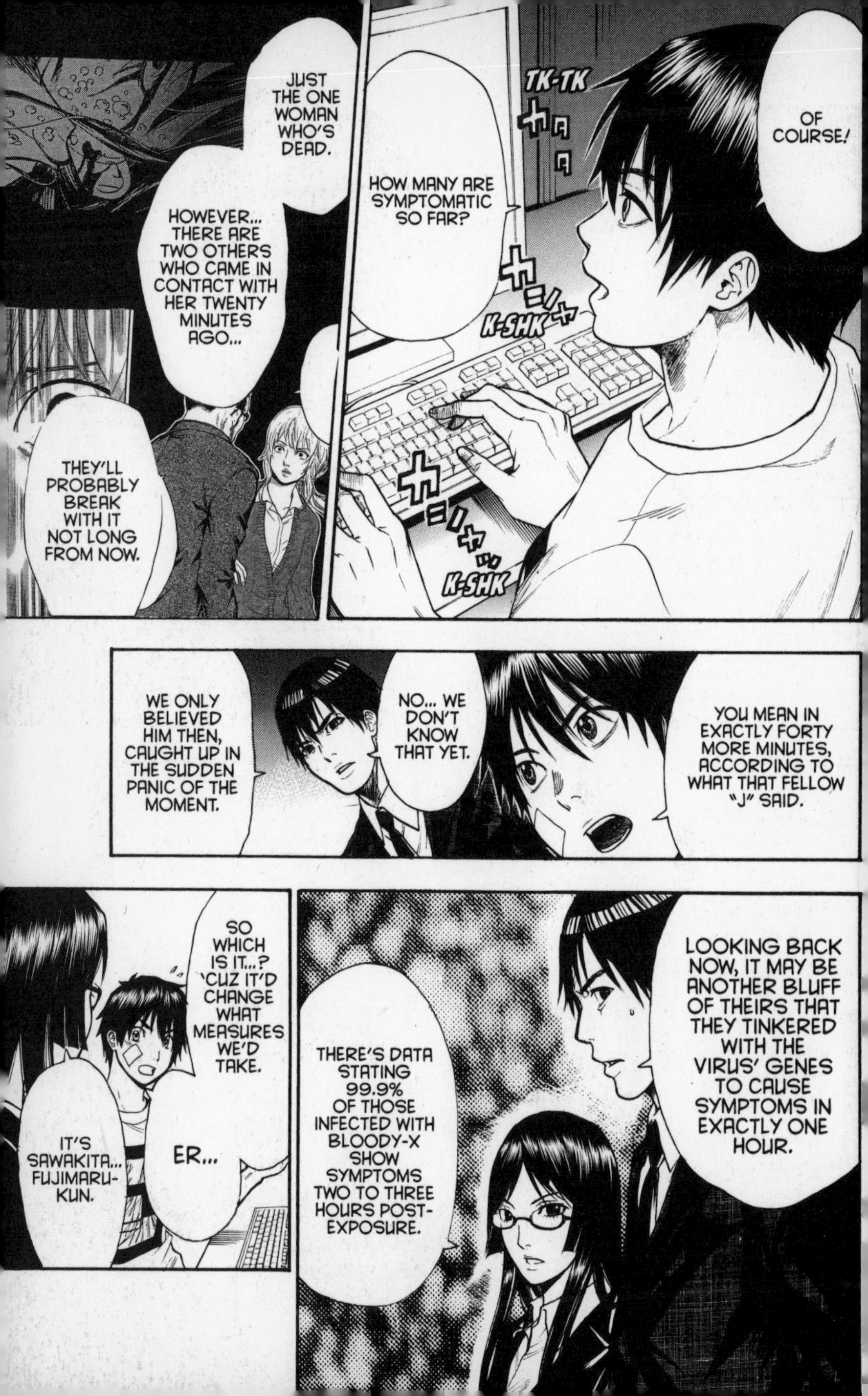
OF COURSE!
TK-TK
HOW MANY ARE SYMPTOMATIC SO FAR?
K-SHK
K-SHK
JUST THE ONE WOMAN WHO'S DEAD.
HOWEVER... THERE ARE TWO OTHERS WHO CAME IN CONTACT WITH HER TWENTY MINUTES AGO...
THEY'LL PROBABLY BREAK WITH IT NOT LONG FROM NOW.
YOU MEAN IN EXACTLY FORTY MORE MINUTES, ACCORDING TO WHAT THAT FELLOW "J" SAID.
NO... WE DON'T KNOW THAT YET.
WE ONLY BELIEVED HIM THEN, CAUGHT UP IN THE SUDDEN PANIC OF THE MOMENT.
LOOKING BACK NOW, IT MAY BE ANOTHER BLUFF OF THEIRS THAT THEY TINKERED WITH THE VIRUS' GENES TO CAUSE SYMPTOMS IN EXACTLY ONE HOUR.
THERE'S DATA STATING 99.9% OF THOSE INFECTED WITH BLOODY-X SHOW SYMPTOMS TWO TO THREE HOURS POST-EXPOSURE.
SO WHICH IS IT...? 'CUZ IT'D CHANGE WHAT MEASURES WE'D TAKE.
ER...
IT'S SAWAKITA... FUJIMARU-KUN.

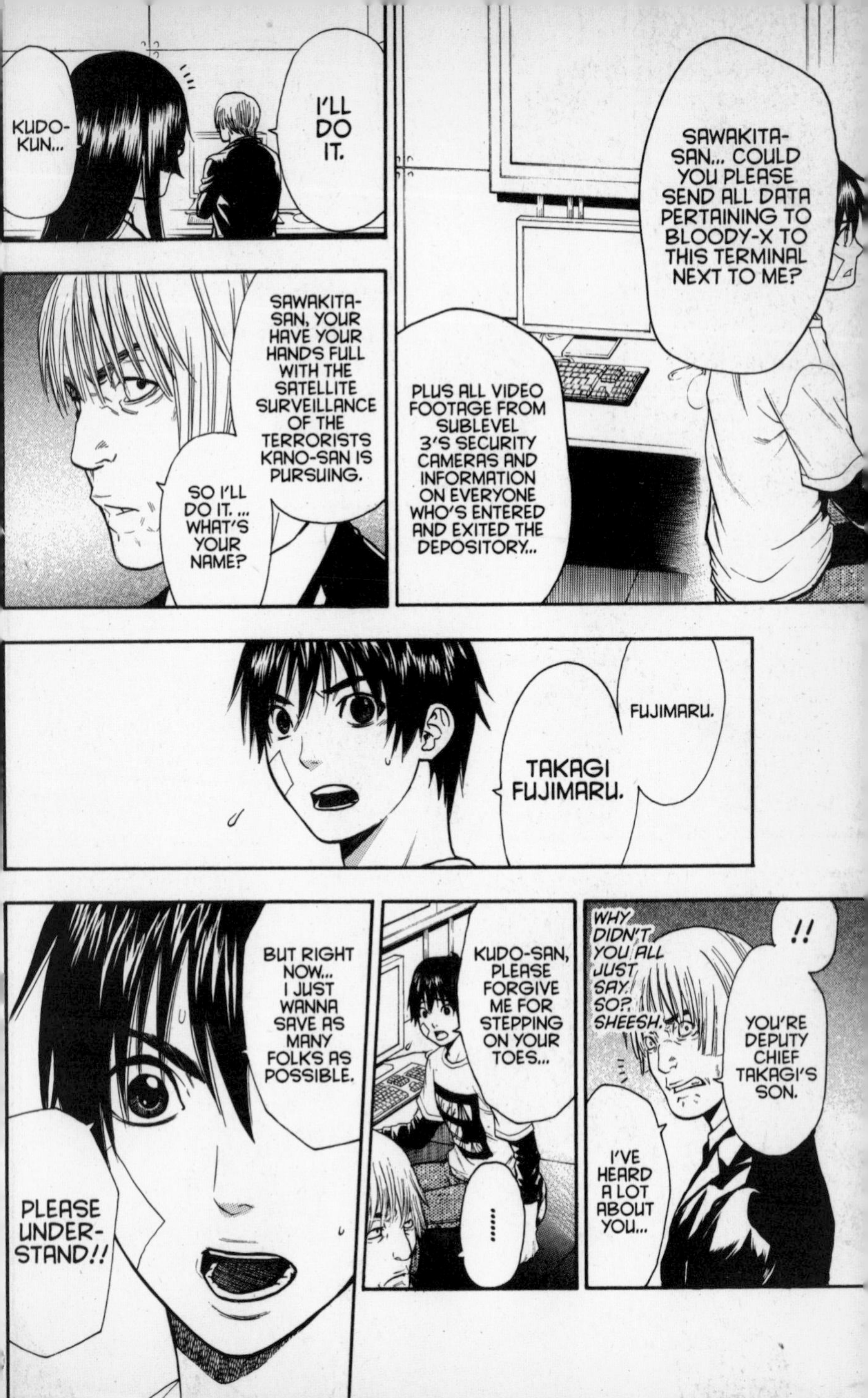
SAWAKITA-SAN... COULD YOU PLEASE SEND ALL DATA PERTAINING TO BLOODY-X TO THIS TERMINAL NEXT TO ME?
PLUS ALL VIDEO FOOTAGE FROM SUBLEVEL 3'S SECURITY CAMERAS AND INFORMATION ON EVERYONE WHO'S ENTERED AND EXITED THE DEPOSITORY...
I'LL DO IT.
KUDO-KUN...
SAWAKITA-SAN, YOUR HAVE YOUR HANDS FULL WITH THE SATELLITE SURVEILLANCE OF THE TERRORISTS KANO-SAN IS PURSUING.
SO I'LL DO IT. ... WHAT'S YOUR NAME?
FUJIMARU.
TAKAGI FUJIMARU.
!!
YOU'RE DEPUTY CHIEF TAKAGI'S SON.
WHY DIDN'T YOU ALL JUST SAY SO? SHEESH.
I'VE HEARD A LOT ABOUT YOU...
KUDO-SAN, PLEASE FORGIVE ME FOR STEPPING ON YOUR TOES...
......
BUT RIGHT NOW... I JUST WANNA SAVE AS MANY FOLKS AS POSSIBLE.
PLEASE UNDERSTAND!!

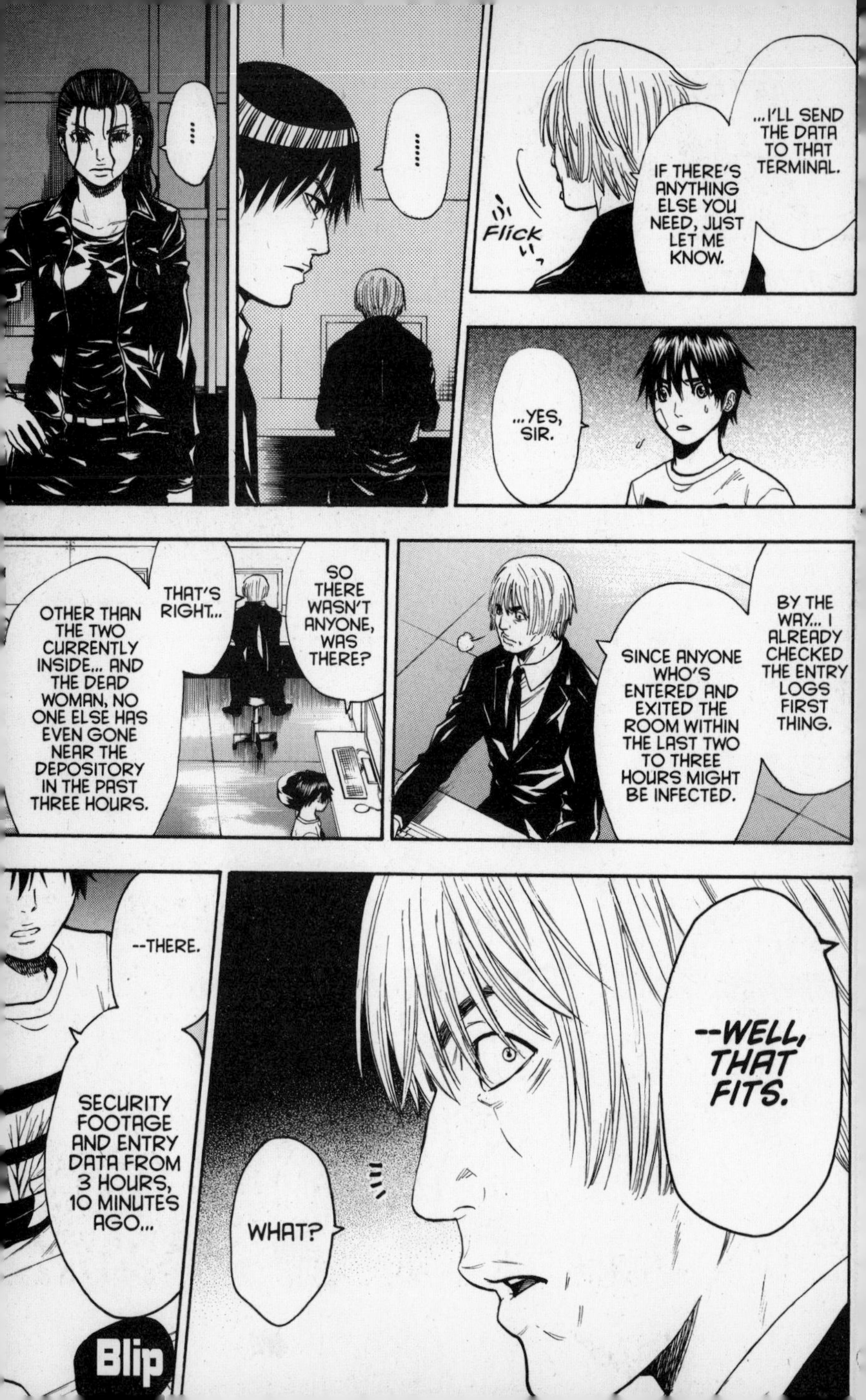

...I'LL SEND THE DATA TO THAT TERMINAL.
IF THERE'S ANYTHING ELSE YOU NEED, JUST LET ME KNOW.
Flick
...YES, SIR.
......
....
BY THE WAY... I ALREADY CHECKED THE ENTRY LOGS FIRST THING.
SINCE ANYONE WHO'S ENTERED AND EXITED THE ROOM WITHIN THE LAST TWO TO THREE HOURS MIGHT BE INFECTED.
SO THERE WASN'T ANYONE, WAS THERE?
THAT'S RIGHT...
OTHER THAN THE TWO CURRENTLY INSIDE... AND THE DEAD WOMAN, NO ONE ELSE HAS EVEN GONE NEAR THE DEPOSITORY IN THE PAST THREE HOURS.
--WELL, THAT FITS.
WHAT?
--THERE.
SECURITY FOOTAGE AND ENTRY DATA FROM 3 HOURS, 10 MINUTES AGO...
Blip

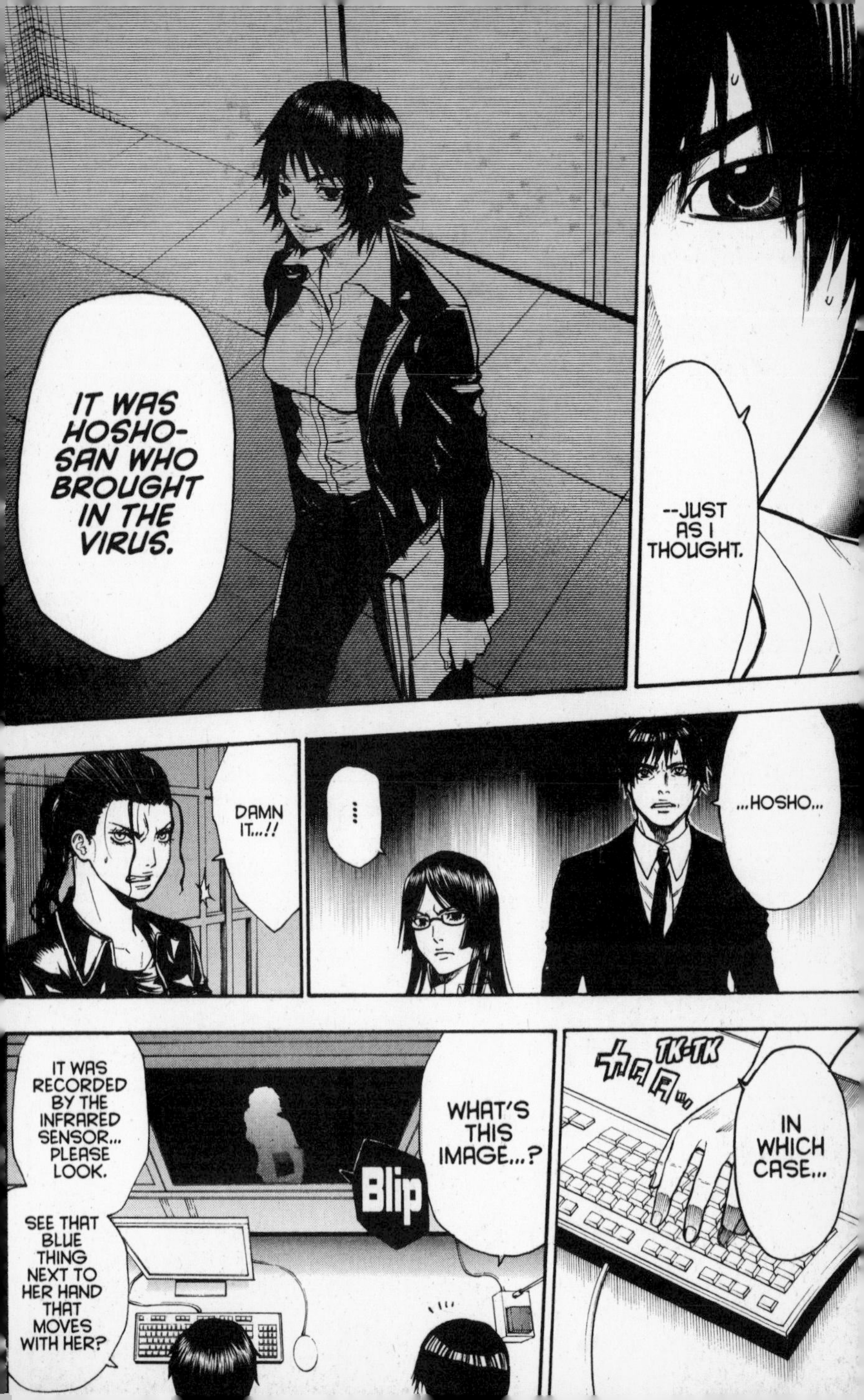
--JUST AS I THOUGHT.
IT WAS HOSHO-SAN WHO BROUGHT IN THE VIRUS.
...HOSHO...
....
DAMN IT...!!
TK-TK
IN WHICH CASE...
Blip
WHAT'S THIS IMAGE...?
IT WAS RECORDED BY THE INFRARED SENSOR... PLEASE LOOK.
SEE THAT BLUE THING NEXT TO HER HAND THAT MOVES WITH HER?

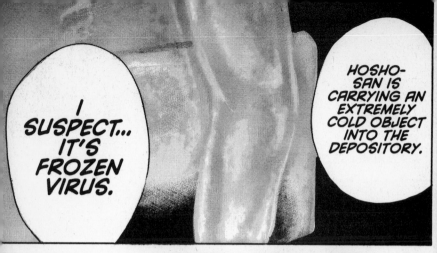

HOSHO-SAN IS CARRYING AN EXTREMELY COLD OBJECT INTO THE DEPOSITORY.
I SUSPECT... IT'S FROZEN VIRUS.
I SEE... AND THAT'S WHY SHE SHUT OFF THE DE-POSITORY'S AIR FLOW AFTERWARDS.
SHE WANTED THE ROOM TEMPERATURE TO RISE... CAUSING THE VIRUS TO THAW, EVAPORATE, AND DIFFUSE...
Tk-tk
AT THIS TEMPERATURE, THE VIRUS OUGHT TO HAVE STARTED SPREADING WITHIN 10 MINUTES...
WHICH MEANS IT TOOK ABOUT 2 HOURS, 40 MINUTES FOR SYMPTOMS TO APPEAR...
SO WHAT "J" SAID ABOUT A ONE-HOUR INTERVAL *WAS* A BLUFF!
SO IT APPEARS.
I THINK IT'S SAFE TO ASSUME THAT AS PER THE ORIGINAL DATA ON BLOODY-X, IT TAKES TWO TO THREE HOURS FROM EXPOSURE TO SYMPTOMS!
U-UN-BELIEVABLE. HE'S EVEN BETTER THAN RUMORED.
IT'S BARELY BEEN FIVE MINUTES SINCE HE SAT DOWN AT THAT TERMINAL...

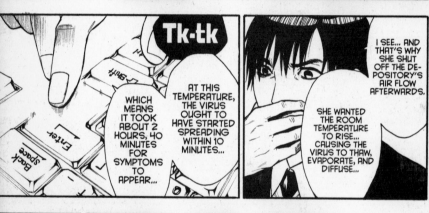

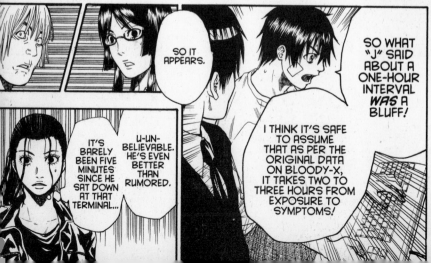

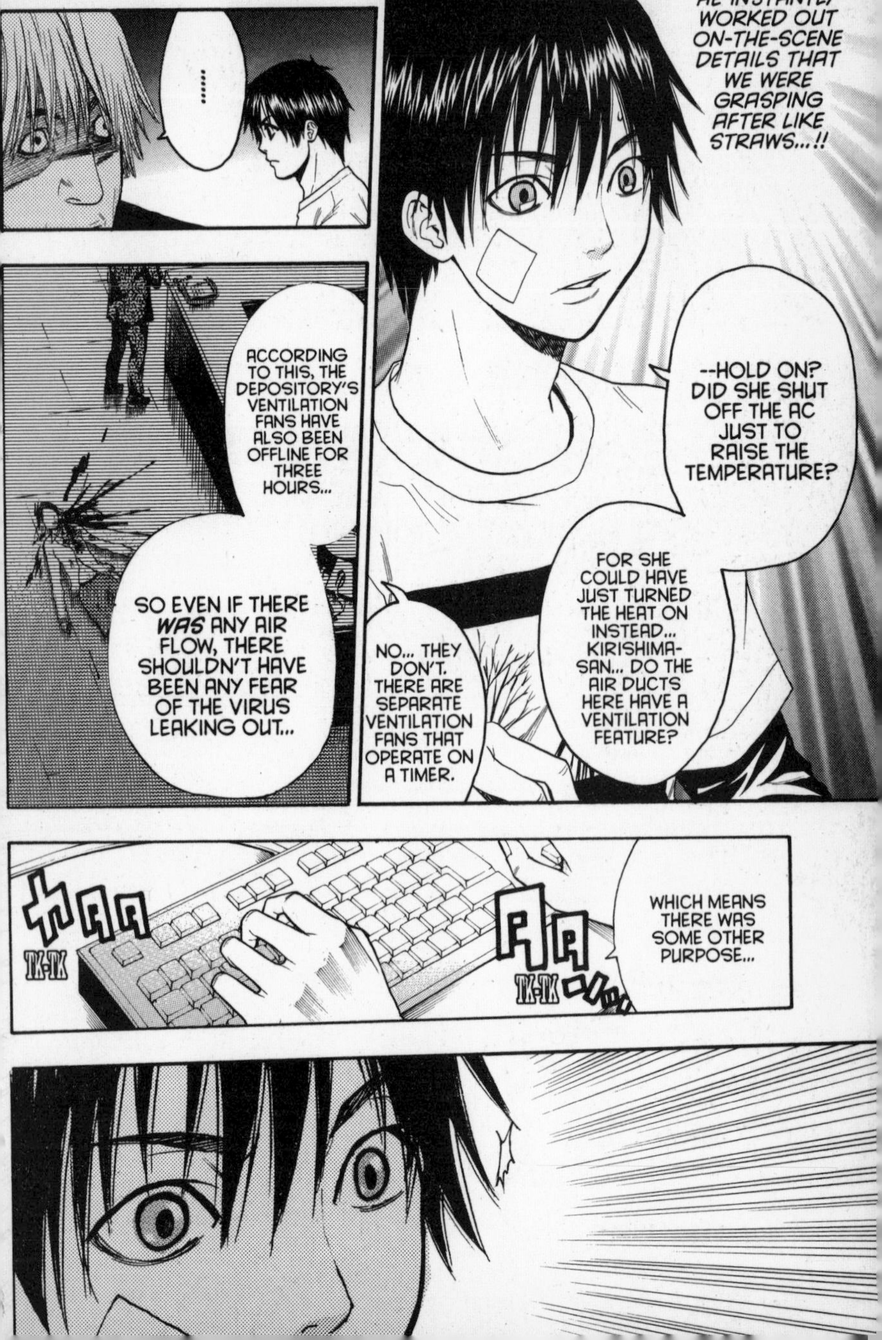

HE INSTANTLY WORKED OUT ON-THE-SCENE DETAILS THAT WE WERE GRASPING AFTER LIKE STRAWS...!!
--HOLD ON? DID SHE SHUT OFF THE AC JUST TO RAISE THE TEMPERATURE?
FOR SHE COULD HAVE JUST TURNED THE HEAT ON INSTEAD... KIRISHIMA-SAN... DO THE AIR DUCTS HERE HAVE A VENTILATION FEATURE?
NO... THEY DON'T. THERE ARE SEPARATE VENTILATION FANS THAT OPERATE ON A TIMER.
......
ACCORDING TO THIS, THE DEPOSITORY'S VENTILATION FANS HAVE ALSO BEEN OFFLINE FOR THREE HOURS...
SO EVEN IF THERE *WAS* ANY AIR FLOW, THERE SHOULDN'T HAVE BEEN ANY FEAR OF THE VIRUS LEAKING OUT...
WHICH MEANS THERE WAS SOME OTHER PURPOSE...
TK-TK
TK-TK

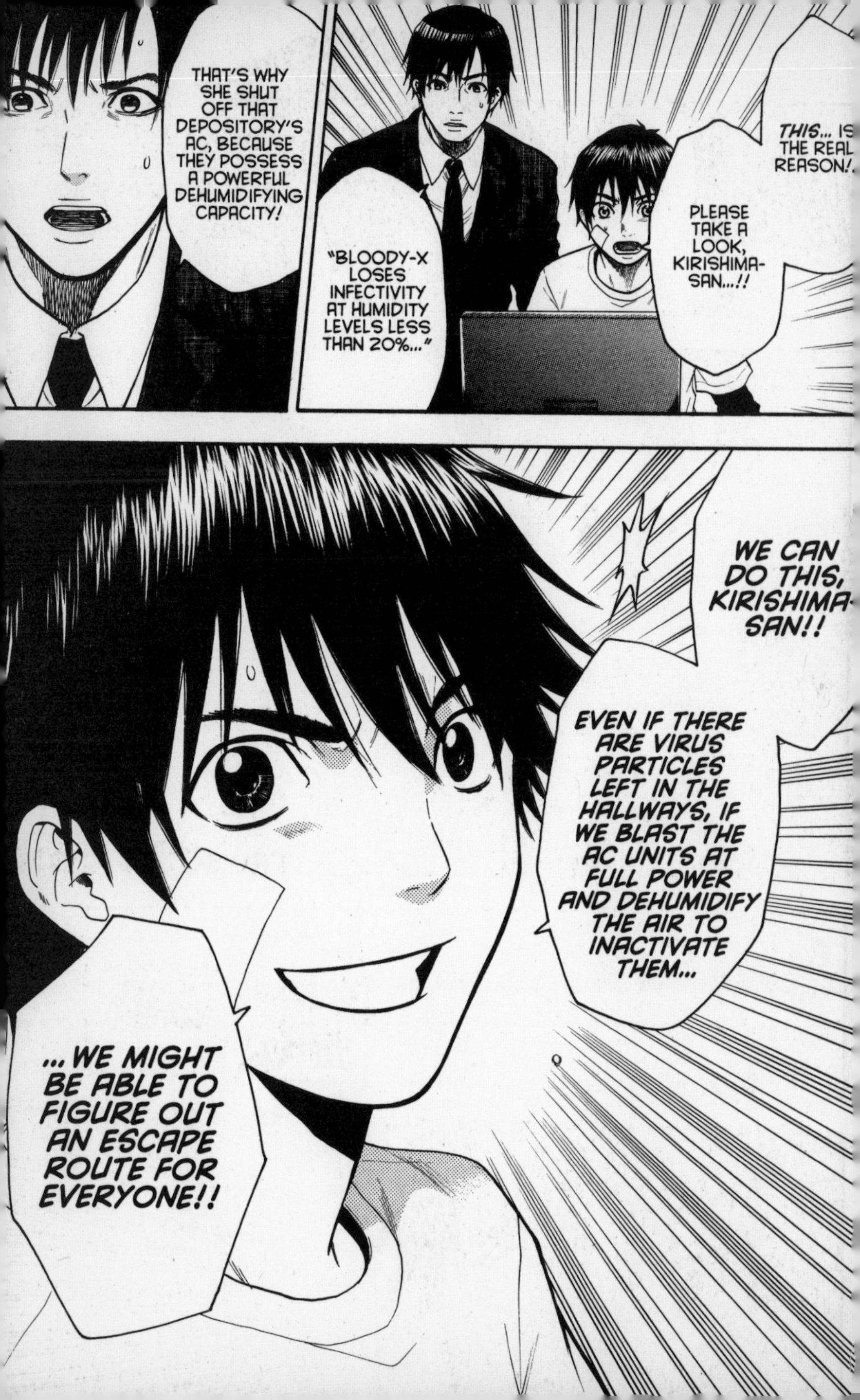
THIS... IS THE REAL REASON!
PLEASE TAKE A LOOK, KIRISHIMA-SAN...!!
"BLOODY-X LOSES INFECTIVITY AT HUMIDITY LEVELS LESS THAN 20%..."
THAT'S WHY SHE SHUT OFF THAT DEPOSITORY'S AC, BECAUSE THEY POSSESS A POWERFUL DEHUMIDIFYING CAPACITY!
WE CAN DO THIS, KIRISHIMA-SAN!!
EVEN IF THERE ARE VIRUS PARTICLES LEFT IN THE HALLWAYS, IF WE BLAST THE AC UNITS AT FULL POWER AND DEHUMIDIFY THE AIR TO INACTIVATE THEM...
...WE MIGHT BE ABLE TO FIGURE OUT AN ESCAPE ROUTE FOR EVERYONE!!

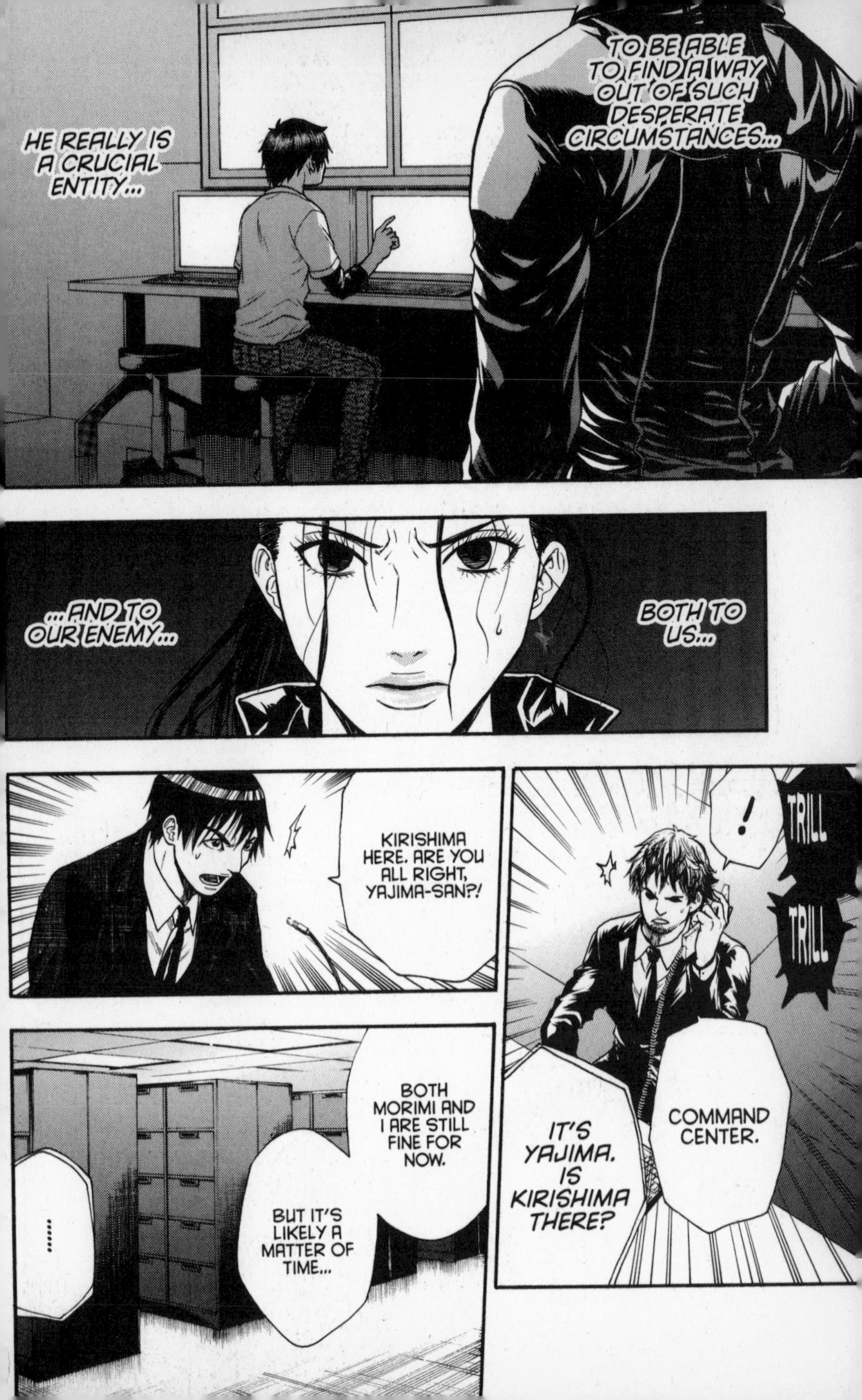
TO BE ABLE TO FIND A WAY OUT OF SUCH DESPERATE CIRCUMSTANCES...
HE REALLY IS A CRUCIAL ENTITY...
BOTH TO US...
...AND TO OUR ENEMY...
TRILL
TRILL
!
COMMAND CENTER.
IT'S YAJIMA. IS KIRISHIMA THERE?
KIRISHIMA HERE. ARE YOU ALL RIGHT, YAJIMA-SAN?!
BOTH MORIMI AND I ARE STILL FINE FOR NOW.
BUT IT'S LIKELY A MATTER OF TIME...
......

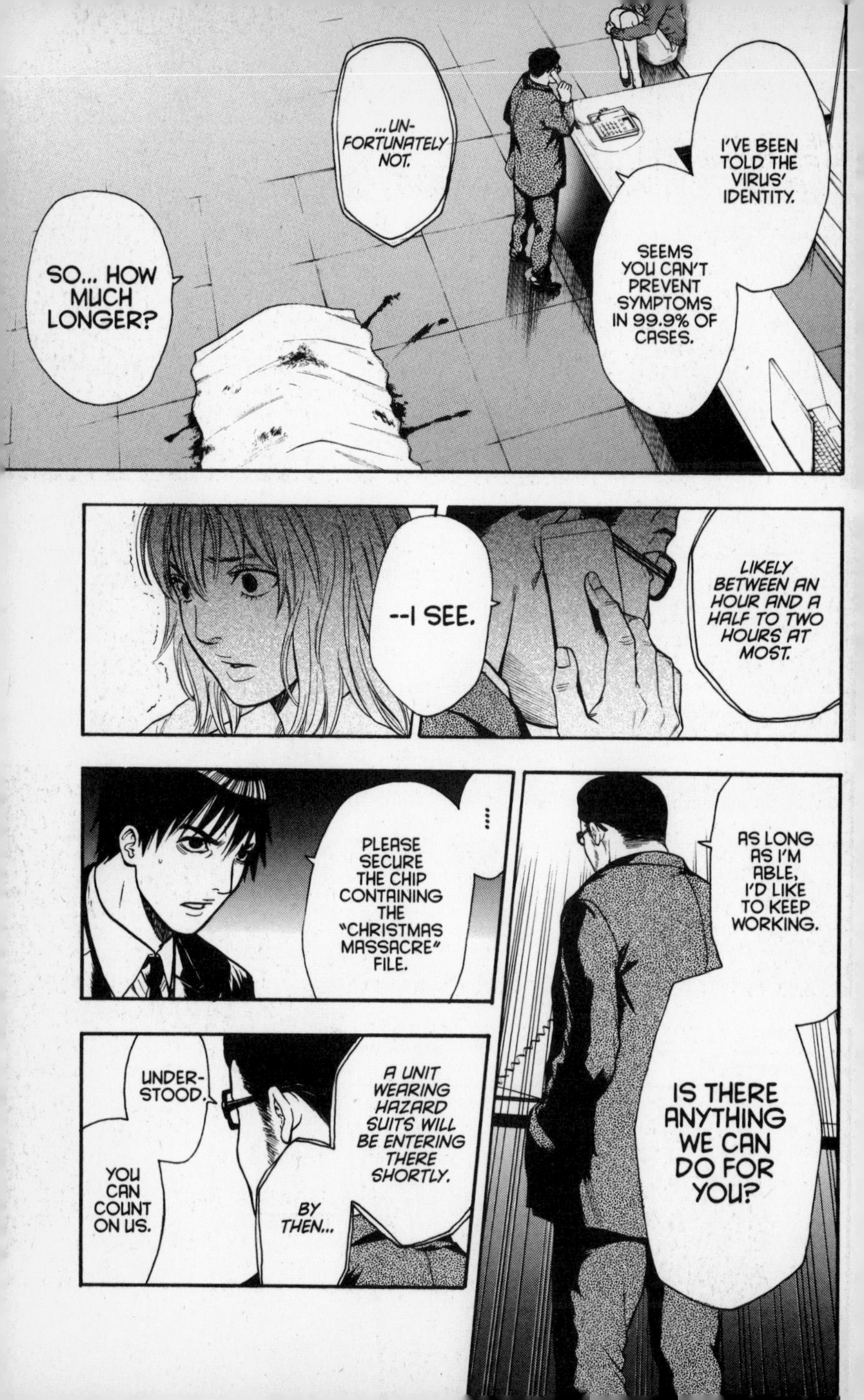
I'VE BEEN TOLD THE VIRUS' IDENTITY.
SEEMS YOU CAN'T PREVENT SYMPTOMS IN 99.9% OF CASES.
...UN-FORTUNATELY NOT.
SO... HOW MUCH LONGER?
LIKELY BETWEEN AN HOUR AND A HALF TO TWO HOURS AT MOST.
--I SEE.
AS LONG AS I'M ABLE, I'D LIKE TO KEEP WORKING.
IS THERE ANYTHING WE CAN DO FOR YOU?
....
PLEASE SECURE THE CHIP CONTAINING THE "CHRISTMAS MASSACRE" FILE.
A UNIT WEARING HAZARD SUITS WILL BE ENTERING THERE SHORTLY.
BY THEN...
UNDER-STOOD.
YOU CAN COUNT ON US.

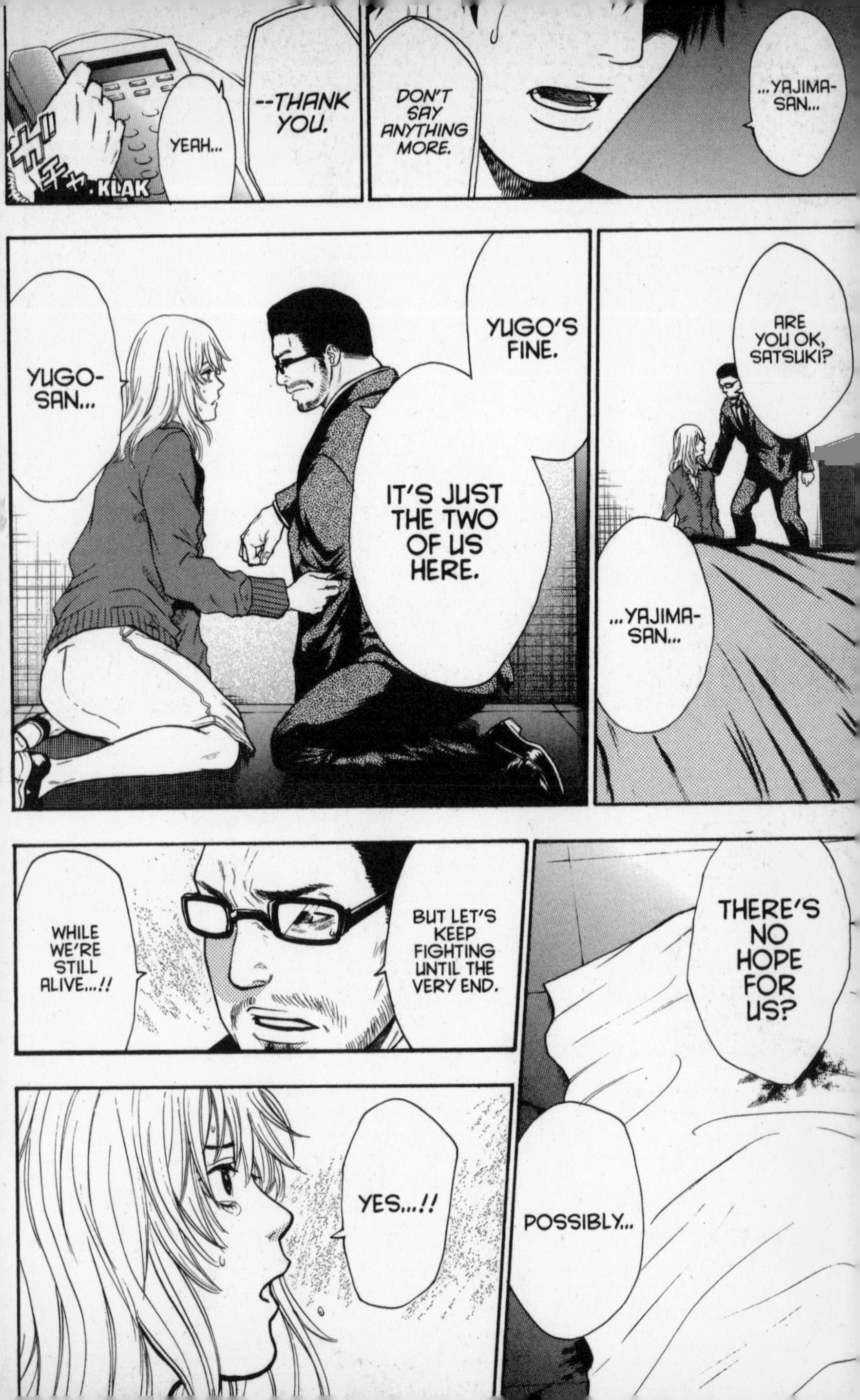
...YAJIMA-SAN...
DON'T SAY ANYTHING MORE.
--THANK YOU.
YEAH...
KLAK
ARE YOU OK, SATSUKI?
...YAJIMA-SAN...
YUGO'S FINE.
IT'S JUST THE TWO OF US HERE.
YUGO-SAN...
THERE'S NO HOPE FOR US?
POSSIBLY...
BUT LET'S KEEP FIGHTING UNTIL THE VERY END.
WHILE WE'RE STILL ALIVE...!!
YES...!!

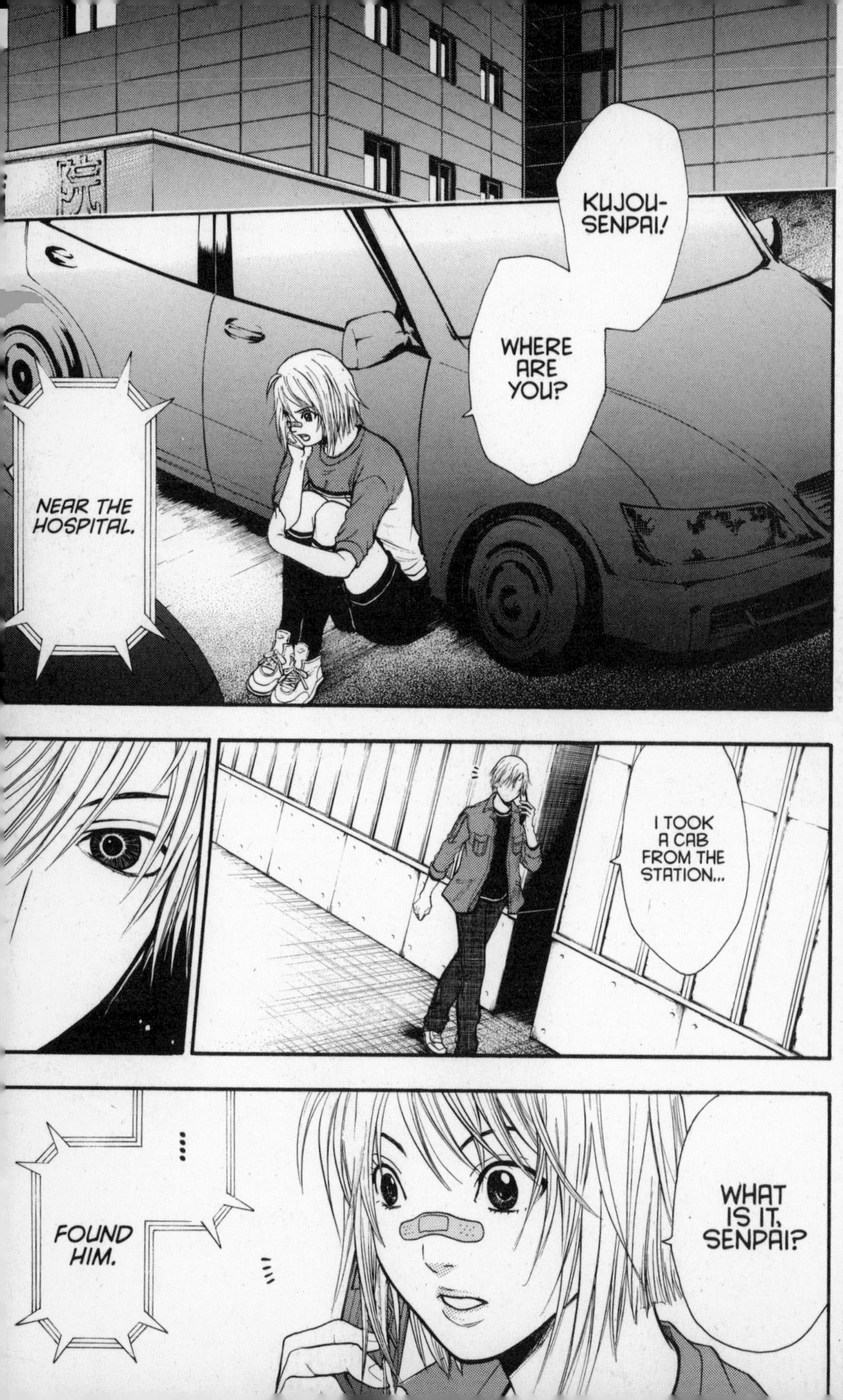
KUJOU-SENPAI!
WHERE ARE YOU?
院
NEAR THE HOSPITAL.
I TOOK A CAB FROM THE STATION...
WHAT IS IT, SENPAI?
....
FOUND HIM.

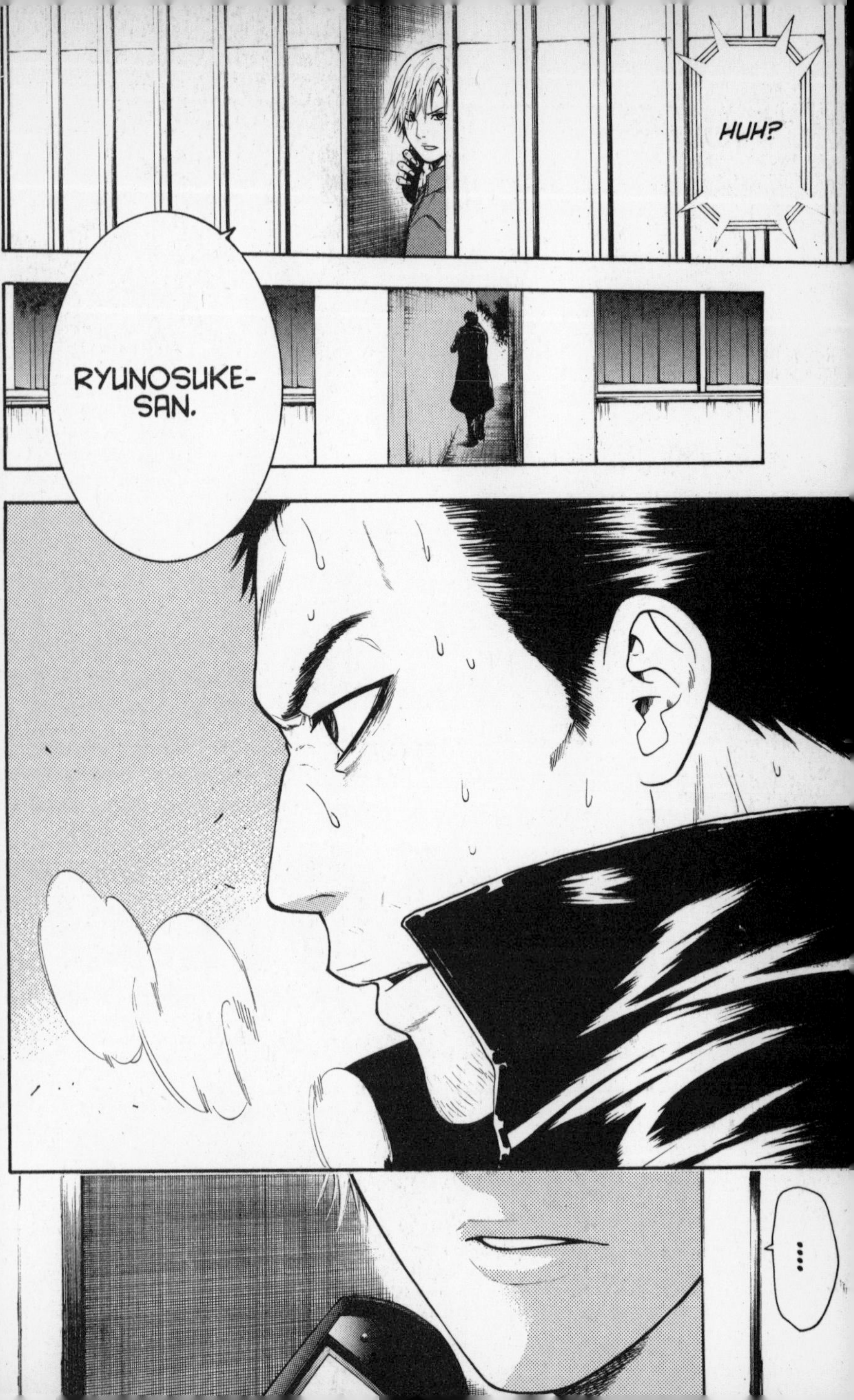
HUH?
RYUNOSUKE-SAN.
....

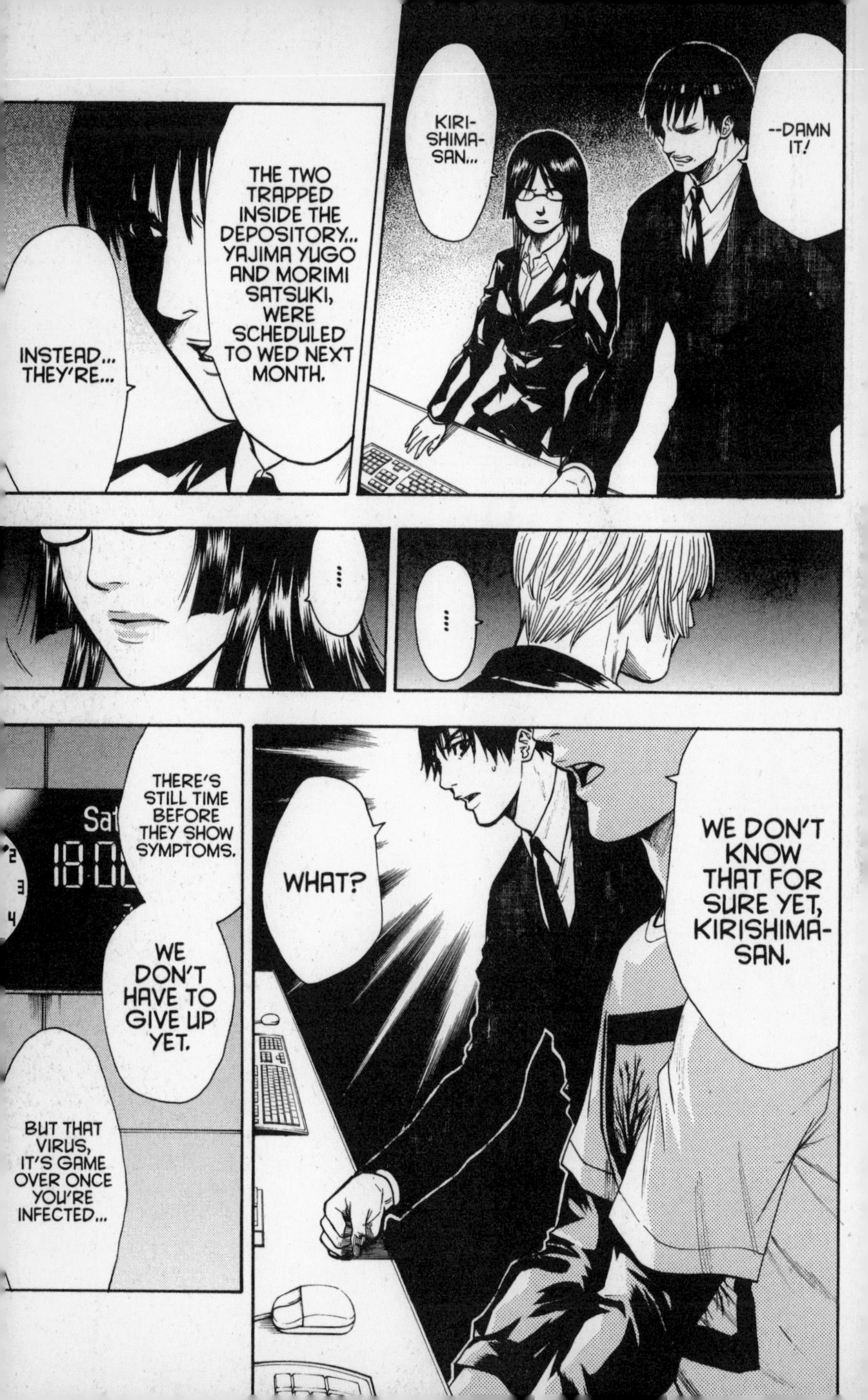
--DAMN IT!
KIRI-SHIMA-SAN...
THE TWO TRAPPED INSIDE THE DEPOSITORY... YAJIMA YUGO AND MORIMI SATSUKI, WERE SCHEDULED TO WED NEXT MONTH.
INSTEAD... THEY'RE...
....
....
WE DON'T KNOW THAT FOR SURE YET, KIRISHIMA-SAN.
WHAT?
THERE'S STILL TIME BEFORE THEY SHOW SYMPTOMS.
WE DON'T HAVE TO GIVE UP YET.
BUT THAT VIRUS, IT'S GAME OVER ONCE YOU'RE INFECTED...

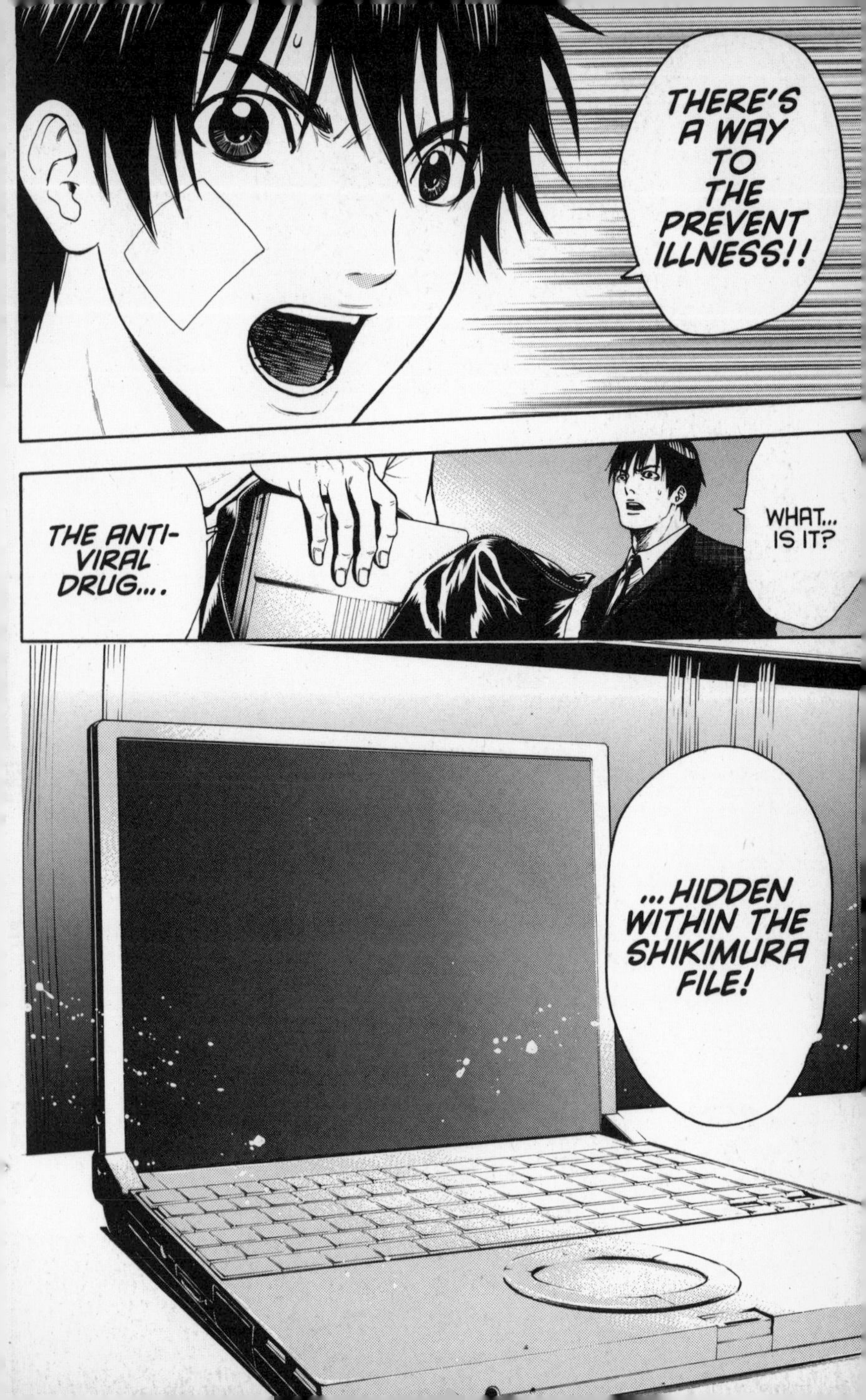
THERE'S A WAY TO THE PREVENT ILLNESS!!
WHAT... IS IT?
THE ANTI-VIRAL DRUG....
...HIDDEN WITHIN THE SHIKIMURA FILE!

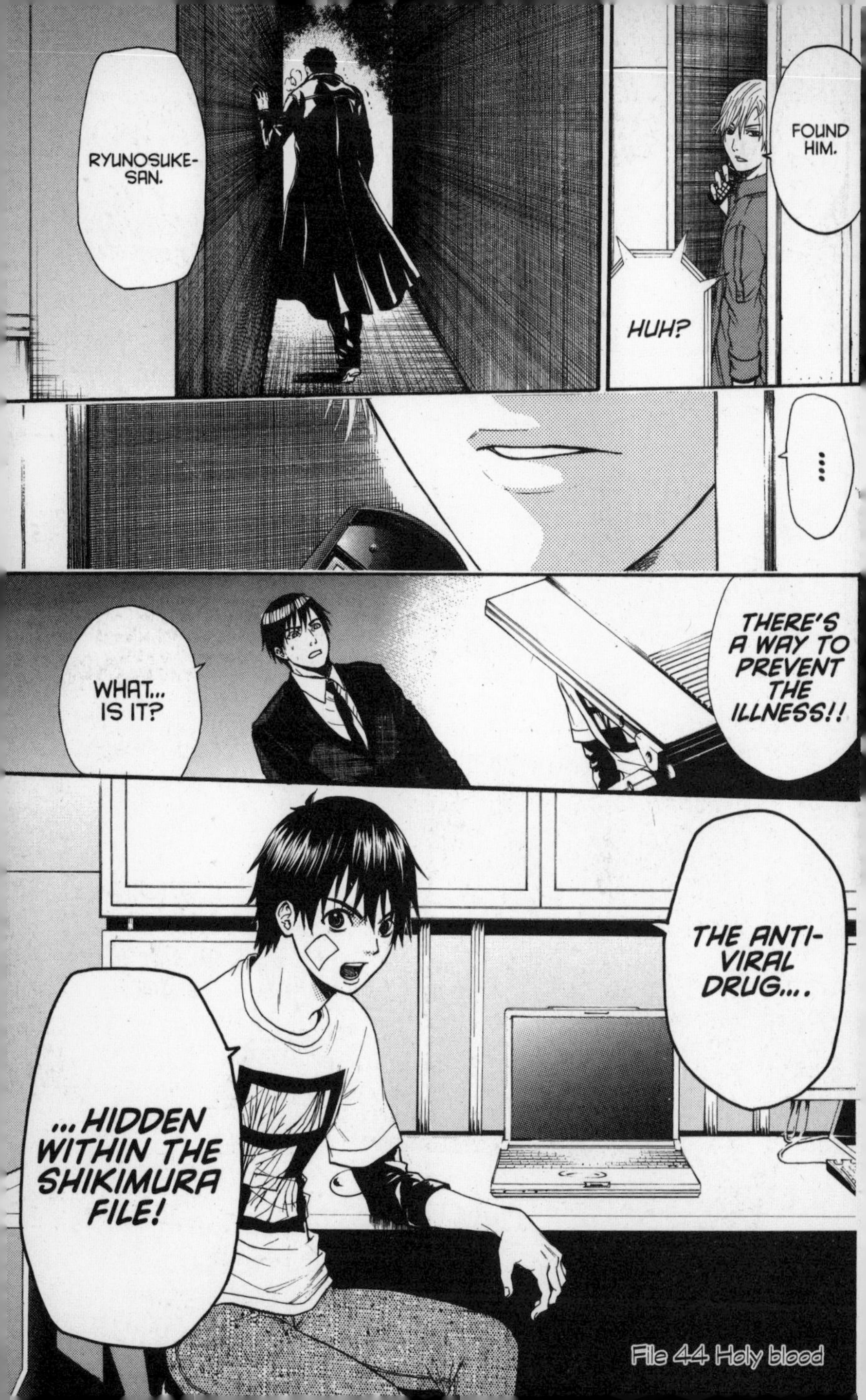

FOUND HIM.
HUH?
RYUNOSUKE-SAN.
....
THERE'S A WAY TO PREVENT THE ILLNESS!!
WHAT... IS IT?
THE ANTI-VIRAL DRUG....
...HIDDEN WITHIN THE SHIKIMURA FILE!
File 44 Holy blood

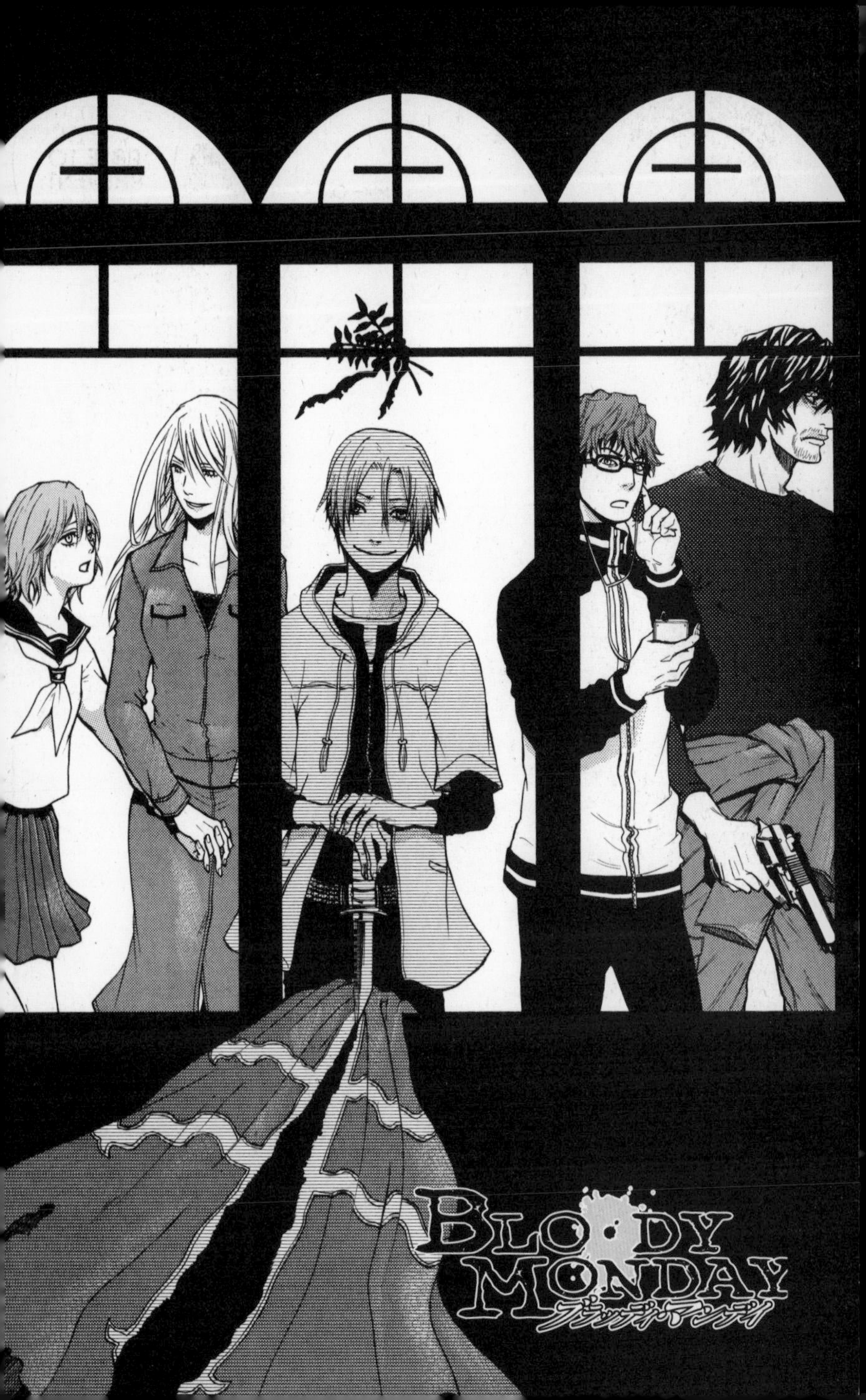
BLOODY MONDAY
ブラッディ・マンデイ

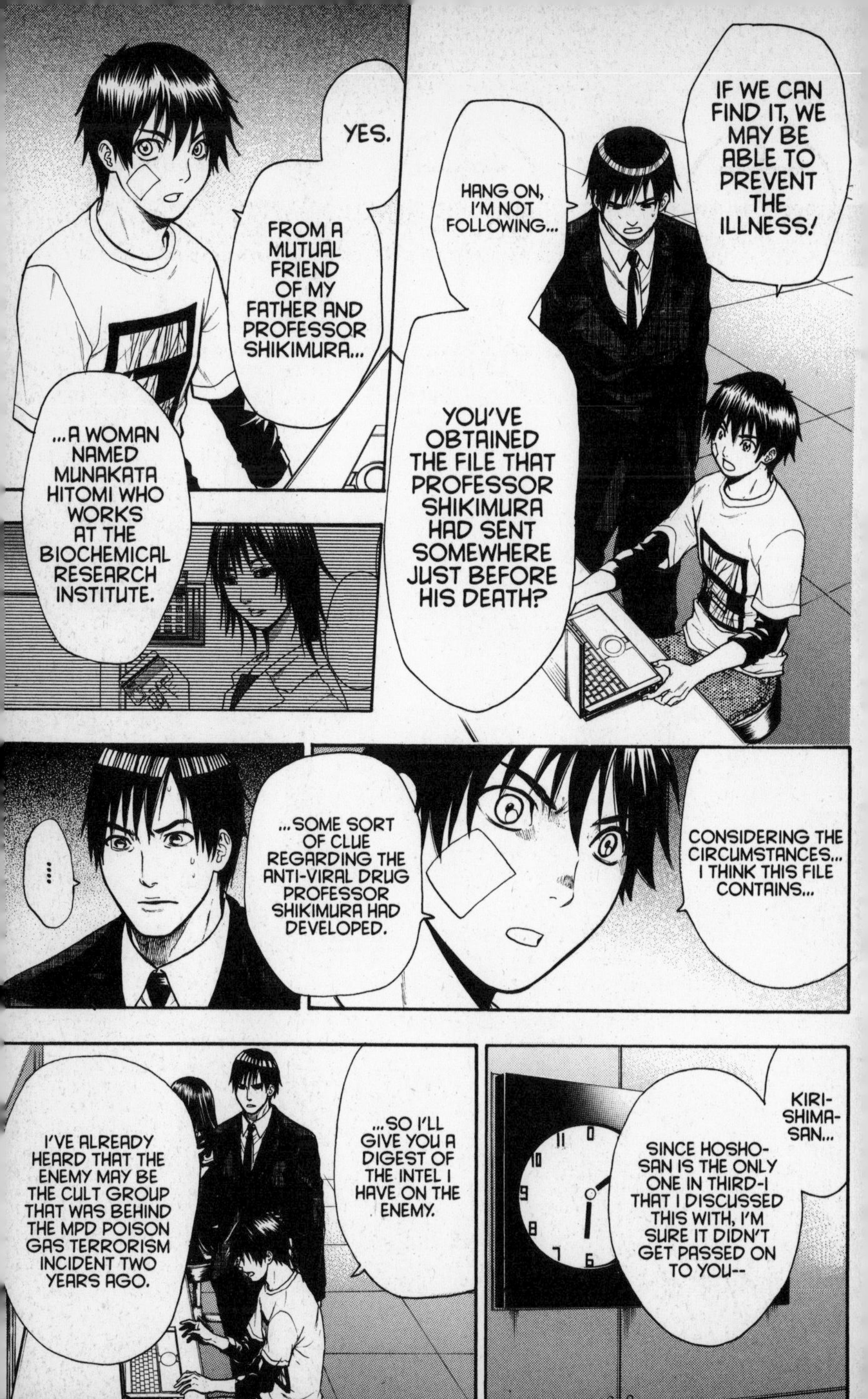
IF WE CAN FIND IT, WE MAY BE ABLE TO PREVENT THE ILLNESS!
HANG ON, I'M NOT FOLLOWING...
YOU'VE OBTAINED THE FILE THAT PROFESSOR SHIKIMURA HAD SENT SOMEWHERE JUST BEFORE HIS DEATH?
YES.
FROM A MUTUAL FRIEND OF MY FATHER AND PROFESSOR SHIKIMURA...
...A WOMAN NAMED MUNAKATA HITOMI WHO WORKS AT THE BIOCHEMICAL RESEARCH INSTITUTE.
CONSIDERING THE CIRCUMSTANCES... I THINK THIS FILE CONTAINS...
...SOME SORT OF CLUE REGARDING THE ANTI-VIRAL DRUG PROFESSOR SHIKIMURA HAD DEVELOPED.
....
KIRI-SHIMA-SAN...
SINCE HOSHO-SAN IS THE ONLY ONE IN THIRD-I THAT I DISCUSSED THIS WITH, I'M SURE IT DIDN'T GET PASSED ON TO YOU--
...SO I'LL GIVE YOU A DIGEST OF THE INTEL I HAVE ON THE ENEMY.
I'VE ALREADY HEARD THAT THE ENEMY MAY BE THE CULT GROUP THAT WAS BEHIND THE MPD POISON GAS TERRORISM INCIDENT TWO YEARS AGO.

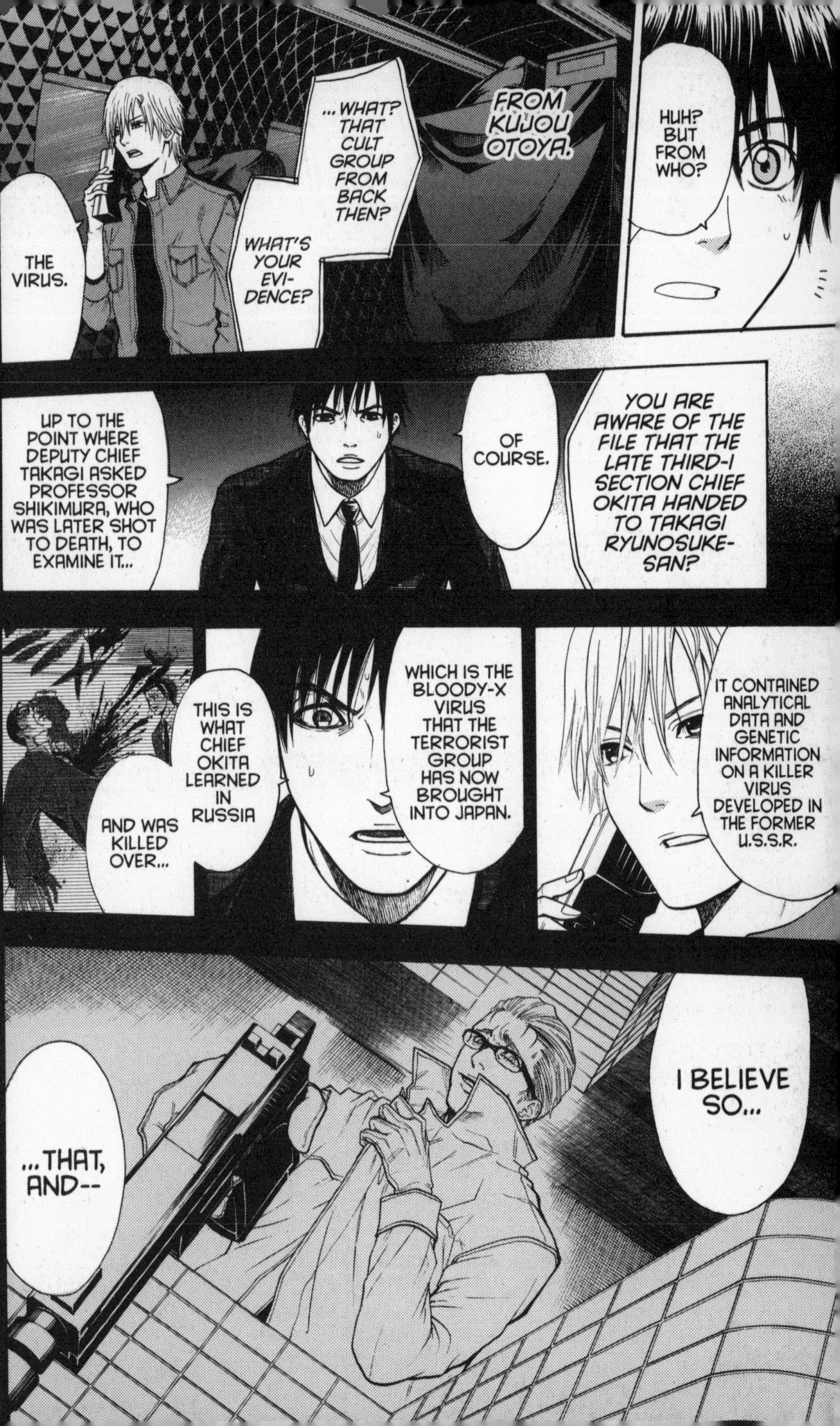
HUH? BUT FROM WHO?
FROM KUJOU OTOYA.
...WHAT? THAT CULT GROUP FROM BACK THEN?
WHAT'S YOUR EVI-DENCE?
THE VIRUS.
YOU ARE AWARE OF THE FILE THAT THE LATE THIRD-I SECTION CHIEF OKITA HANDED TO TAKAGI RYUNOSUKE-SAN?
OF COURSE.
UP TO THE POINT WHERE DEPUTY CHIEF TAKAGI ASKED PROFESSOR SHIKIMURA, WHO WAS LATER SHOT TO DEATH, TO EXAMINE IT...
IT CONTAINED ANALYTICAL DATA AND GENETIC INFORMATION ON A KILLER VIRUS DEVELOPED IN THE FORMER U.S.S.R.
WHICH IS THE BLOODY-X VIRUS THAT THE TERRORIST GROUP HAS NOW BROUGHT INTO JAPAN.
THIS IS WHAT CHIEF OKITA LEARNED IN RUSSIA
AND WAS KILLED OVER...
I BELIEVE SO...
...THAT, AND--

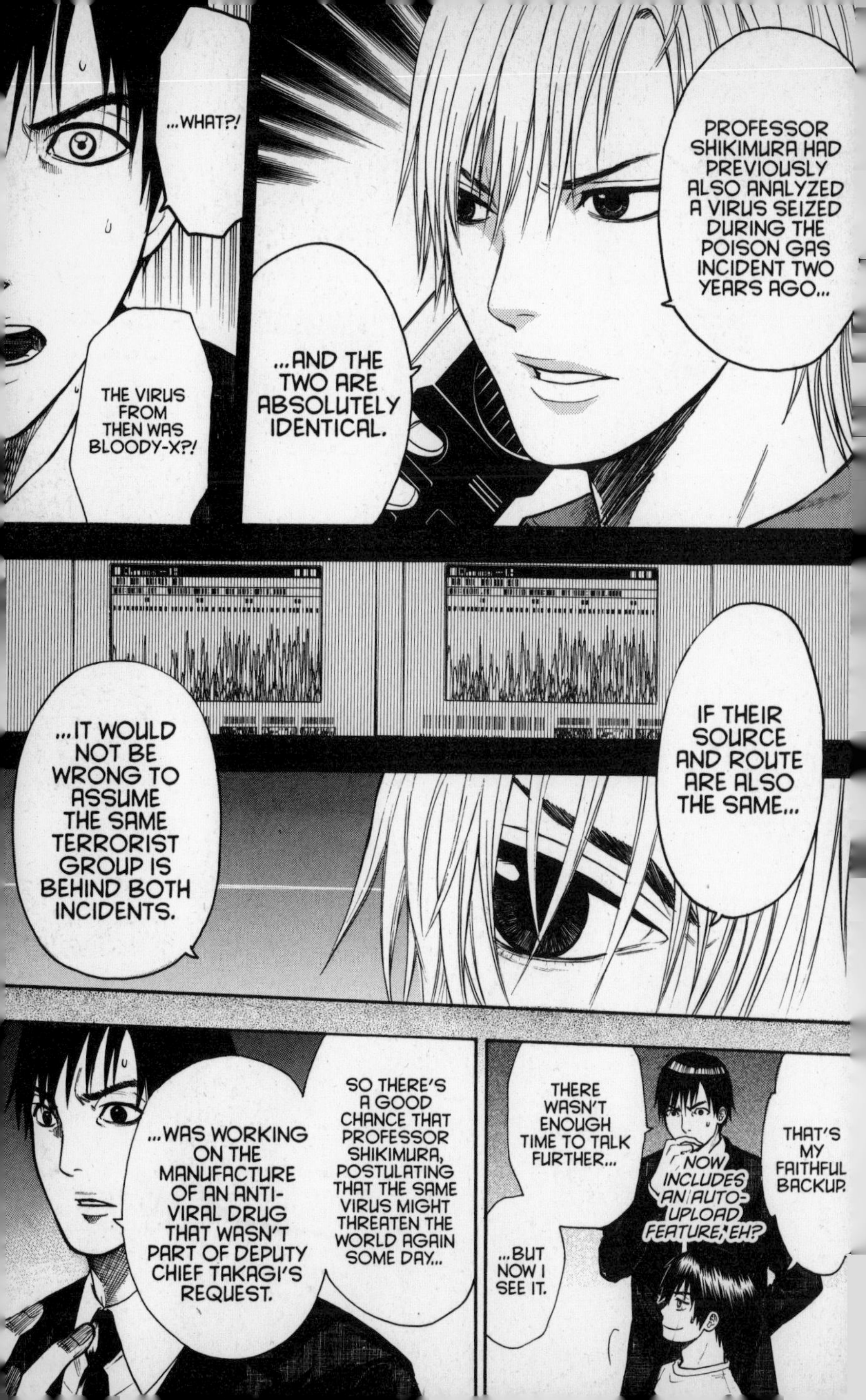

PROFESSOR SHIKIMURA HAD PREVIOUSLY ALSO ANALYZED A VIRUS SEIZED DURING THE POISON GAS INCIDENT TWO YEARS AGO...
...AND THE TWO ARE ABSOLUTELY IDENTICAL.
...WHAT?!
THE VIRUS FROM THEN WAS BLOODY-X?!
IF THEIR SOURCE AND ROUTE ARE ALSO THE SAME...
...IT WOULD NOT BE WRONG TO ASSUME THE SAME TERRORIST GROUP IS BEHIND BOTH INCIDENTS.
THAT'S MY FAITHFUL BACKUP.
NOW INCLUDES AN AUTO-UPLOAD FEATURE, EH?
THERE WASN'T ENOUGH TIME TO TALK FURTHER...
...BUT NOW I SEE IT.
SO THERE'S A GOOD CHANCE THAT PROFESSOR SHIKIMURA, POSTULATING THAT THE SAME VIRUS MIGHT THREATEN THE WORLD AGAIN SOME DAY...
...WAS WORKING ON THE MANUFACTURE OF AN ANTI-VIRAL DRUG THAT WASN'T PART OF DEPUTY CHIEF TAKAGI'S REQUEST.

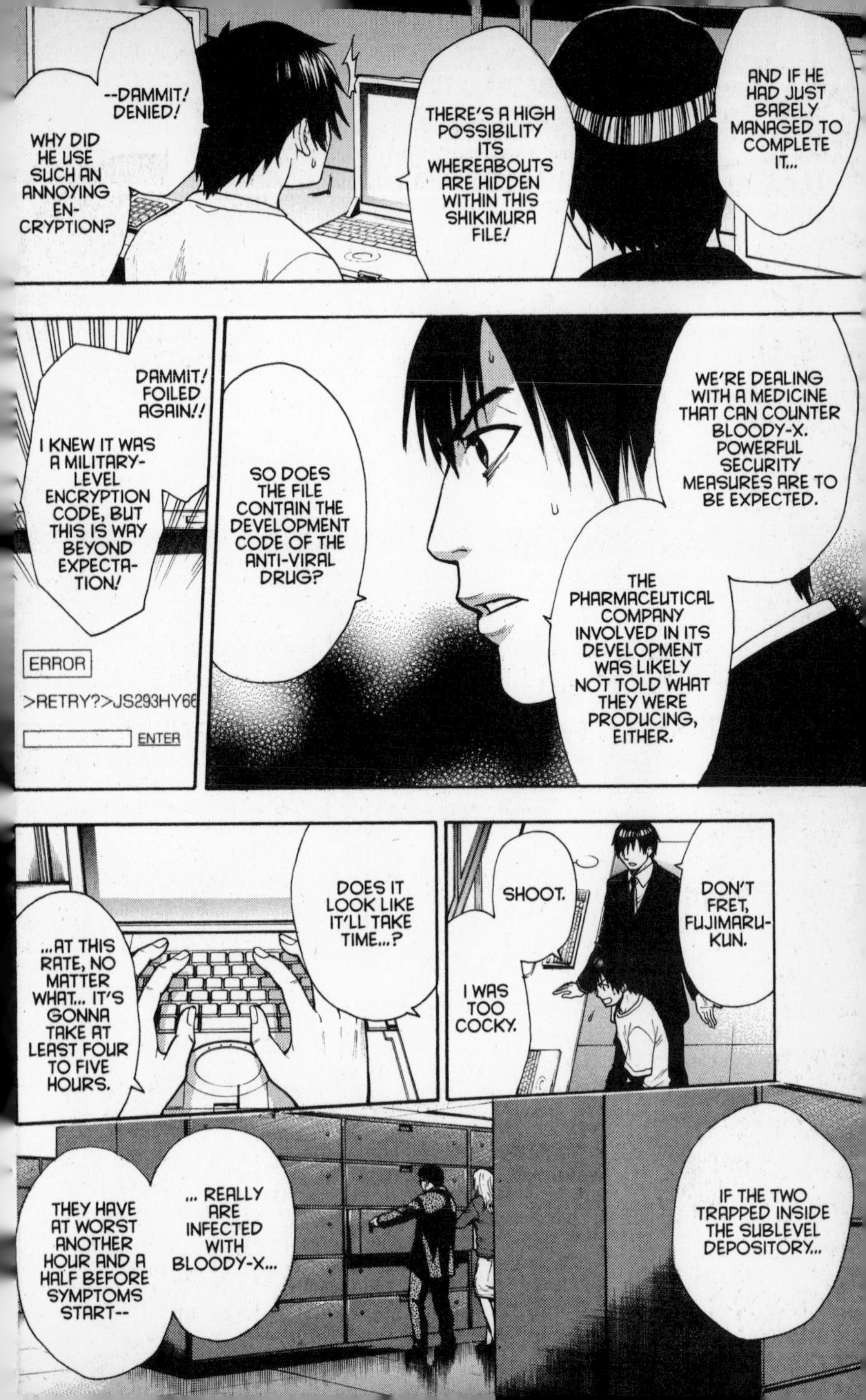
AND IF HE HAD JUST BARELY MANAGED TO COMPLETE IT...
THERE'S A HIGH POSSIBILITY ITS WHEREABOUTS ARE HIDDEN WITHIN THIS SHIKIMURA FILE!
--DAMMIT! DENIED!
WHY DID HE USE SUCH AN ANNOYING EN-CRYPTION?
WE'RE DEALING WITH A MEDICINE THAT CAN COUNTER BLOODY-X. POWERFUL SECURITY MEASURES ARE TO BE EXPECTED.
THE PHARMACEUTICAL COMPANY INVOLVED IN ITS DEVELOPMENT WAS LIKELY NOT TOLD WHAT THEY WERE PRODUCING, EITHER.
SO DOES THE FILE CONTAIN THE DEVELOPMENT CODE OF THE ANTI-VIRAL DRUG?
DAMMIT! FOILED AGAIN!!
I KNEW IT WAS A MILITARY-LEVEL ENCRYPTION CODE, BUT THIS IS WAY BEYOND EXPECTA-TION!
ERROR
>RETRY?>JS293HY66
ENTER
DON'T FRET, FUJIMARU-KUN.
SHOOT.
I WAS TOO COCKY.
DOES IT LOOK LIKE IT'LL TAKE TIME...?
...AT THIS RATE, NO MATTER WHAT... IT'S GONNA TAKE AT LEAST FOUR TO FIVE HOURS.
IF THE TWO TRAPPED INSIDE THE SUBLEVEL DEPOSITORY...
... REALLY ARE INFECTED WITH BLOODY-X...
THEY HAVE AT WORST ANOTHER HOUR AND A HALF BEFORE SYMPTOMS START--

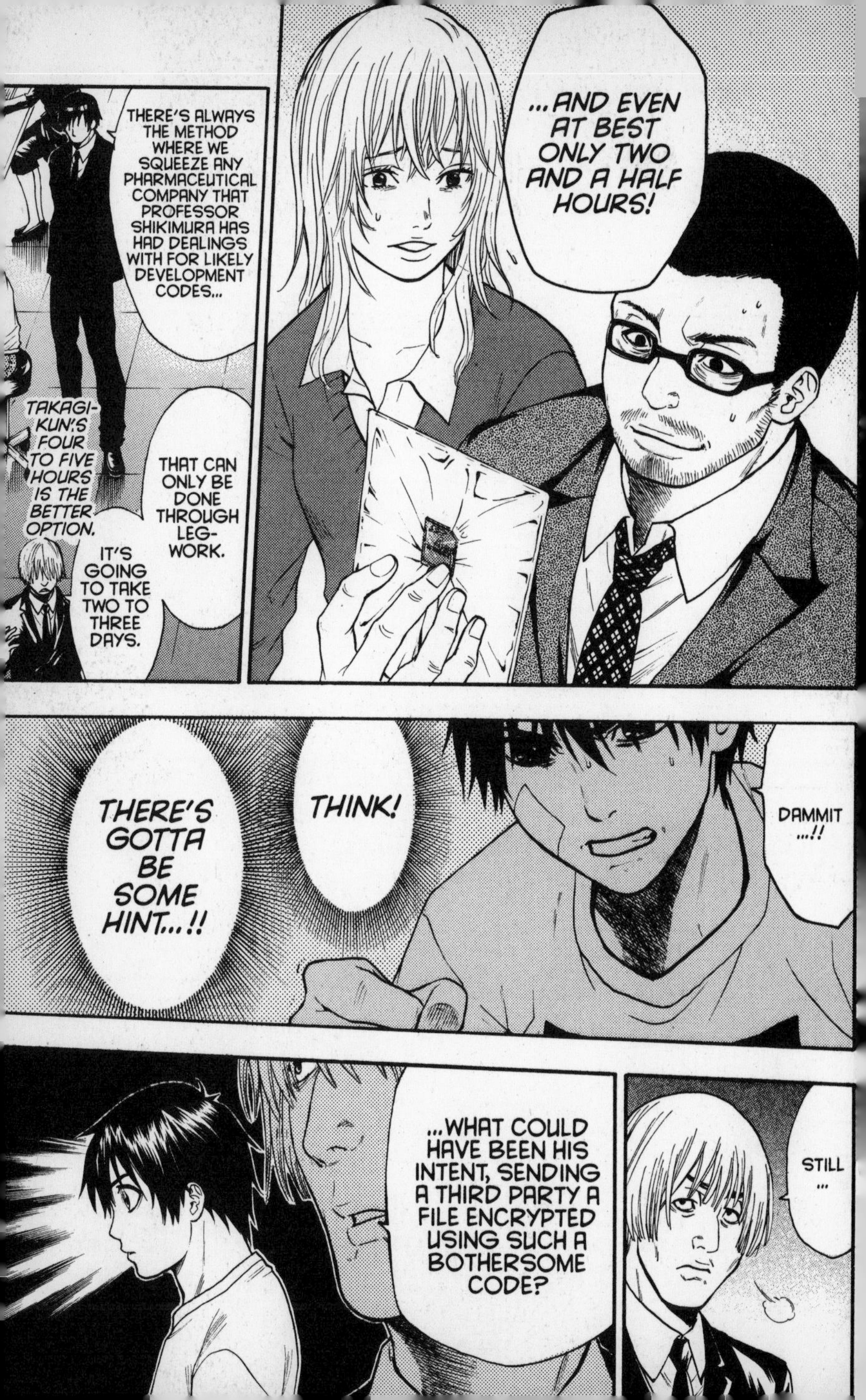
...AND EVEN AT BEST ONLY TWO AND A HALF HOURS!
THERE'S ALWAYS THE METHOD WHERE WE SQUEEZE ANY PHARMACEUTICAL COMPANY THAT PROFESSOR SHIKIMURA HAS HAD DEALINGS WITH FOR LIKELY DEVELOPMENT CODES...
THAT CAN ONLY BE DONE THROUGH LEG-WORK.
IT'S GOING TO TAKE TWO TO THREE DAYS.
TAKAGI-KUN'S FOUR TO FIVE HOURS IS THE BETTER OPTION.
DAMMIT ...!!
THINK!
THERE'S GOTTA BE SOME HINT...!!
STILL ...
...WHAT COULD HAVE BEEN HIS INTENT, SENDING A THIRD PARTY A FILE ENCRYPTED USING SUCH A BOTHERSOME CODE?

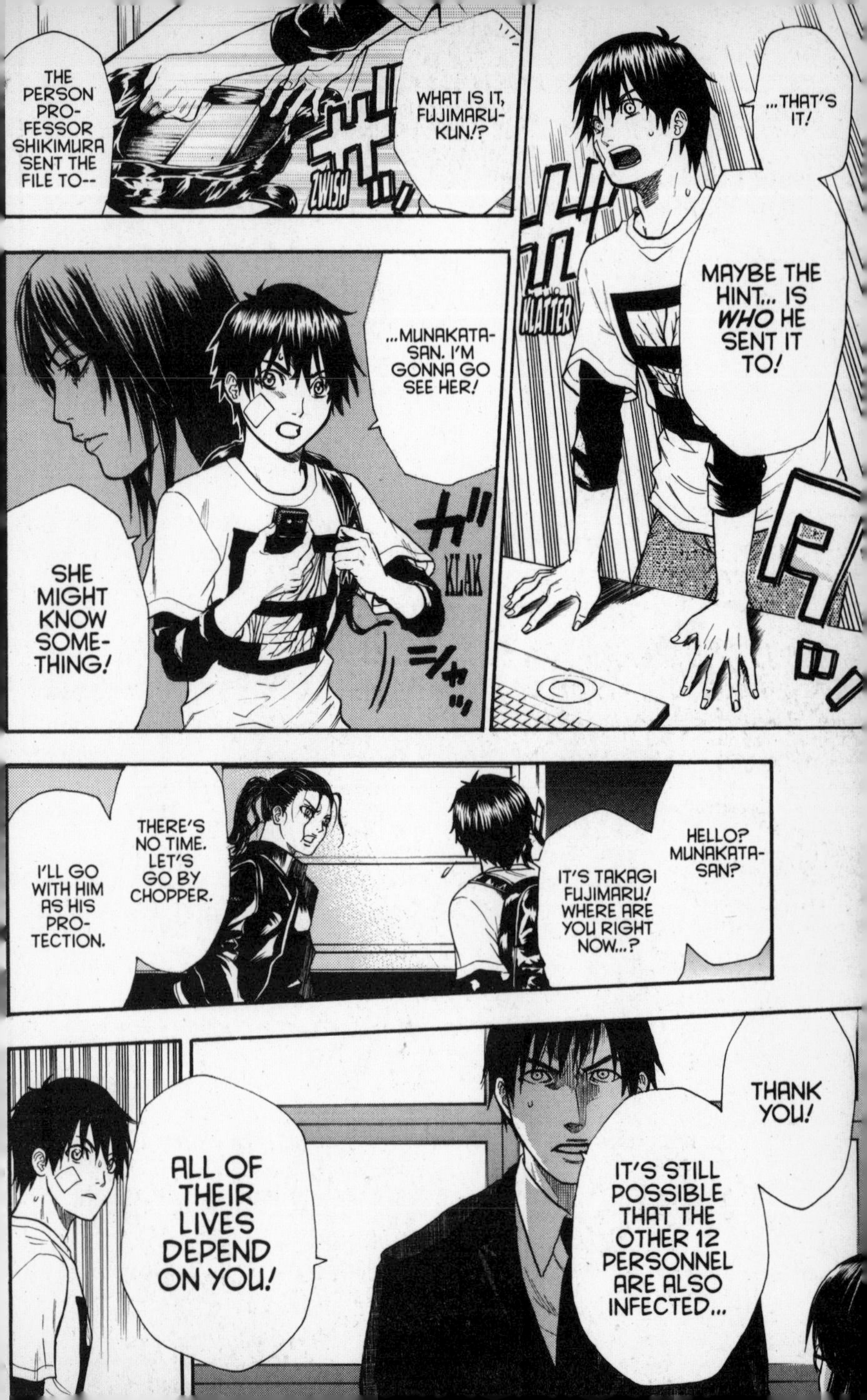
...THAT'S IT!
KLATTER
MAYBE THE HINT... IS *WHO* HE SENT IT TO!
WHAT IS IT, FUJIMARU-KUN!?
ZWISH
THE PERSON PROFESSOR SHIKIMURA SENT THE FILE TO--
...MUNAKATA-SAN. I'M GONNA GO SEE HER!
KLAK
SHE MIGHT KNOW SOMETHING!
HELLO? MUNAKATA-SAN?
IT'S TAKAGI FUJIMARU! WHERE ARE YOU RIGHT NOW...?
THERE'S NO TIME. LET'S GO BY CHOPPER.
I'LL GO WITH HIM AS HIS PROTECTION.
THANK YOU!
IT'S STILL POSSIBLE THAT THE OTHER 12 PERSONNEL ARE ALSO INFECTED...
ALL OF THEIR LIVES DEPEND ON YOU!

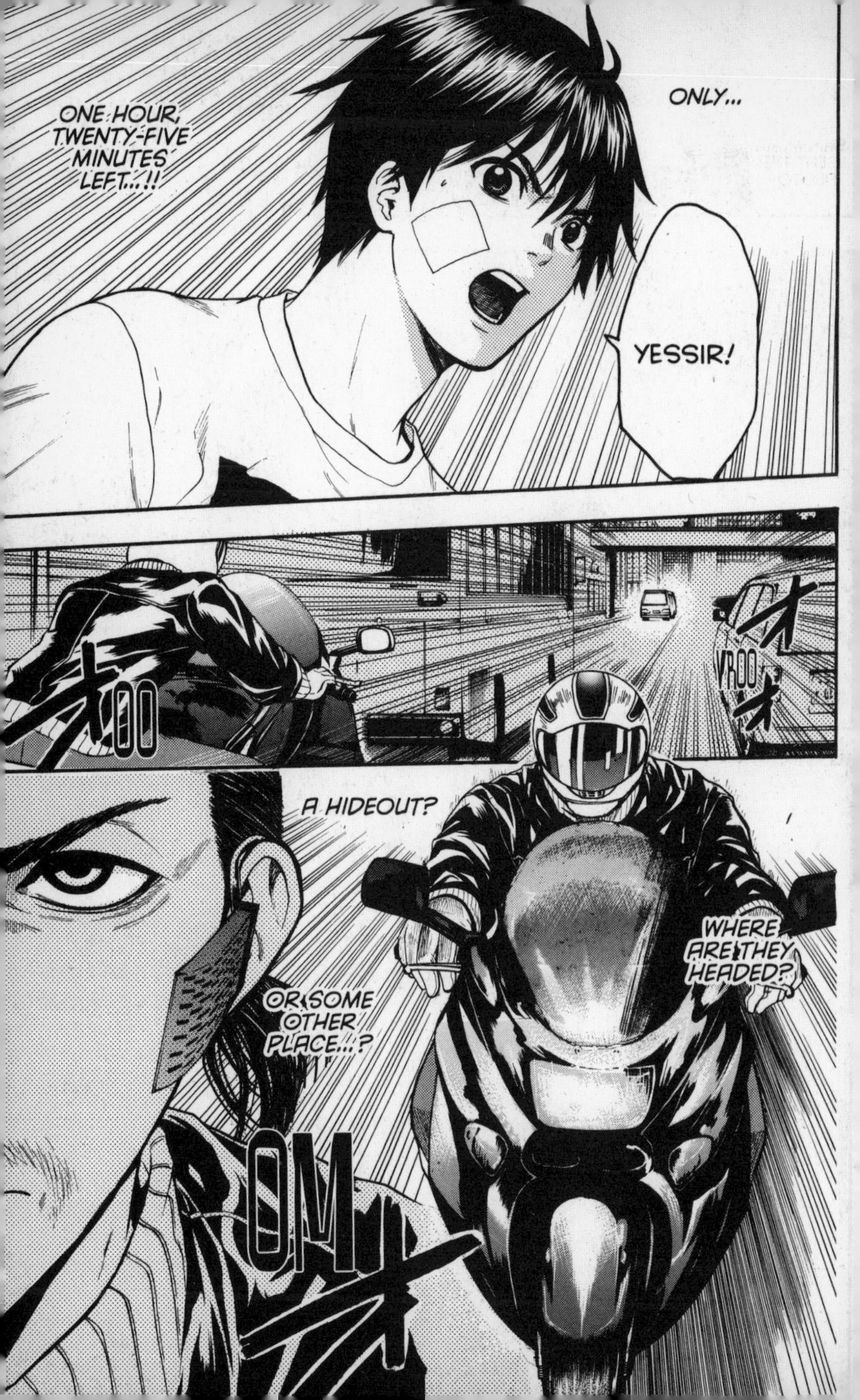
ONLY...
YESSIR!
ONE HOUR, TWENTY-FIVE MINUTES LEFT...!!
VROO
OO
WHERE ARE THEY HEADED?
A HIDEOUT?
OR SOME OTHER PLACE...?
OM

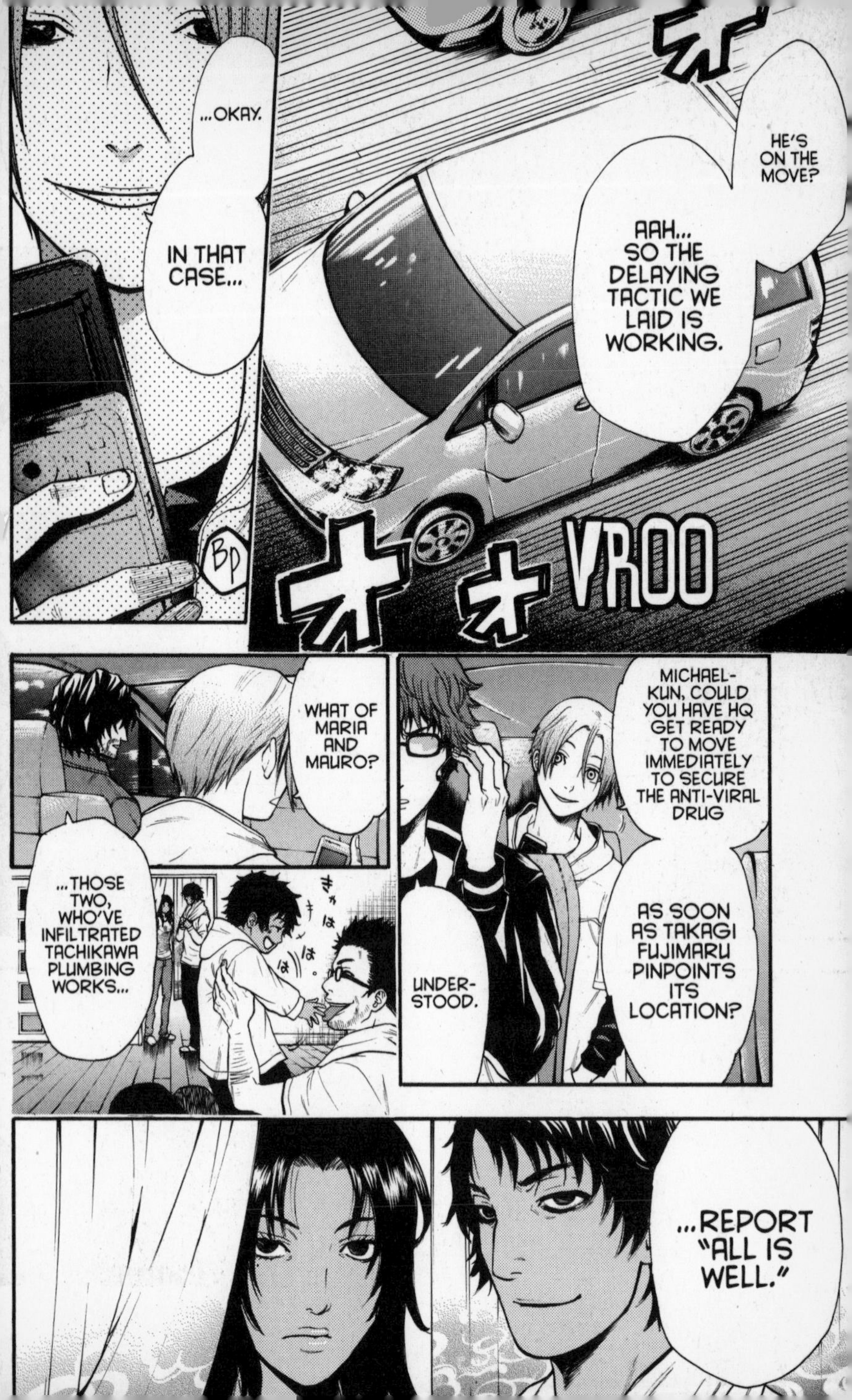
HE'S ON THE MOVE?
AAH... SO THE DELAYING TACTIC WE LAID IS WORKING.
VROO
...OKAY.
IN THAT CASE...
BP
MICHAEL-KUN, COULD YOU HAVE HQ GET READY TO MOVE IMMEDIATELY TO SECURE THE ANTI-VIRAL DRUG
AS SOON AS TAKAGI FUJIMARU PINPOINTS ITS LOCATION?
UNDER-STOOD.
WHAT OF MARIA AND MAURO?
...THOSE TWO, WHO'VE INFILTRATED TACHIKAWA PLUMBING WORKS...
...REPORT "ALL IS WELL."

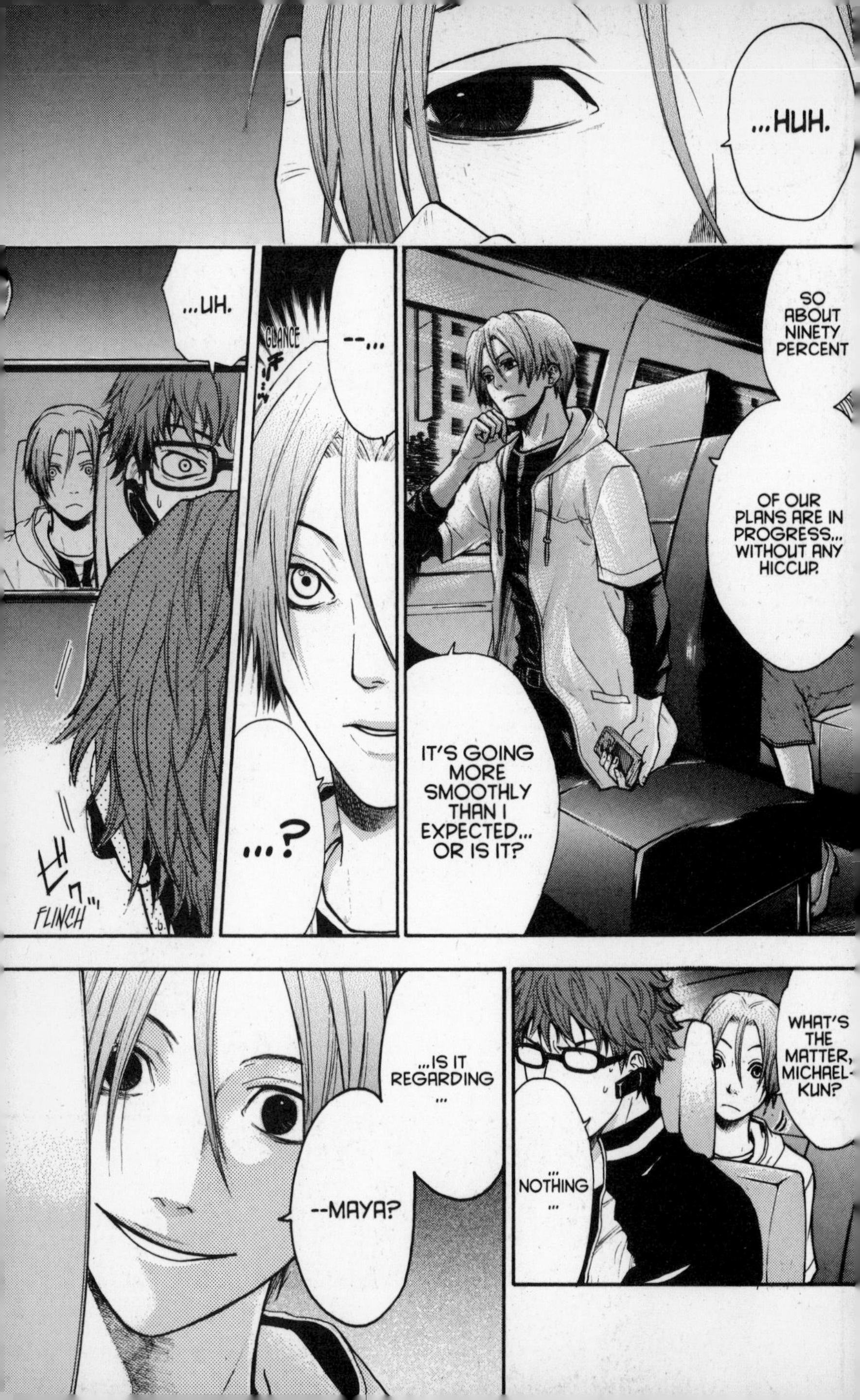
...HUH.
SO ABOUT NINETY PERCENT
OF OUR PLANS ARE IN PROGRESS... WITHOUT ANY HICCUP.
IT'S GOING MORE SMOOTHLY THAN I EXPECTED... OR IS IT?
GLANCE
--...
...?
...UH.
FLINCH
WHAT'S THE MATTER, MICHAEL-KUN?
... NOTHING ...
...IS IT REGARDING ...
--MAYA?

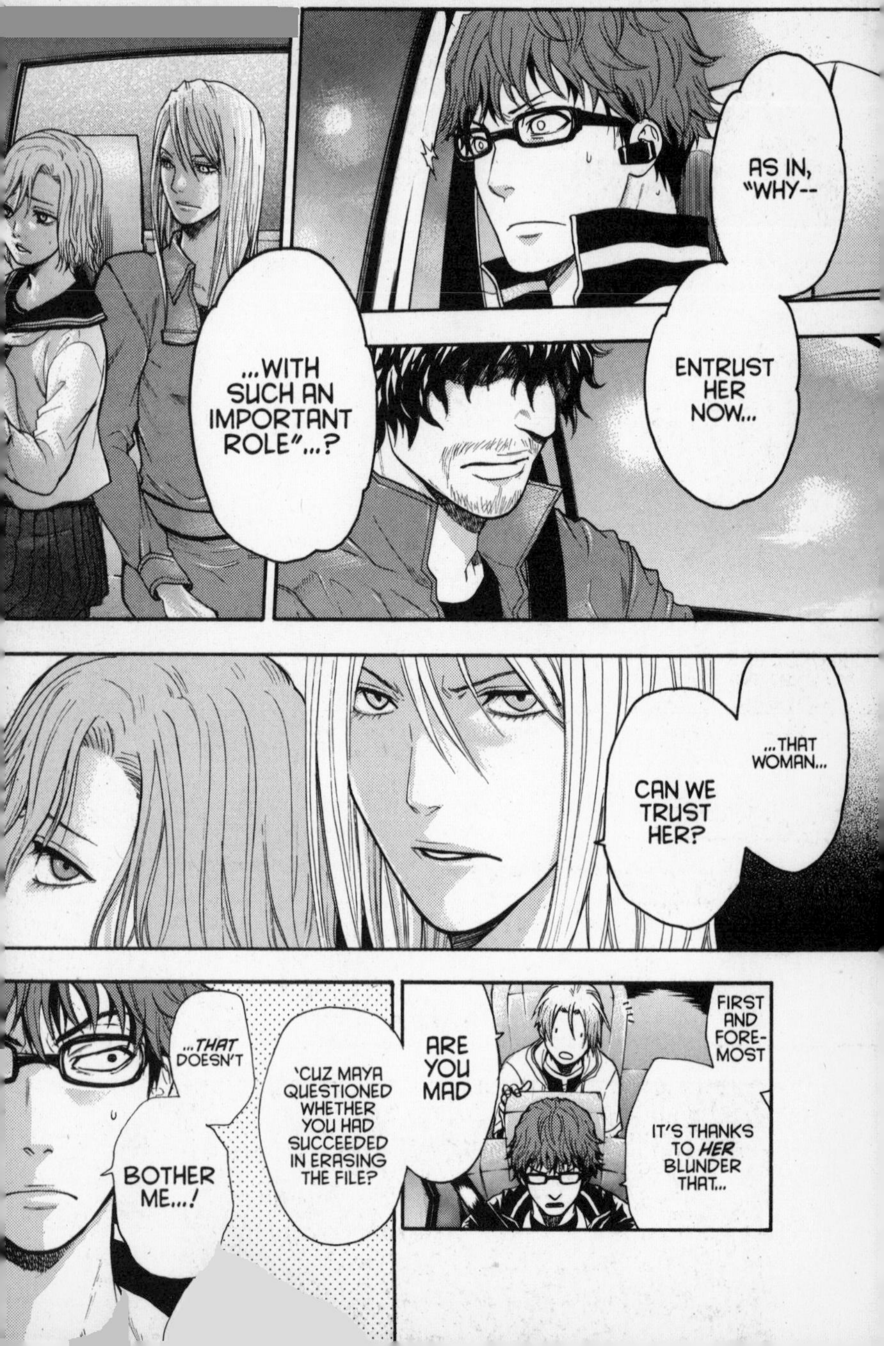
AS IN, "WHY--
ENTRUST HER NOW...
...WITH SUCH AN IMPORTANT ROLE"...?
...THAT WOMAN...
CAN WE TRUST HER?
FIRST AND FORE-MOST
IT'S THANKS TO *HER* BLUNDER THAT...
ARE YOU MAD
'CUZ MAYA QUESTIONED WHETHER YOU HAD SUCCEEDED IN ERASING THE FILE?
...*THAT* DOESN'T
BOTHER ME...!

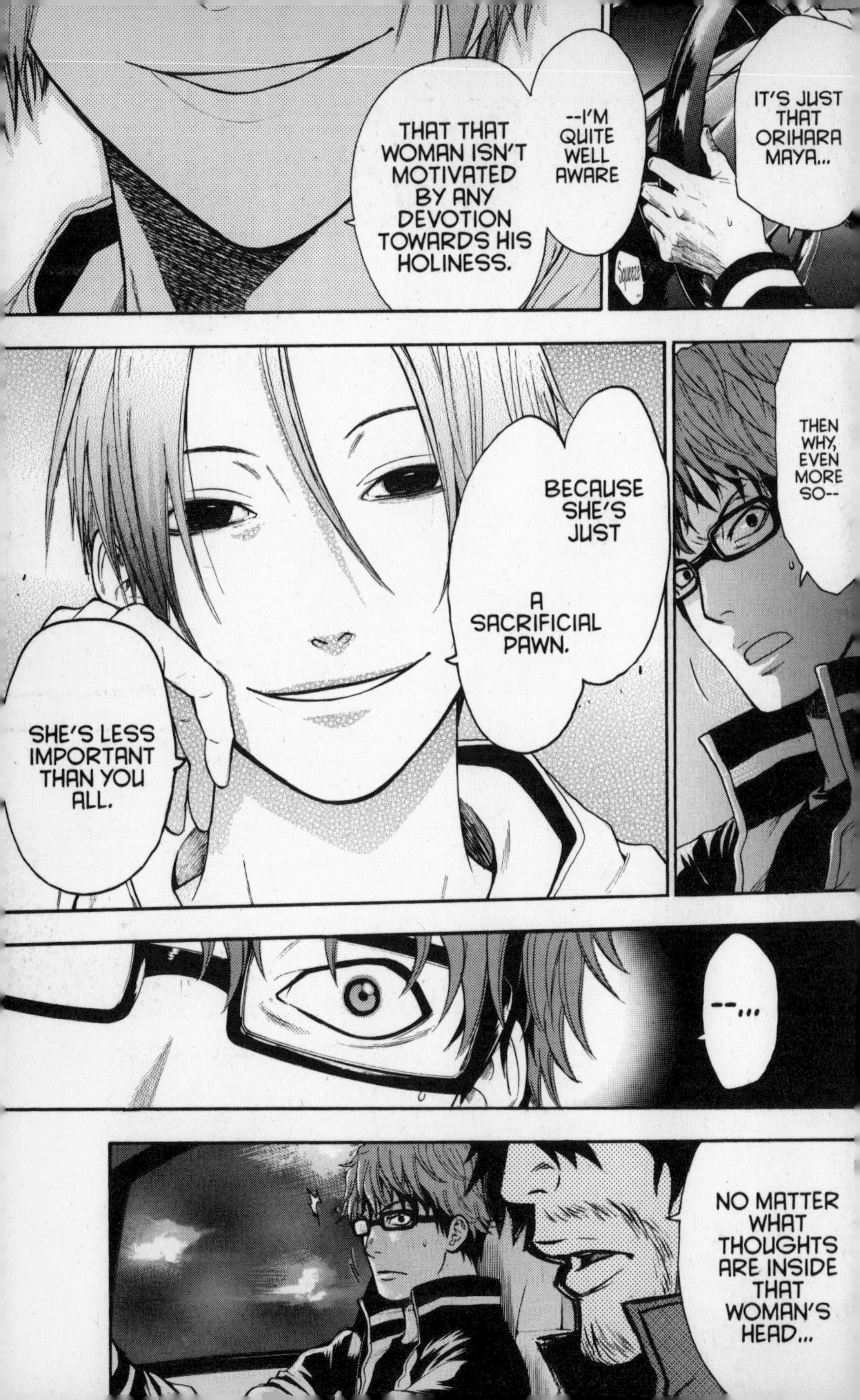
IT'S JUST THAT ORIHARA MAYA...
Squeeze
--I'M QUITE WELL AWARE
THAT THAT WOMAN ISN'T MOTIVATED BY ANY DEVOTION TOWARDS HIS HOLINESS.
THEN WHY, EVEN MORE SO--
BECAUSE SHE'S JUST
A SACRIFICIAL PAWN.
SHE'S LESS IMPORTANT THAN YOU ALL.
--...
NO MATTER WHAT THOUGHTS ARE INSIDE THAT WOMAN'S HEAD...

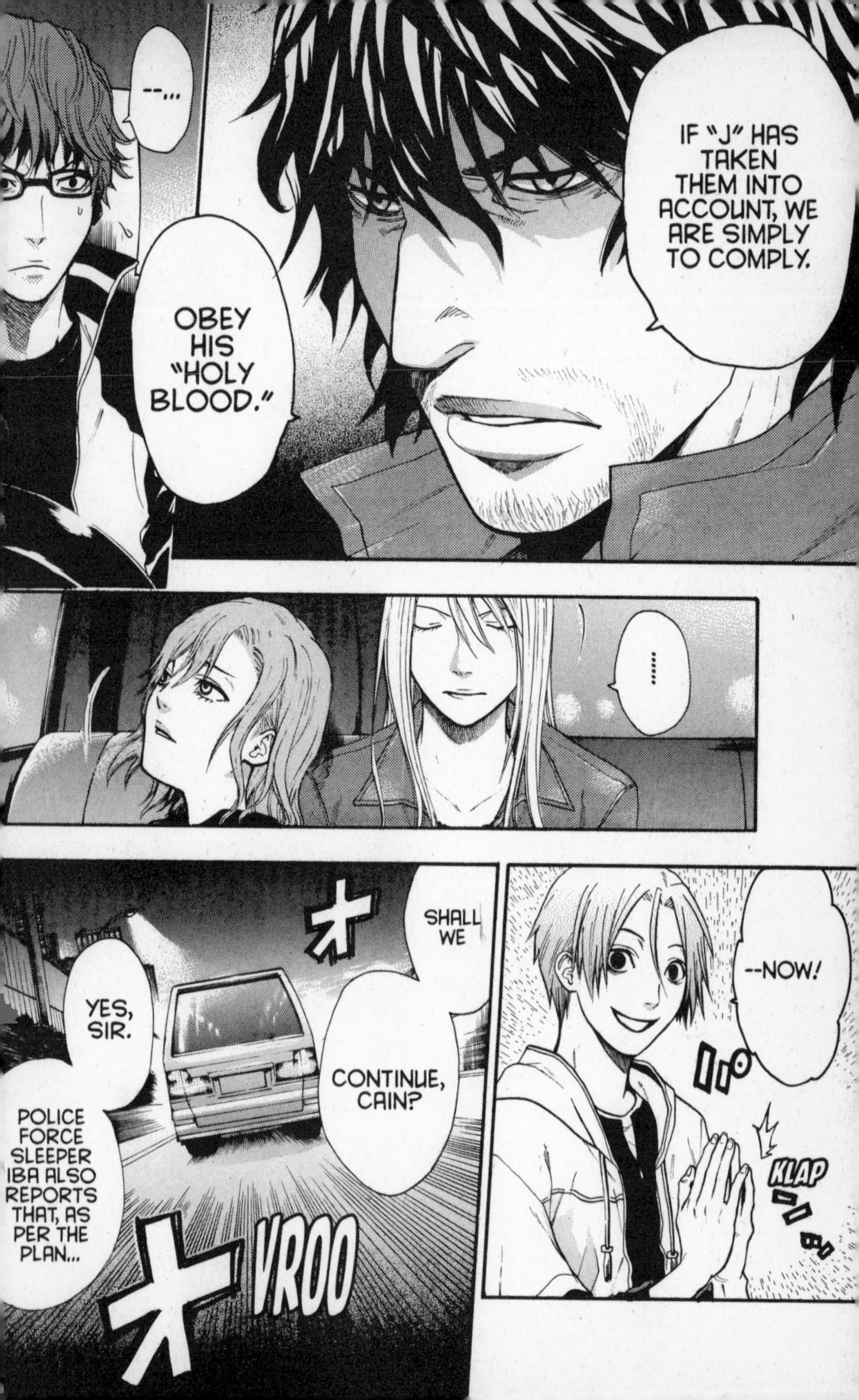
IF "J" HAS TAKEN THEM INTO ACCOUNT, WE ARE SIMPLY TO COMPLY.
OBEY HIS "HOLY BLOOD."
--...
......
--NOW!
KLAP
SHALL WE
CONTINUE, CAIN?
YES, SIR.
POLICE FORCE SLEEPER IBA ALSO REPORTS THAT, AS PER THE PLAN...
VROO

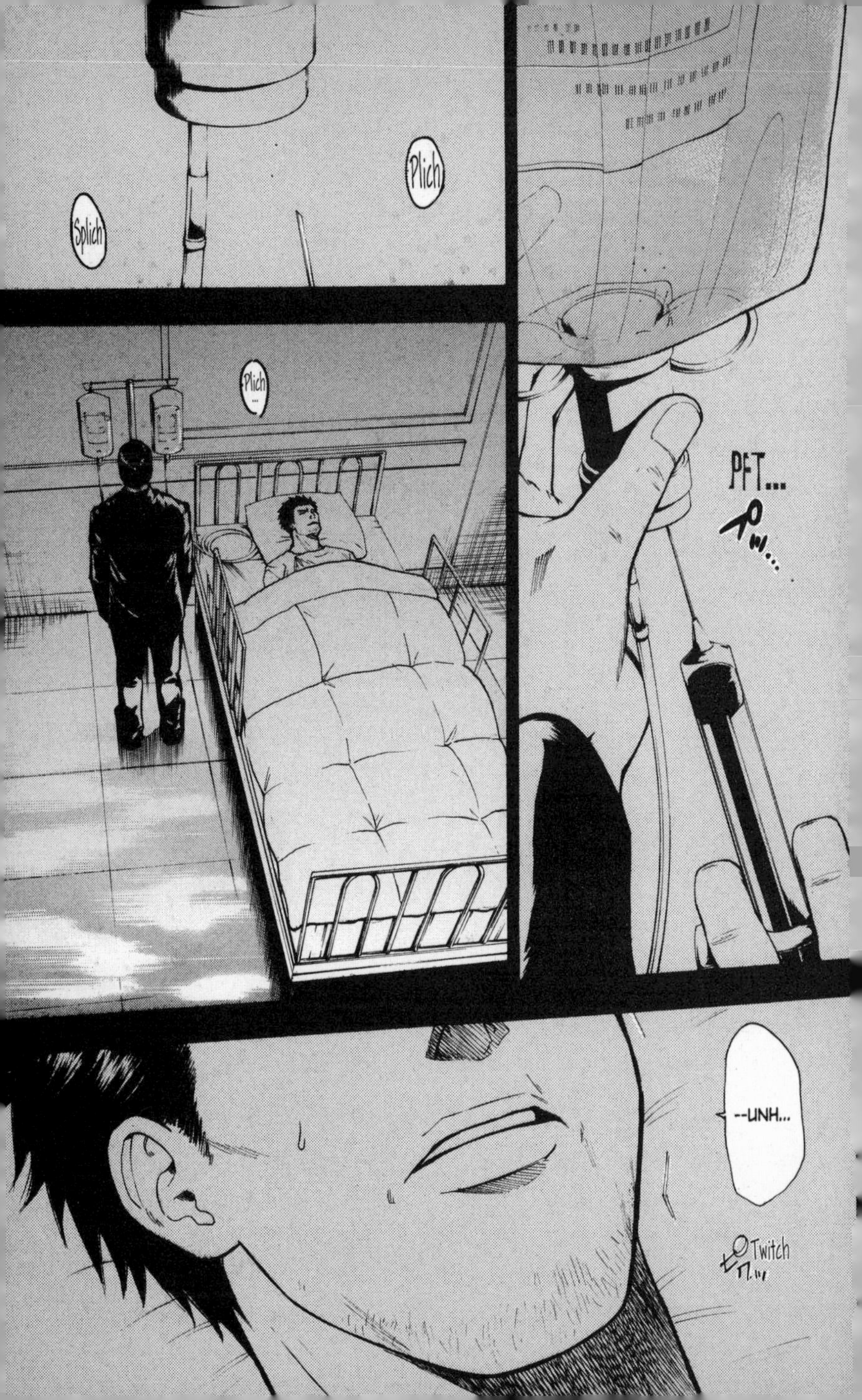
PFT...
Plich
Splich
Plich ...
--UNH...
Twitch

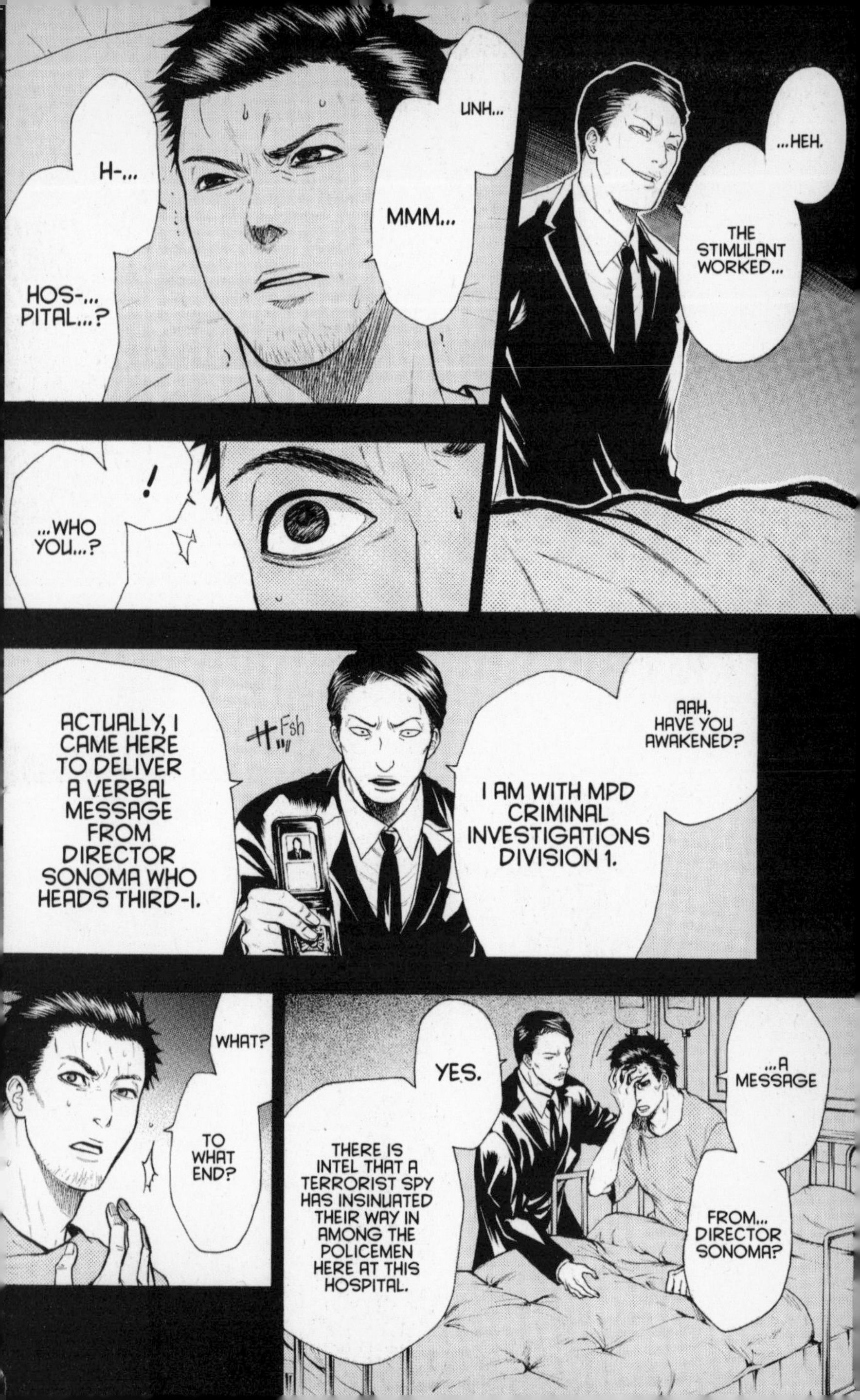
...HEH.
THE STIMULANT WORKED...
UNH...
MMM...
H-...
HOS-... PITAL...?
!
...WHO YOU...?
AAH, HAVE YOU AWAKENED?
I AM WITH MPD CRIMINAL INVESTIGATIONS DIVISION 1.
Fsh
ACTUALLY, I CAME HERE TO DELIVER A VERBAL MESSAGE FROM DIRECTOR SONOMA WHO HEADS THIRD-I.
...A MESSAGE
FROM... DIRECTOR SONOMA?
YES.
THERE IS INTEL THAT A TERRORIST SPY HAS INSINUATED THEIR WAY IN AMONG THE POLICEMEN HERE AT THIS HOSPITAL.
WHAT?
TO WHAT END?

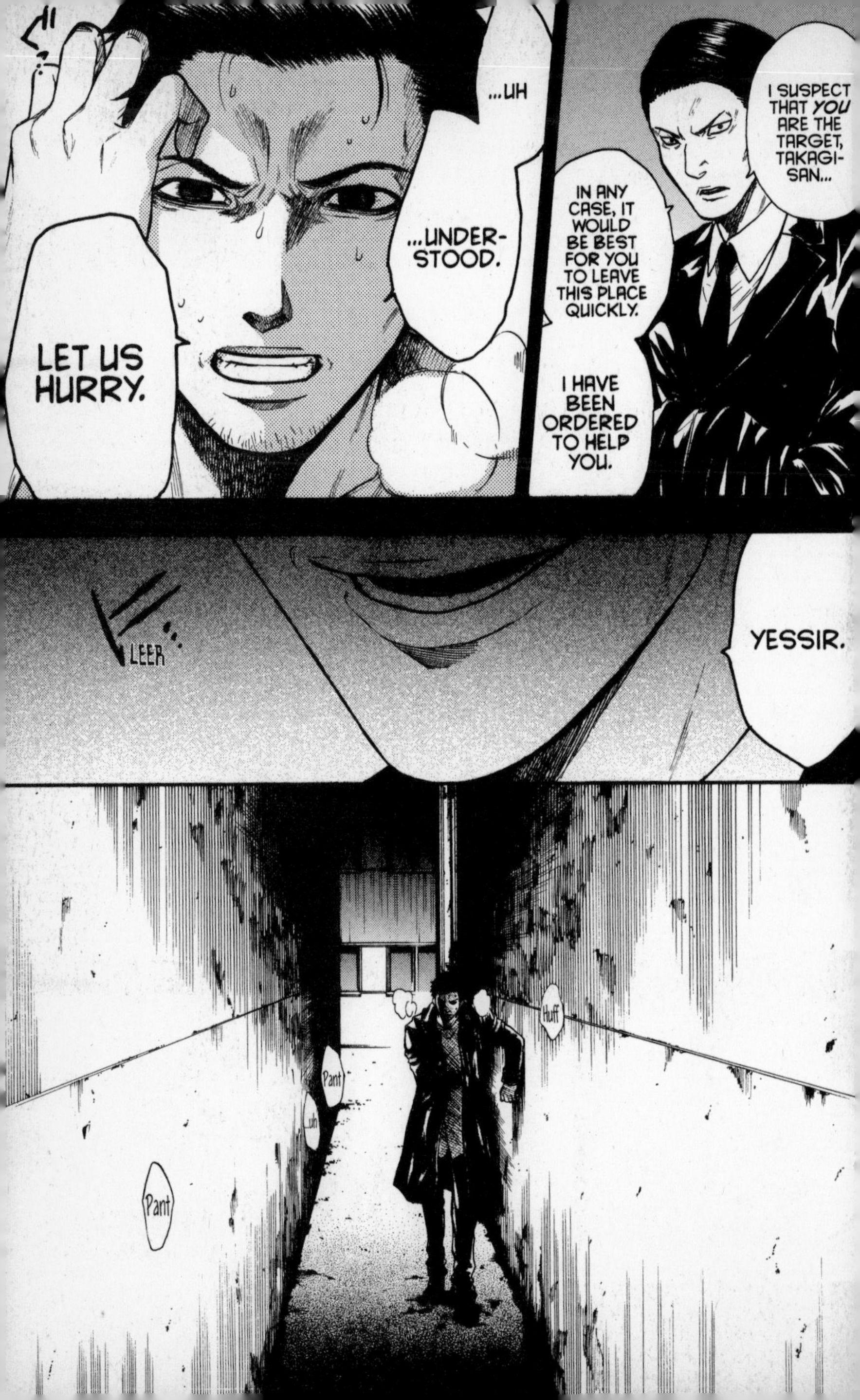
I SUSPECT THAT *YOU* ARE THE TARGET, TAKAGI-SAN...
IN ANY CASE, IT WOULD BE BEST FOR YOU TO LEAVE THIS PLACE QUICKLY.
I HAVE BEEN ORDERED TO HELP YOU.
...UH
...UNDERSTOOD.
LET US HURRY.
YESSIR.
LEER
Huff
Pant
...uh
Pant

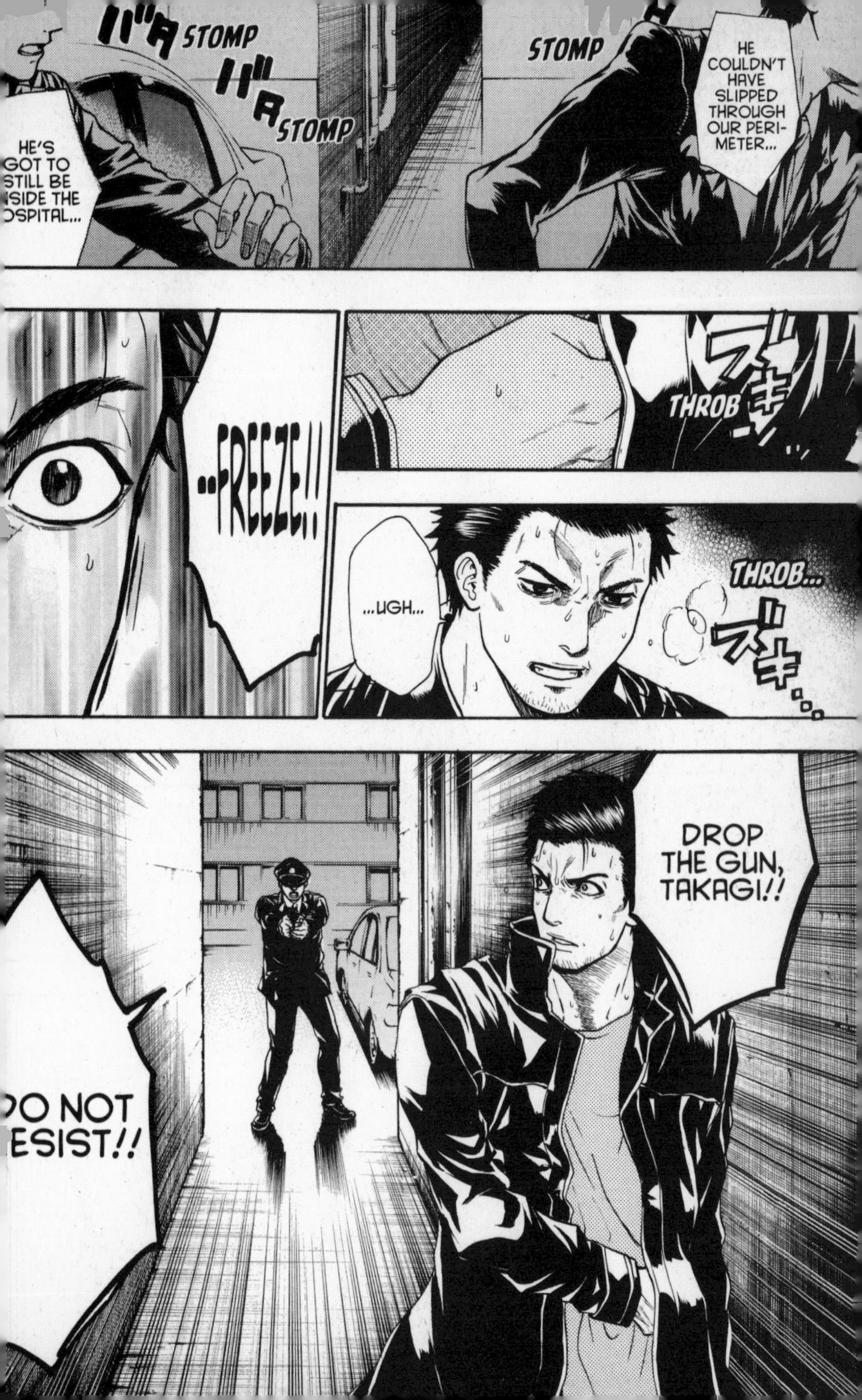
STOMP
HE COULDN'T HAVE SLIPPED THROUGH OUR PERIMETER...
バタ STOMP
バタ STOMP
HE'S GOT TO STILL BE SIDE THE OSPITAL...
ズキ THROB
...UGH...
THROB...
ズキ...
..FREEZE!!
DROP THE GUN, TAKAGI!!
O NOT ESIST!!

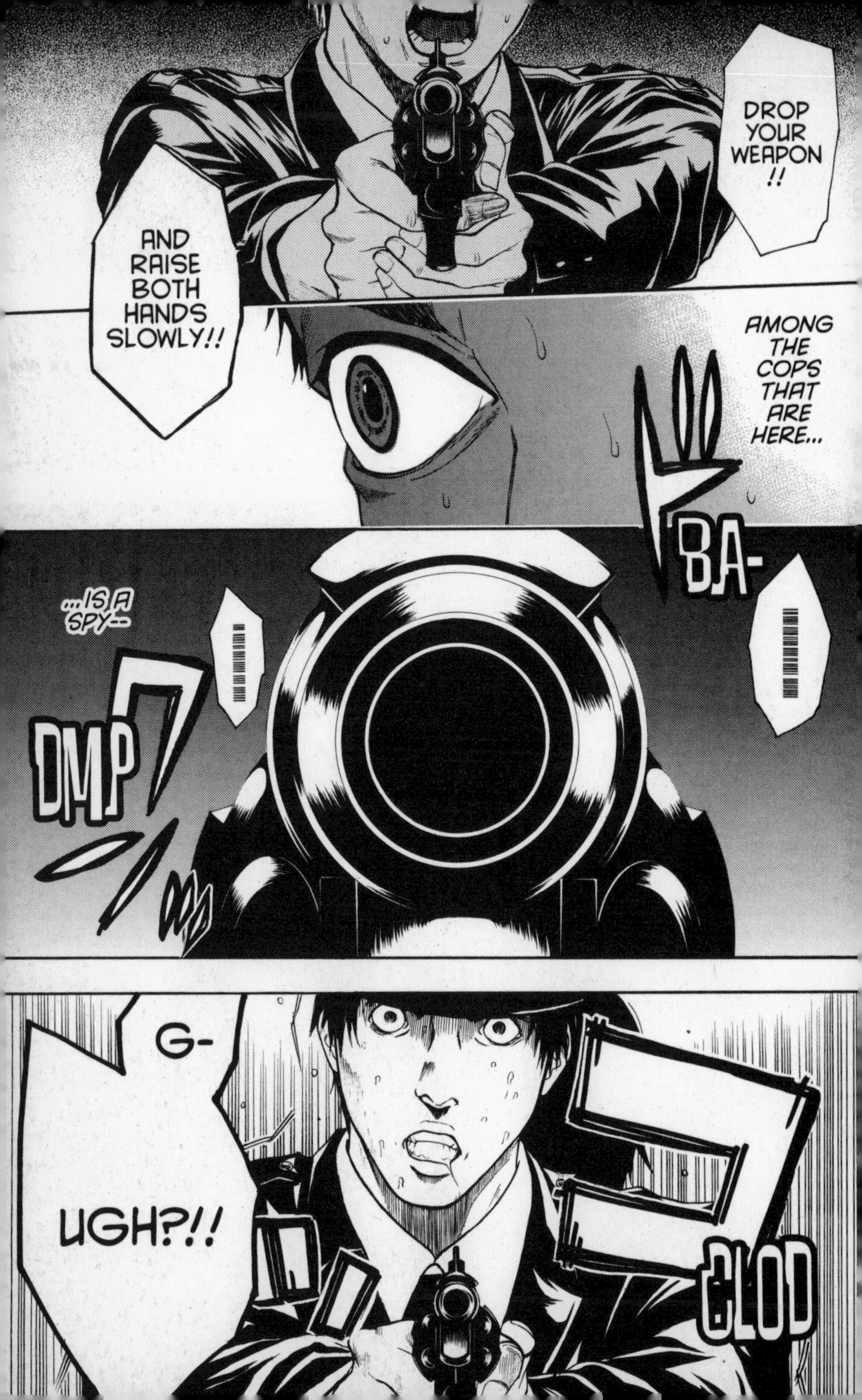
DROP YOUR WEAPON!!
AND RAISE BOTH HANDS SLOWLY!!
AMONG THE COPS THAT ARE HERE...
BA-
...IS A SPY--
DMP
CLOD
G-
UGH?!!

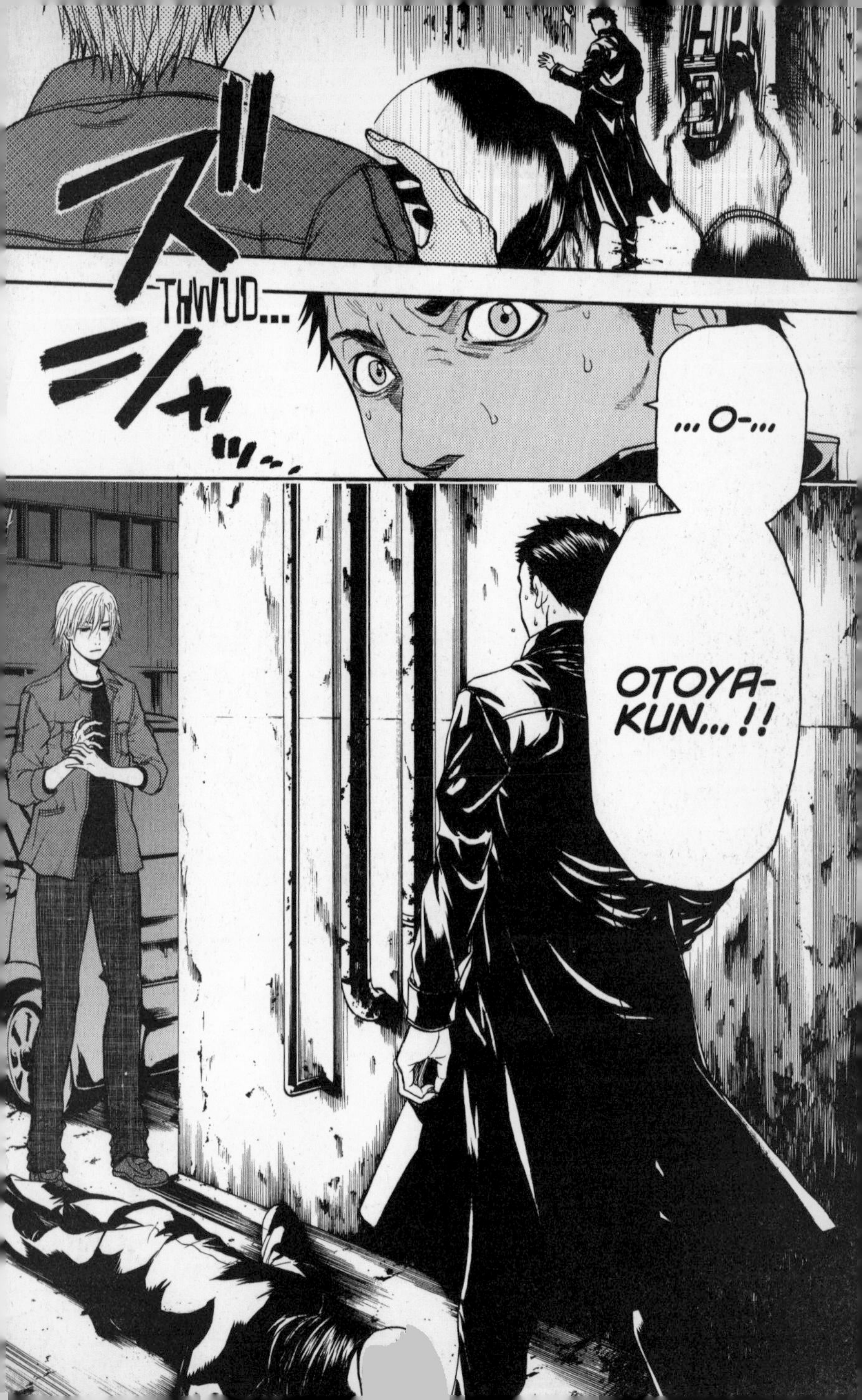
ズ
THWUD...
シャッ...
...O-...
OTOYA-KUN...!!

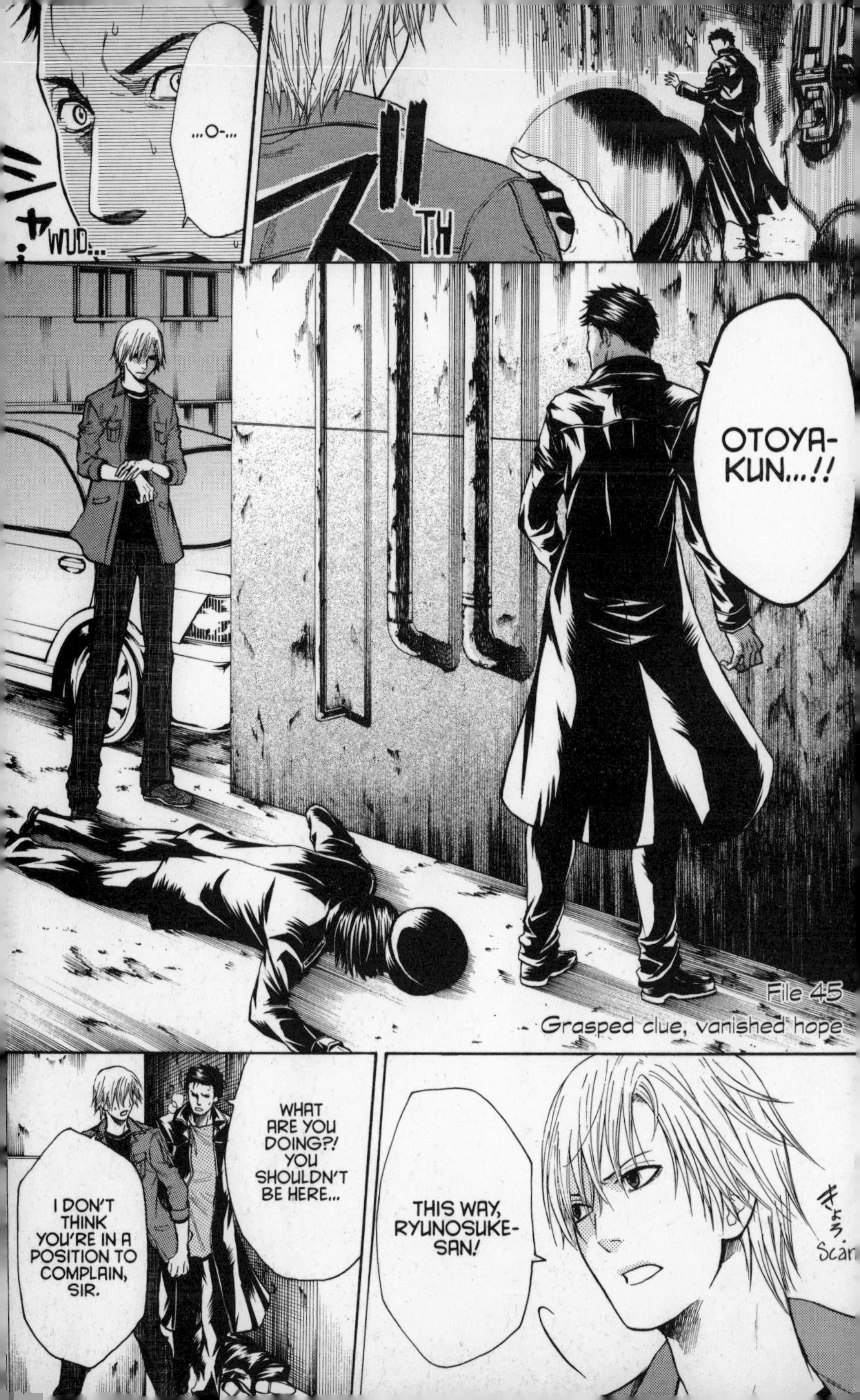

TH
...O-...
WUD...
OTOYA-KUN...!!
File 45
Grasped clue, vanished hope
Scan
THIS WAY, RYUNOSUKE-SAN!
WHAT ARE YOU DOING?! YOU SHOULDN'T BE HERE...
I DON'T THINK YOU'RE IN A POSITION TO COMPLAIN, SIR.

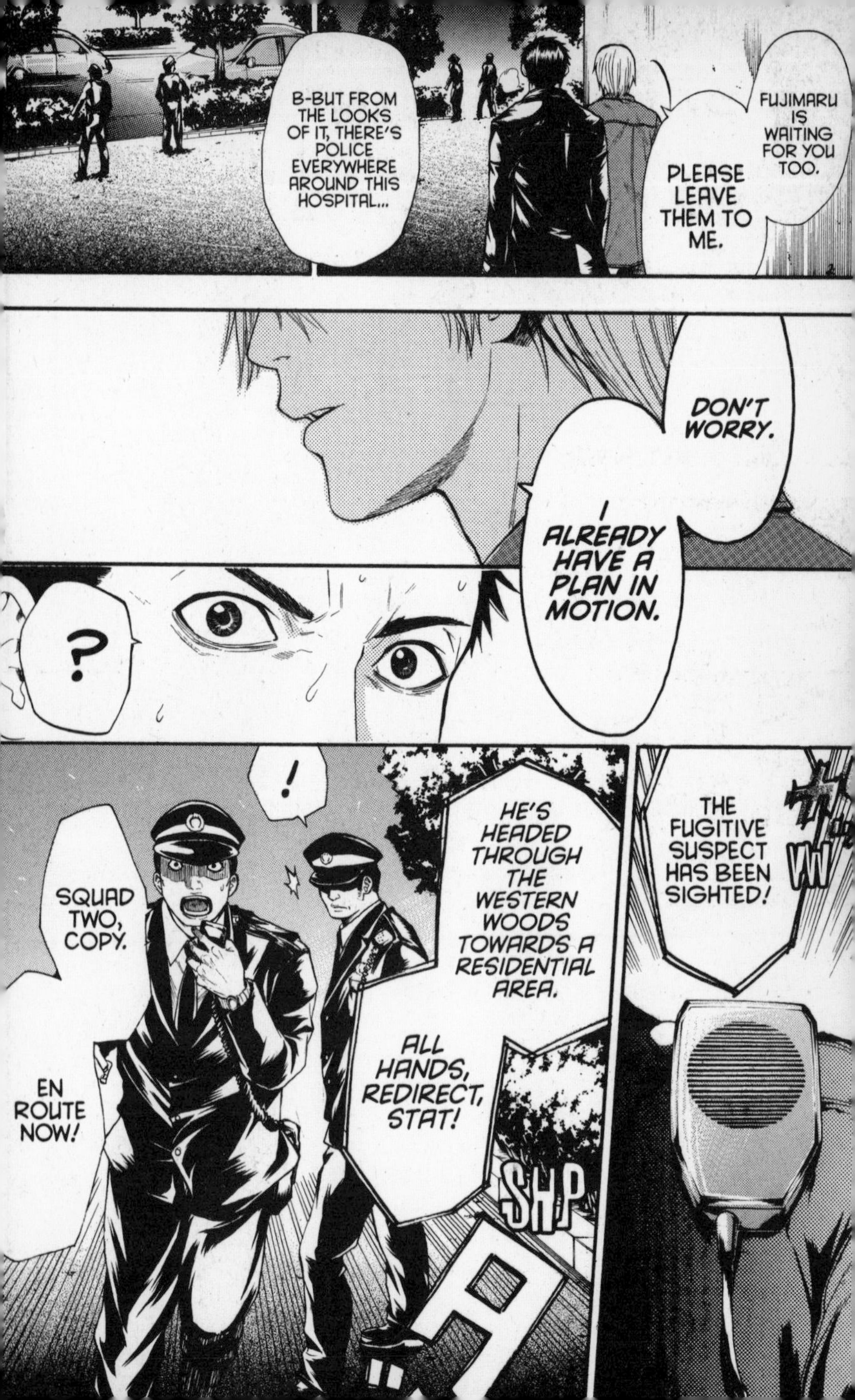
FUJIMARU IS WAITING FOR YOU TOO.
PLEASE LEAVE THEM TO ME.
B-BUT FROM THE LOOKS OF IT, THERE'S POLICE EVERYWHERE AROUND THIS HOSPITAL...
DON'T WORRY.
I ALREADY HAVE A PLAN IN MOTION.
?
THE FUGITIVE SUSPECT HAS BEEN SIGHTED!
HE'S HEADED THROUGH THE WESTERN WOODS TOWARDS A RESIDENTIAL AREA.
ALL HANDS, REDIRECT, STAT!
SHP
!
SQUAD TWO, COPY.
EN ROUTE NOW!

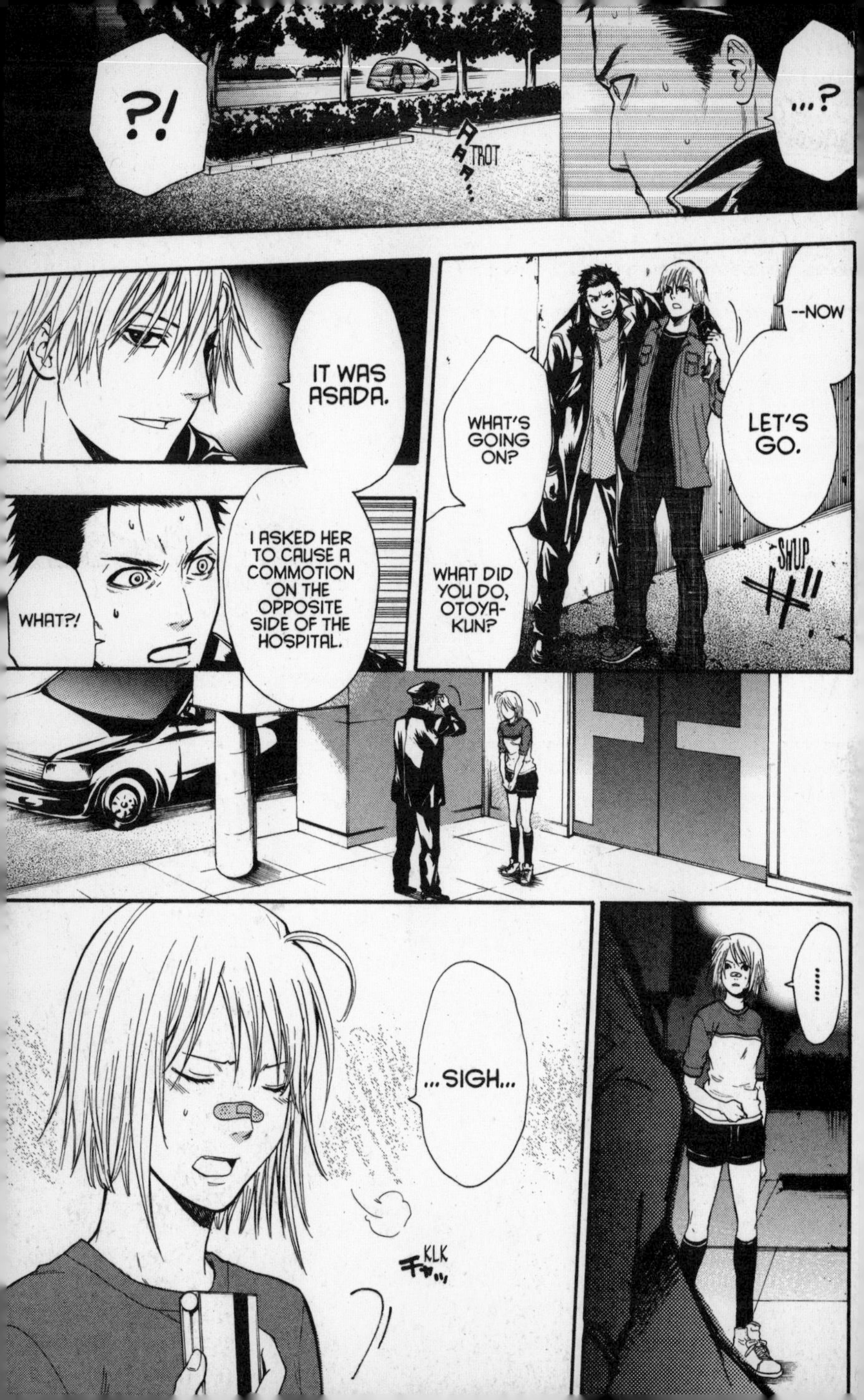
...?
?!
TROT
--NOW LET'S GO.
SHUP
WHAT'S GOING ON?
WHAT DID YOU DO, OTOYA-KUN?
IT WAS ASADA.
I ASKED HER TO CAUSE A COMMOTION ON THE OPPOSITE SIDE OF THE HOSPITAL.
WHAT?!
......
...SIGH...
KLK

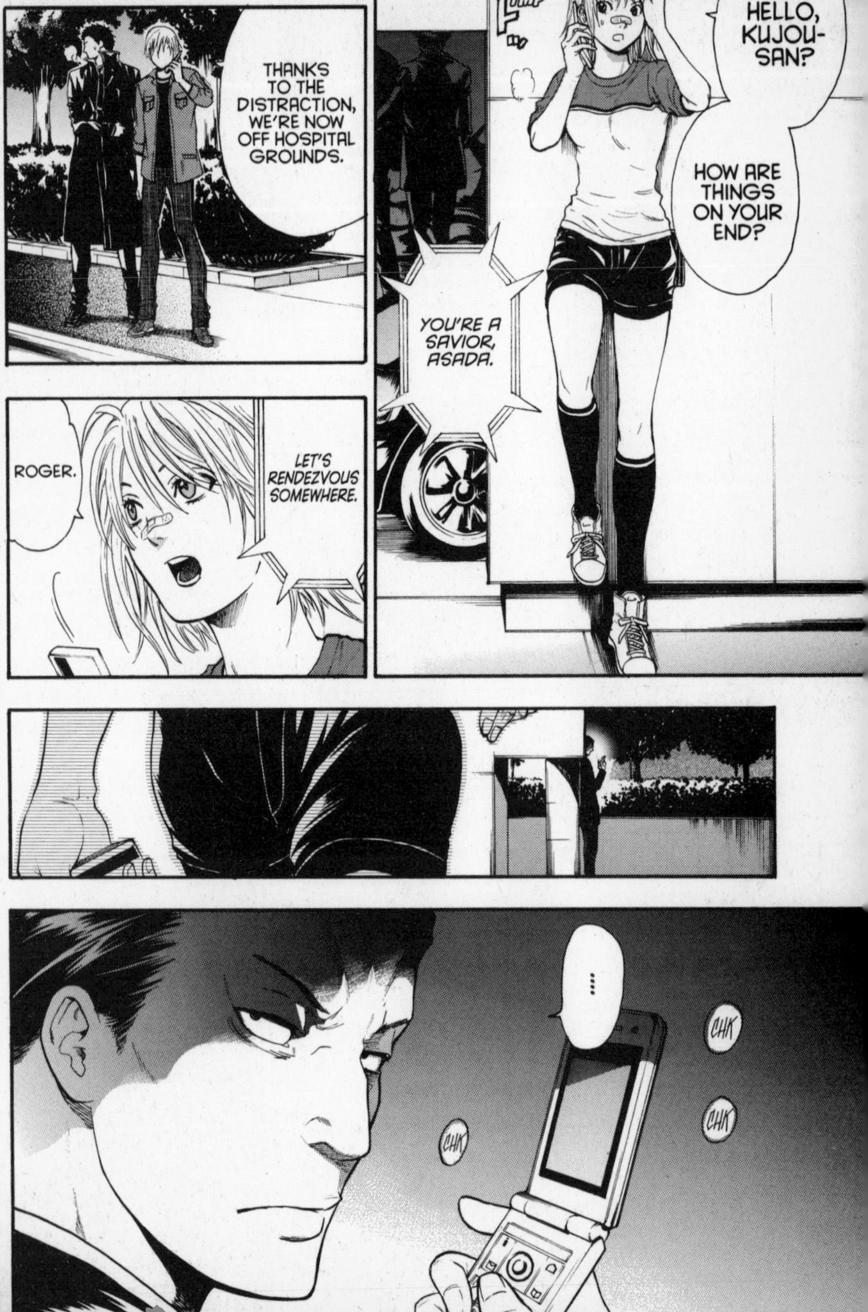

TMP
HELLO, KUJOU-SAN?
HOW ARE THINGS ON YOUR END?
YOU'RE A SAVIOR, ASADA.
THANKS TO THE DISTRACTION, WE'RE NOW OFF HOSPITAL GROUNDS.
LET'S RENDEZVOUS SOMEWHERE.
ROGER.
....
CHK
CHK
CHK

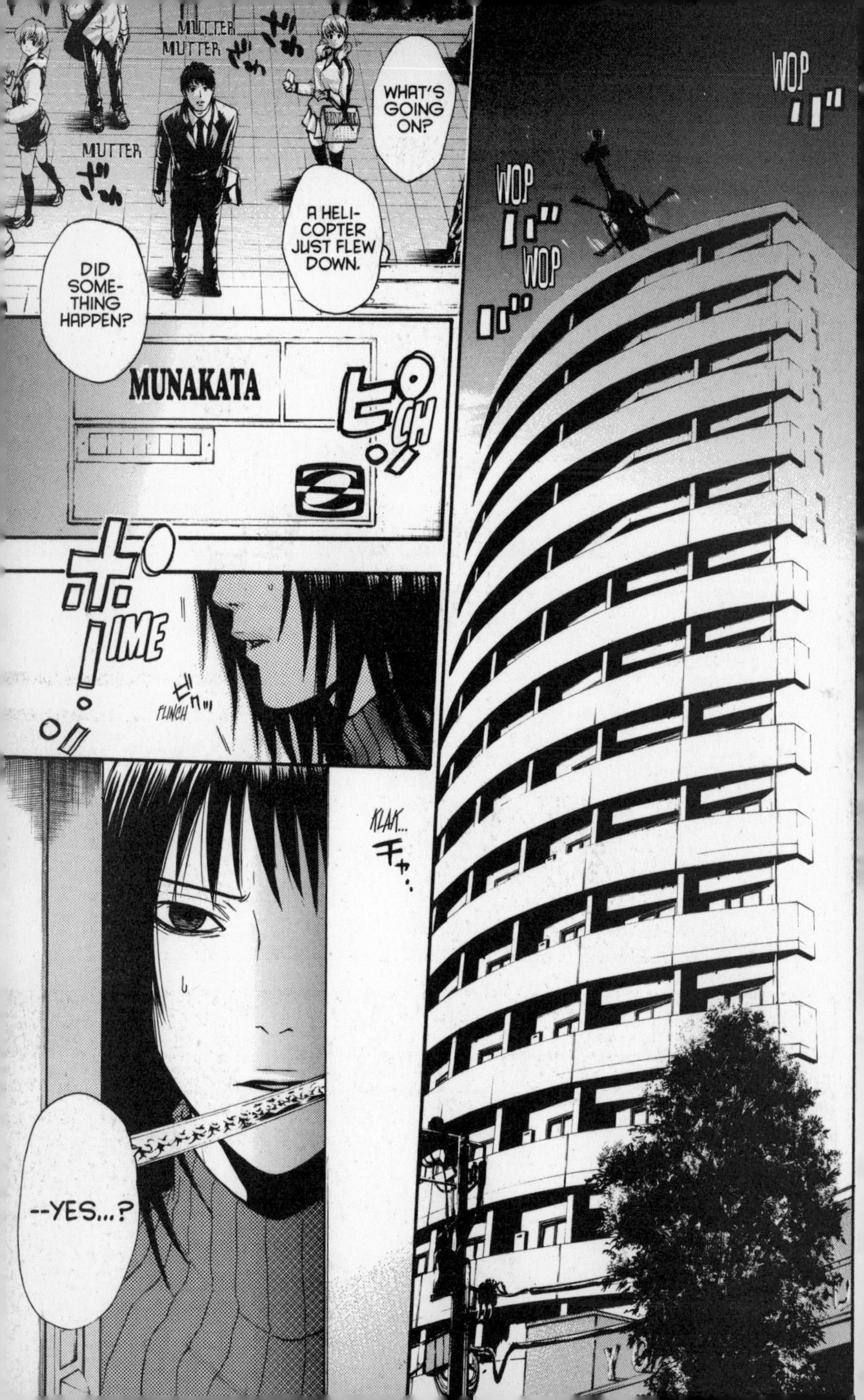

WOP
WOP
WOP
WHAT'S GOING ON?
A HELI-COPTER JUST FLEW DOWN.
MUTTER MUTTER
MUTTER
DID SOME-THING HAPPEN?
MUNAKATA
CH
IME
FLINCH
KLAK...
--YES...?

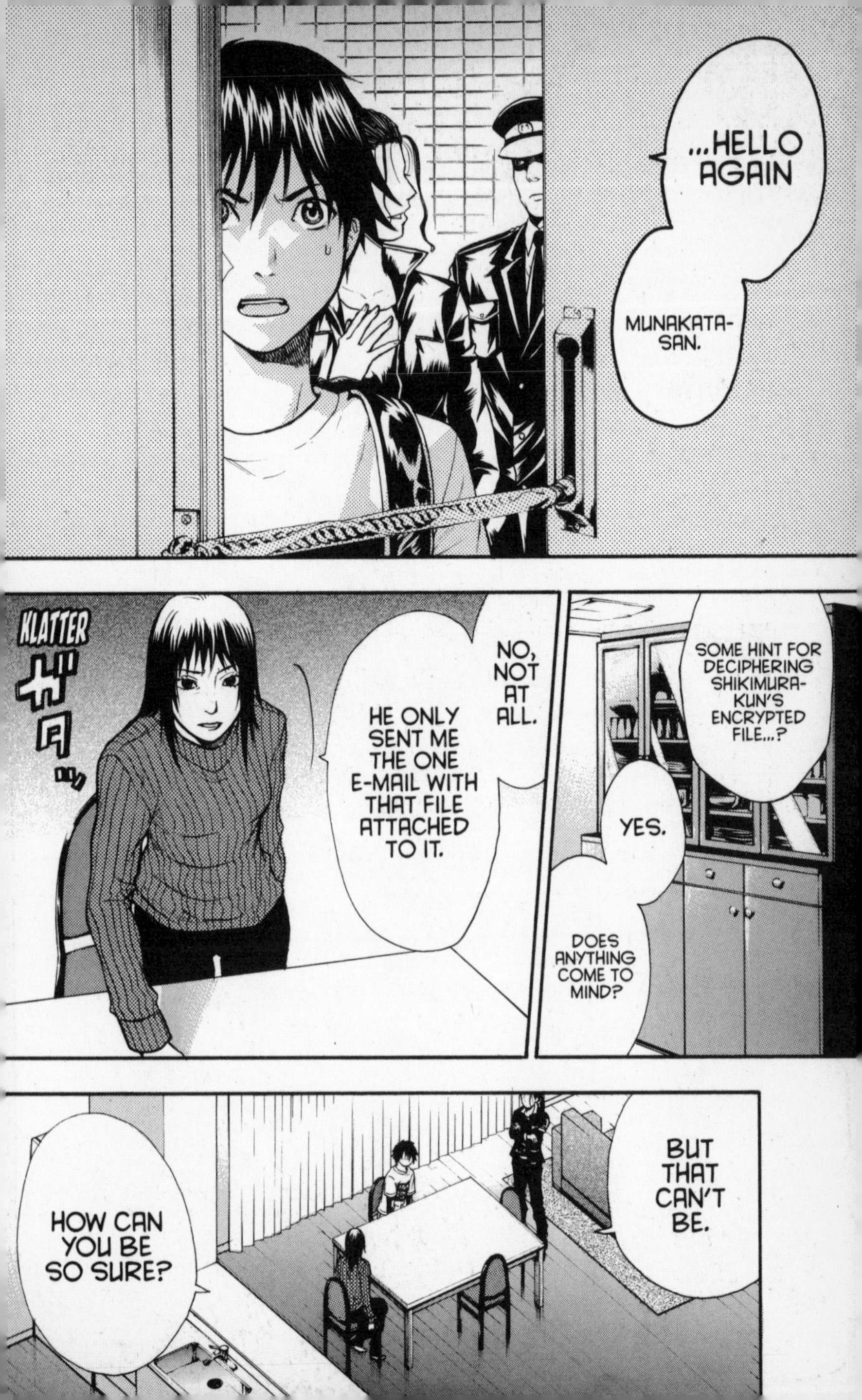
...HELLO AGAIN
MUNAKATA-SAN.
SOME HINT FOR DECIPHERING SHIKIMURA-KUN'S ENCRYPTED FILE...?
YES.
DOES ANYTHING COME TO MIND?
NO, NOT AT ALL.
HE ONLY SENT ME THE ONE E-MAIL WITH THAT FILE ATTACHED TO IT.
KLATTER
ガタッ
BUT THAT CAN'T BE.
HOW CAN YOU BE SO SURE?

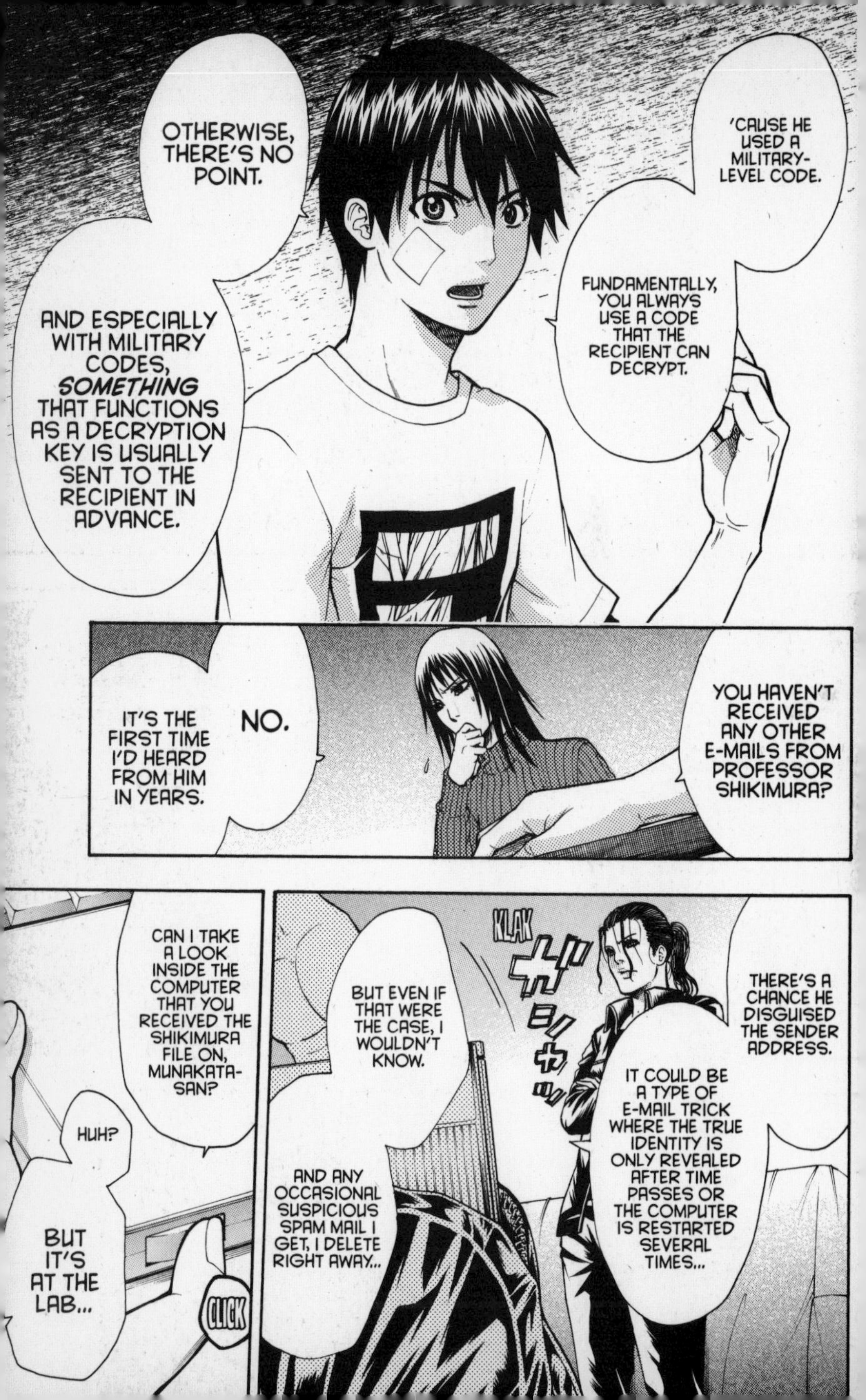
'CAUSE HE USED A MILITARY-LEVEL CODE.
FUNDAMENTALLY, YOU ALWAYS USE A CODE THAT THE RECIPIENT CAN DECRYPT.
OTHERWISE, THERE'S NO POINT.
AND ESPECIALLY WITH MILITARY CODES, *SOMETHING* THAT FUNCTIONS AS A DECRYPTION KEY IS USUALLY SENT TO THE RECIPIENT IN ADVANCE.
YOU HAVEN'T RECEIVED ANY OTHER E-MAILS FROM PROFESSOR SHIKIMURA?
NO.
IT'S THE FIRST TIME I'D HEARD FROM HIM IN YEARS.
THERE'S A CHANCE HE DISGUISED THE SENDER ADDRESS.
KLAK
IT COULD BE A TYPE OF E-MAIL TRICK WHERE THE TRUE IDENTITY IS ONLY REVEALED AFTER TIME PASSES OR THE COMPUTER IS RESTARTED SEVERAL TIMES...
BUT EVEN IF THAT WERE THE CASE, I WOULDN'T KNOW.
AND ANY OCCASIONAL SUSPICIOUS SPAM MAIL I GET, I DELETE RIGHT AWAY...
CAN I TAKE A LOOK INSIDE THE COMPUTER THAT YOU RECEIVED THE SHIKIMURA FILE ON, MUNAKATA-SAN?
HUH?
BUT IT'S AT THE LAB...
CLICK

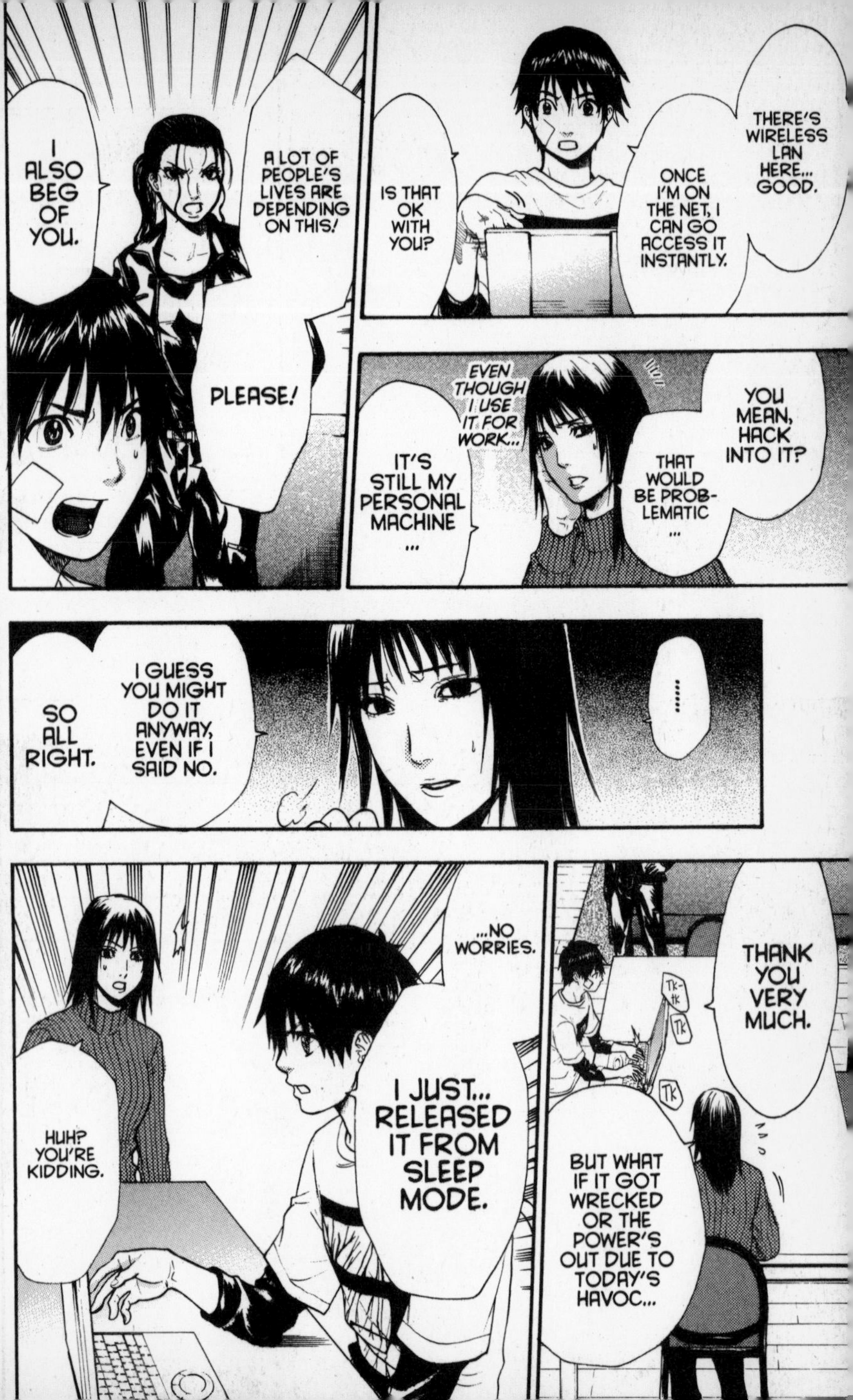
THERE'S WIRELESS LAN HERE... GOOD.
ONCE I'M ON THE NET, I CAN GO ACCESS IT INSTANTLY.
IS THAT OK WITH YOU?
YOU MEAN, HACK INTO IT?
THAT WOULD BE PROB-LEMATIC ...
EVEN THOUGH I USE IT FOR WORK...
IT'S STILL MY PERSONAL MACHINE ...
A LOT OF PEOPLE'S LIVES ARE DEPENDING ON THIS!
I ALSO BEG OF YOU.
PLEASE!
......
I GUESS YOU MIGHT DO IT ANYWAY, EVEN IF I SAID NO.
SO ALL RIGHT.
THANK YOU VERY MUCH.
TK-TK
TK
TK
BUT WHAT IF IT GOT WRECKED OR THE POWER'S OUT DUE TO TODAY'S HAVOC...
...NO WORRIES.
I JUST... RELEASED IT FROM SLEEP MODE.
HUH? YOU'RE KIDDING.

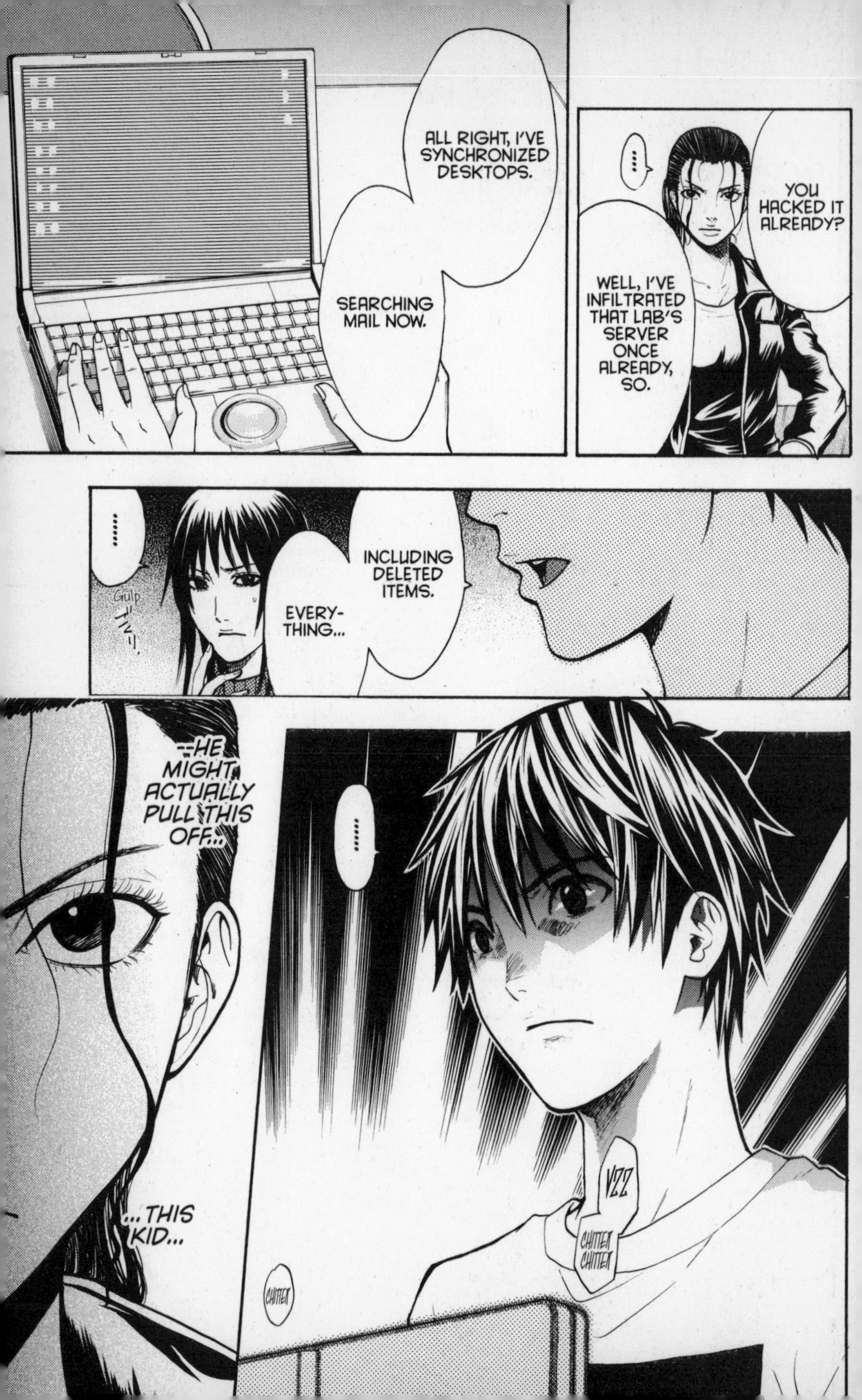
......
YOU HACKED IT ALREADY?
WELL, I'VE INFILTRATED THAT LAB'S SERVER ONCE ALREADY, SO.
ALL RIGHT, I'VE SYNCHRONIZED DESKTOPS.
SEARCHING MAIL NOW.
INCLUDING DELETED ITEMS.
EVERY-THING...
......
Gulp
......
VZZ
CHITTER CHITTER
CHITTER
—HE MIGHT ACTUALLY PULL THIS OFF...
...THIS KID...

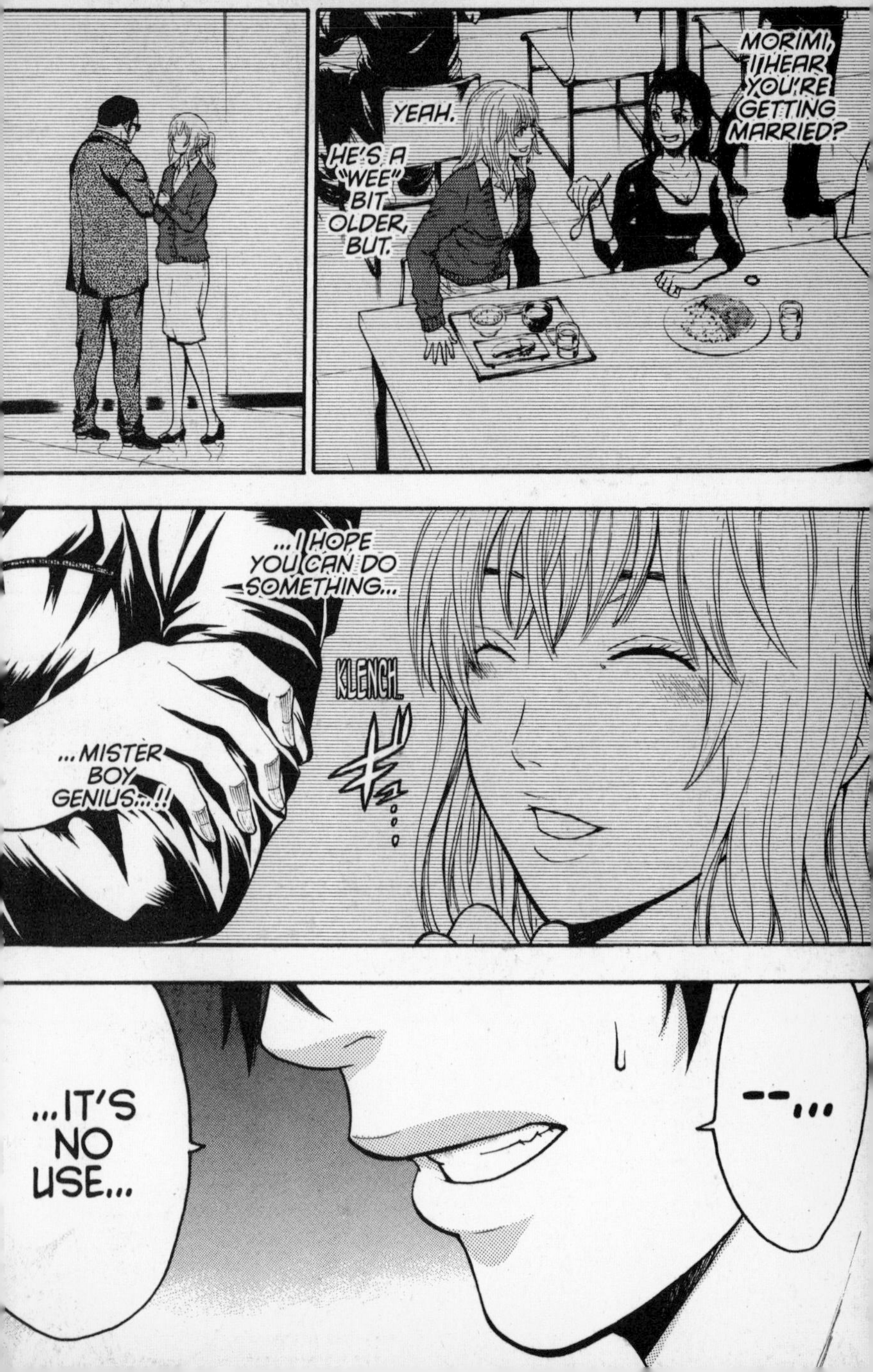
MORIMI, I HEAR YOU'RE GETTING MARRIED?
YEAH.
HE'S A "WEE" BIT OLDER, BUT.
...I HOPE YOU CAN DO SOMETHING...
KLENCH...
...MISTER BOY GENIUS...!!
--...
...IT'S NO USE...

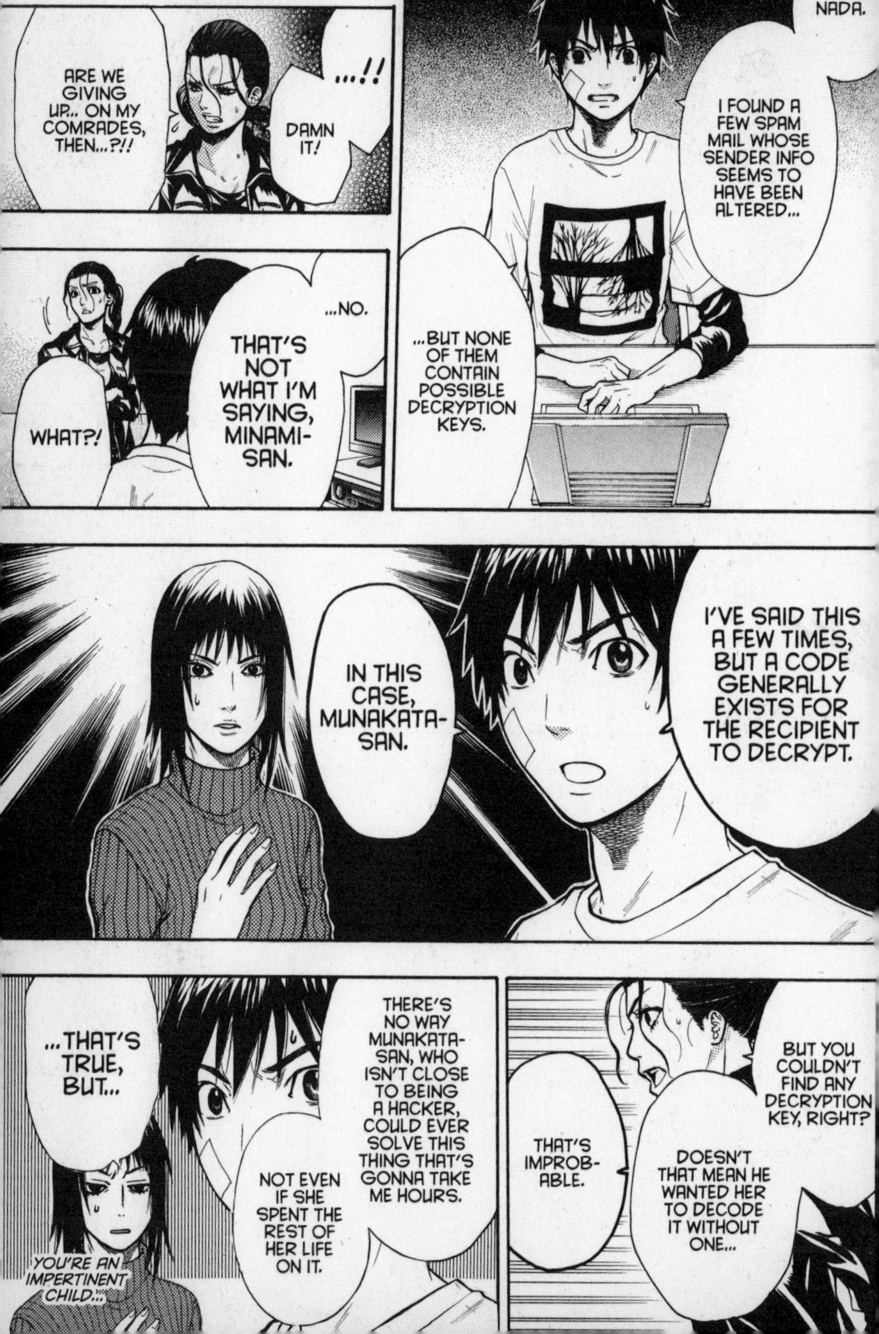
NADA.
I FOUND A FEW SPAM MAIL WHOSE SENDER INFO SEEMS TO HAVE BEEN ALTERED...
...BUT NONE OF THEM CONTAIN POSSIBLE DECRYPTION KEYS.
...!!
DAMN IT!
ARE WE GIVING UP... ON MY COMRADES, THEN...?!!
...NO.
THAT'S NOT WHAT I'M SAYING, MINAMI-SAN.
WHAT?!
I'VE SAID THIS A FEW TIMES, BUT A CODE GENERALLY EXISTS FOR THE RECIPIENT TO DECRYPT.
IN THIS CASE, MUNAKATA-SAN.
BUT YOU COULDN'T FIND ANY DECRYPTION KEY, RIGHT?
DOESN'T THAT MEAN HE WANTED HER TO DECODE IT WITHOUT ONE...
THAT'S IMPROB-ABLE.
THERE'S NO WAY MUNAKATA-SAN, WHO ISN'T CLOSE TO BEING A HACKER, COULD EVER SOLVE THIS THING THAT'S GONNA TAKE ME HOURS.
NOT EVEN IF SHE SPENT THE REST OF HER LIFE ON IT.
...THAT'S TRUE, BUT...
YOU'RE AN IMPERTINENT CHILD...

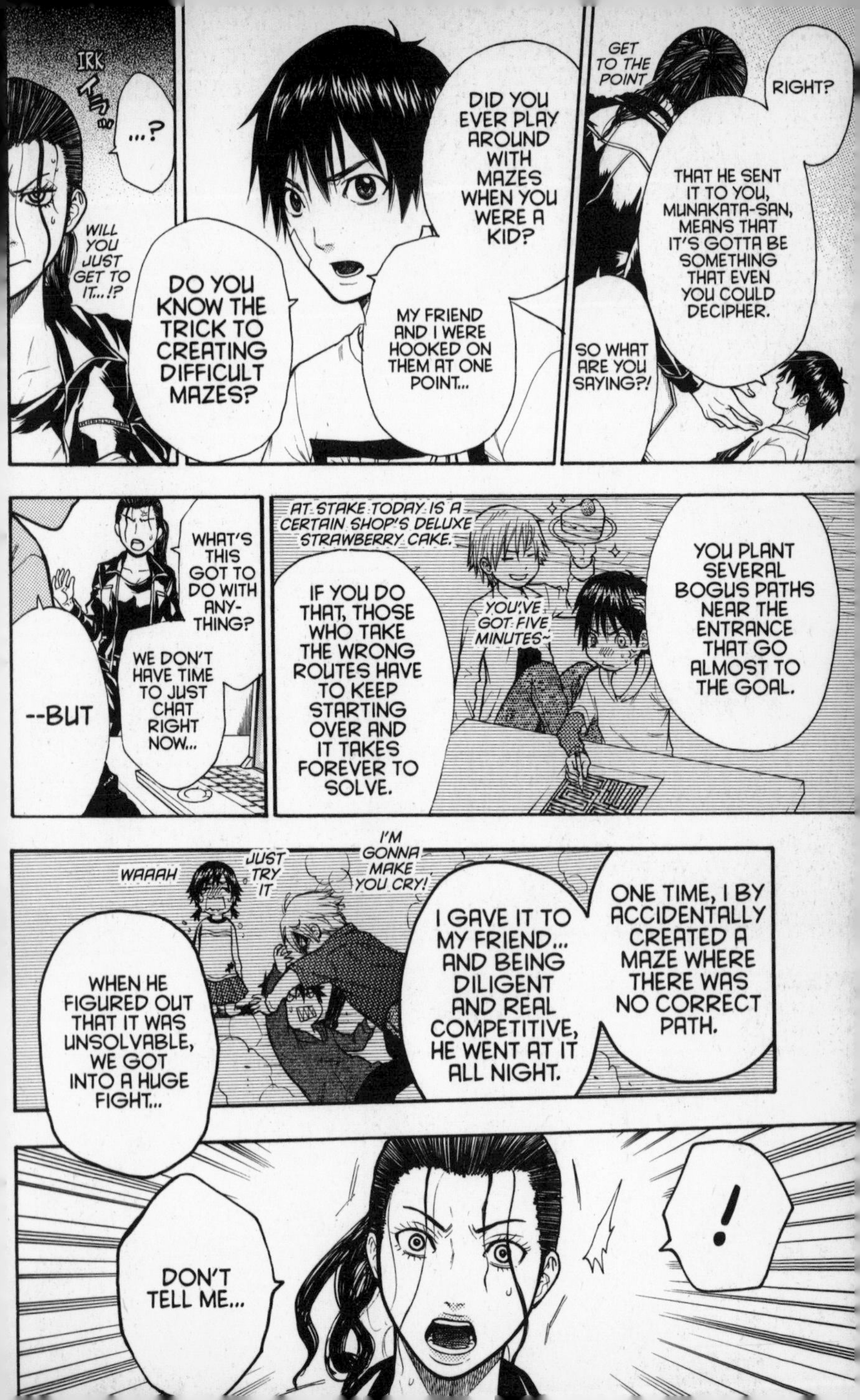
GET TO THE POINT
RIGHT?
THAT HE SENT IT TO YOU, MUNAKATA-SAN, MEANS THAT IT'S GOTTA BE SOMETHING THAT EVEN YOU COULD DECIPHER.
SO WHAT ARE YOU SAYING?!
DID YOU EVER PLAY AROUND WITH MAZES WHEN YOU WERE A KID?
MY FRIEND AND I WERE HOOKED ON THEM AT ONE POINT...
DO YOU KNOW THE TRICK TO CREATING DIFFICULT MAZES?
IRK
...?
WILL YOU JUST GET TO IT...!?
YOU PLANT SEVERAL BOGUS PATHS NEAR THE ENTRANCE THAT GO ALMOST TO THE GOAL.
AT STAKE TODAY IS A CERTAIN SHOP'S DELUXE STRAWBERRY CAKE.
YOU'VE GOT FIVE MINUTES~
IF YOU DO THAT, THOSE WHO TAKE THE WRONG ROUTES HAVE TO KEEP STARTING OVER AND IT TAKES FOREVER TO SOLVE.
WHAT'S THIS GOT TO DO WITH ANY-THING?
WE DON'T HAVE TIME TO JUST CHAT RIGHT NOW...
--BUT
ONE TIME, I BY ACCIDENTALLY CREATED A MAZE WHERE THERE WAS NO CORRECT PATH.
I GAVE IT TO MY FRIEND... AND BEING DILIGENT AND REAL COMPETITIVE, HE WENT AT IT ALL NIGHT.
I'M GONNA MAKE YOU CRY!
JUST TRY IT
WAAAH
WHEN HE FIGURED OUT THAT IT WAS UNSOLVABLE, WE GOT INTO A HUGE FIGHT...
!
DON'T TELL ME...

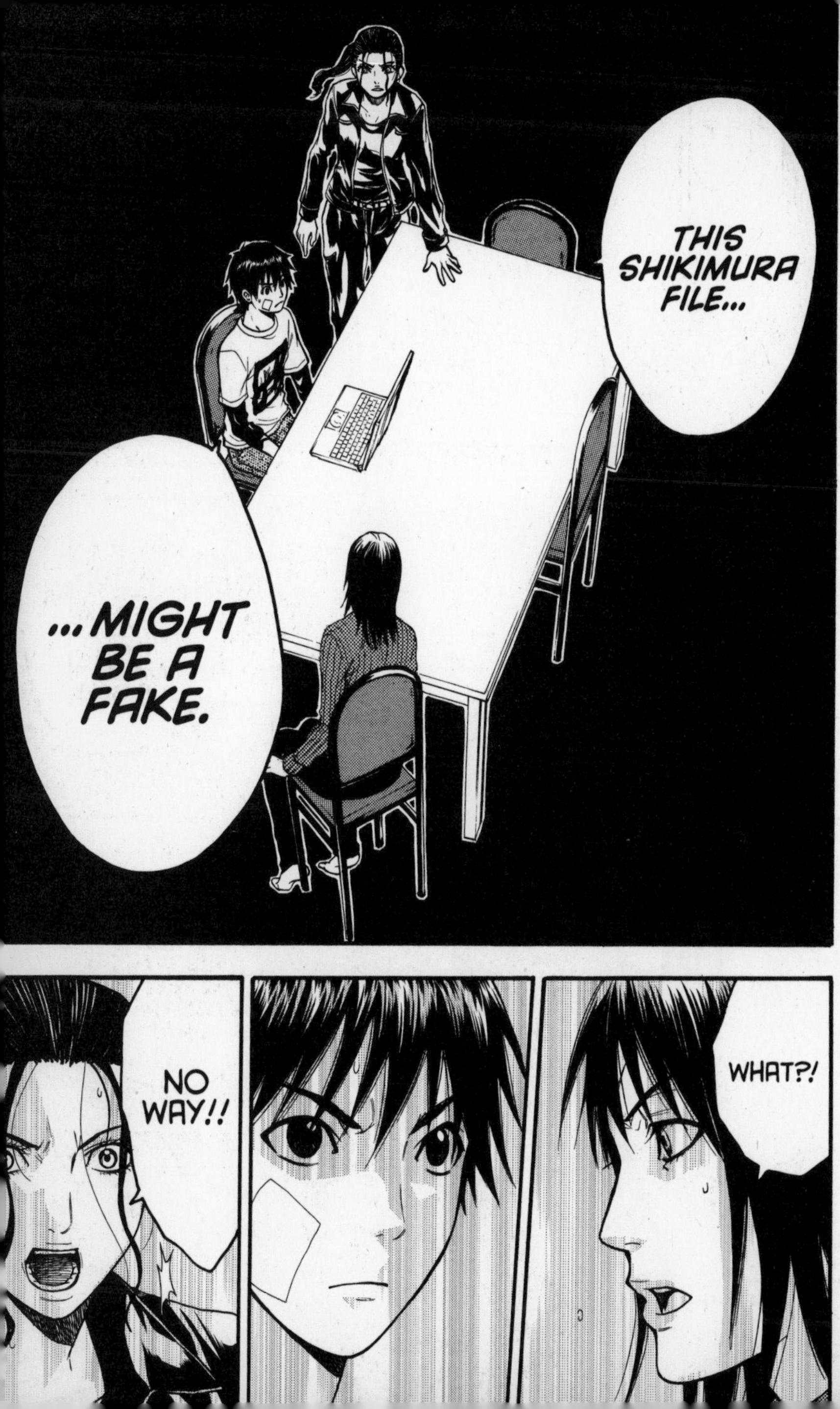
THIS SHIKIMURA FILE...
...MIGHT BE A FAKE.
WHAT?!
NO WAY!!

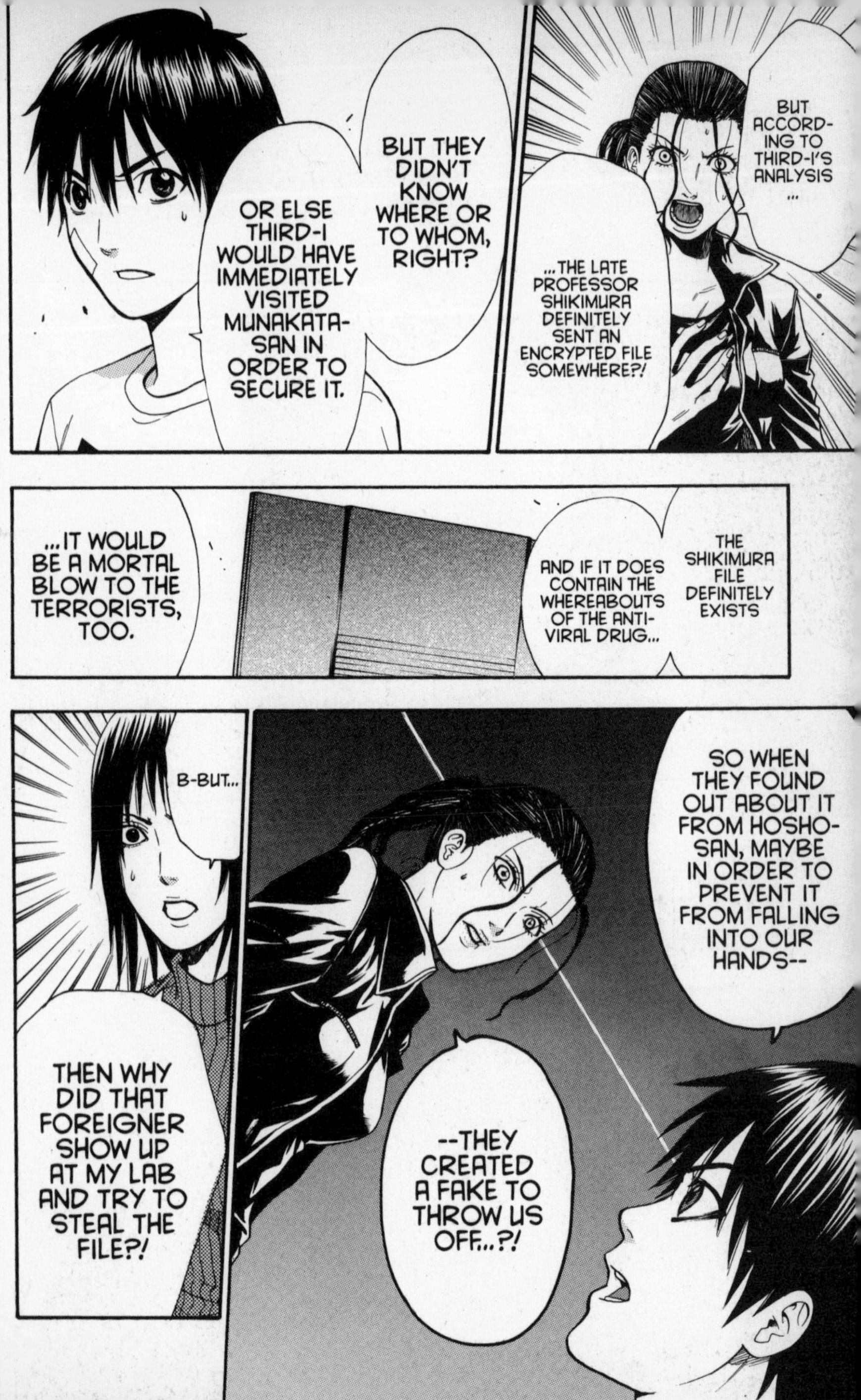
BUT ACCORDING TO THIRD-I'S ANALYSIS...
...THE LATE PROFESSOR SHIKIMURA DEFINITELY SENT AN ENCRYPTED FILE SOMEWHERE?!
BUT THEY DIDN'T KNOW WHERE OR TO WHOM, RIGHT?
OR ELSE THIRD-I WOULD HAVE IMMEDIATELY VISITED MUNAKATA-SAN IN ORDER TO SECURE IT.
THE SHIKIMURA FILE DEFINITELY EXISTS
AND IF IT DOES CONTAIN THE WHEREABOUTS OF THE ANTI-VIRAL DRUG...
...IT WOULD BE A MORTAL BLOW TO THE TERRORISTS, TOO.
SO WHEN THEY FOUND OUT ABOUT IT FROM HOSHO-SAN, MAYBE IN ORDER TO PREVENT IT FROM FALLING INTO OUR HANDS--
--THEY CREATED A FAKE TO THROW US OFF...?!
B-BUT...
THEN WHY DID THAT FOREIGNER SHOW UP AT MY LAB AND TRY TO STEAL THE FILE?!

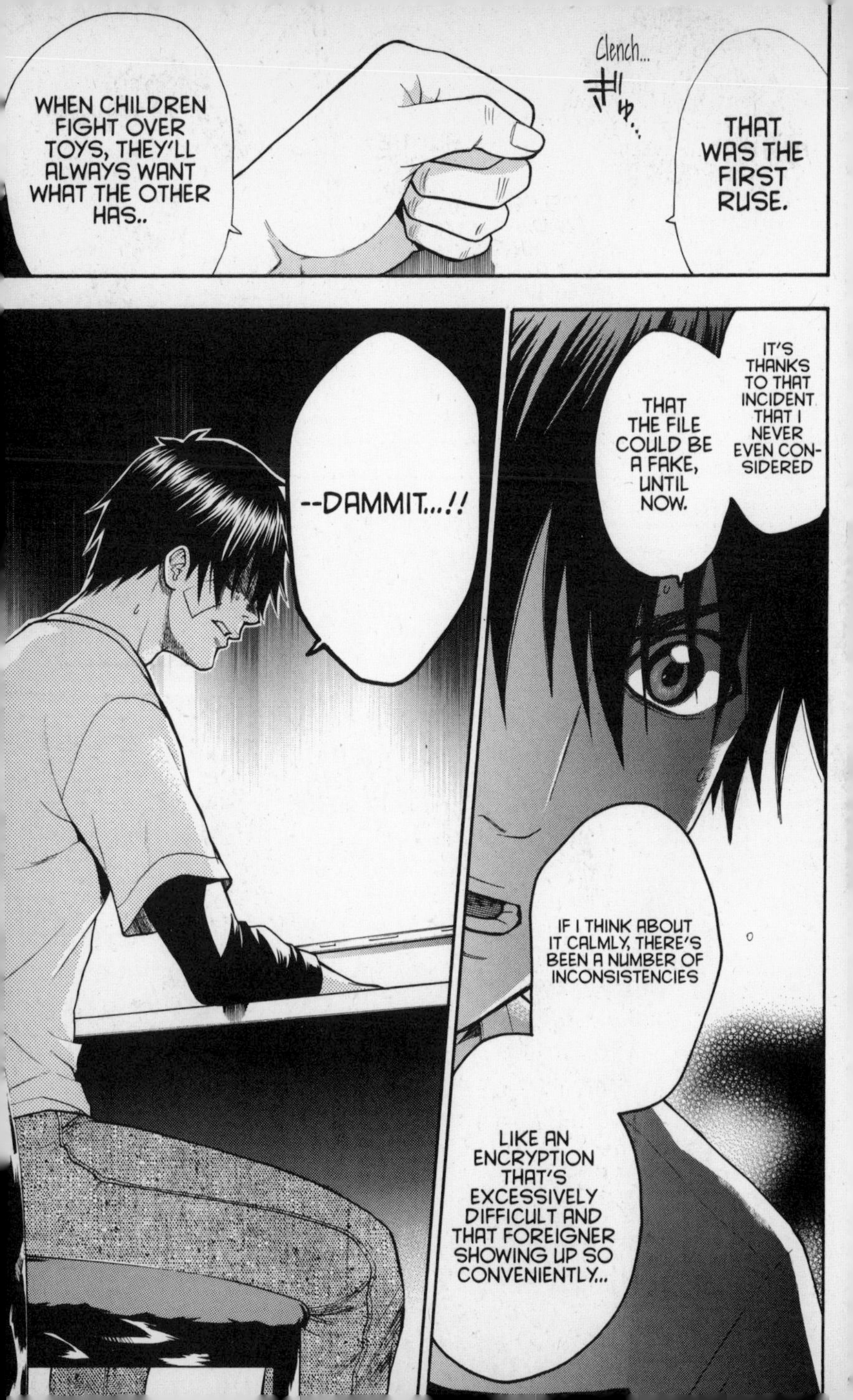
THAT WAS THE FIRST RUSE.
Clench...
WHEN CHILDREN FIGHT OVER TOYS, THEY'LL ALWAYS WANT WHAT THE OTHER HAS..
IT'S THANKS TO THAT INCIDENT THAT I NEVER EVEN CONSIDERED
THAT THE FILE COULD BE A FAKE, UNTIL NOW.
IF I THINK ABOUT IT CALMLY, THERE'S BEEN A NUMBER OF INCONSISTENCIES
LIKE AN ENCRYPTION THAT'S EXCESSIVELY DIFFICULT AND THAT FOREIGNER SHOWING UP SO CONVENIENTLY...
--DAMMIT...!!

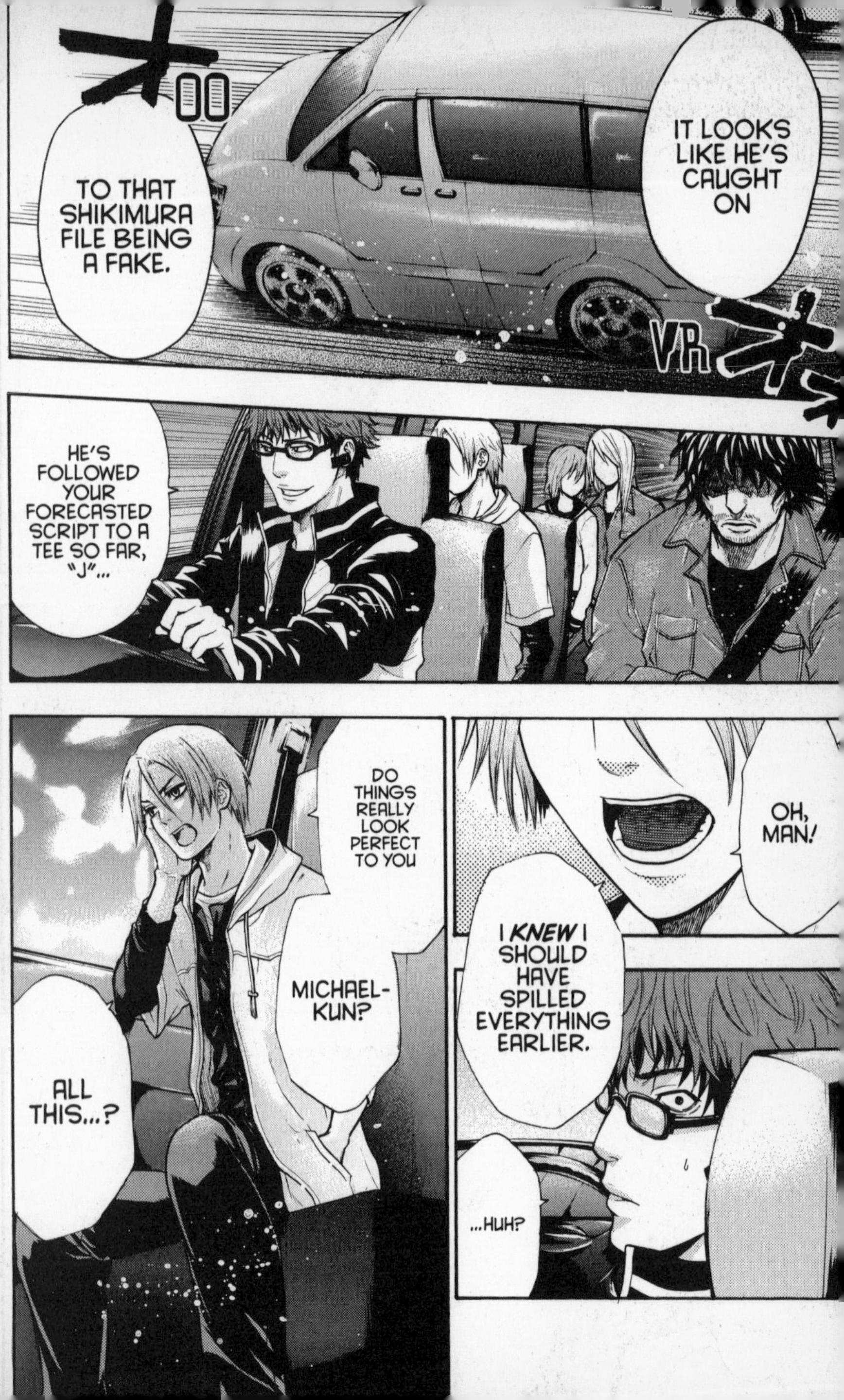
IT LOOKS LIKE HE'S CAUGHT ON
VR
OO
TO THAT SHIKIMURA FILE BEING A FAKE.
HE'S FOLLOWED YOUR FORECASTED SCRIPT TO A TEE SO FAR, "J"...
OH, MAN!
I *KNEW* I SHOULD HAVE SPILLED EVERYTHING EARLIER.
...HUH?
DO THINGS REALLY LOOK PERFECT TO YOU
MICHAEL-KUN?
ALL THIS...?

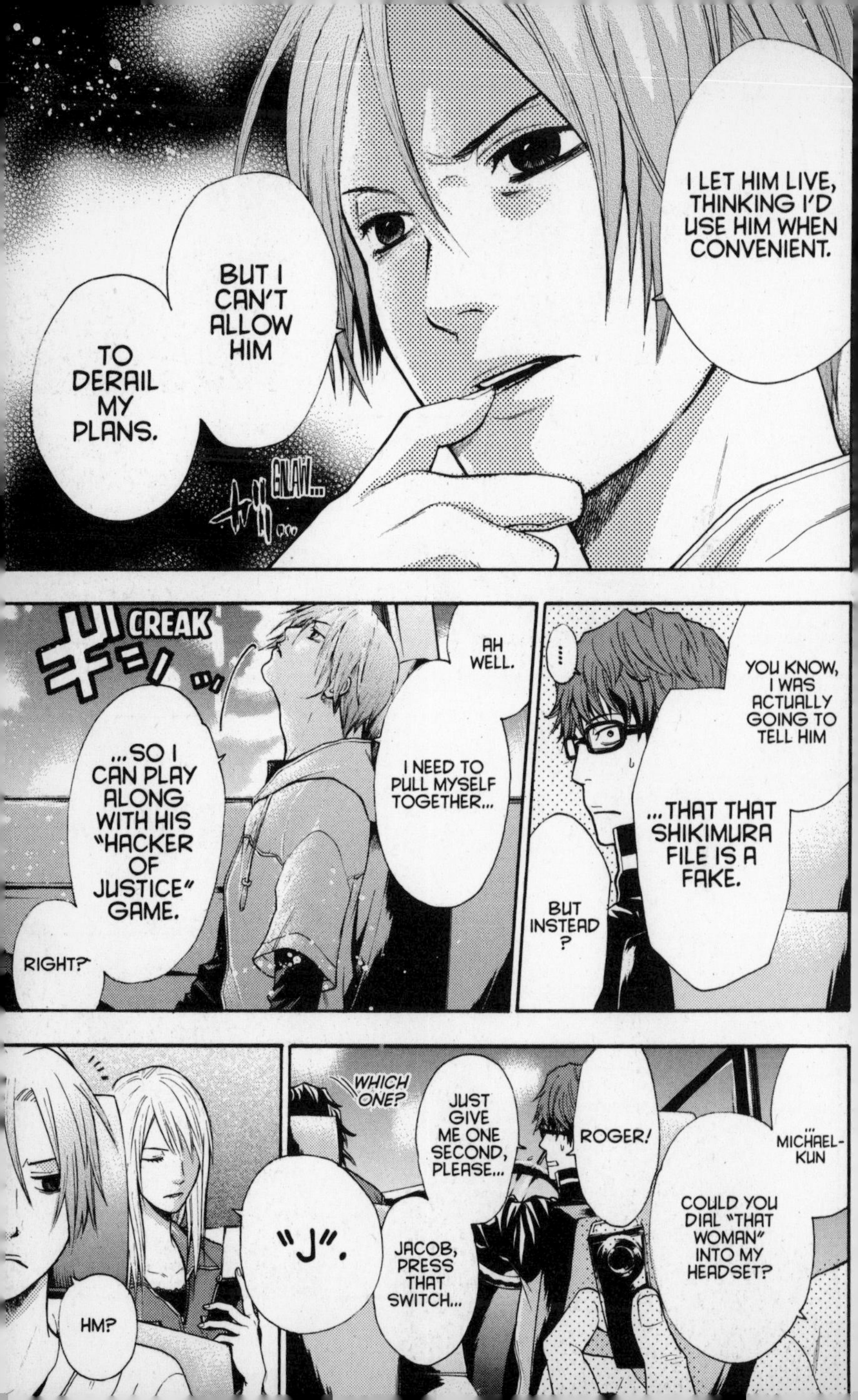
I LET HIM LIVE, THINKING I'D USE HIM WHEN CONVENIENT.
BUT I CAN'T ALLOW HIM
TO DERAIL MY PLANS.
GNAW...
...
YOU KNOW, I WAS ACTUALLY GOING TO TELL HIM
...THAT THAT SHIKIMURA FILE IS A FAKE.
BUT INSTEAD?
CREAK
AH WELL.
I NEED TO PULL MYSELF TOGETHER...
...SO I CAN PLAY ALONG WITH HIS "HACKER OF JUSTICE" GAME.
RIGHT?
...MICHAEL-KUN
COULD YOU DIAL "THAT WOMAN" INTO MY HEADSET?
ROGER!
JUST GIVE ME ONE SECOND, PLEASE...
WHICH ONE?
JACOB, PRESS THAT SWITCH...
"J".
!
HM?

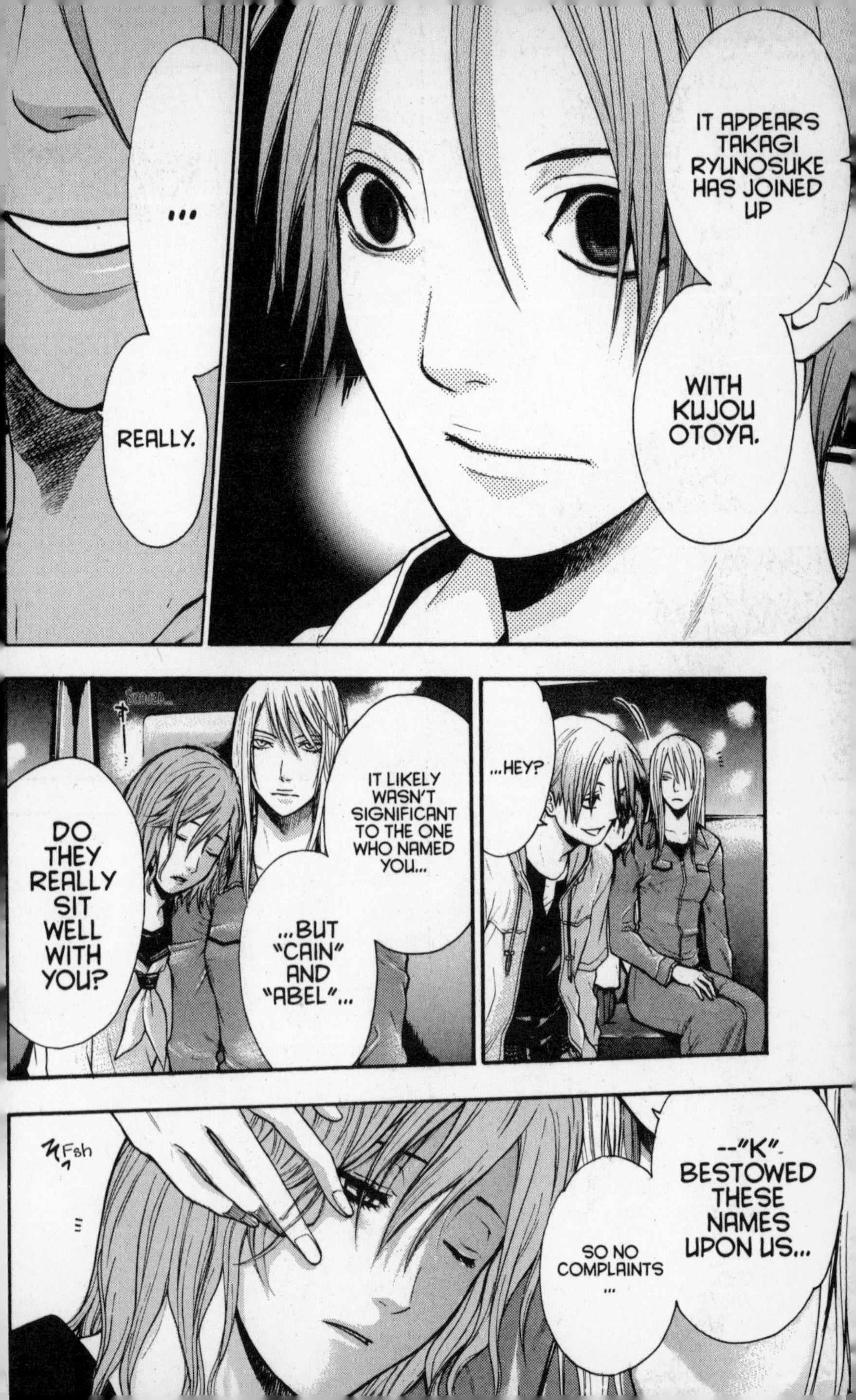
IT APPEARS TAKAGI RYUNOSUKE HAS JOINED UP
WITH KUJOU OTOYA.
...
REALLY.
...HEY?
Snooze...
IT LIKELY WASN'T SIGNIFICANT TO THE ONE WHO NAMED YOU...
...BUT "CAIN" AND "ABEL"...
DO THEY REALLY SIT WELL WITH YOU?
--"K" BESTOWED THESE NAMES UPON US...
SO NO COMPLAINTS ...
Fsh

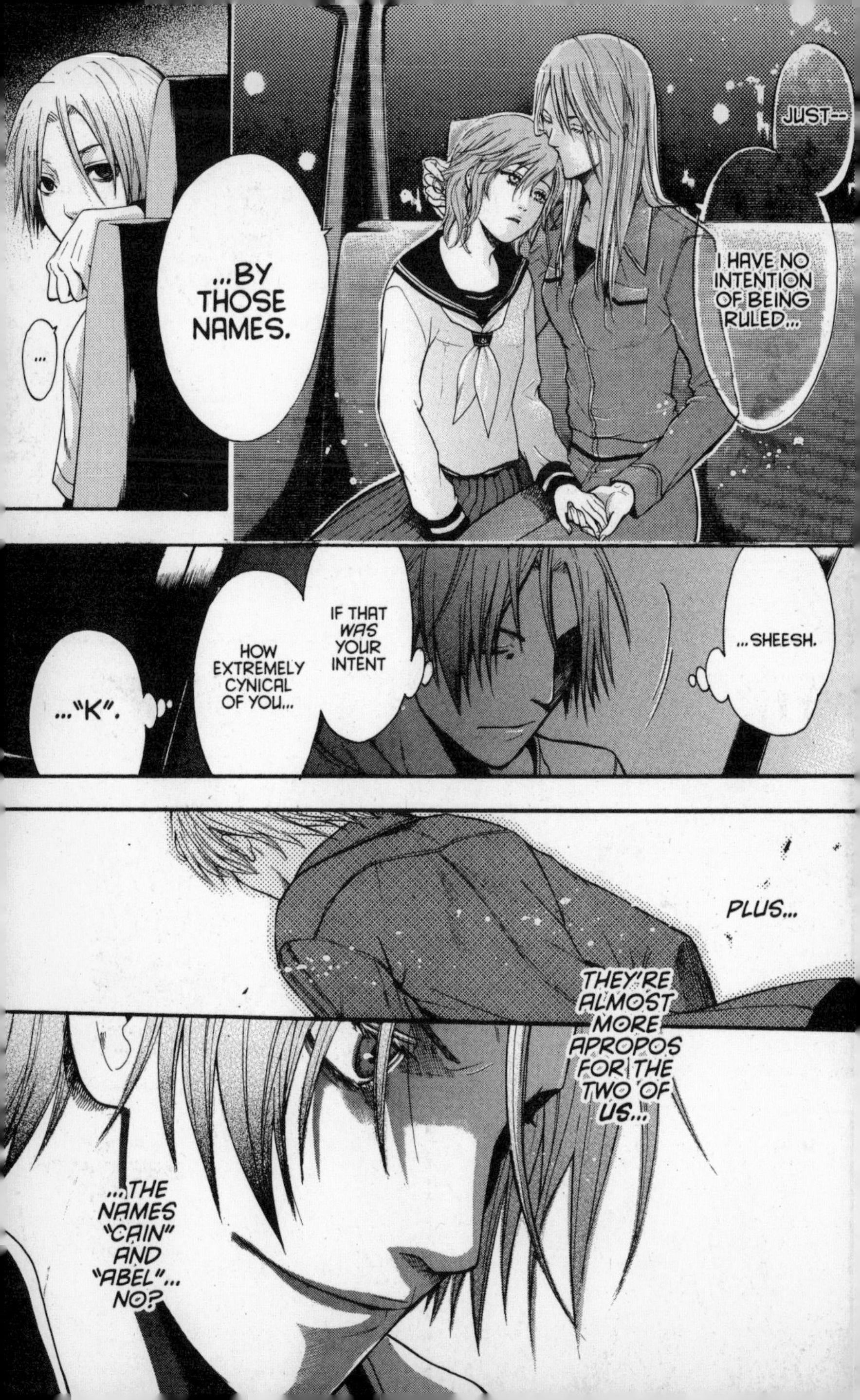
JUST--
I HAVE NO INTENTION OF BEING RULED...
...BY THOSE NAMES.
...
...SHEESH.
IF THAT WAS YOUR INTENT
HOW EXTREMELY CYNICAL OF YOU...
..."K".
PLUS...
THEY'RE ALMOST MORE APROPOS FOR THE TWO OF US...
...THE NAMES "CAIN" AND "ABEL"... NO?

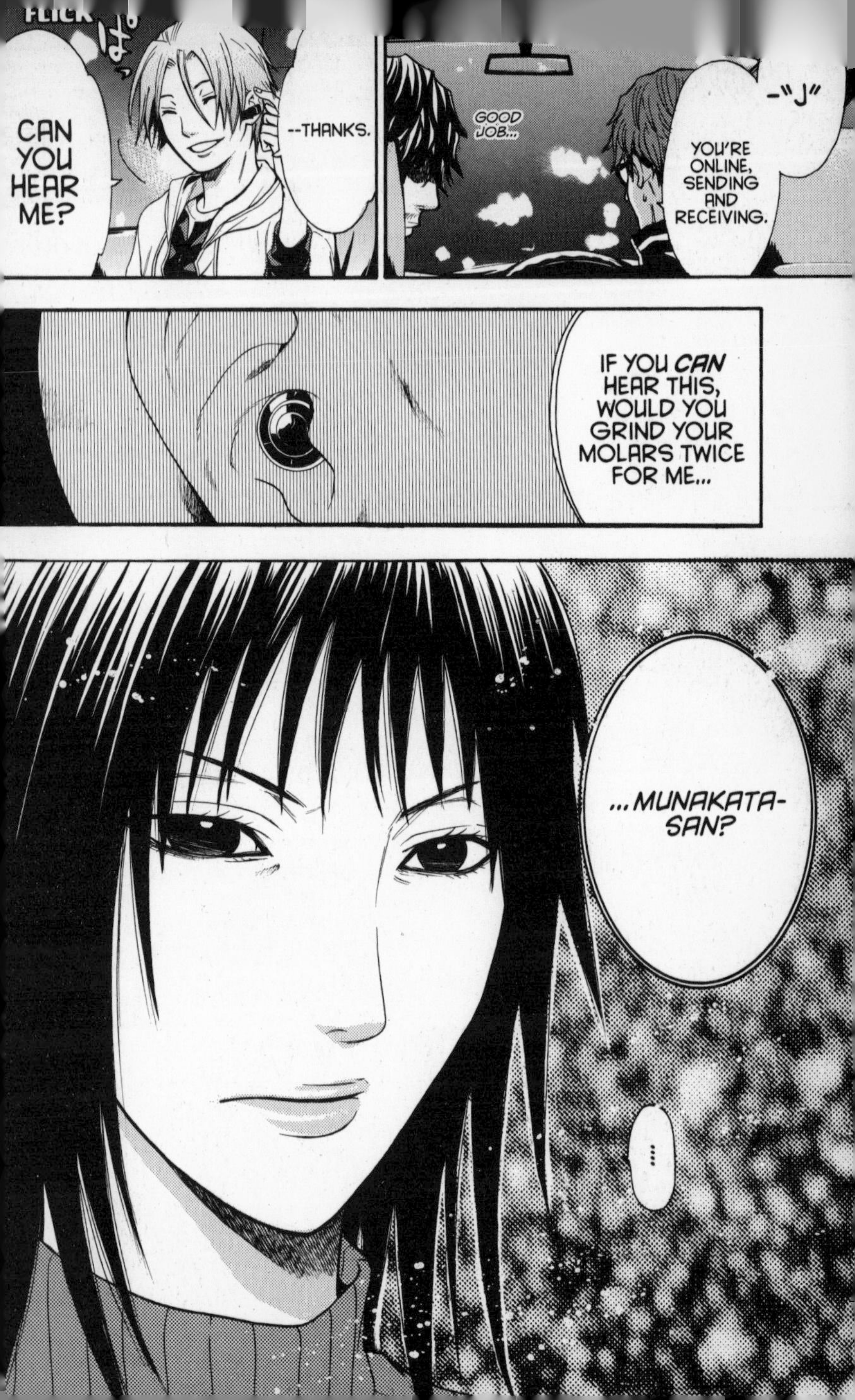
-"J"
YOU'RE ONLINE, SENDING AND RECEIVING.
GOOD JOB...
--THANKS.
FLICK
CAN YOU HEAR ME?
IF YOU *CAN* HEAR THIS, WOULD YOU GRIND YOUR MOLARS TWICE FOR ME...
...MUNAKATA-SAN?
......

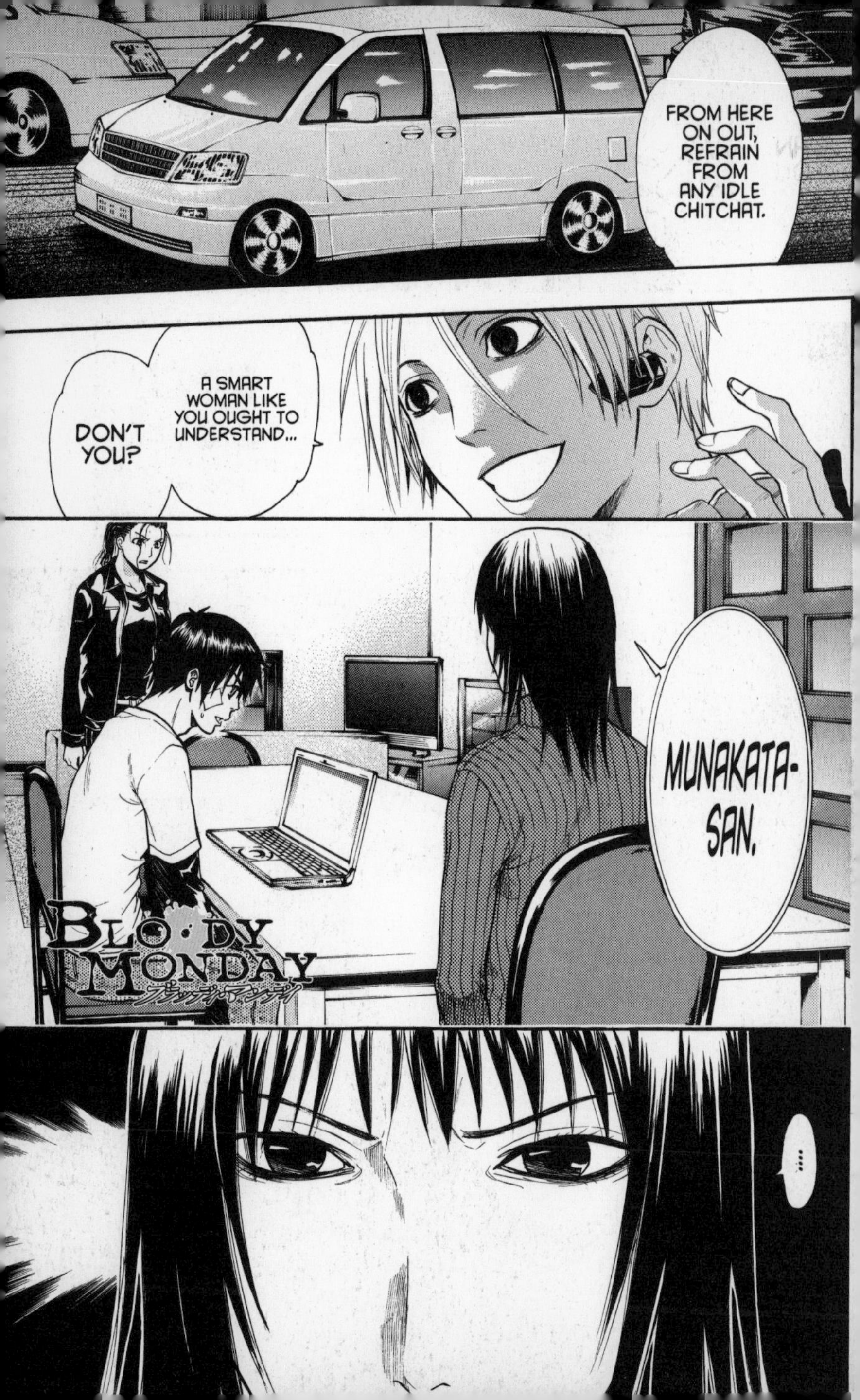
FROM HERE ON OUT, REFRAIN FROM ANY IDLE CHITCHAT.
A SMART WOMAN LIKE YOU OUGHT TO UNDERSTAND...
DON'T YOU?
MUNAKATA-SAN.
.....

File 46

Boxed in by the enemy

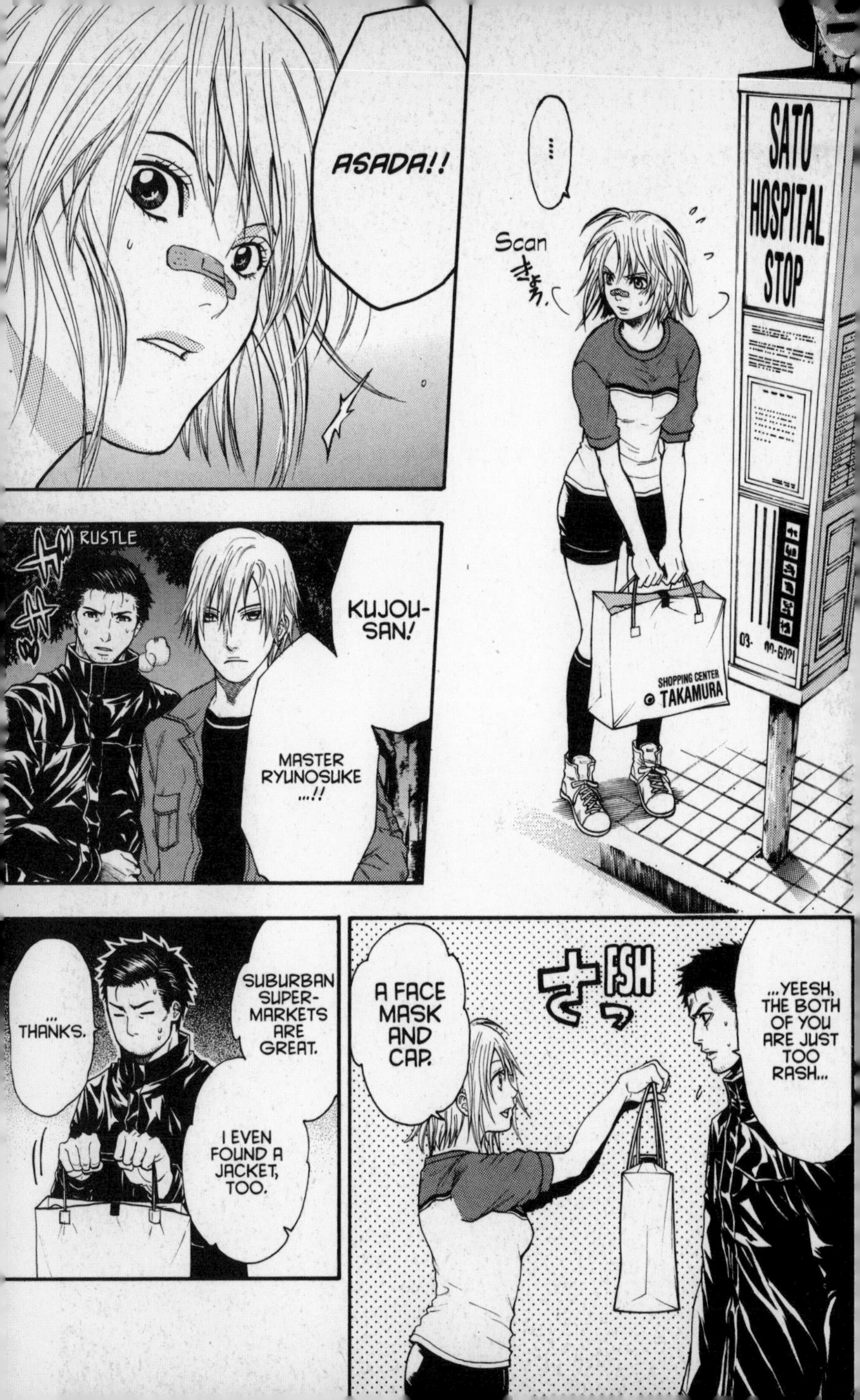
SATO HOSPITAL STOP
......
Scan
SHOPPING CENTER TAKAMURA
ASADA!!
KUJOU-SAN!
MASTER RYUNOSUKE ...!!
RUSTLE
...YEESH, THE BOTH OF YOU ARE JUST TOO RASH...
FSH
A FACE MASK AND CAP.
SUBURBAN SUPER-MARKETS ARE GREAT.
I EVEN FOUND A JACKET, TOO.
... THANKS.

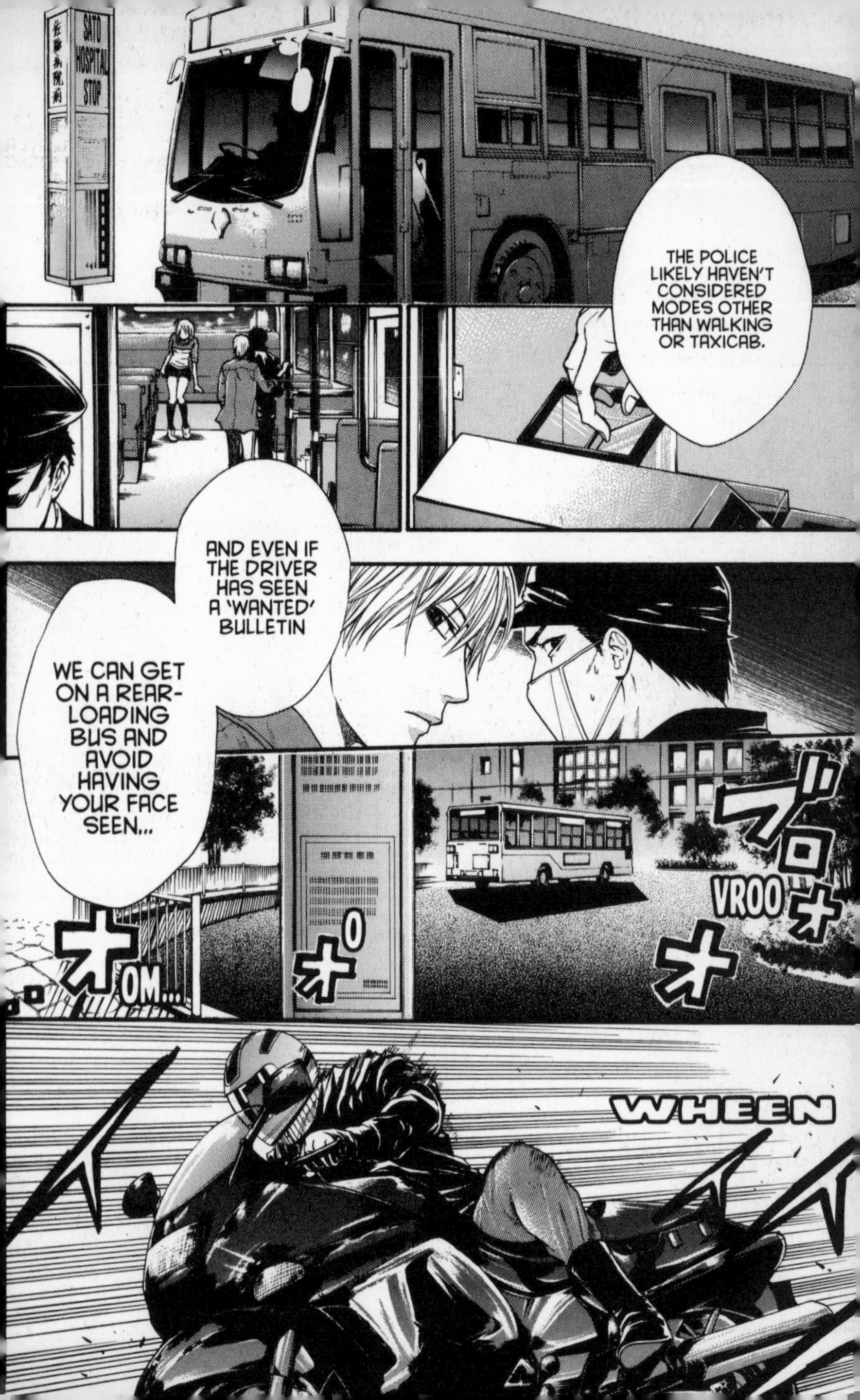

佐藤病院前
SATO HOSPITAL STOP
THE POLICE LIKELY HAVEN'T CONSIDERED MODES OTHER THAN WALKING OR TAXICAB.
AND EVEN IF THE DRIVER HAS SEEN A 'WANTED' BULLETIN
WE CAN GET ON A REAR-LOADING BUS AND AVOID HAVING YOUR FACE SEEN...
ブロオオ
VROO
オ
O
オ
OM...
WHEEN

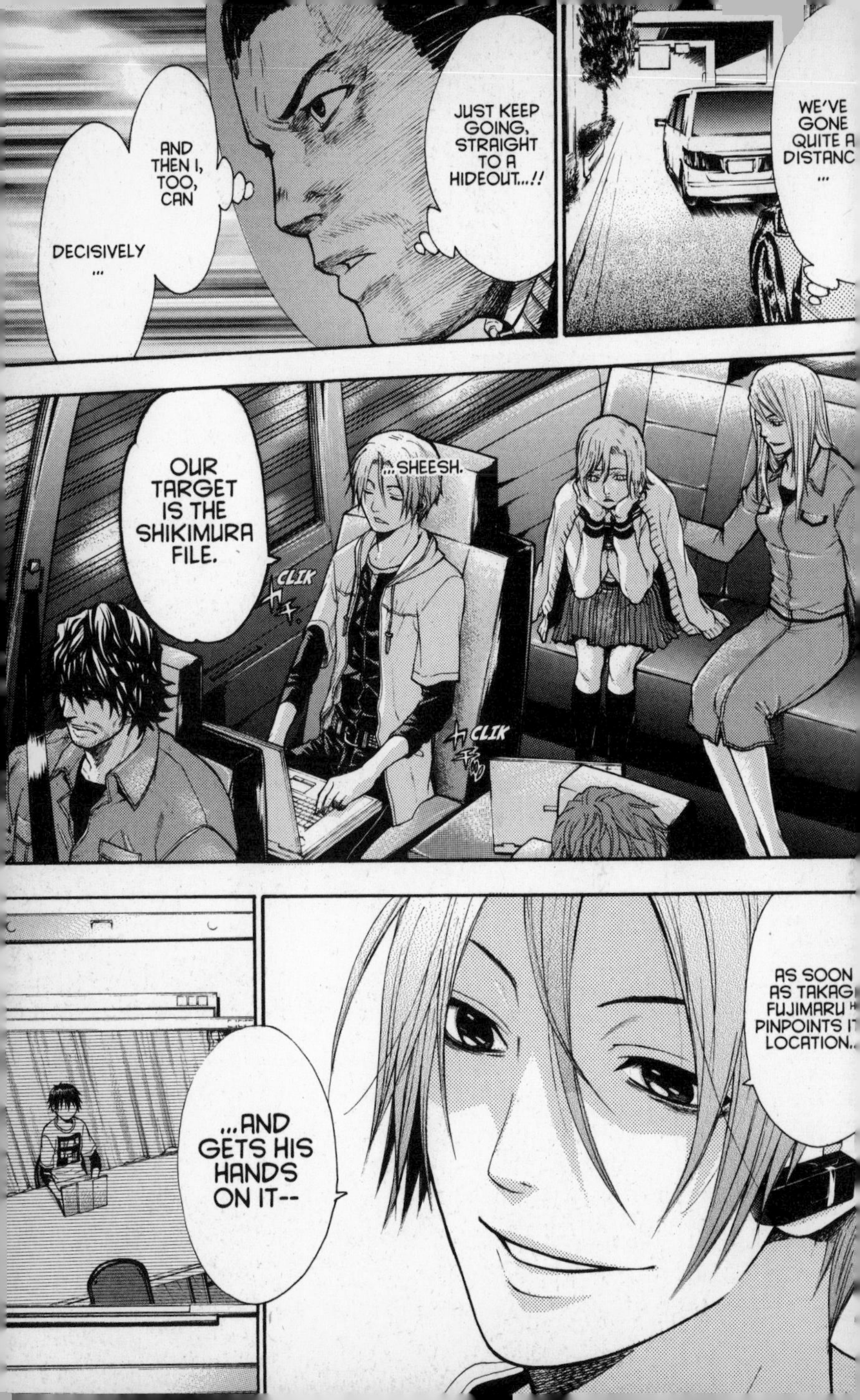
WE'VE GONE QUITE A DISTANC ...
JUST KEEP GOING, STRAIGHT TO A HIDEOUT...!!
AND THEN I, TOO, CAN
DECISIVELY ...
...SHEESH.
OUR TARGET IS THE SHIKIMURA FILE.
CLIK
CLIK
AS SOON AS TAKAG FUJIMARU PINPOINTS IT LOCATION..
...AND GETS HIS HANDS ON IT--

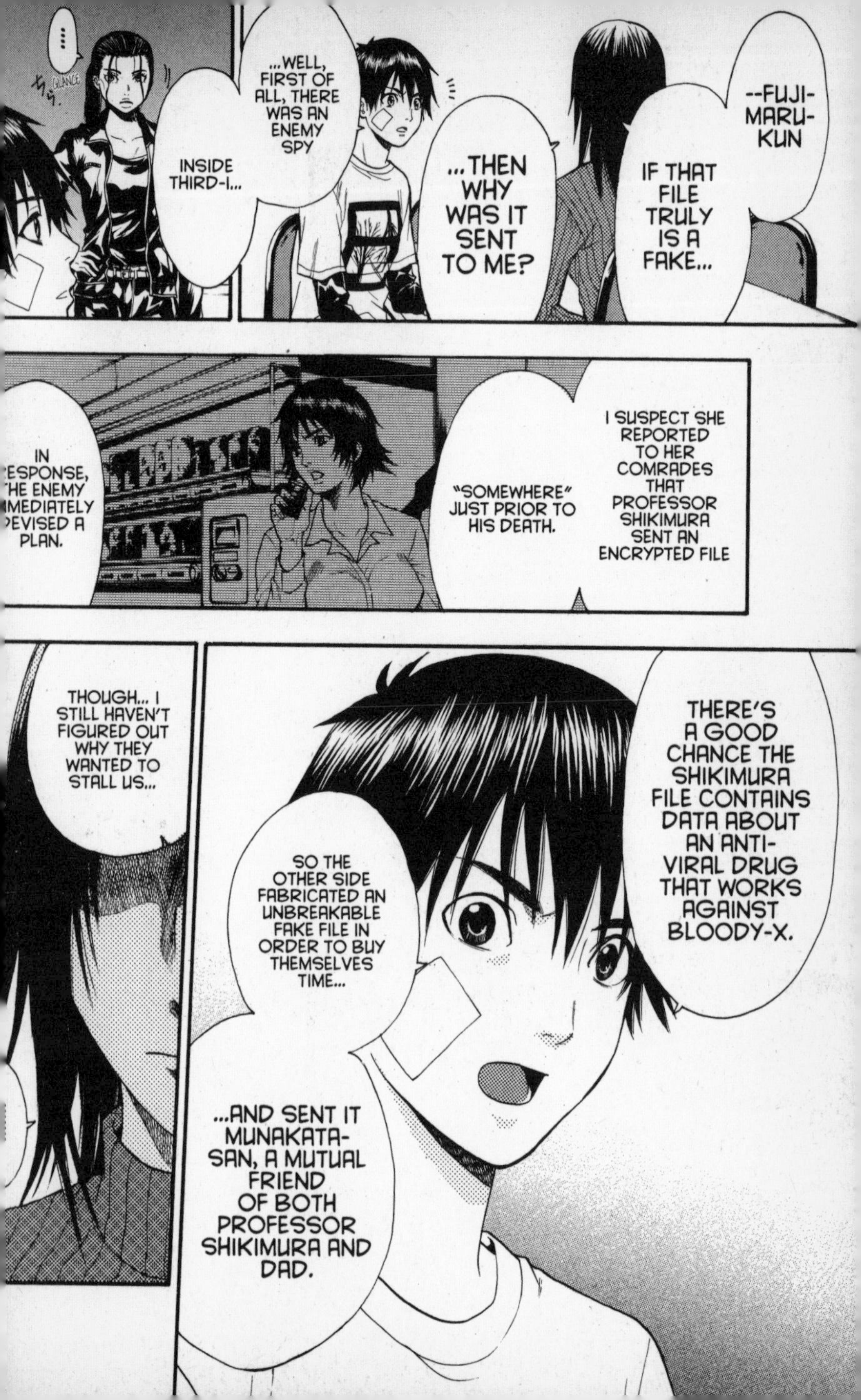
--FUJI-MARU-KUN
IF THAT FILE TRULY IS A FAKE...
...THEN WHY WAS IT SENT TO ME?
...WELL, FIRST OF ALL, THERE WAS AN ENEMY SPY
INSIDE THIRD-I...
GLANCE
....
I SUSPECT SHE REPORTED TO HER COMRADES THAT PROFESSOR SHIKIMURA SENT AN ENCRYPTED FILE
"SOMEWHERE" JUST PRIOR TO HIS DEATH.
IN ESPONSE, THE ENEMY MEDIATELY EVISED A PLAN.
THERE'S A GOOD CHANCE THE SHIKIMURA FILE CONTAINS DATA ABOUT AN ANTI-VIRAL DRUG THAT WORKS AGAINST BLOODY-X.
SO THE OTHER SIDE FABRICATED AN UNBREAKABLE FAKE FILE IN ORDER TO BUY THEMSELVES TIME...
...AND SENT IT MUNAKATA-SAN, A MUTUAL FRIEND OF BOTH PROFESSOR SHIKIMURA AND DAD.
THOUGH... I STILL HAVEN'T FIGURED OUT WHY THEY WANTED TO STALL US...

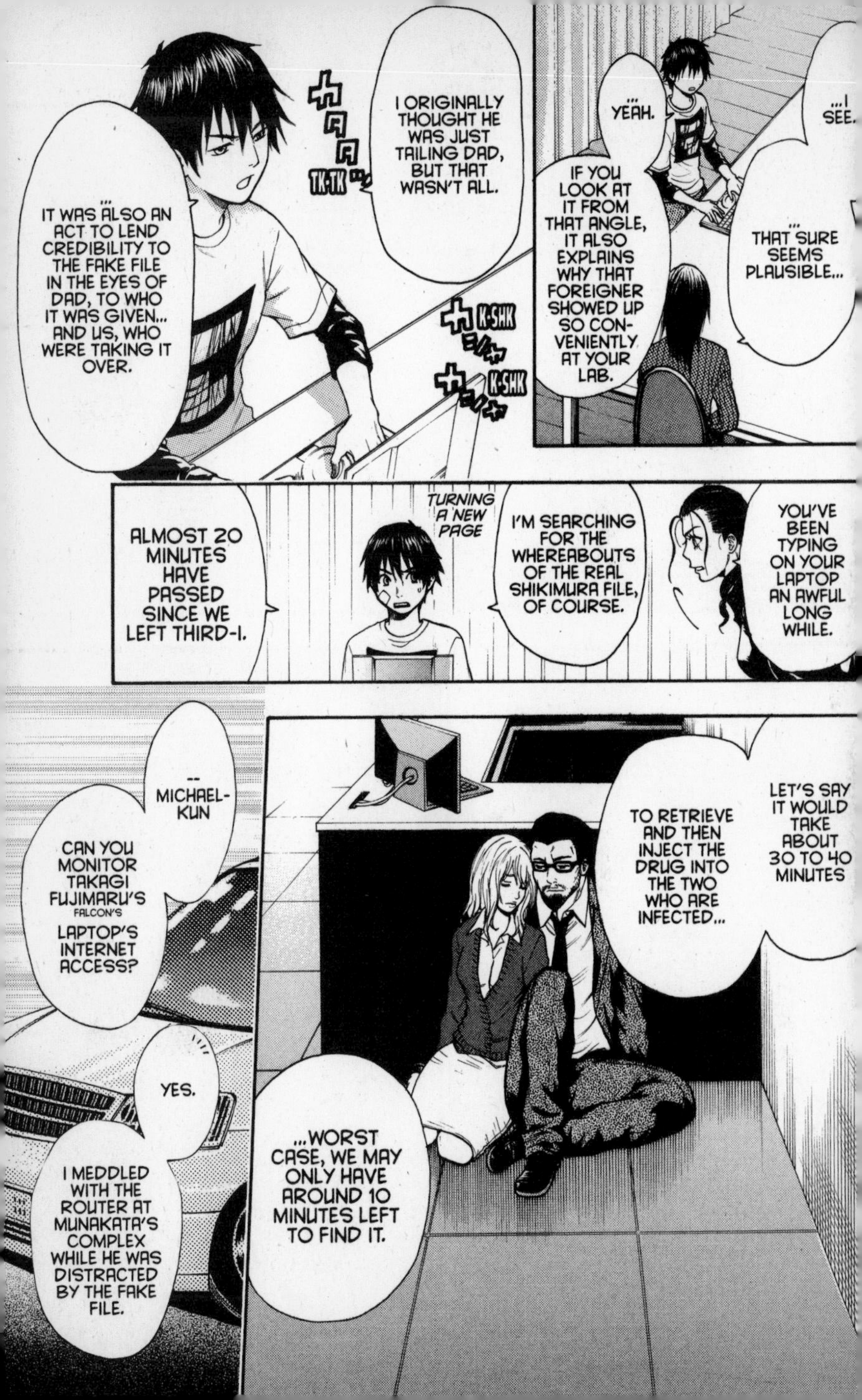
...I SEE.
...YEAH.
IF YOU LOOK AT IT FROM THAT ANGLE, IT ALSO EXPLAINS WHY THAT FOREIGNER SHOWED UP SO CONVENIENTLY AT YOUR LAB.
...THAT SURE SEEMS PLAUSIBLE...
K-SHK
K-SHK
TK-TK
I ORIGINALLY THOUGHT HE WAS JUST TAILING DAD, BUT THAT WASN'T ALL.
...IT WAS ALSO AN ACT TO LEND CREDIBILITY TO THE FAKE FILE IN THE EYES OF DAD, TO WHO IT WAS GIVEN... AND US, WHO WERE TAKING IT OVER.
YOU'VE BEEN TYPING ON YOUR LAPTOP AN AWFUL LONG WHILE.
I'M SEARCHING FOR THE WHEREABOUTS OF THE REAL SHIKIMURA FILE, OF COURSE.
TURNING A NEW PAGE
ALMOST 20 MINUTES HAVE PASSED SINCE WE LEFT THIRD-I.
LET'S SAY IT WOULD TAKE ABOUT 30 TO 40 MINUTES
TO RETRIEVE AND THEN INJECT THE DRUG INTO THE TWO WHO ARE INFECTED...
...WORST CASE, WE MAY ONLY HAVE AROUND 10 MINUTES LEFT TO FIND IT.
--MICHAEL-KUN
CAN YOU MONITOR TAKAGI FUJIMARU'S LAPTOP'S INTERNET ACCESS?
FALCON'S
YES.
I MEDDLED WITH THE ROUTER AT MUNAKATA'S COMPLEX WHILE HE WAS DISTRACTED BY THE FAKE FILE.

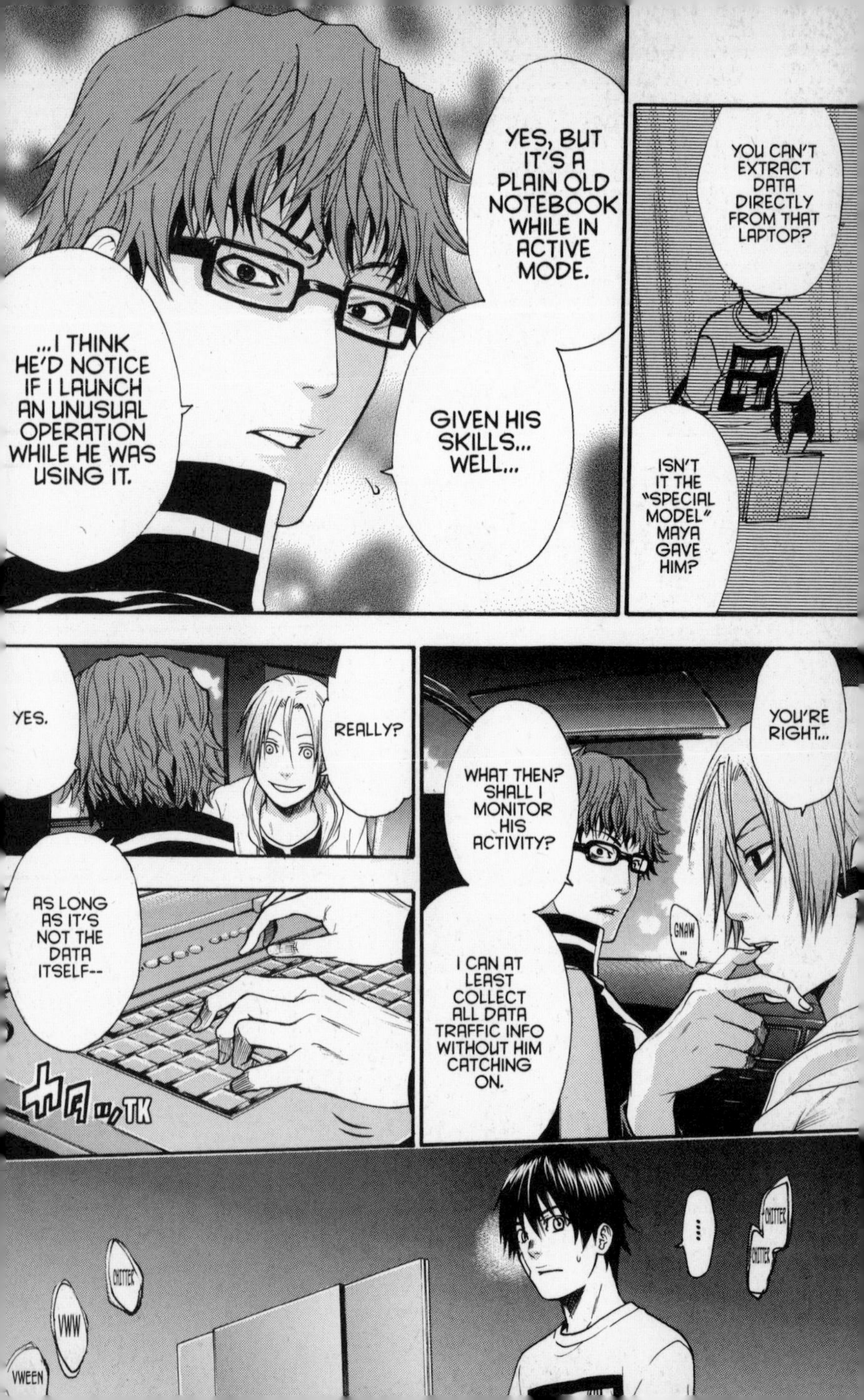
YOU CAN'T EXTRACT DATA DIRECTLY FROM THAT LAPTOP?
ISN'T IT THE "SPECIAL MODEL" MAYA GAVE HIM?
YES, BUT IT'S A PLAIN OLD NOTEBOOK WHILE IN ACTIVE MODE.
GIVEN HIS SKILLS... WELL...
...I THINK HE'D NOTICE IF I LAUNCH AN UNUSUAL OPERATION WHILE HE WAS USING IT.
YOU'RE RIGHT...
GNAW...
WHAT THEN? SHALL I MONITOR HIS ACTIVITY?
I CAN AT LEAST COLLECT ALL DATA TRAFFIC INFO WITHOUT HIM CATCHING ON.
REALLY?
YES.
AS LONG AS IT'S NOT THE DATA ITSELF--
TK
CHITTER
CHITTER
....
CHITTER
VWW
VWEEN

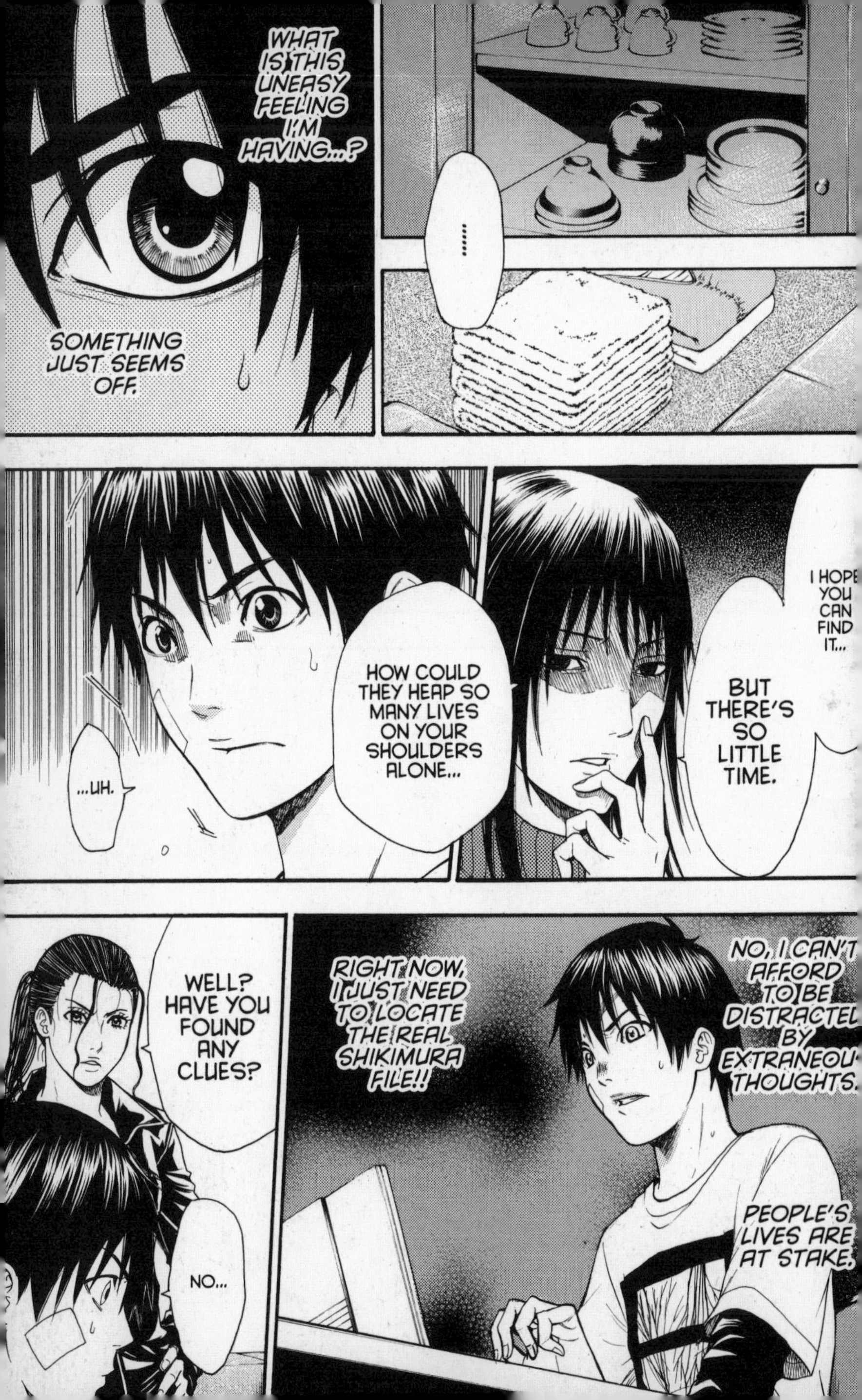
......
WHAT IS THIS UNEASY FEELING I'M HAVING...?
SOMETHING JUST SEEMS OFF.
I HOPE YOU CAN FIND IT...
BUT THERE'S SO LITTLE TIME.
HOW COULD THEY HEAP SO MANY LIVES ON YOUR SHOULDERS ALONE...
...UH.
NO, I CAN'T AFFORD TO BE DISTRACTE BY EXTRANEOU THOUGHTS.
PEOPLE'S LIVES ARE AT STAKE.
RIGHT NOW, I JUST NEED TO LOCATE THE REAL SHIKIMURA FILE!!
WELL? HAVE YOU FOUND ANY CLUES?
NO...

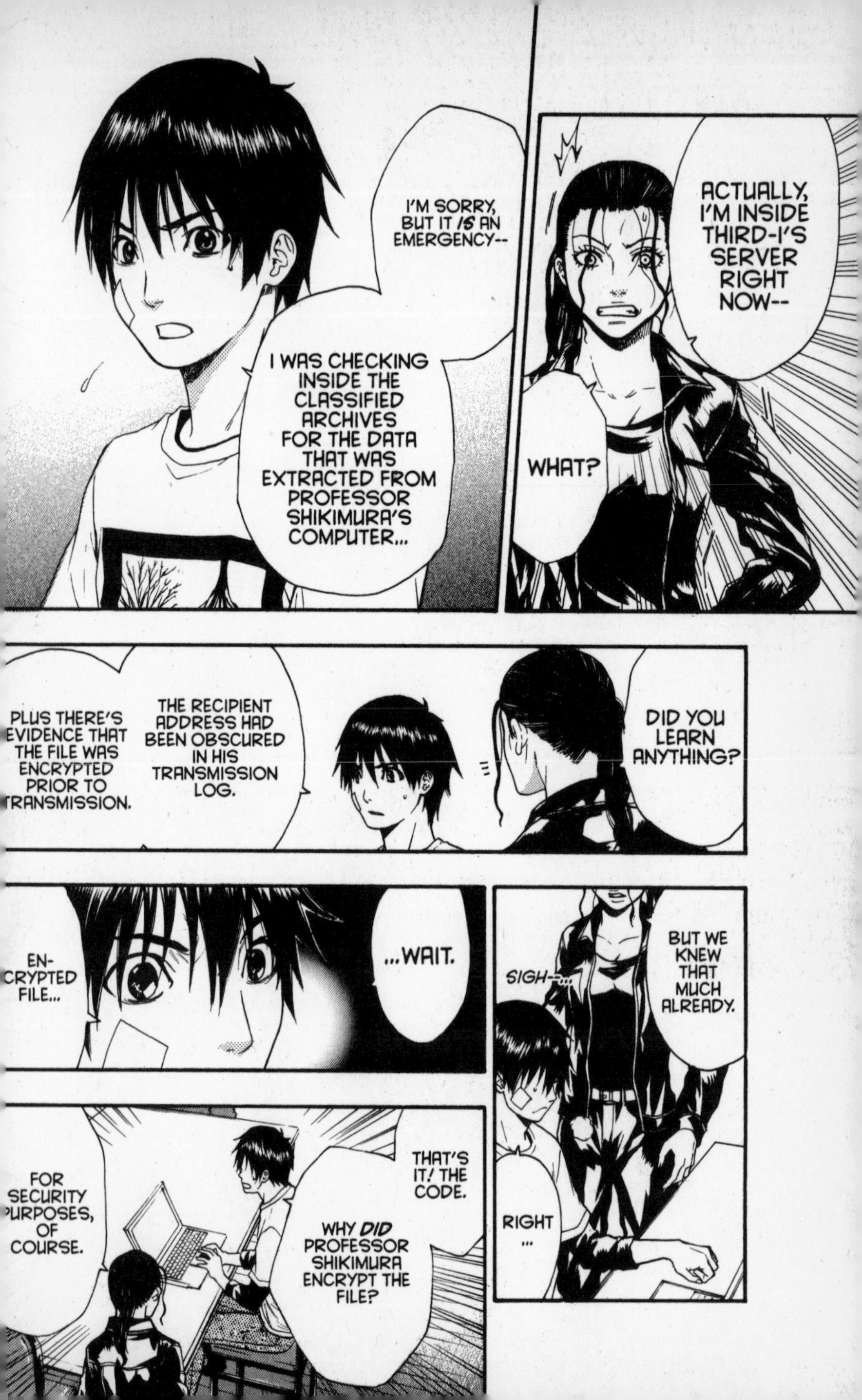
ACTUALLY, I'M INSIDE THIRD-I'S SERVER RIGHT NOW--
WHAT?
I'M SORRY, BUT IT *IS* AN EMERGENCY--
I WAS CHECKING INSIDE THE CLASSIFIED ARCHIVES FOR THE DATA THAT WAS EXTRACTED FROM PROFESSOR SHIKIMURA'S COMPUTER...
DID YOU LEARN ANYTHING?
THE RECIPIENT ADDRESS HAD BEEN OBSCURED IN HIS TRANSMISSION LOG.
PLUS THERE'S EVIDENCE THAT THE FILE WAS ENCRYPTED PRIOR TO TRANSMISSION.
BUT WE KNEW THAT MUCH ALREADY.
SIGH--...
RIGHT ...
...WAIT.
EN-CRYPTED FILE...
THAT'S IT! THE CODE.
WHY *DID* PROFESSOR SHIKIMURA ENCRYPT THE FILE?
FOR SECURITY PURPOSES, OF COURSE.

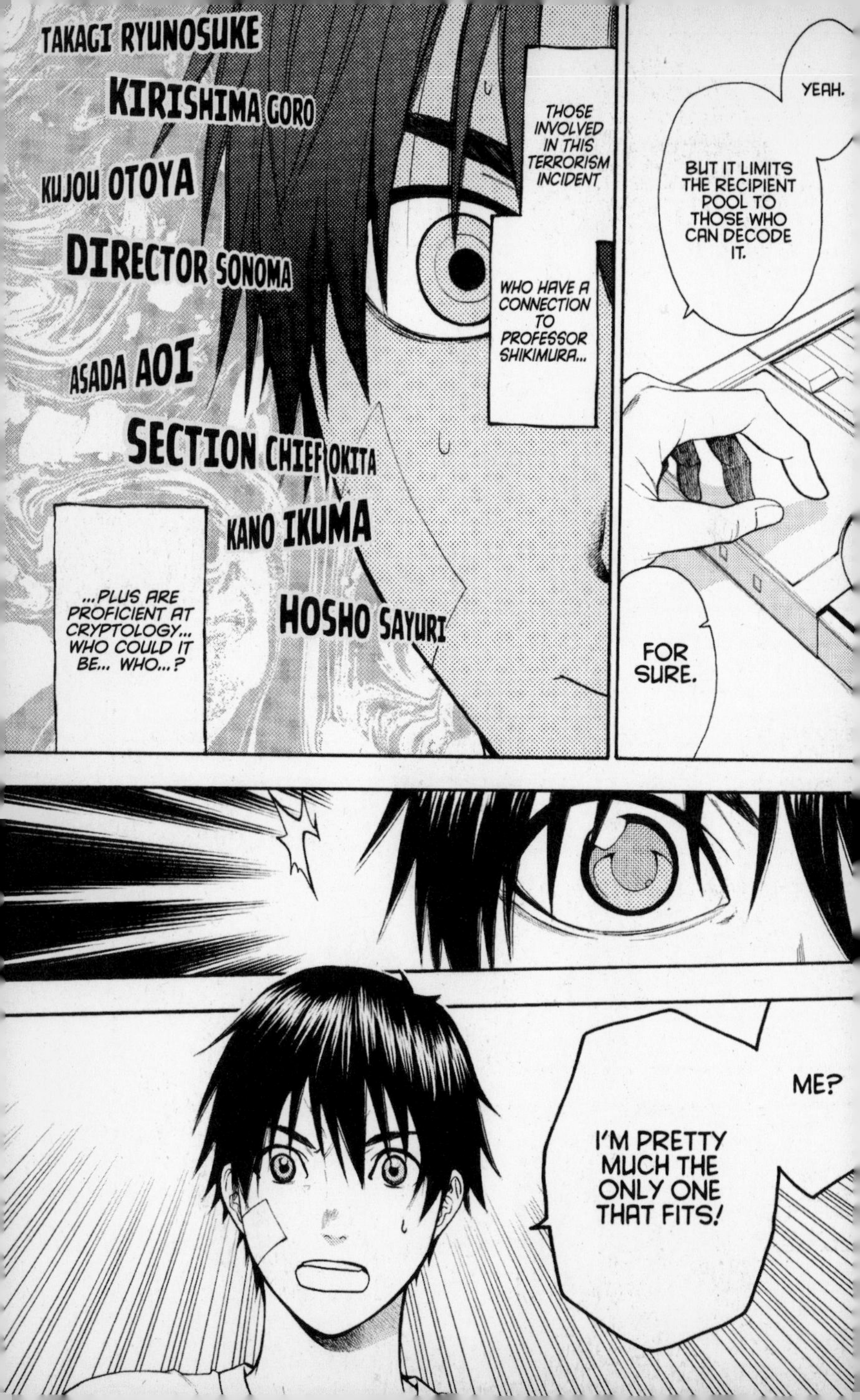
YEAH.
BUT IT LIMITS THE RECIPIENT POOL TO THOSE WHO CAN DECODE IT.
FOR SURE.
THOSE INVOLVED IN THIS TERRORISM INCIDENT
WHO HAVE A CONNECTION TO PROFESSOR SHIKIMURA...
TAKAGI RYUNOSUKE
KIRISHIMA GORO
KUJOU OTOYA
DIRECTOR SONOMA
ASADA AOI
SECTION CHIEF OKITA
KANO IKUMA
HOSHO SAYURI
...PLUS ARE PROFICIENT AT CRYPTOLOGY... WHO COULD IT BE... WHO...?
ME?
I'M PRETTY MUCH THE ONLY ONE THAT FITS!

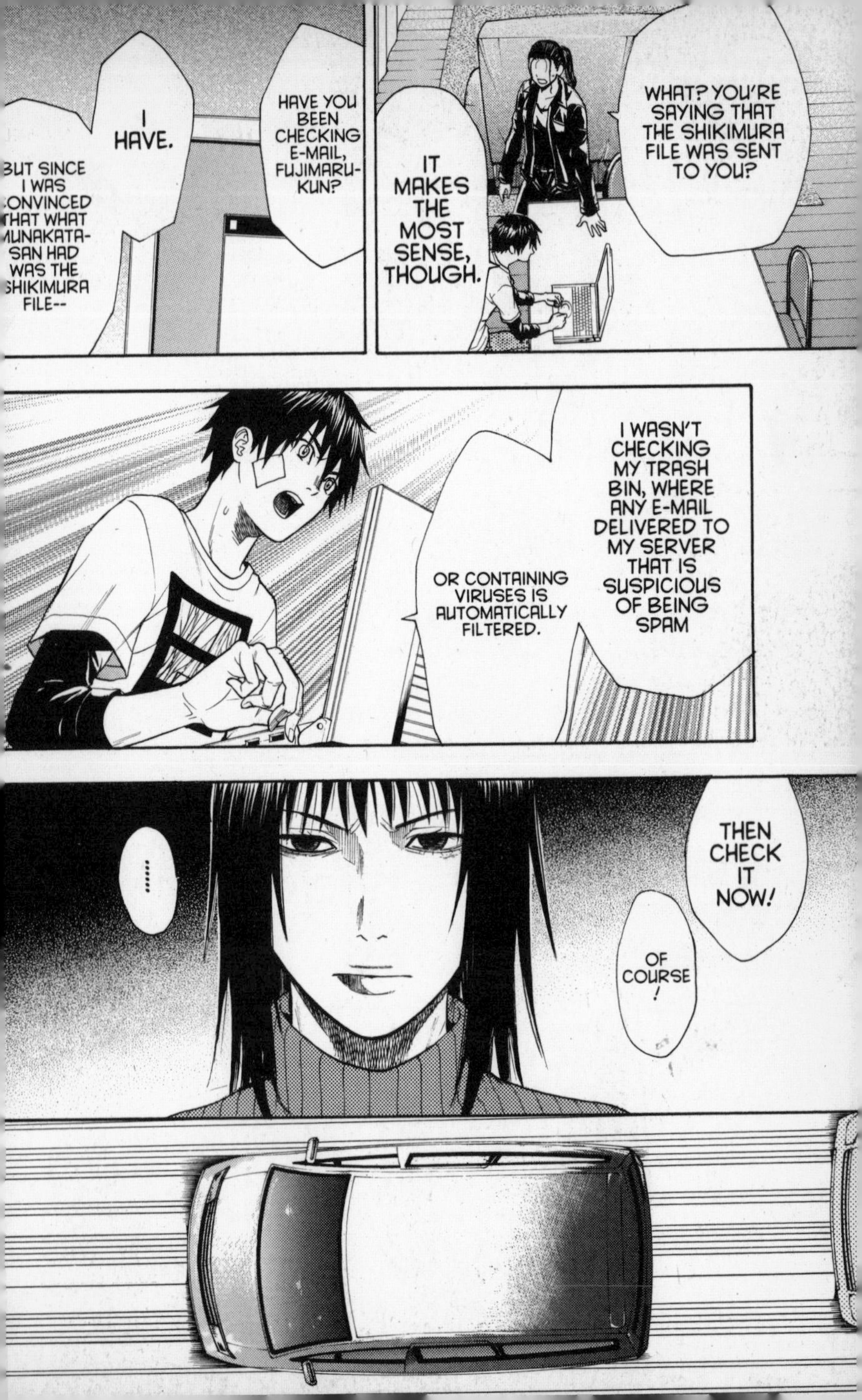
WHAT? YOU'RE SAYING THAT THE SHIKIMURA FILE WAS SENT TO YOU?
IT MAKES THE MOST SENSE, THOUGH.
HAVE YOU BEEN CHECKING E-MAIL, FUJIMARU-KUN?
I HAVE.
BUT SINCE I WAS CONVINCED THAT WHAT MUNAKATA-SAN HAD WAS THE SHIKIMURA FILE--
I WASN'T CHECKING MY TRASH BIN, WHERE ANY E-MAIL DELIVERED TO MY SERVER THAT IS SUSPICIOUS OF BEING SPAM
OR CONTAINING VIRUSES IS AUTOMATICALLY FILTERED.
THEN CHECK IT NOW!
OF COURSE!
......

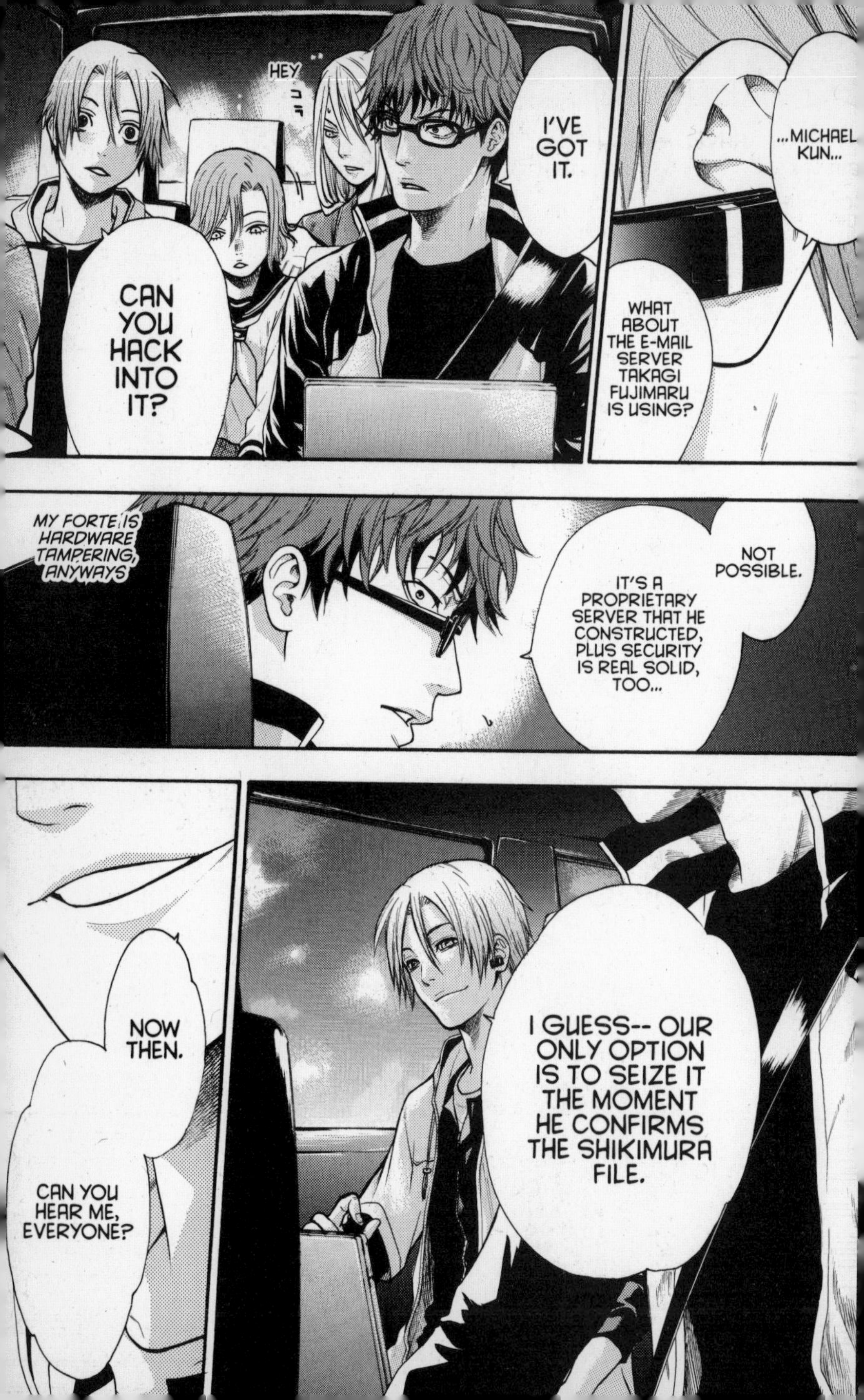
...MICHAEL KUN...
WHAT ABOUT THE E-MAIL SERVER TAKAGI FUJIMARU IS USING?
I'VE GOT IT.
HEY
コラ
CAN YOU HACK INTO IT?
NOT POSSIBLE.
IT'S A PROPRIETARY SERVER THAT HE CONSTRUCTED, PLUS SECURITY IS REAL SOLID, TOO...
MY FORTE IS HARDWARE TAMPERING, ANYWAYS
I GUESS-- OUR ONLY OPTION IS TO SEIZE IT THE MOMENT HE CONFIRMS THE SHIKIMURA FILE.
NOW THEN.
CAN YOU HEAR ME, EVERYONE?

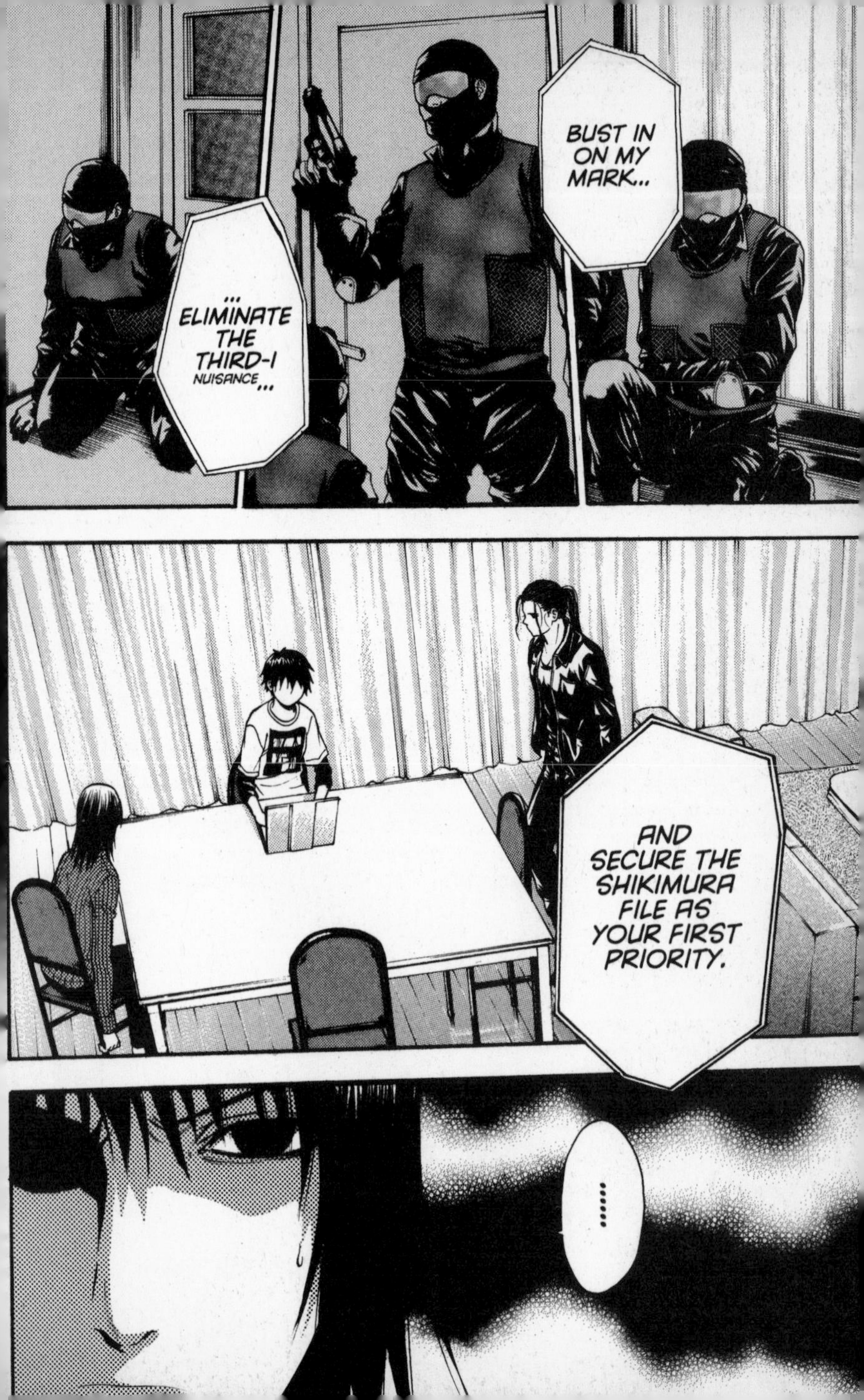
BUST IN ON MY MARK...
...ELIMINATE THE THIRD-I NUISANCE...
AND SECURE THE SHIKIMURA FILE AS YOUR FIRST PRIORITY.
......

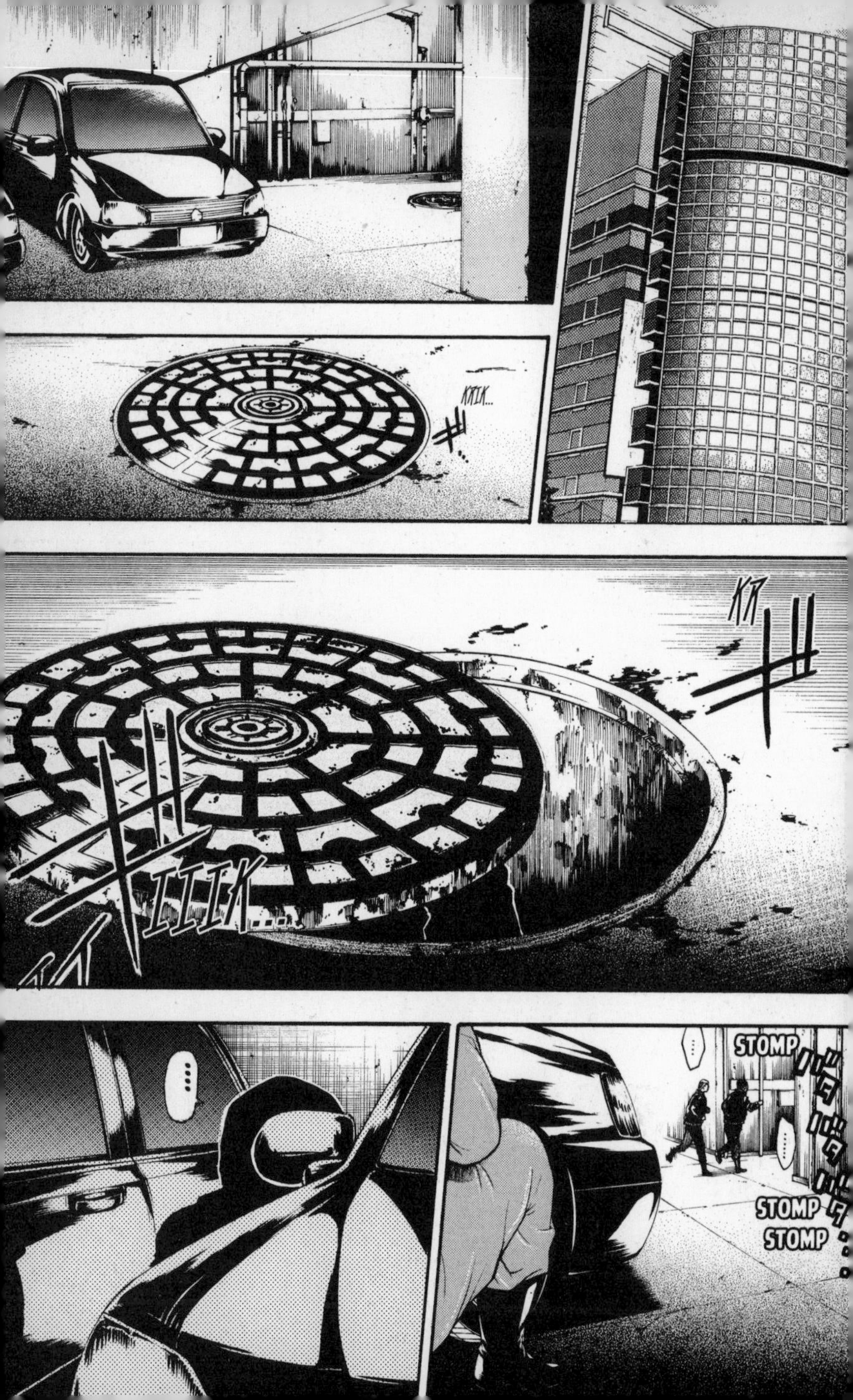
KRIK...
KR
KIIIK...
...
STOMP
...
STOMP
STOMP
....

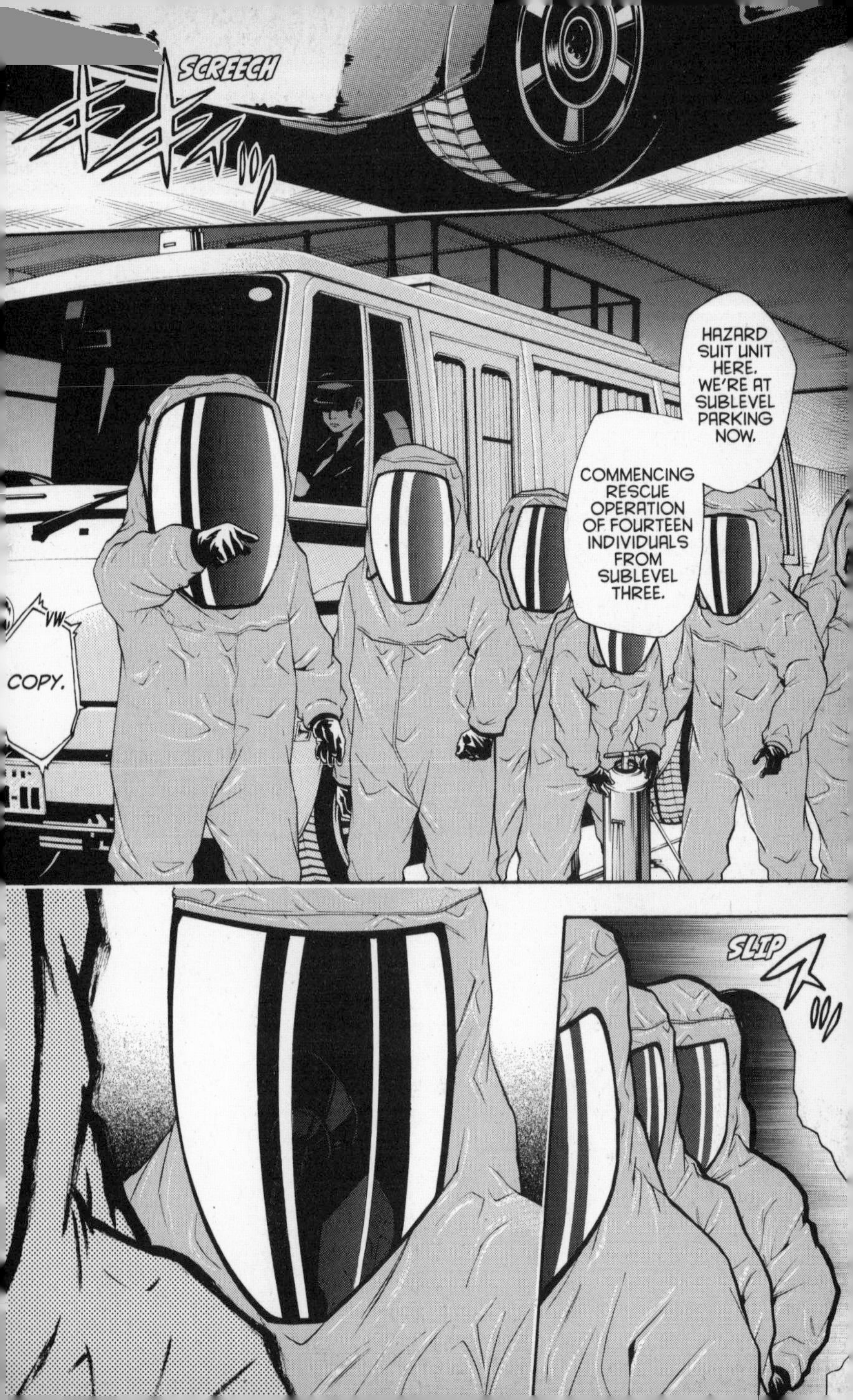
SCREECH
HAZARD SUIT UNIT HERE. WE'RE AT SUBLEVEL PARKING NOW.
COMMENCING RESCUE OPERATION OF FOURTEEN INDIVIDUALS FROM SUBLEVEL THREE.
VW
COPY.
SLIP

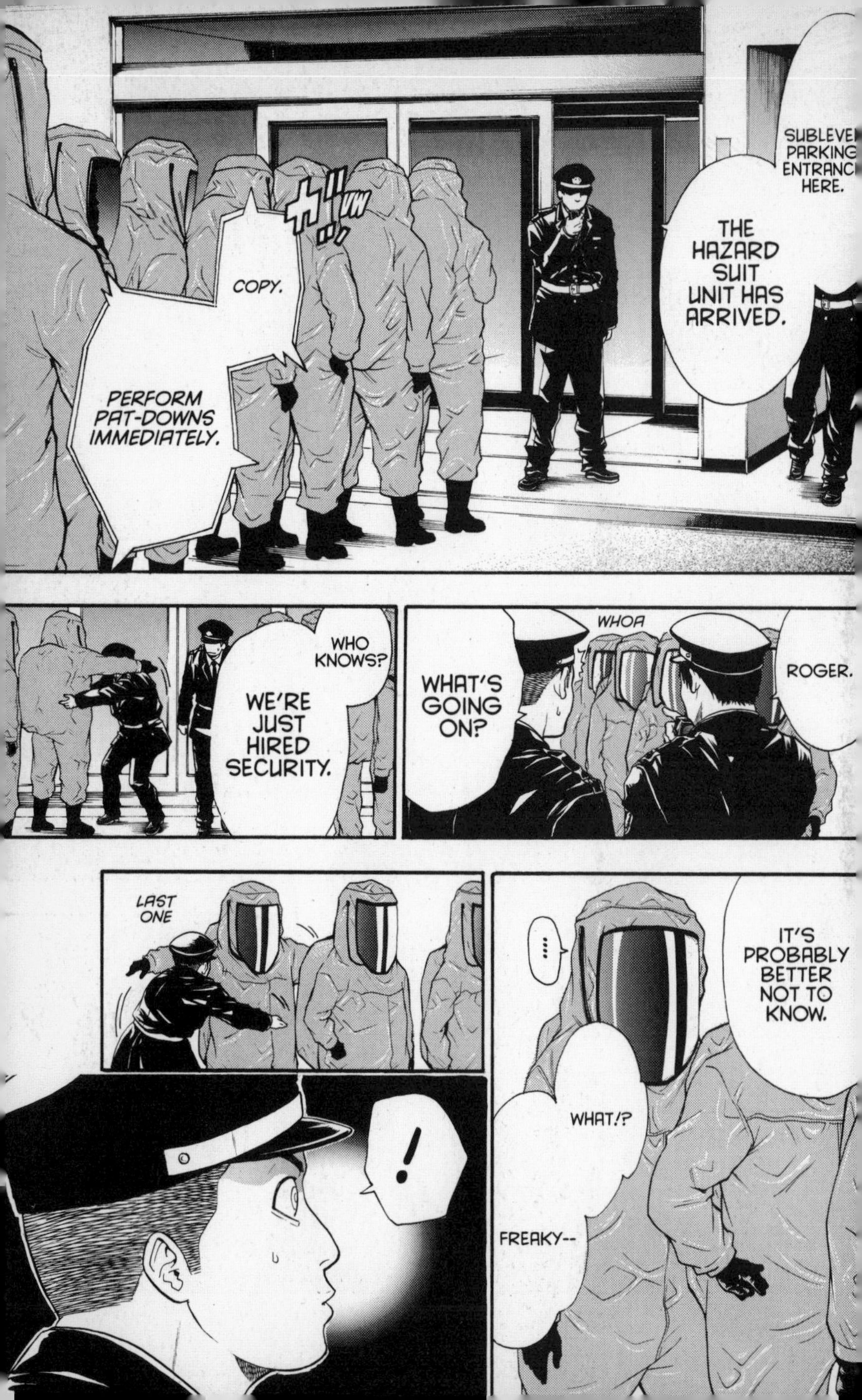
SUBLEVE PARKING ENTRANC HERE.
THE HAZARD SUIT UNIT HAS ARRIVED.
VW
COPY.
PERFORM PAT-DOWNS IMMEDIATELY.
ROGER.
WHOA
WHAT'S GOING ON?
WHO KNOWS?
WE'RE JUST HIRED SECURITY.
IT'S PROBABLY BETTER NOT TO KNOW.
....
WHAT!?
FREAKY--
LAST ONE
!

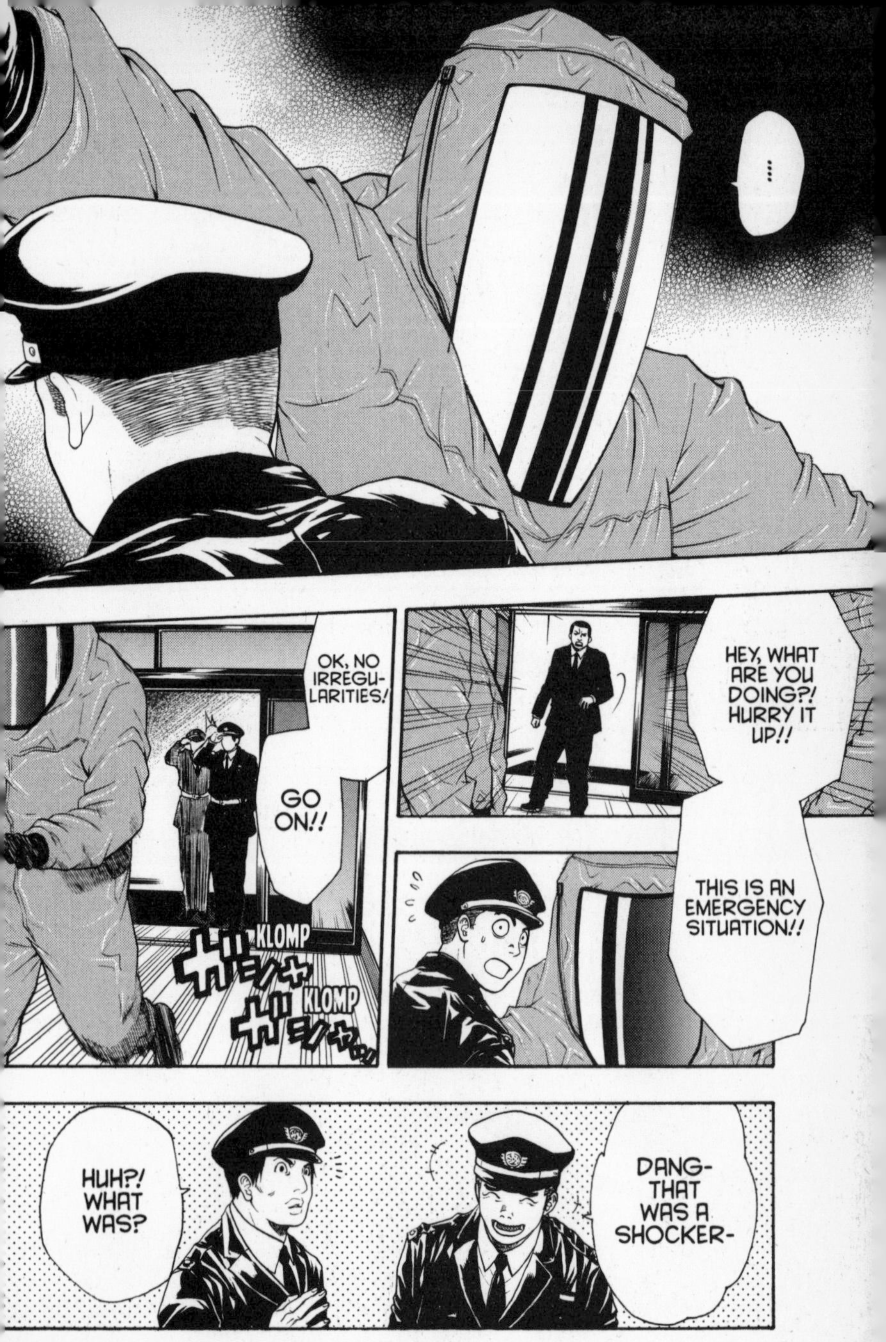
....
HEY, WHAT ARE YOU DOING?! HURRY IT UP!!
THIS IS AN EMERGENCY SITUATION!!
OK, NO IRREGU-LARITIES!
GO ON!!
KLOMP
KLOMP
DANG-THAT WAS A SHOCKER-
HUH?! WHAT WAS?

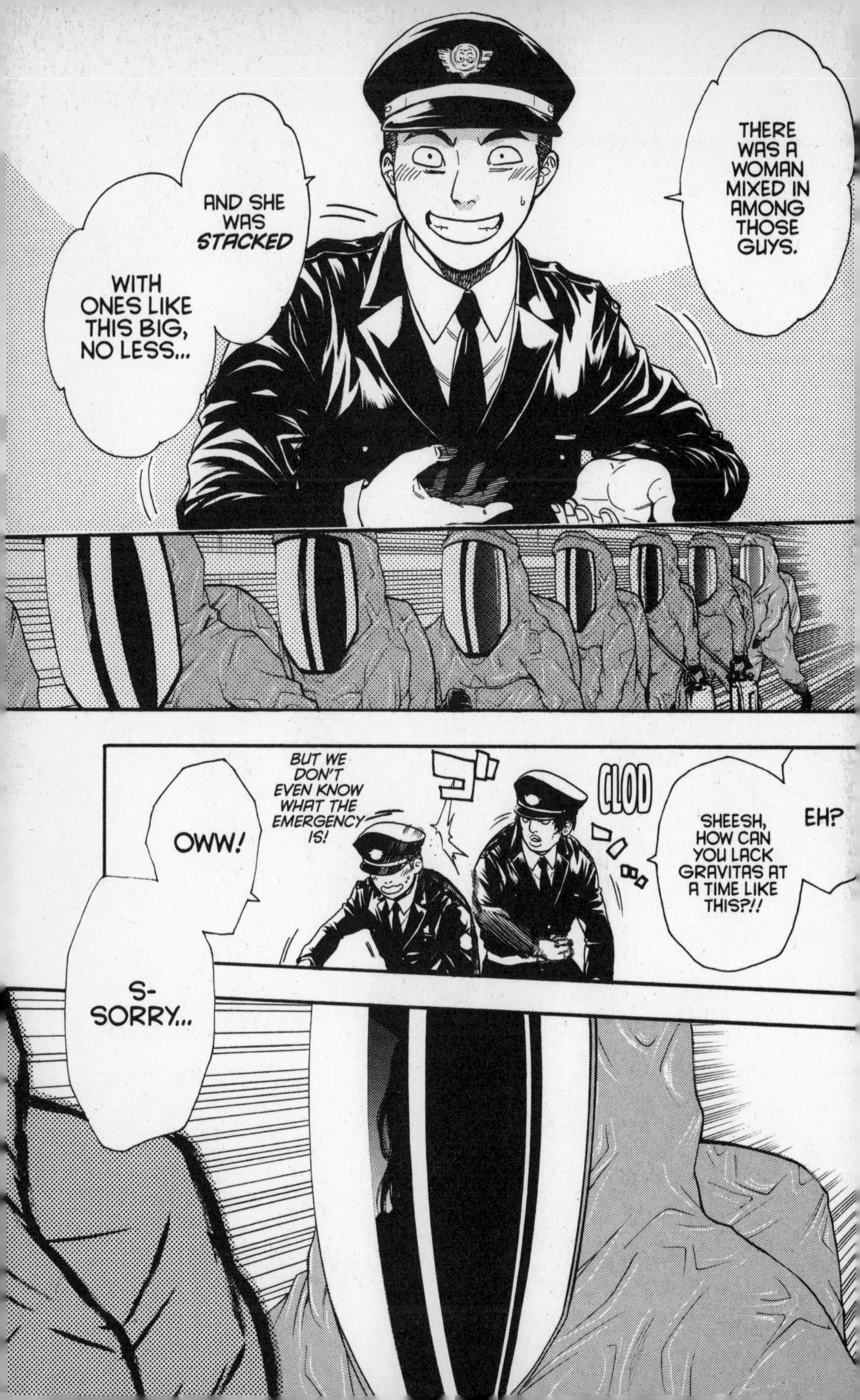
THERE WAS A WOMAN MIXED IN AMONG THOSE GUYS.
AND SHE WAS *STACKED*
WITH ONES LIKE THIS BIG, NO LESS...
EH?
SHEESH, HOW CAN YOU LACK GRAVITAS AT A TIME LIKE THIS?!!
CLOD
BUT WE DON'T EVEN KNOW WHAT THE EMERGENCY IS!
OWW!
S- SORRY...

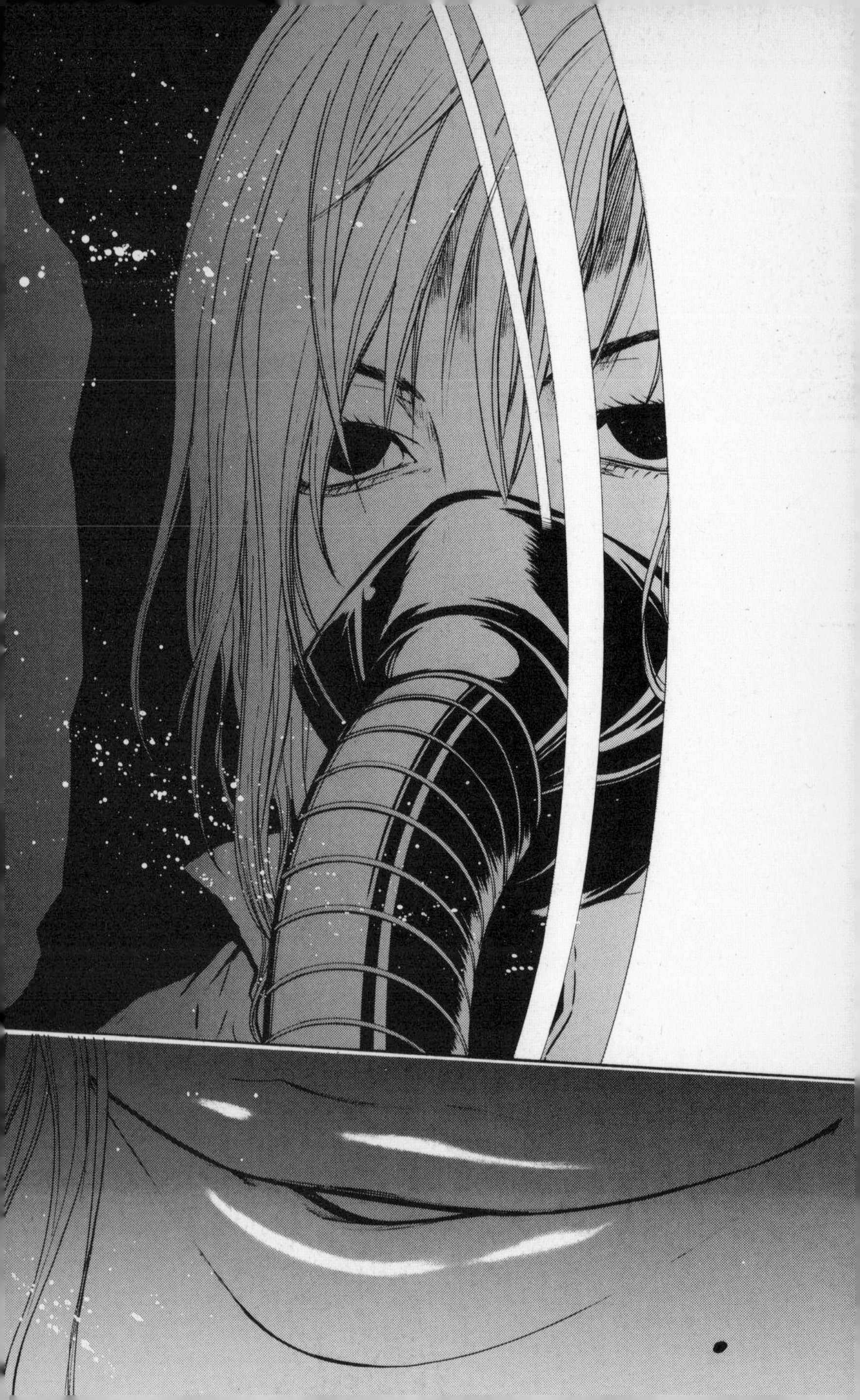

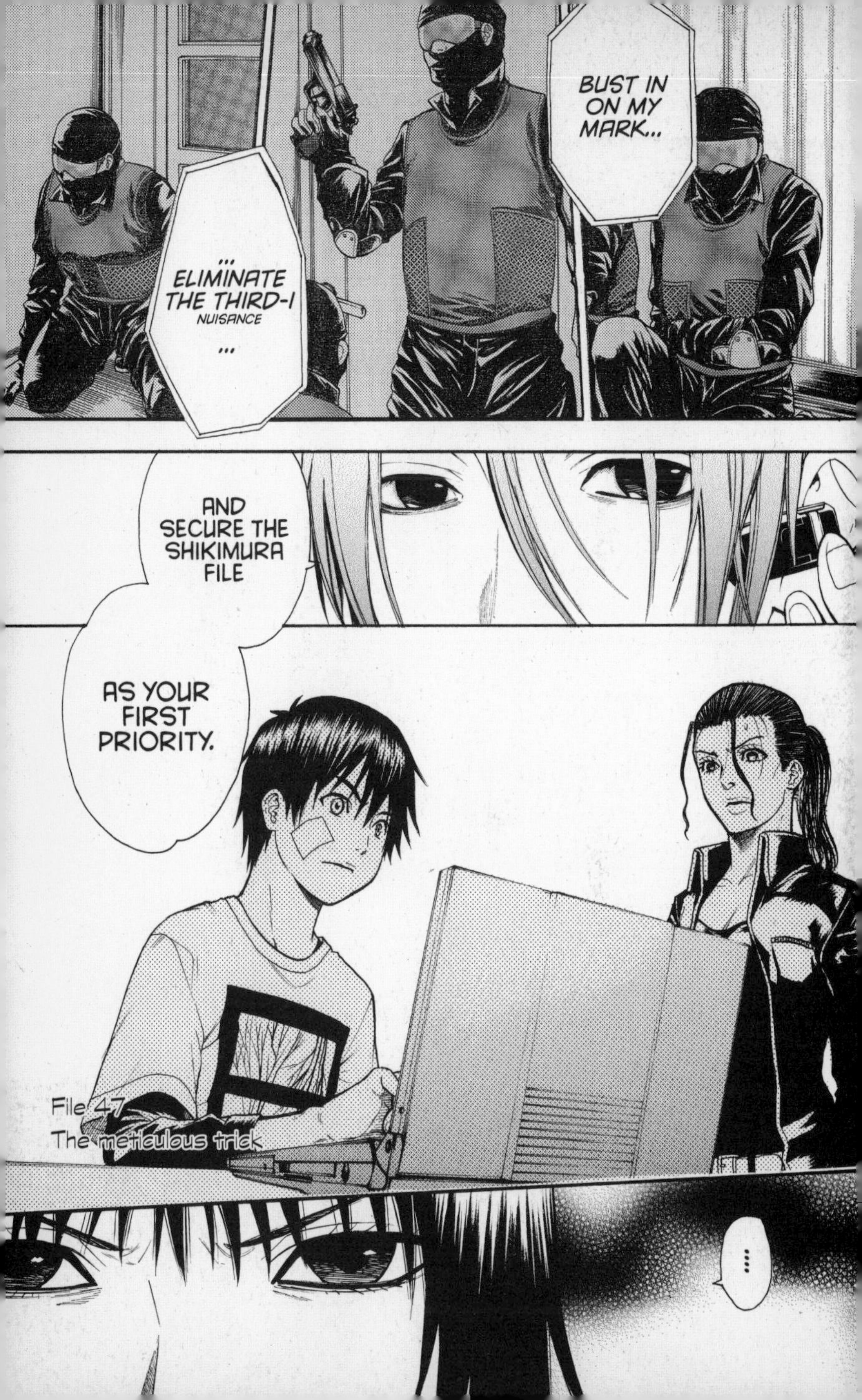
BUST IN ON MY MARK...
...ELIMINATE THE THIRD-I NUISANCE ...
AND SECURE THE SHIKIMURA FILE
AS YOUR FIRST PRIORITY.
File 47
The meticulous trick
...

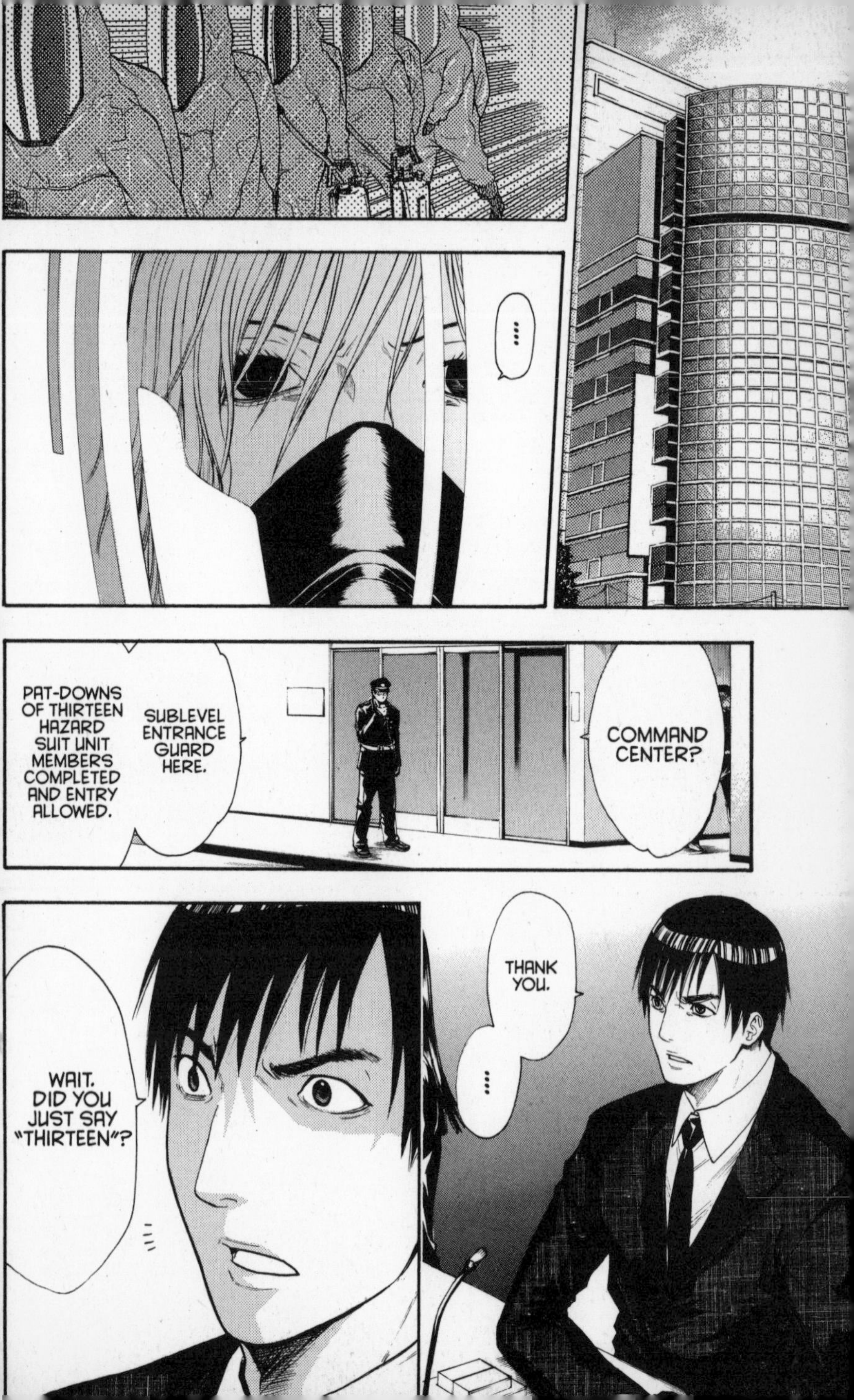
....
COMMAND CENTER?
SUBLEVEL ENTRANCE GUARD HERE.
PAT-DOWNS OF THIRTEEN HAZARD SUIT UNIT MEMBERS COMPLETED AND ENTRY ALLOWED.
THANK YOU.
....
WAIT. DID YOU JUST SAY "THIRTEEN"?

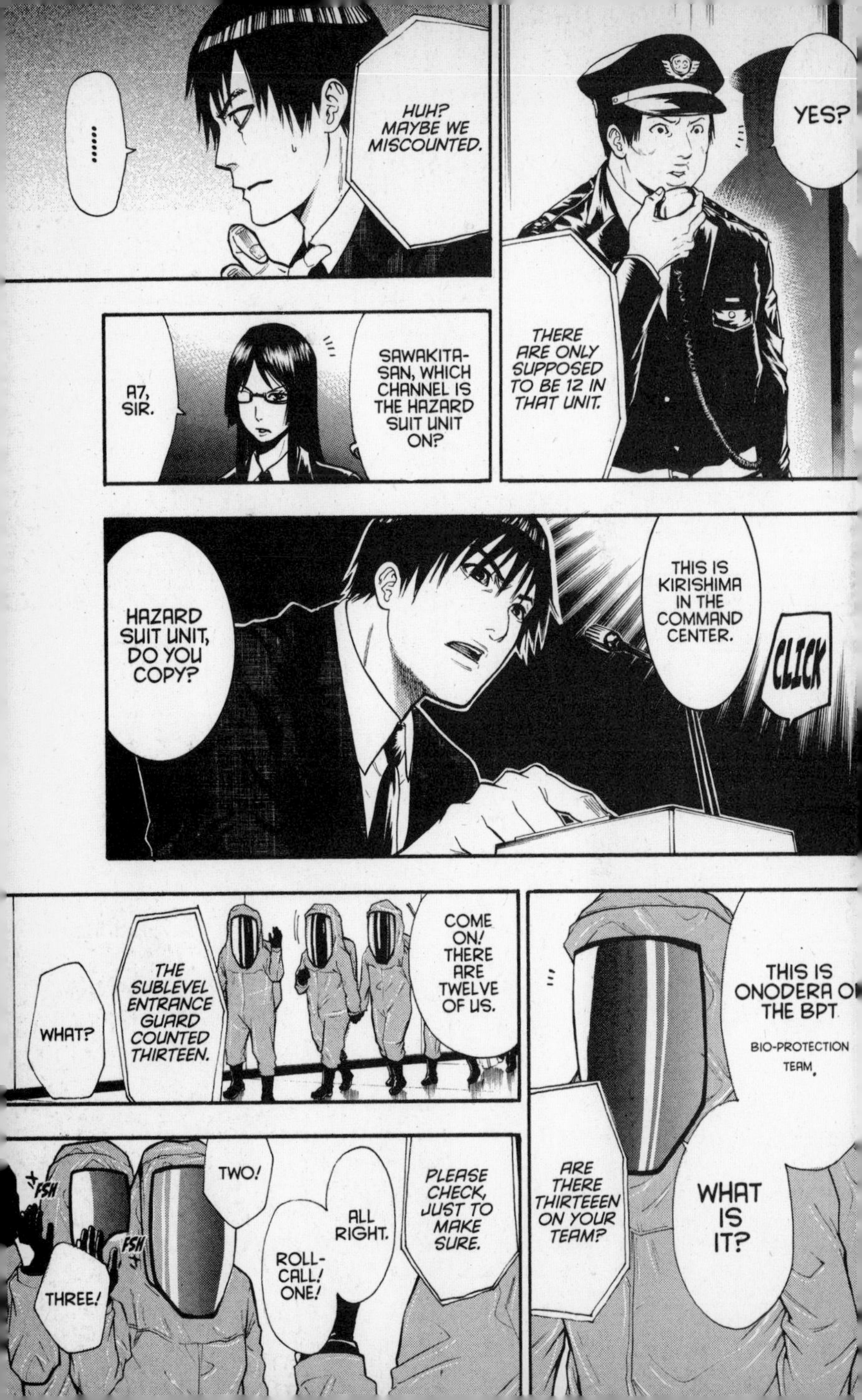
YES?
THERE ARE ONLY SUPPOSED TO BE 12 IN THAT UNIT.
HUH? MAYBE WE MISCOUNTED.
......
SAWAKITA-SAN, WHICH CHANNEL IS THE HAZARD SUIT UNIT ON?
A7, SIR.
THIS IS KIRISHIMA IN THE COMMAND CENTER.
CLICK
HAZARD SUIT UNIT, DO YOU COPY?
THIS IS ONODERA O THE BPT.
BIO-PROTECTION TEAM.
WHAT IS IT?
ARE THERE THIRTEEEN ON YOUR TEAM?
COME ON! THERE ARE TWELVE OF US.
THE SUBLEVEL ENTRANCE GUARD COUNTED THIRTEEN.
WHAT?
PLEASE CHECK, JUST TO MAKE SURE.
ALL RIGHT.
ROLL-CALL! ONE!
TWO!
FSH
THREE!
FSH

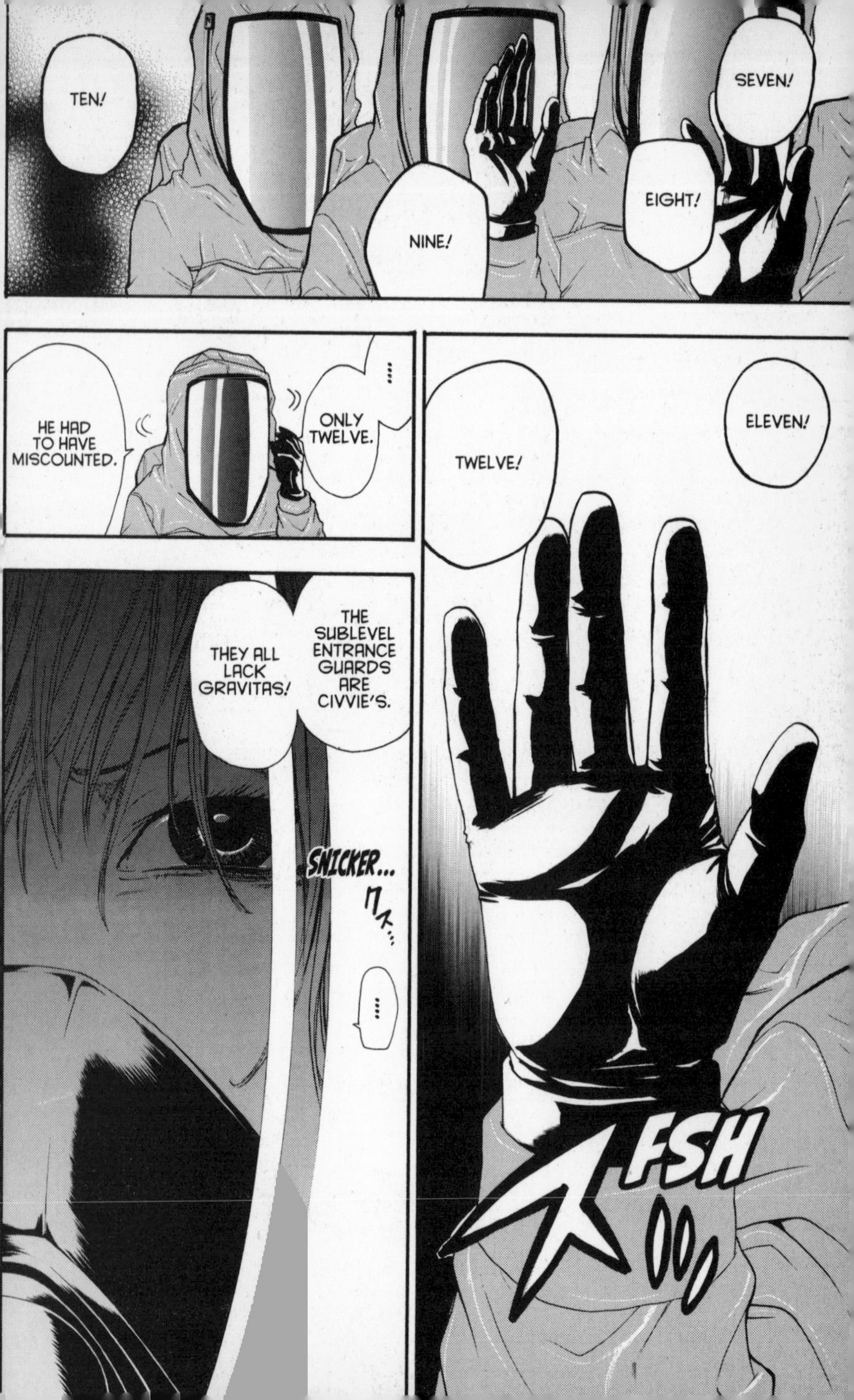
SEVEN!
EIGHT!
NINE!
TEN!
ELEVEN!
TWELVE!
FSH
...
ONLY TWELVE.
HE HAD TO HAVE MISCOUNTED.
THE SUBLEVEL ENTRANCE GUARDS ARE CIVVIE'S.
THEY ALL LACK GRAVITAS!
SNICKER...
クス…
...

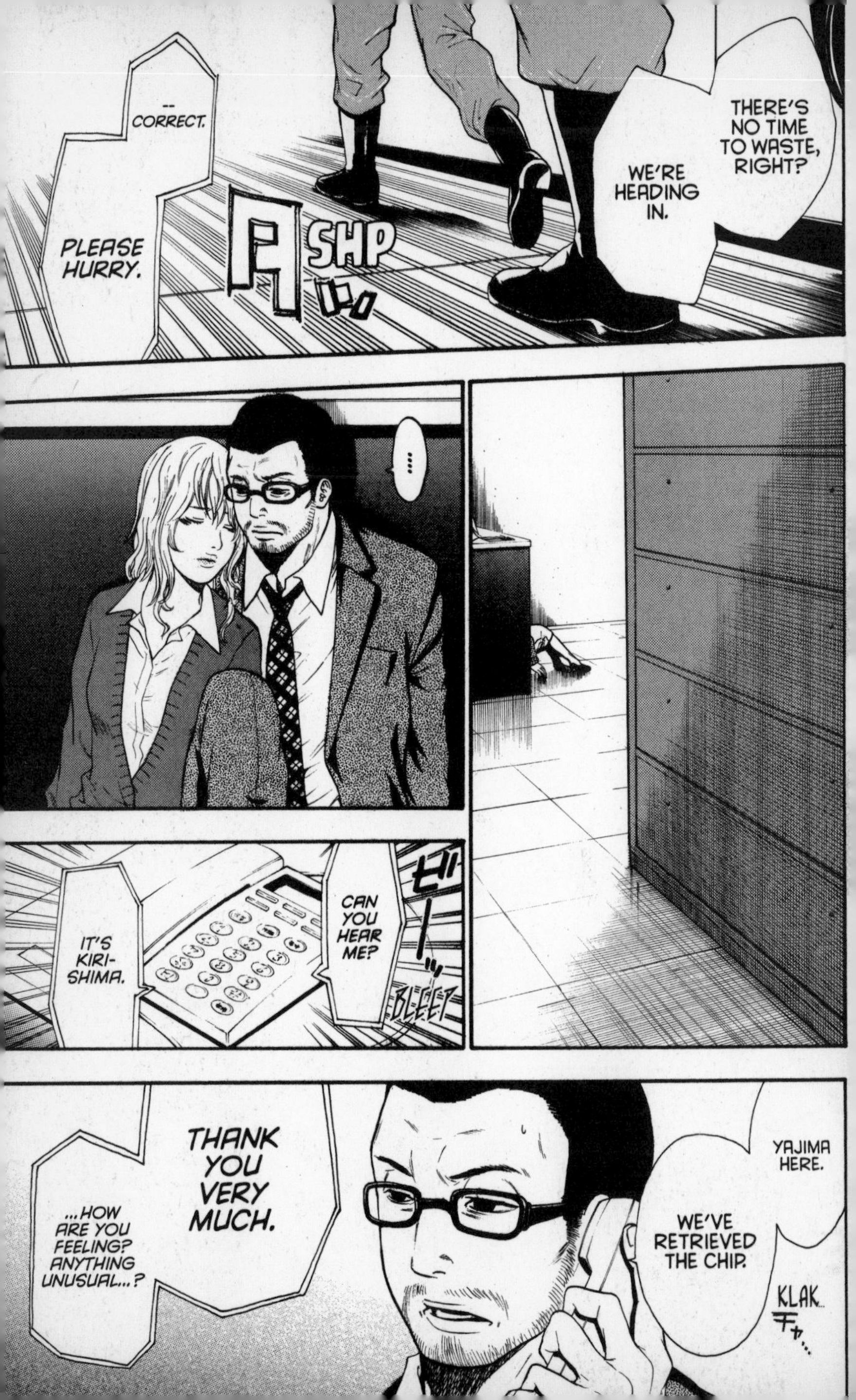
THERE'S NO TIME TO WASTE, RIGHT?
WE'RE HEADING IN.
SHP
-- CORRECT.
PLEASE HURRY.
....
BLEEEP
CAN YOU HEAR ME?
IT'S KIRI-SHIMA.
YAJIMA HERE.
WE'VE RETRIEVED THE CHIP.
KLAK...
チャ...
THANK YOU VERY MUCH.
...HOW ARE YOU FEELING? ANYTHING UNUSUAL...?

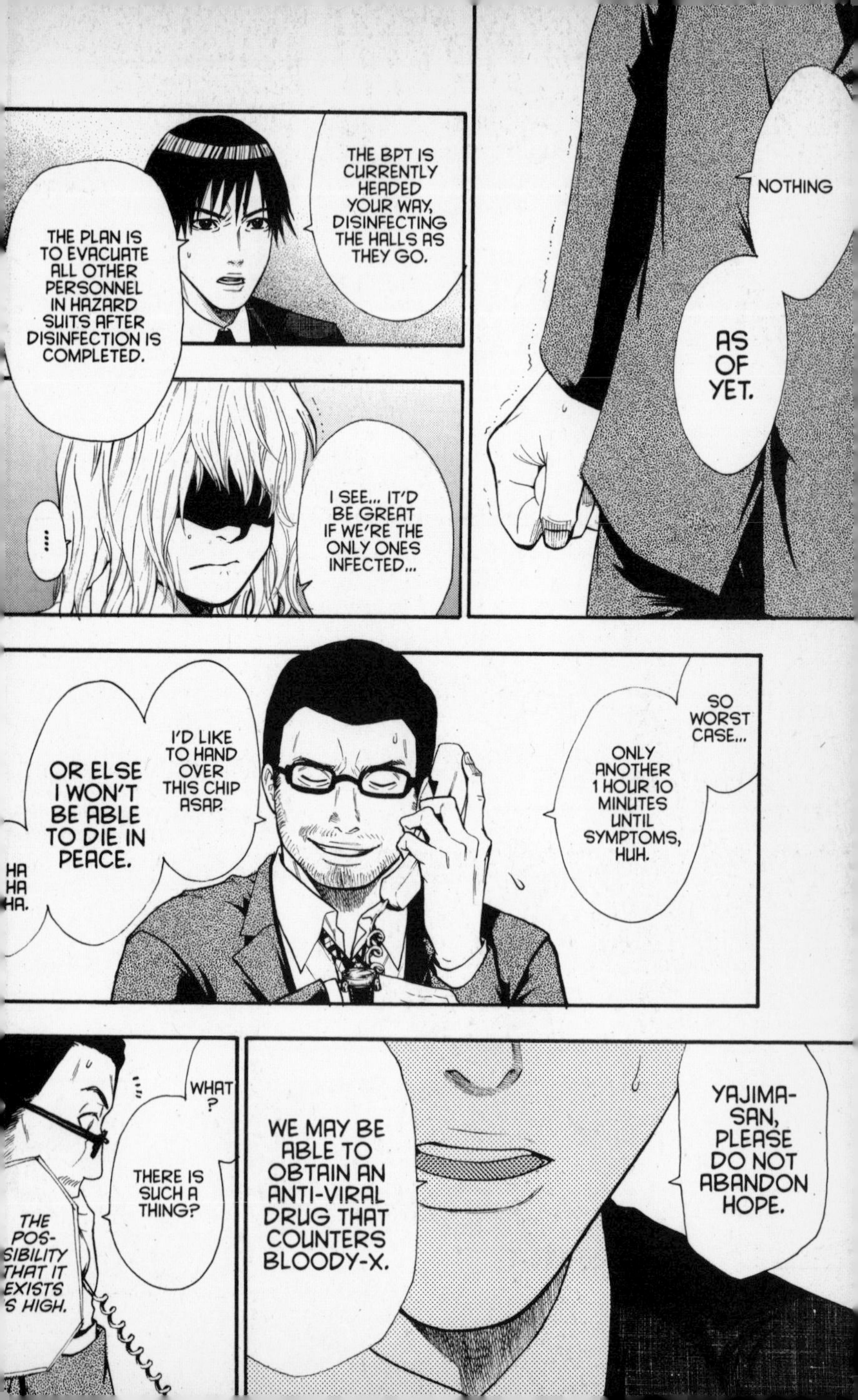
NOTHING
AS OF YET.
THE BPT IS CURRENTLY HEADED YOUR WAY, DISINFECTING THE HALLS AS THEY GO.
THE PLAN IS TO EVACUATE ALL OTHER PERSONNEL IN HAZARD SUITS AFTER DISINFECTION IS COMPLETED.
I SEE... IT'D BE GREAT IF WE'RE THE ONLY ONES INFECTED...
....
SO WORST CASE...
ONLY ANOTHER 1 HOUR 10 MINUTES UNTIL SYMPTOMS, HUH.
I'D LIKE TO HAND OVER THIS CHIP ASAP.
OR ELSE I WON'T BE ABLE TO DIE IN PEACE.
HA HA HA.
YAJIMA-SAN, PLEASE DO NOT ABANDON HOPE.
WE MAY BE ABLE TO OBTAIN AN ANTI-VIRAL DRUG THAT COUNTERS BLOODY-X.
WHAT?
...
THERE IS SUCH A THING?
THE POS-SIBILITY THAT IT EXISTS S HIGH.

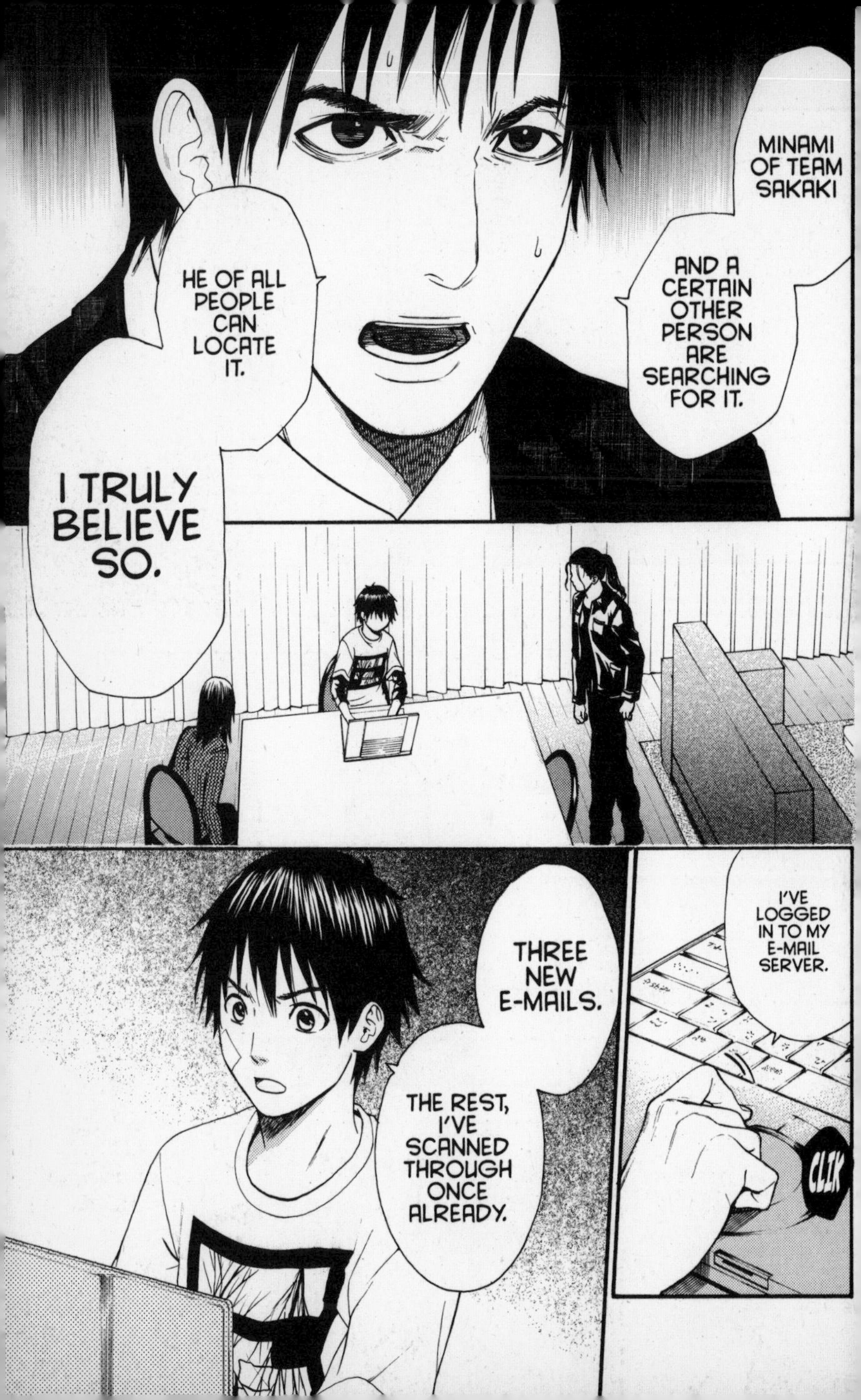
MINAMI OF TEAM SAKAKI
AND A CERTAIN OTHER PERSON ARE SEARCHING FOR IT.
HE OF ALL PEOPLE CAN LOCATE IT.
I TRULY BELIEVE SO.
I'VE LOGGED IN TO MY E-MAIL SERVER.
CLIK
THREE NEW E-MAILS.
THE REST, I'VE SCANNED THROUGH ONCE ALREADY.

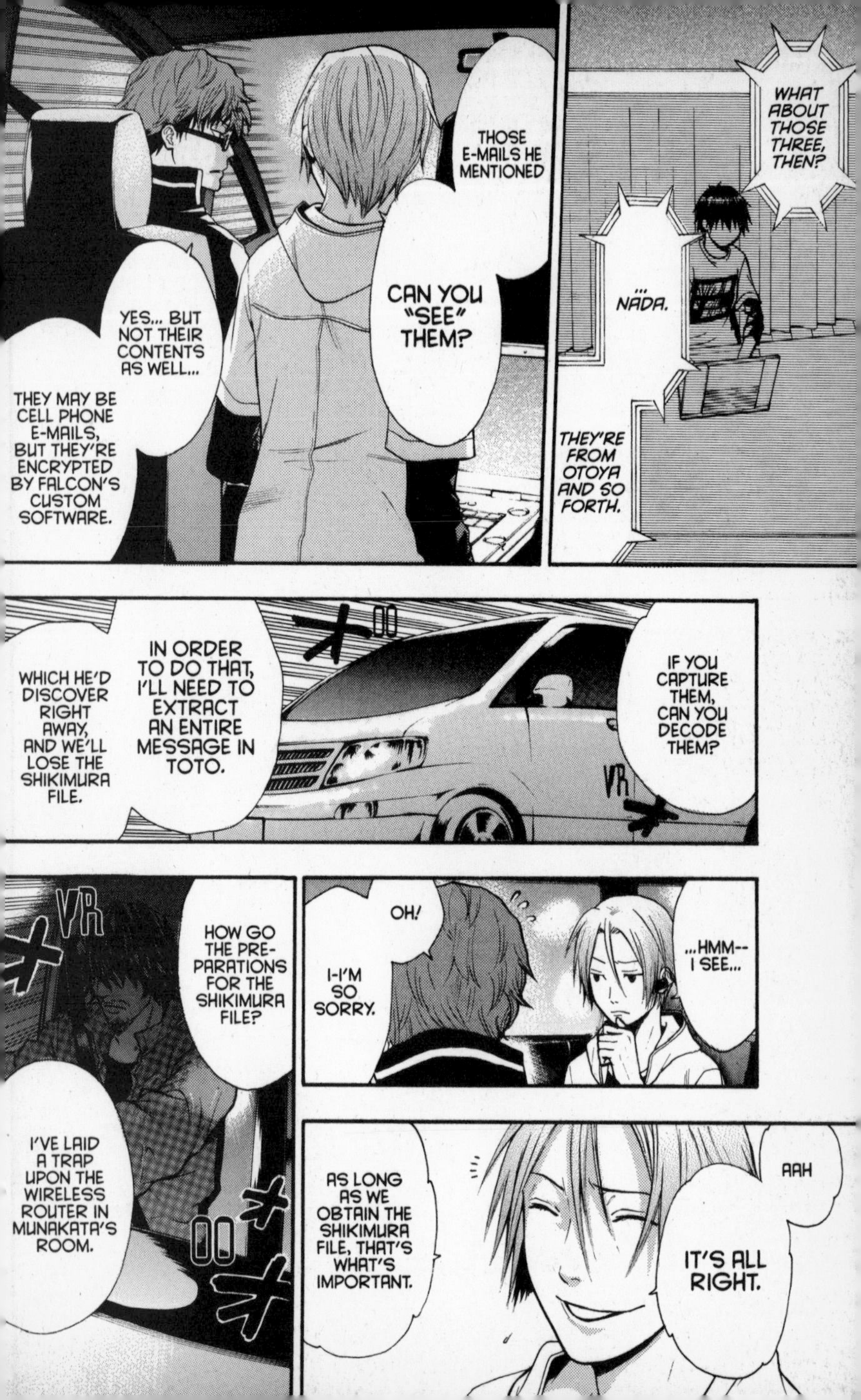
WHAT ABOUT THOSE THREE, THEN?
...NADA.
THEY'RE FROM OTOYA AND SO FORTH.
THOSE E-MAILS HE MENTIONED
CAN YOU "SEE" THEM?
YES... BUT NOT THEIR CONTENTS AS WELL...
THEY MAY BE CELL PHONE E-MAILS, BUT THEY'RE ENCRYPTED BY FALCON'S CUSTOM SOFTWARE.
IF YOU CAPTURE THEM, CAN YOU DECODE THEM?
IN ORDER TO DO THAT, I'LL NEED TO EXTRACT AN ENTIRE MESSAGE IN TOTO.
WHICH HE'D DISCOVER RIGHT AWAY, AND WE'LL LOSE THE SHIKIMURA FILE.
VR
...HMM-- I SEE...
OH!
I-I'M SO SORRY.
AAH
IT'S ALL RIGHT.
AS LONG AS WE OBTAIN THE SHIKIMURA FILE, THAT'S WHAT'S IMPORTANT.
VR
HOW GO THE PRE-PARATIONS FOR THE SHIKIMURA FILE?
I'VE LAID A TRAP UPON THE WIRELESS ROUTER IN MUNAKATA'S ROOM.

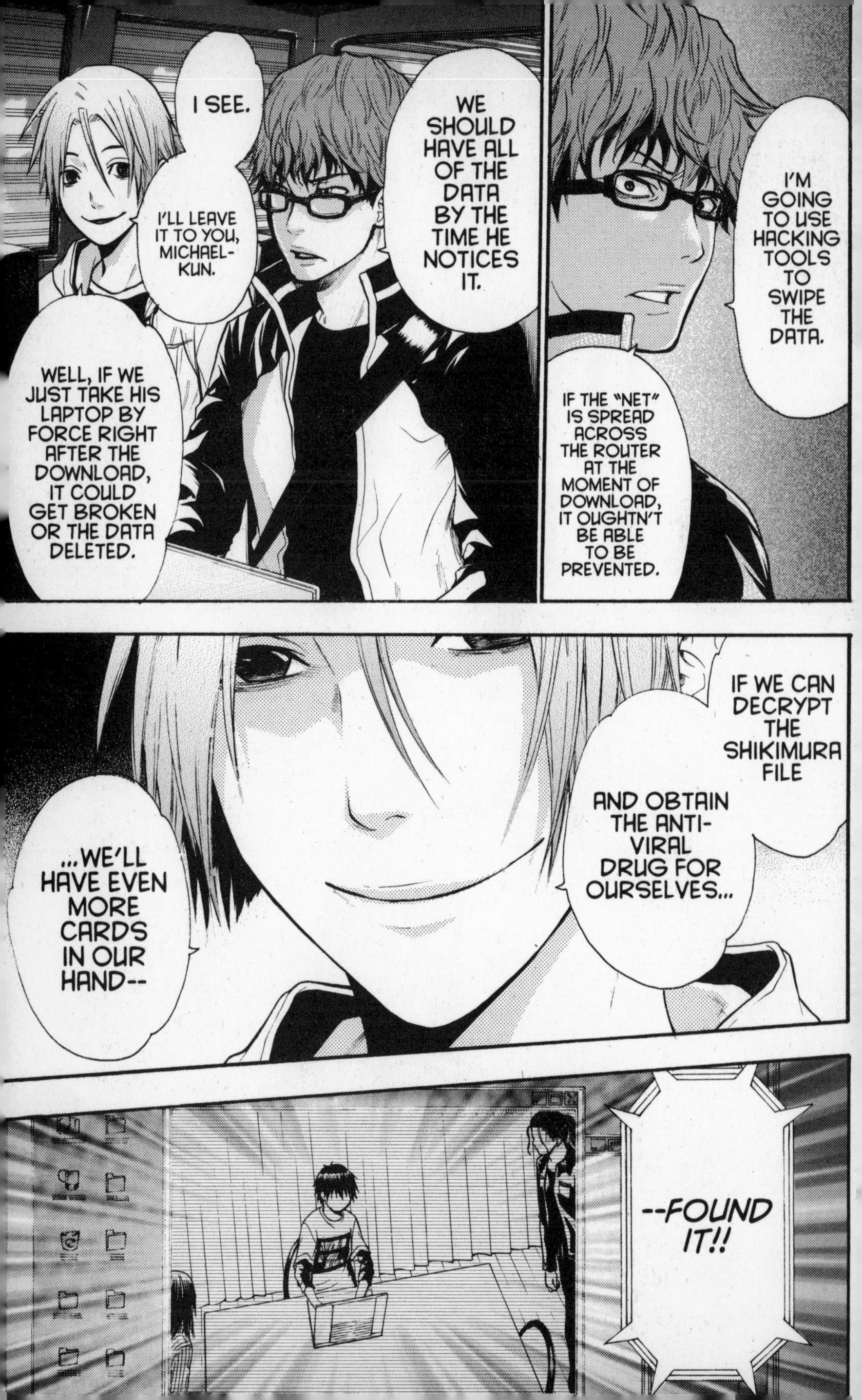
I'M GOING TO USE HACKING TOOLS TO SWIPE THE DATA.
IF THE "NET" IS SPREAD ACROSS THE ROUTER AT THE MOMENT OF DOWNLOAD, IT OUGHTN'T BE ABLE TO BE PREVENTED.
WE SHOULD HAVE ALL OF THE DATA BY THE TIME HE NOTICES IT.
I SEE.
I'LL LEAVE IT TO YOU, MICHAEL-KUN.
WELL, IF WE JUST TAKE HIS LAPTOP BY FORCE RIGHT AFTER THE DOWNLOAD, IT COULD GET BROKEN OR THE DATA DELETED.
IF WE CAN DECRYPT THE SHIKIMURA FILE
AND OBTAIN THE ANTI-VIRAL DRUG FOR OURSELVES...
...WE'LL HAVE EVEN MORE CARDS IN OUR HAND--
--FOUND IT!!

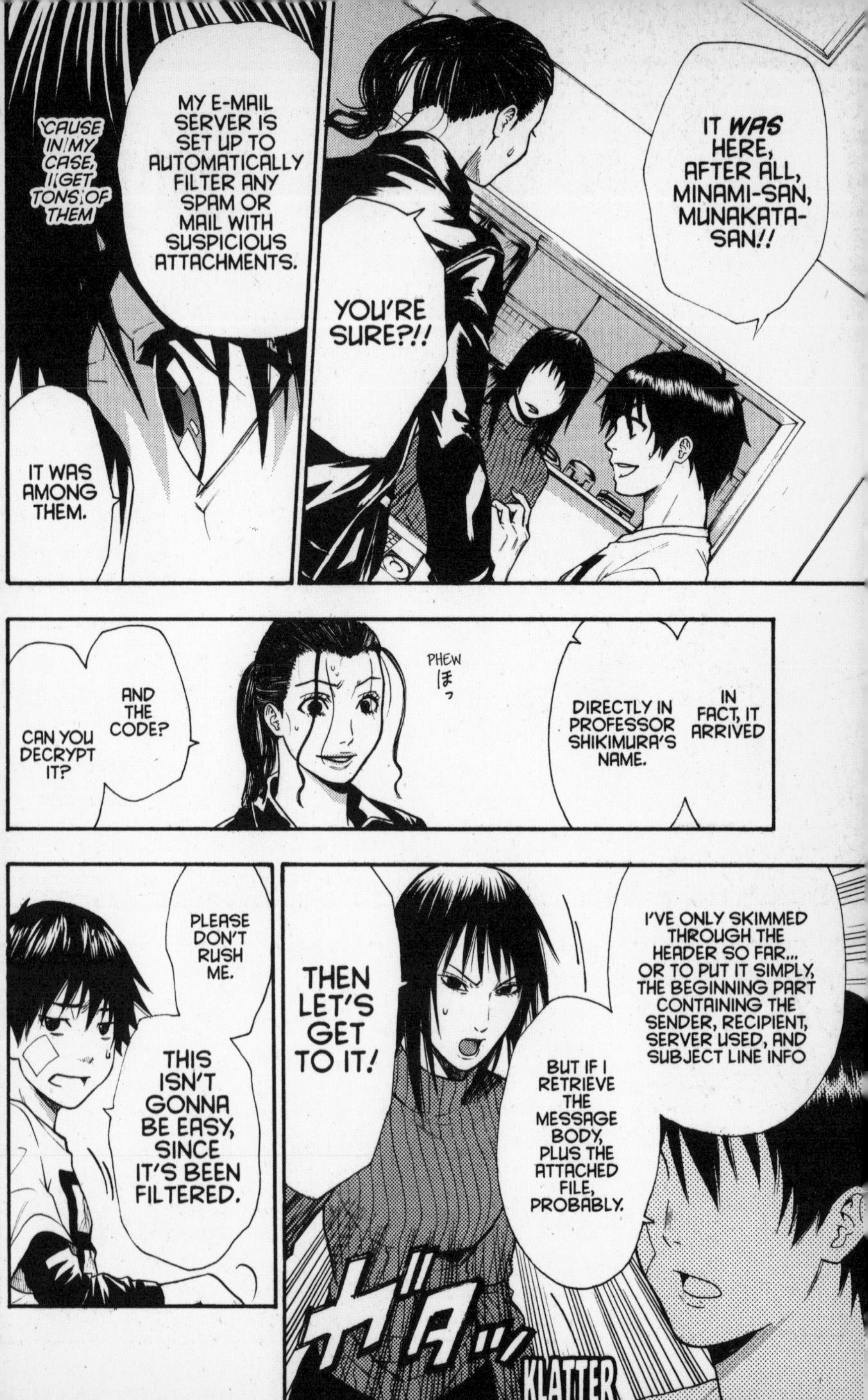

IT *WAS* HERE, AFTER ALL, MINAMI-SAN, MUNAKATA-SAN!!
YOU'RE SURE?!!
MY E-MAIL SERVER IS SET UP TO AUTOMATICALLY FILTER ANY SPAM OR MAIL WITH SUSPICIOUS ATTACHMENTS.
'CAUSE IN MY CASE, I GET TONS OF THEM
IT WAS AMONG THEM.
IN FACT, IT ARRIVED
DIRECTLY IN PROFESSOR SHIKIMURA'S NAME.
PHEW
ほっ
AND THE CODE?
CAN YOU DECRYPT IT?
I'VE ONLY SKIMMED THROUGH THE HEADER SO FAR... OR TO PUT IT SIMPLY, THE BEGINNING PART CONTAINING THE SENDER, RECIPIENT, SERVER USED, AND SUBJECT LINE INFO
BUT IF I RETRIEVE THE MESSAGE BODY, PLUS THE ATTACHED FILE, PROBABLY.
THEN LET'S GET TO IT!
ガタッ
KLATTER
PLEASE DON'T RUSH ME.
THIS ISN'T GONNA BE EASY, SINCE IT'S BEEN FILTERED.

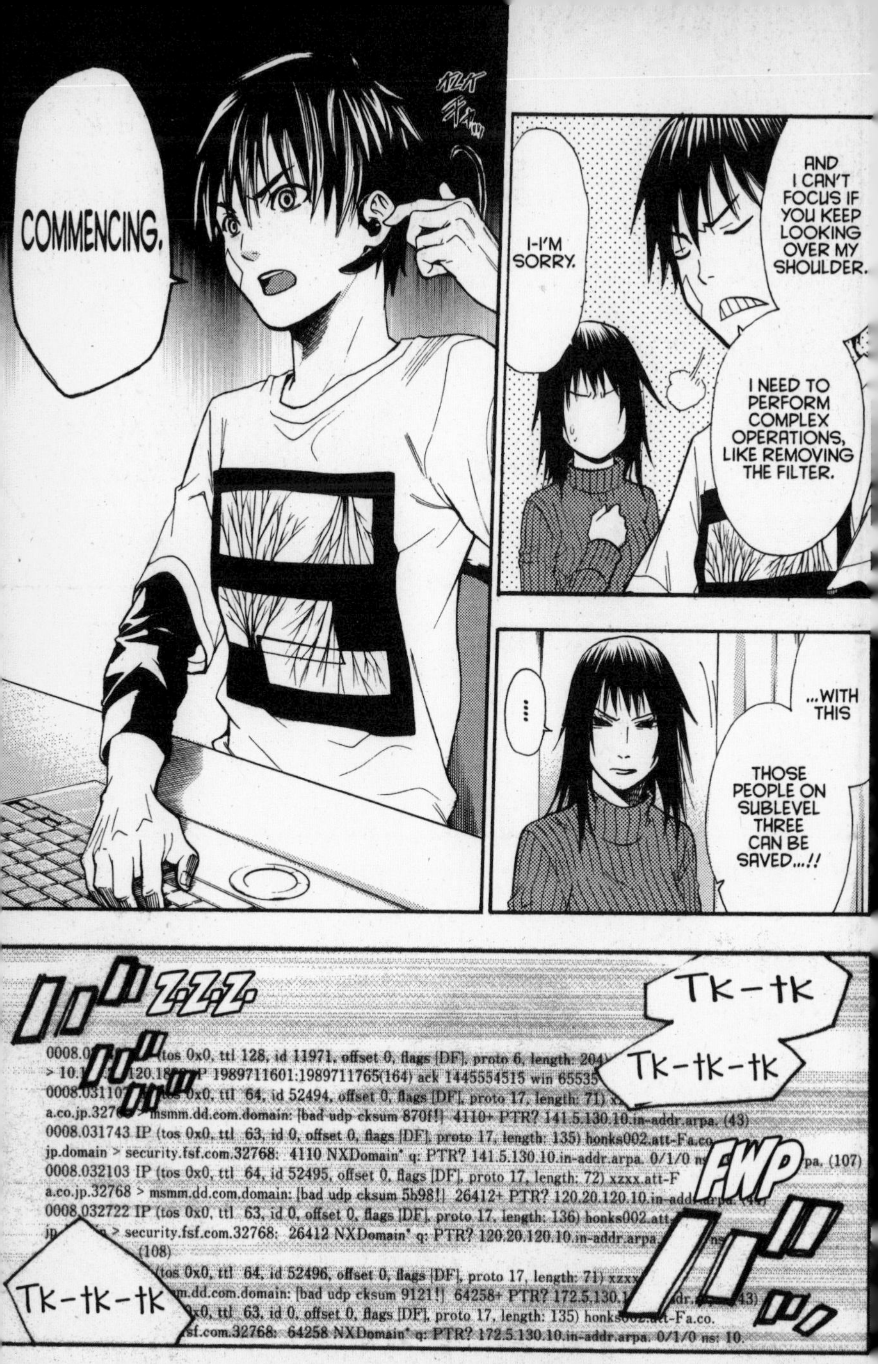
AND I CAN'T FOCUS IF YOU KEEP LOOKING OVER MY SHOULDER.
I NEED TO PERFORM COMPLEX OPERATIONS, LIKE REMOVING THE FILTER.
I-I'M SORRY.
...WITH THIS
THOSE PEOPLE ON SUBLEVEL THREE CAN BE SAVED...!!
....
COMMENCING.
Tk-tk
Tk-tk-tk
FWP
Tk-tk-tk
0008.031743 IP (tos 0x0, ttl 63, id 0, offset 0, flags [DF], proto 17, length: 135) honks002.att-Fa.co.
jp.domain > security.fsf.com.32768: 4110 NXDomain* q: PTR? 141.5.130.10.in-addr.arpa. 0/1/0
0008.032103 IP (tos 0x0, ttl 64, id 52495, offset 0, flags [DF], proto 17, length: 72) xzxx.att-F
a.co.jp.32768 > msmm.dd.com.domain: [bad udp cksum 5b98!] 26412+ PTR? 120.20.120.10.in-addr.arpa.
0008.032722 IP (tos 0x0, ttl 63, id 0, offset 0, flags [DF], proto 17, length: 136) honks002.att-
> security.fsf.com.32768: 26412 NXDomain* q: PTR? 120.20.120.10.in-addr.arpa.

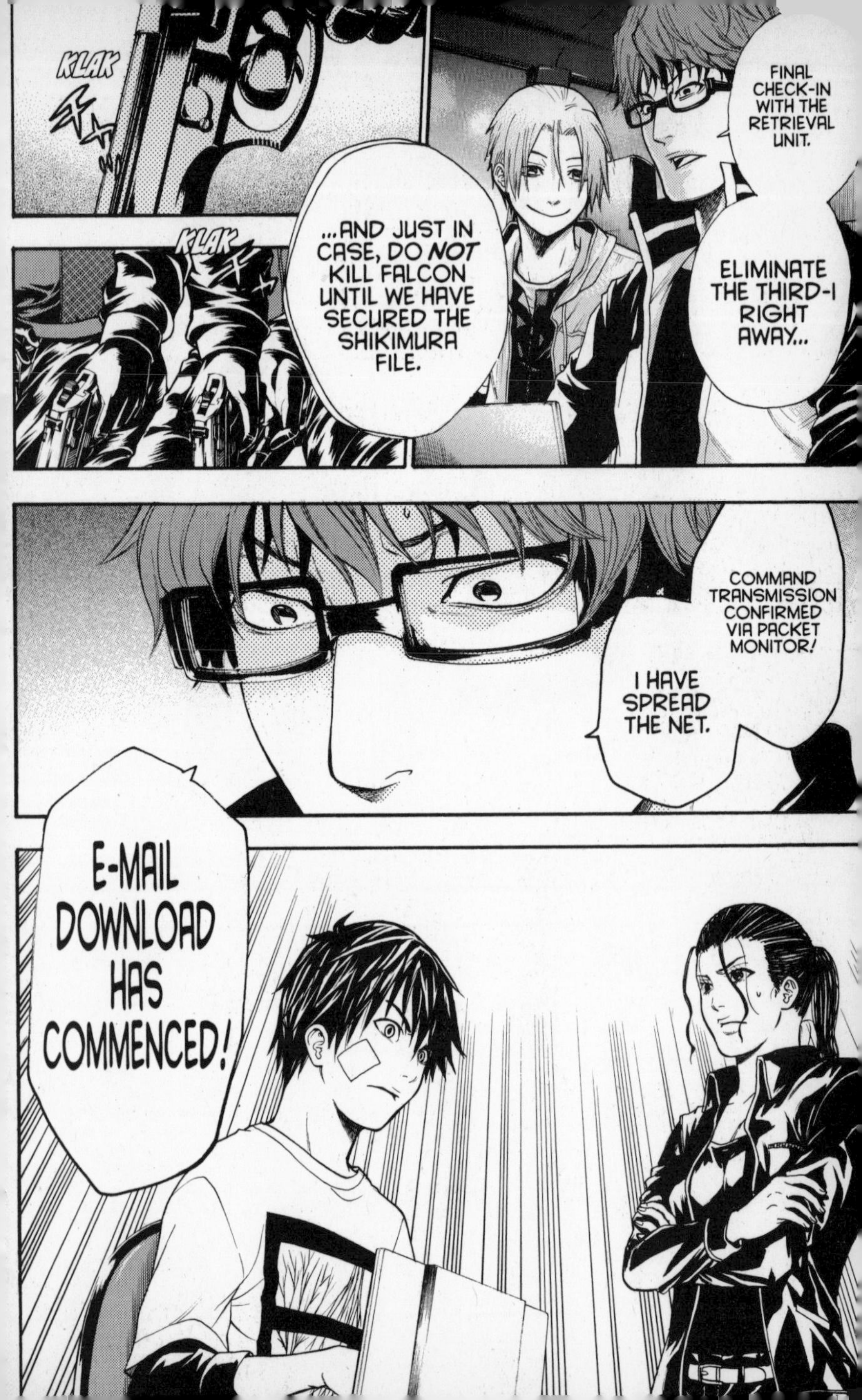
FINAL CHECK-IN WITH THE RETRIEVAL UNIT.
ELIMINATE THE THIRD-I RIGHT AWAY...
...AND JUST IN CASE, DO *NOT* KILL FALCON UNTIL WE HAVE SECURED THE SHIKIMURA FILE.
KLAK
KLAK
COMMAND TRANSMISSION CONFIRMED VIA PACKET MONITOR!
I HAVE SPREAD THE NET.
E-MAIL DOWNLOAD HAS COMMENCED!

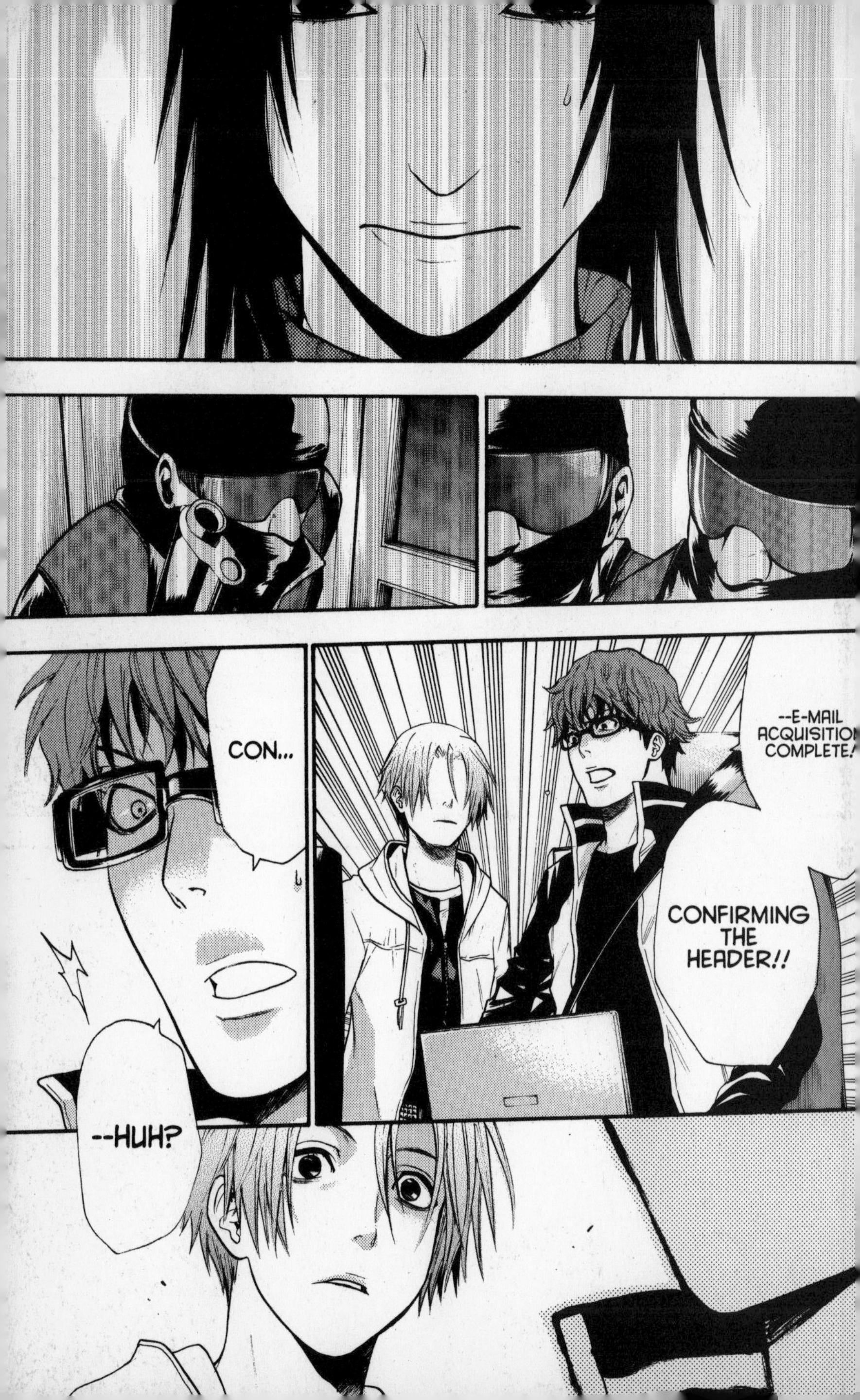
--E-MAIL ACQUISITIO COMPLETE!
CONFIRMING THE HEADER!!
CON...
--HUH?

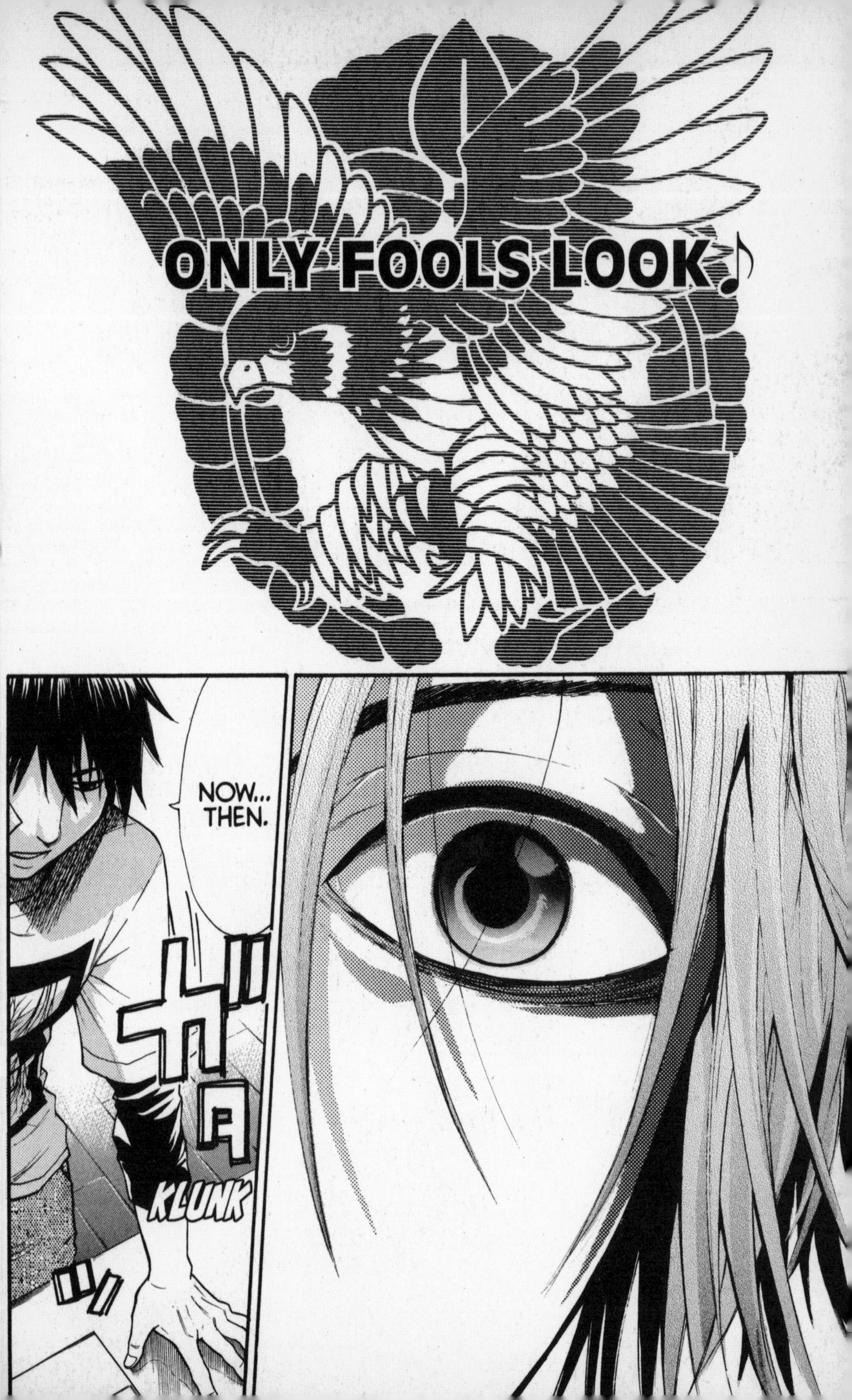
ONLY FOOLS LOOK♪
NOW... THEN.
KLUNK

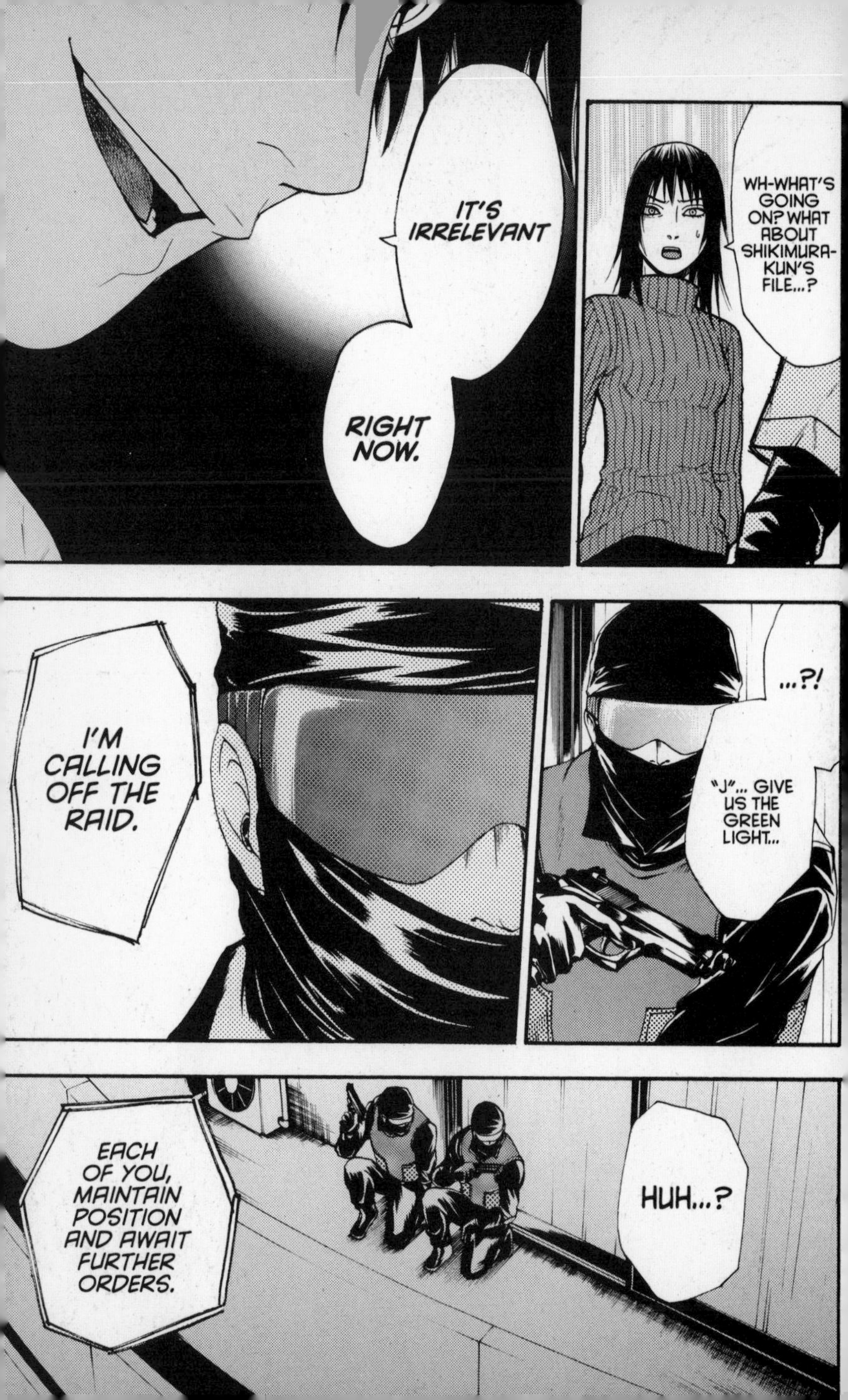
WH-WHAT'S GOING ON? WHAT ABOUT SHIKIMURA-KUN'S FILE...?
IT'S IRRELEVANT
RIGHT NOW.
...?!
"J"... GIVE US THE GREEN LIGHT...
I'M CALLING OFF THE RAID.
HUH...?
EACH OF YOU, MAINTAIN POSITION AND AWAIT FURTHER ORDERS.

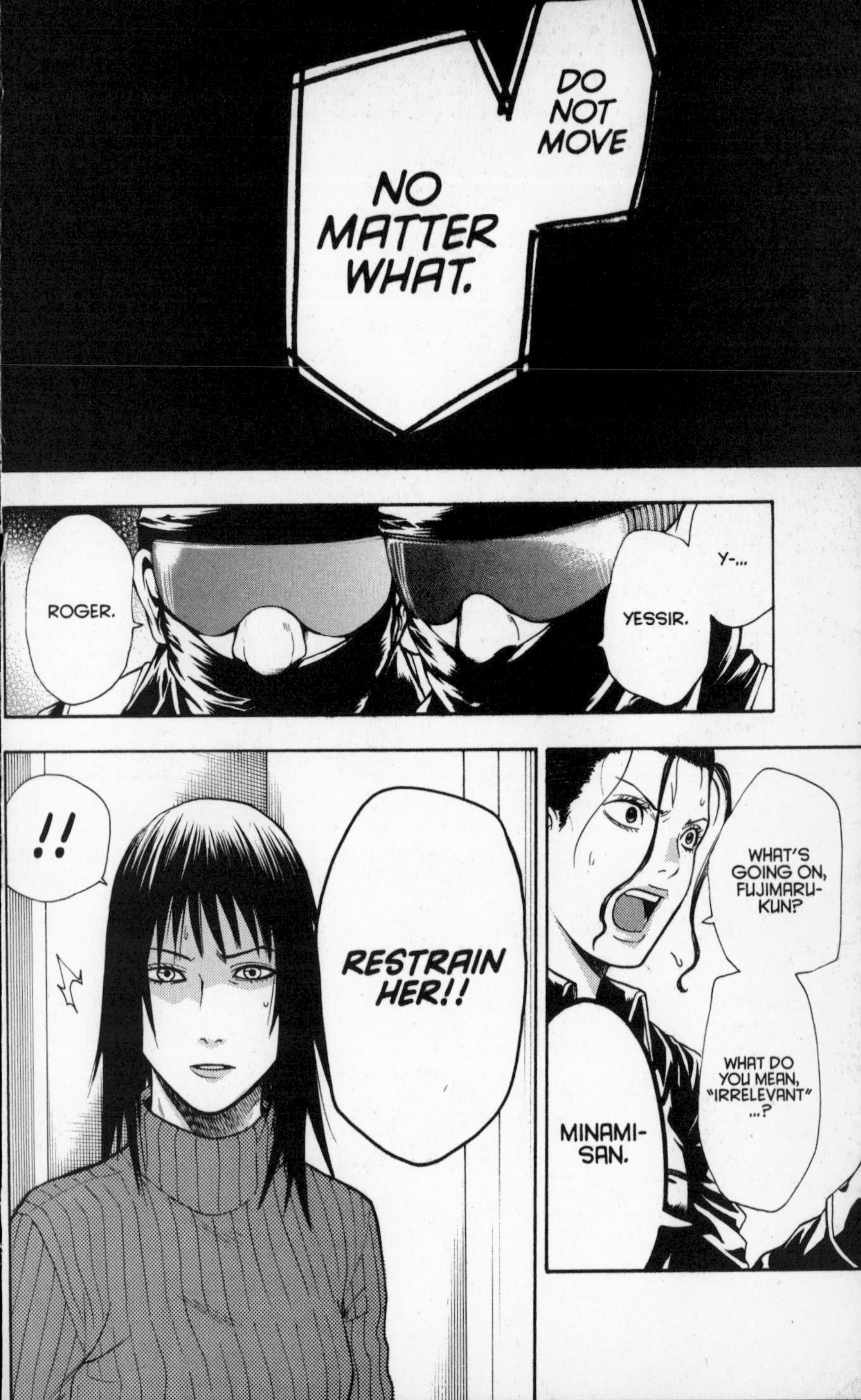
DO NOT MOVE
NO MATTER WHAT.
Y-...
YESSIR.
ROGER.
WHAT'S GOING ON, FUJIMARU-KUN?
WHAT DO YOU MEAN, "IRRELEVANT" ...?
MINAMI-SAN.
RESTRAIN HER!!
!!

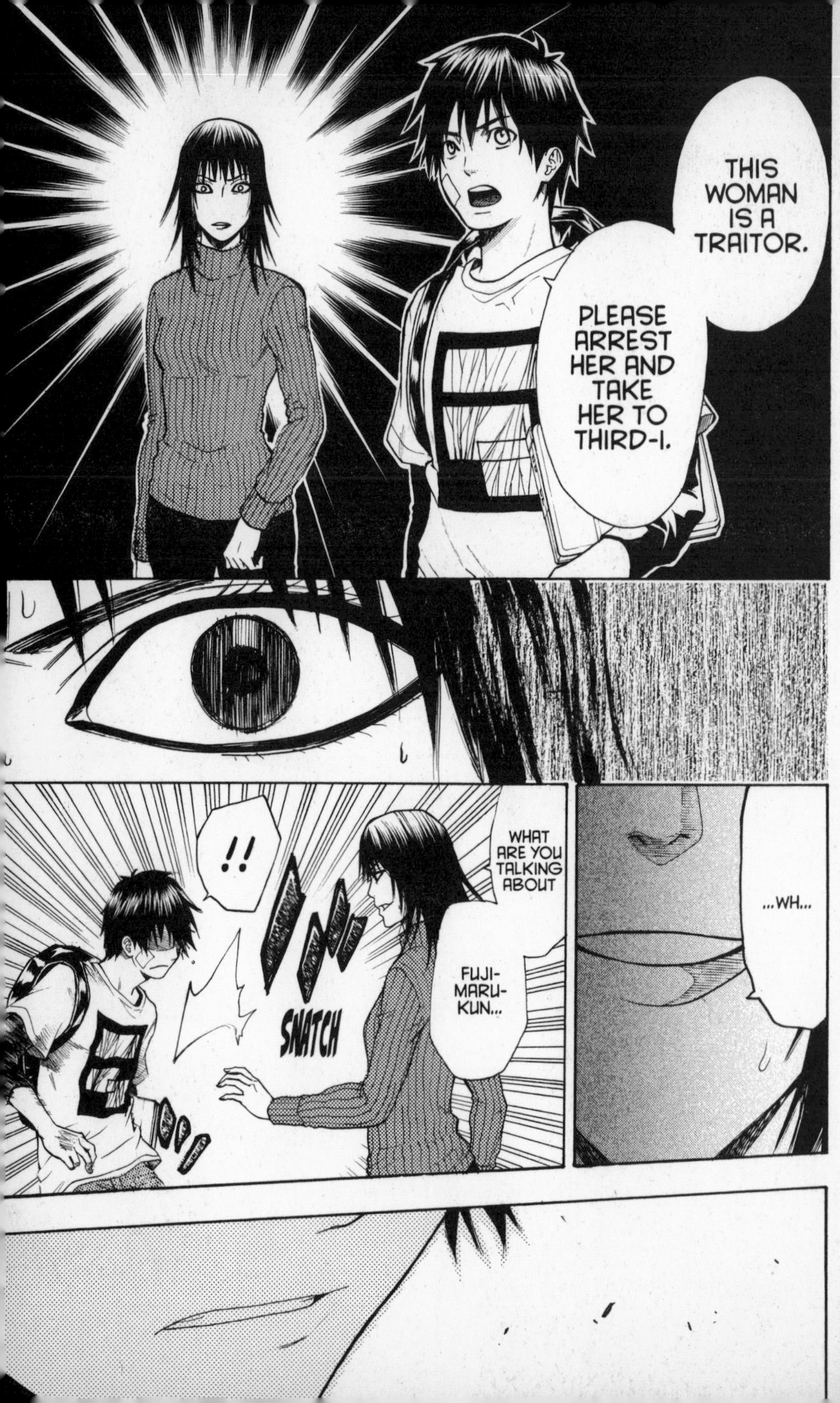
THIS WOMAN IS A TRAITOR.
PLEASE ARREST HER AND TAKE HER TO THIRD-I.
...WH...
WHAT ARE YOU TALKING ABOUT
FUJI-MARU-KUN...
!!
SNATCH

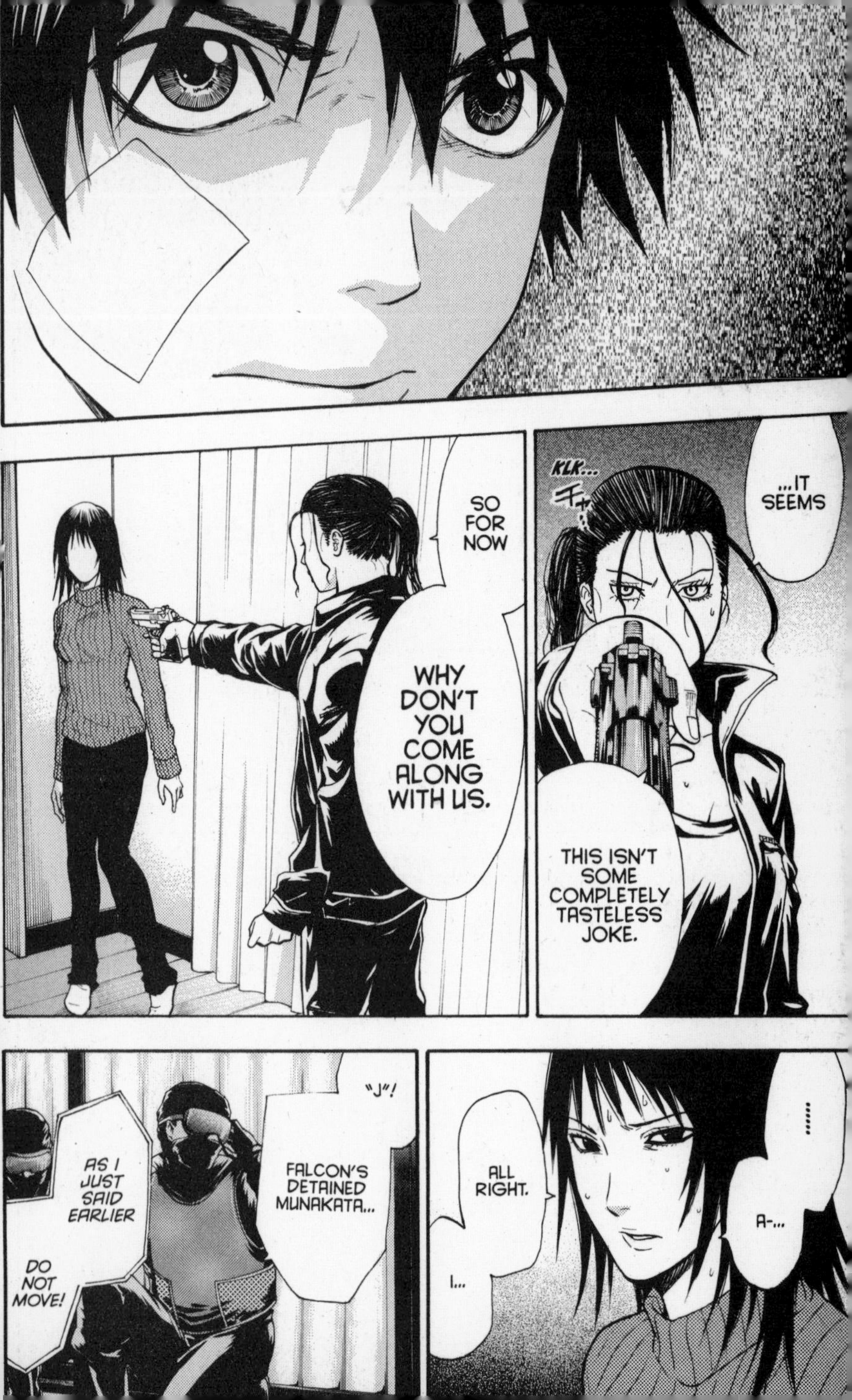
...IT SEEMS
KLK...
チャ
THIS ISN'T SOME COMPLETELY TASTELESS JOKE.
SO FOR NOW
WHY DON'T YOU COME ALONG WITH US.
......
ALL RIGHT.
A-...
I...
"J"!
FALCON'S DETAINED MUNAKATA...
AS I JUST SAID EARLIER
DO NOT MOVE!

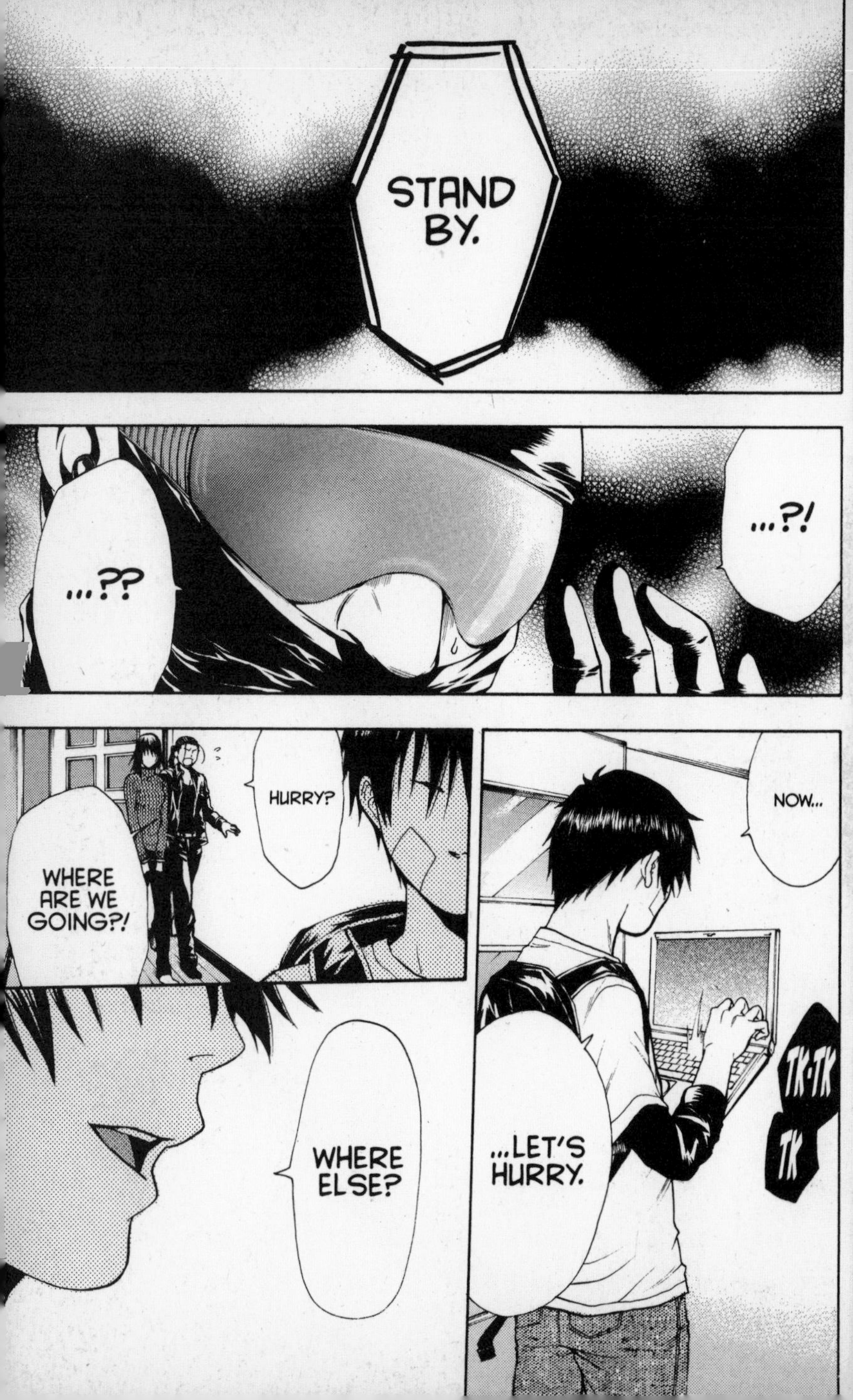
STAND BY.
...?!
...??
NOW...
...LET'S HURRY.
TK-TK
TK
HURRY?
WHERE ARE WE GOING?!
WHERE ELSE?

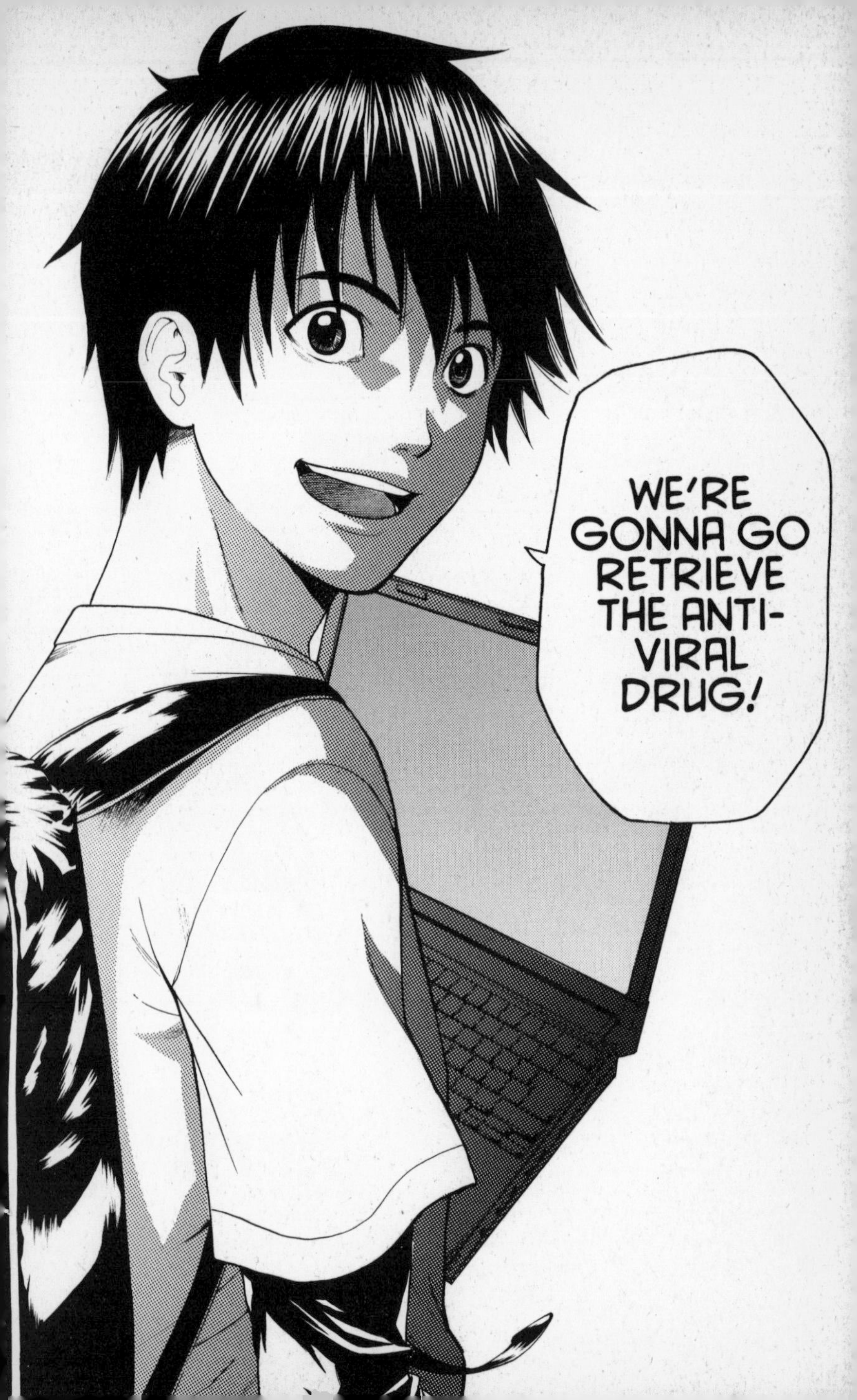
WE'RE GONNA GO RETRIEVE THE ANTI-VIRAL DRUG!

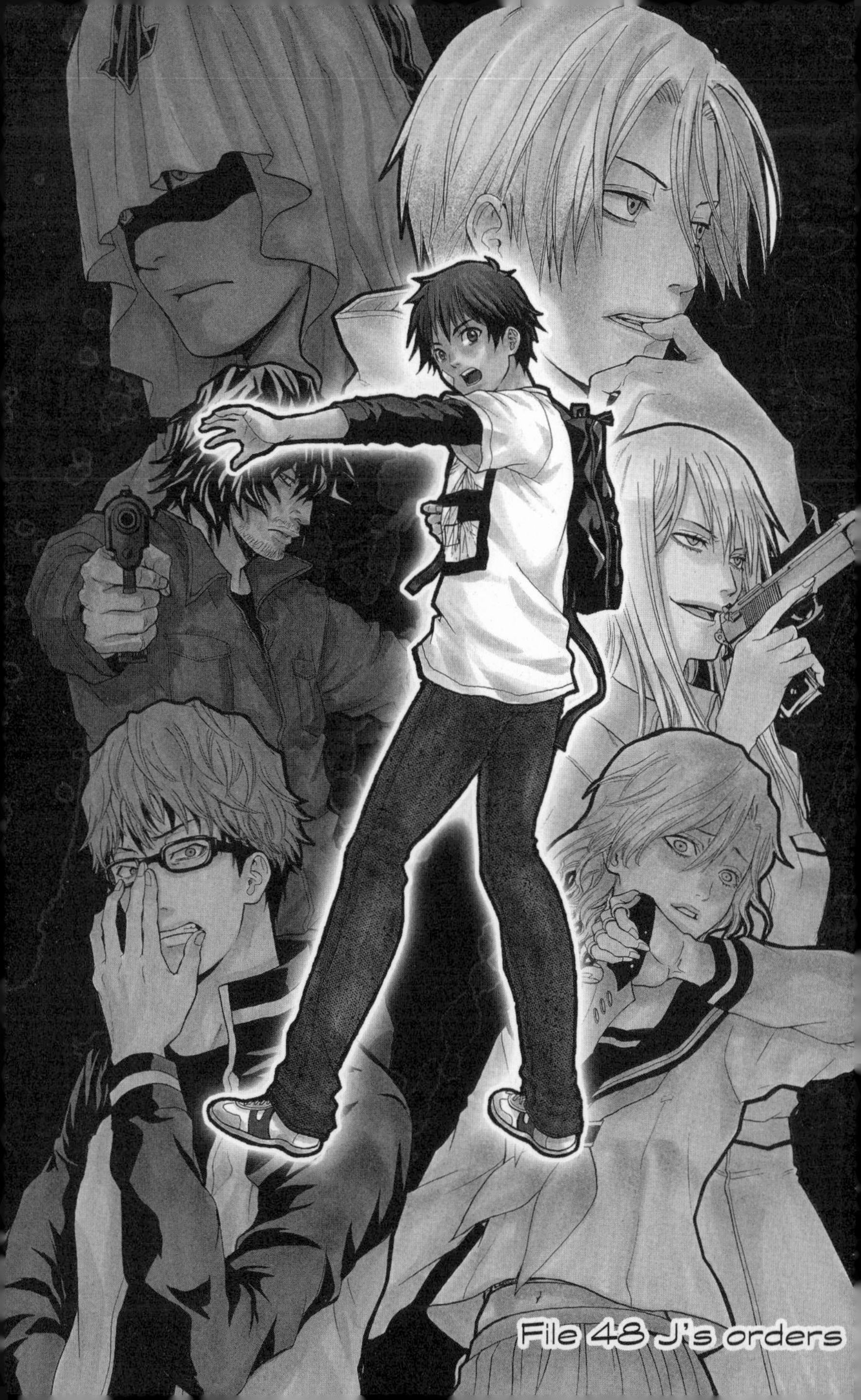
File 48 J's orders

BLOODY MONDAY

- GLOSSARY OF TERMS · LIST 13 -

GUI (Graphical user interface) p176
A type of user interface (the interaction between a human user and computer hardware or software) where icons and other visual images are utilized to present information to the user and basic operations can be performed using a mouse.

Fortran p176
A programming language used for scientific computing (numeric computation). Its special feature is that numerical formulas can be inputted almost exactly as they appear on paper.

COBOL p176
A programming language used for business applications. Its code is similar to normal English text, and it is widely used for accounting and other file-oriented applications.

Security hole p178
A weakness in the security system of a network or a computer that arises from a software configuration or programming error.

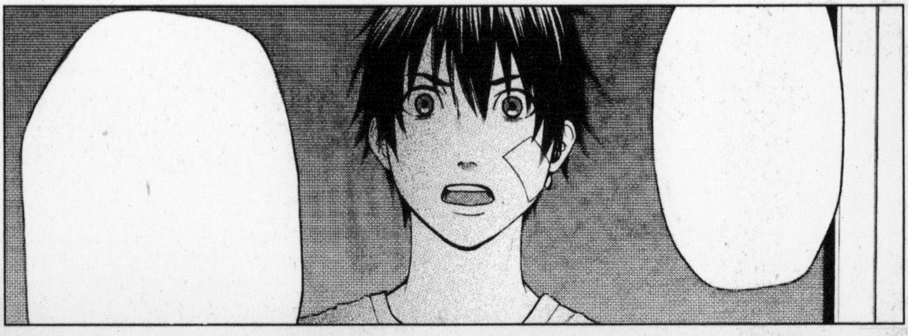

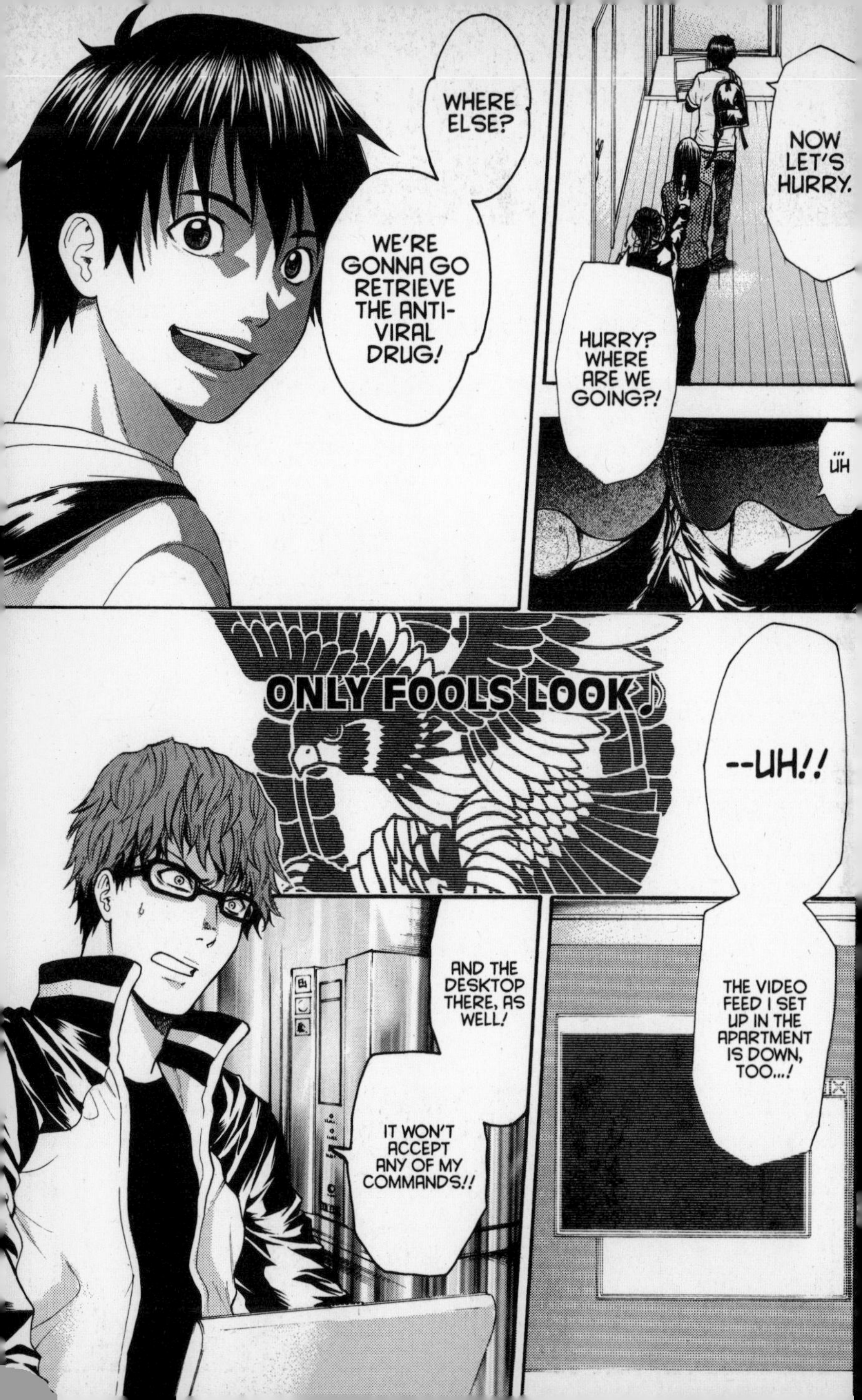
NOW LET'S HURRY.
HURRY? WHERE ARE WE GOING?!
...UH
WHERE ELSE?
WE'RE GONNA GO RETRIEVE THE ANTI-VIRAL DRUG!
ONLY FOOLS LOOK♪
--UH!!
THE VIDEO FEED I SET UP IN THE APARTMENT IS DOWN, TOO...!
AND THE DESKTOP THERE, AS WELL!
IT WON'T ACCEPT ANY OF MY COMMANDS!!

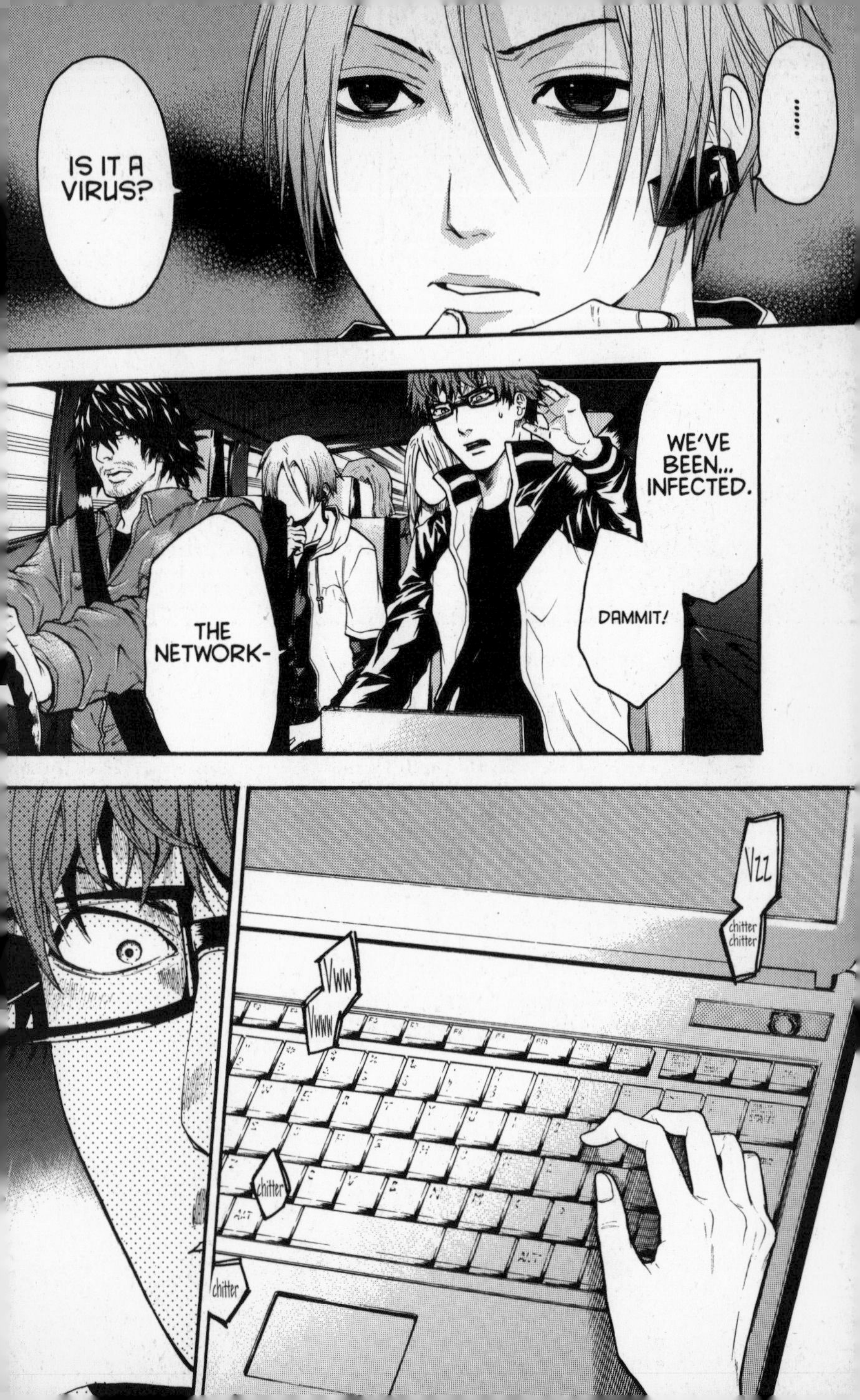
......
IS IT A VIRUS?
WE'VE BEEN... INFECTED.
DAMMIT!
THE NETWORK-
Vzz
chitter chitter
Vwww
Vwww
chitter
chitter

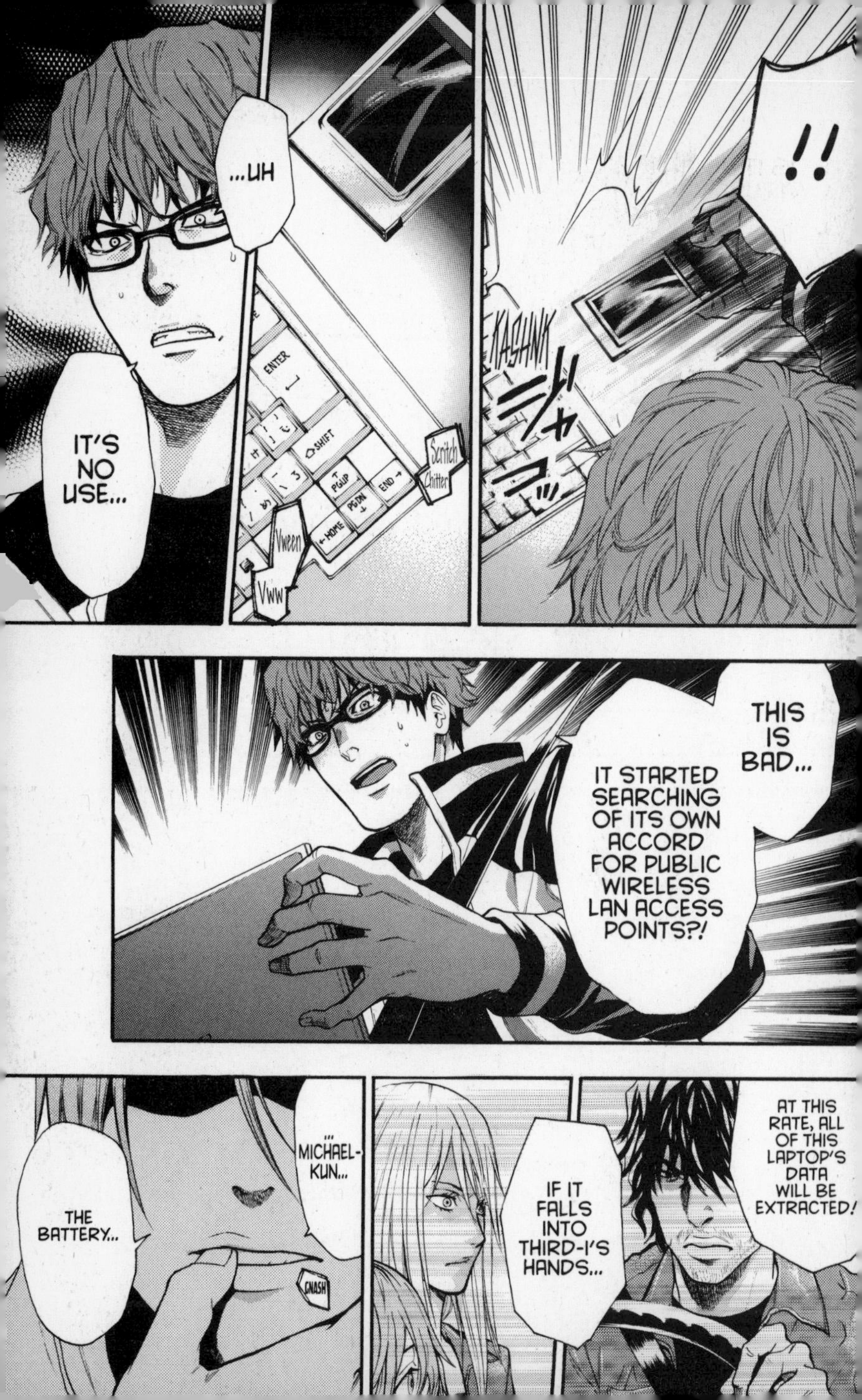
!!
KASHNK
...UH
Scritch
Chitter
Vween
Vww
IT'S NO USE...
THIS IS BAD...
IT STARTED SEARCHING OF ITS OWN ACCORD FOR PUBLIC WIRELESS LAN ACCESS POINTS?!
AT THIS RATE, ALL OF THIS LAPTOP'S DATA WILL BE EXTRACTED!
IF IT FALLS INTO THIRD-I'S HANDS...
... MICHAEL-KUN...
GNASH
THE BATTERY...

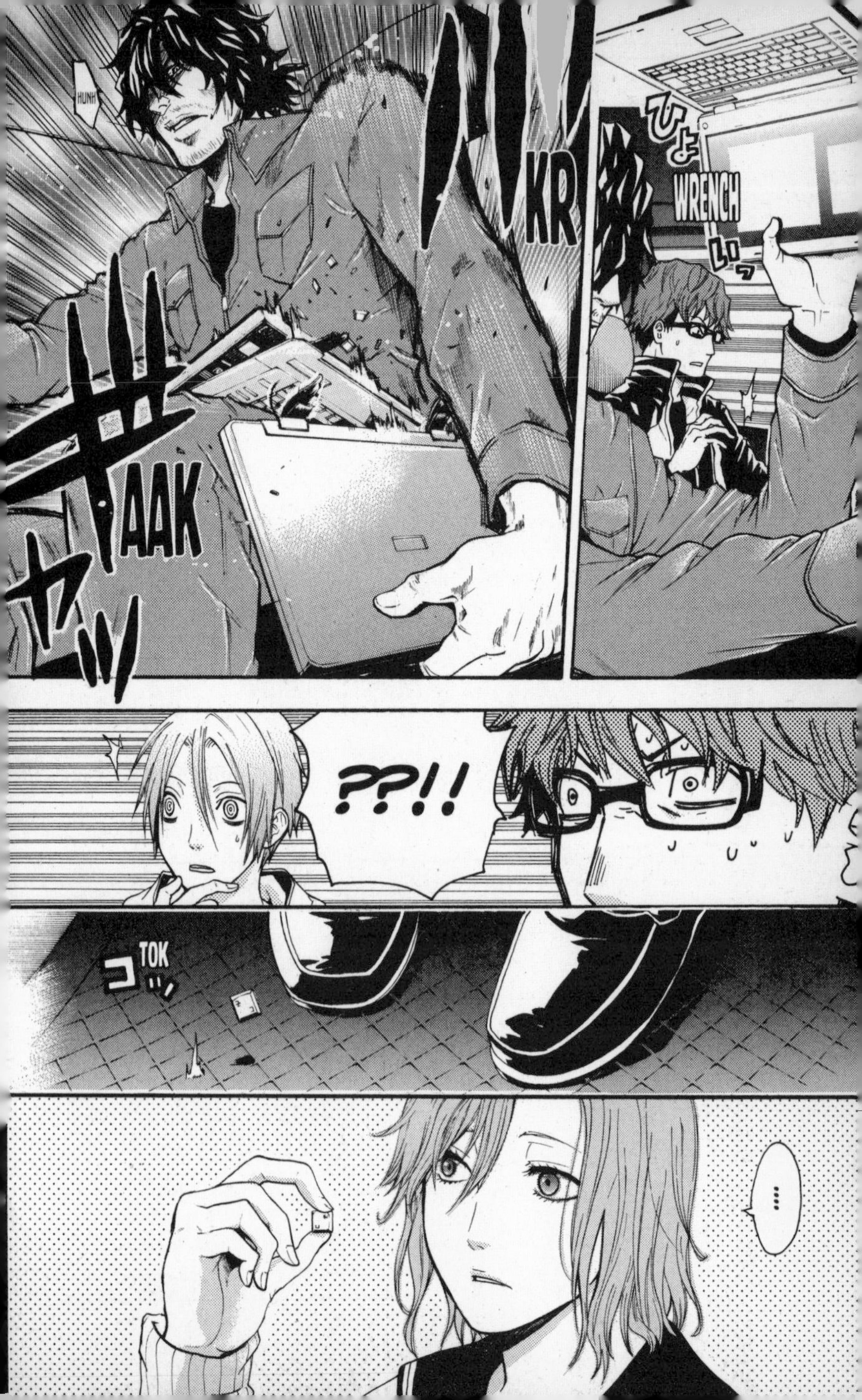

WRENCH
HUNH
KR
AAK
??!!
TOK
...

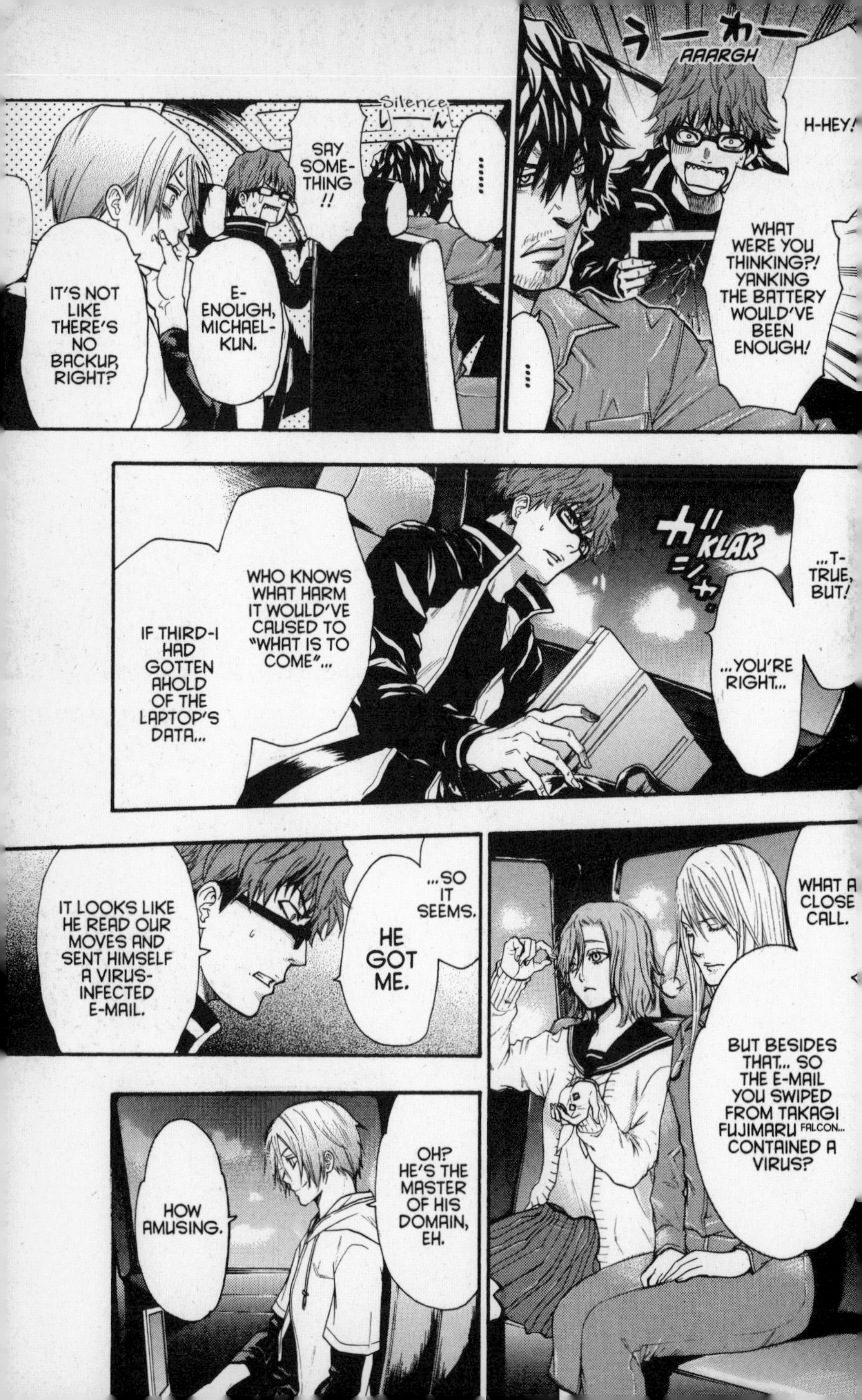
AAARGH
H-HEY!
WHAT WERE YOU THINKING?! YANKING THE BATTERY WOULD'VE BEEN ENOUGH!
....
Silence
......
SAY SOME-THING !!
E-ENOUGH, MICHAEL-KUN.
IT'S NOT LIKE THERE'S NO BACKUP, RIGHT?
...T-TRUE, BUT!
KLAK
...YOU'RE RIGHT...
WHO KNOWS WHAT HARM IT WOULD'VE CAUSED TO "WHAT IS TO COME"...
IF THIRD-I HAD GOTTEN AHOLD OF THE LAPTOP'S DATA...
WHAT A CLOSE CALL.
BUT BESIDES THAT... SO THE E-MAIL YOU SWIPED FROM TAKAGI FUJIMARU FALCON... CONTAINED A VIRUS?
...SO IT SEEMS.
HE GOT ME.
IT LOOKS LIKE HE READ OUR MOVES AND SENT HIMSELF A VIRUS-INFECTED E-MAIL.
OH? HE'S THE MASTER OF HIS DOMAIN, EH.
HOW AMUSING.

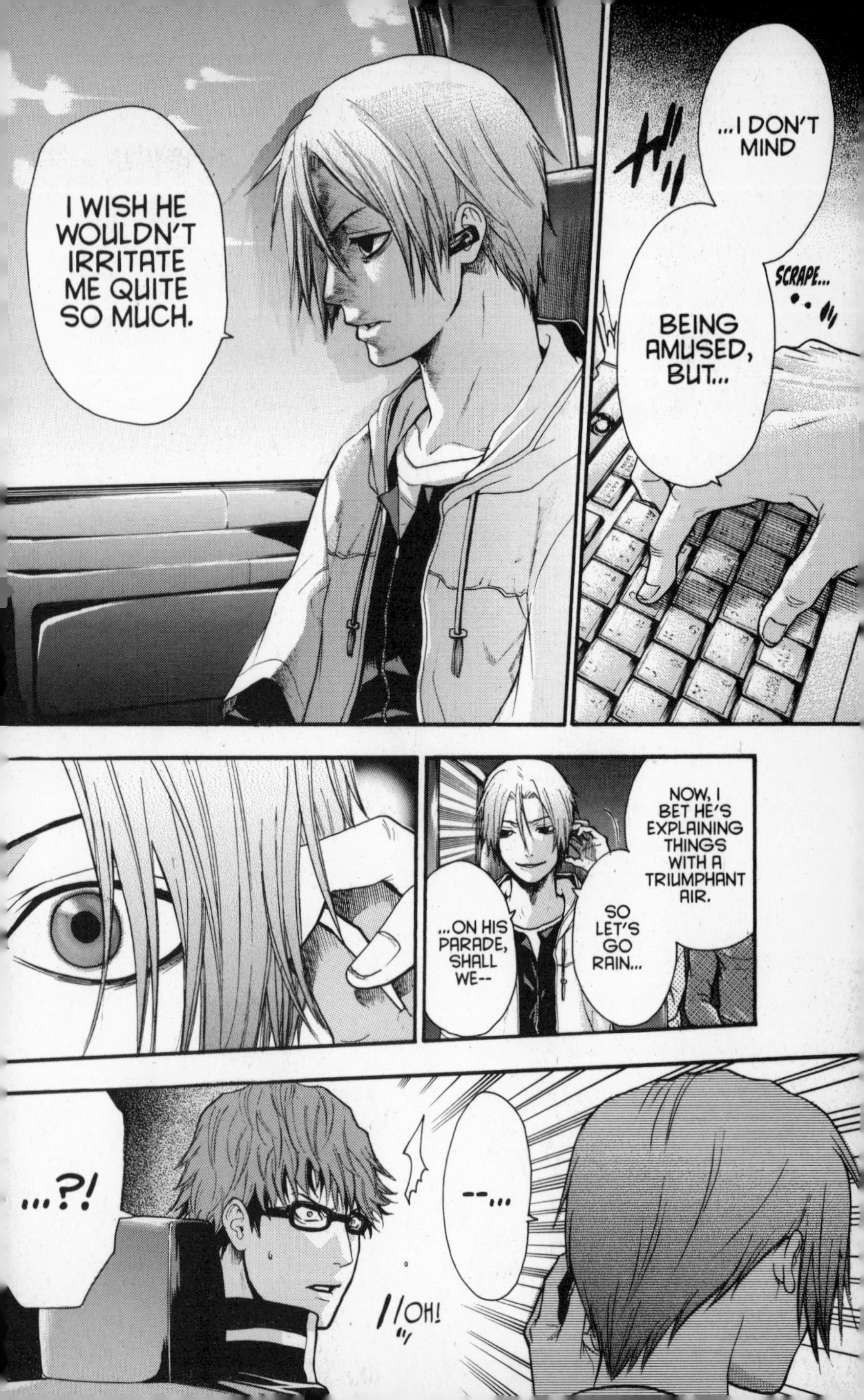
...I DON'T MIND
BEING AMUSED, BUT...
SCRAPE...
I WISH HE WOULDN'T IRRITATE ME QUITE SO MUCH.
NOW, I BET HE'S EXPLAINING THINGS WITH A TRIUMPHANT AIR.
SO LET'S GO RAIN...
...ON HIS PARADE, SHALL WE--
--...
OH!
...?!

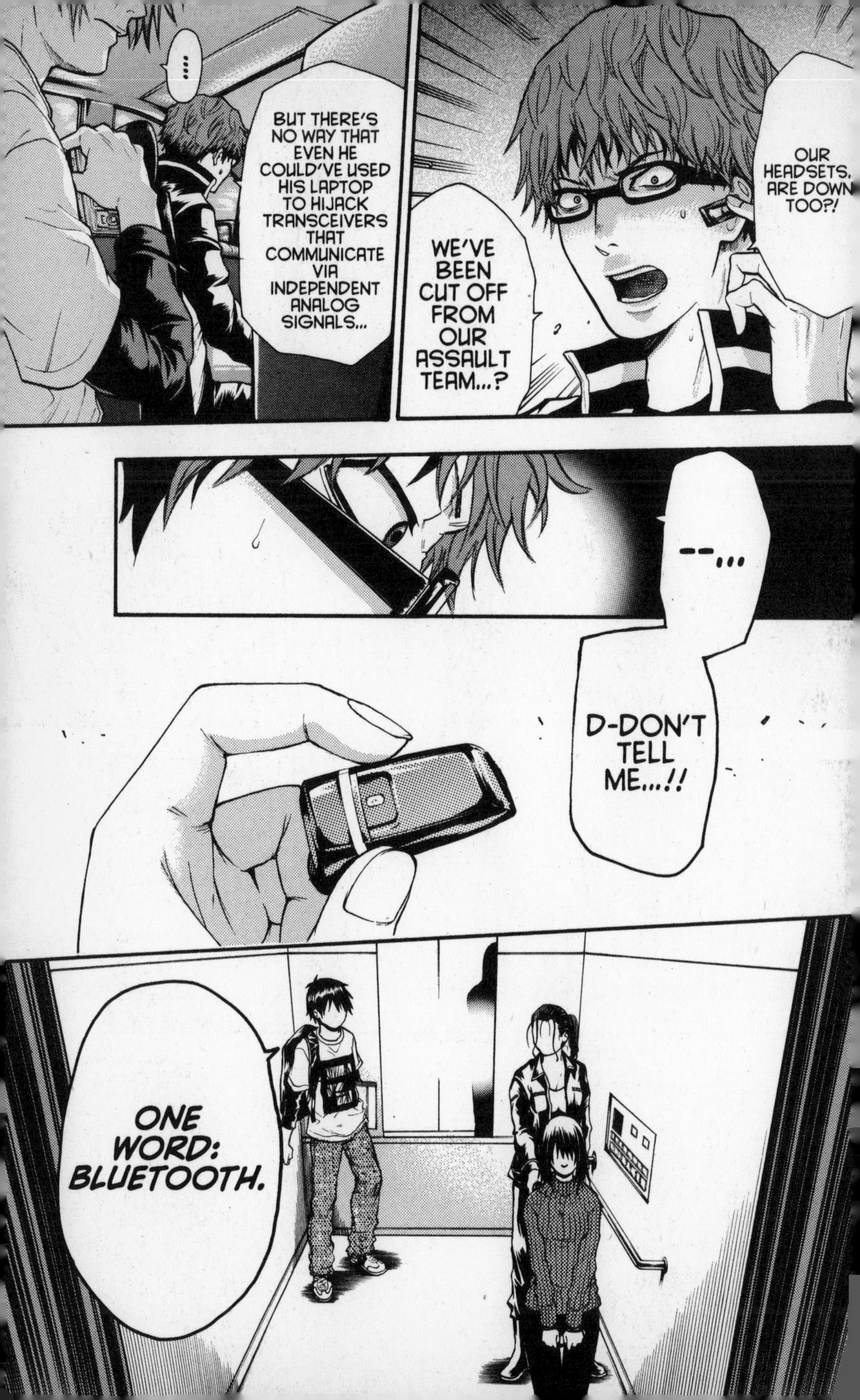
OUR HEADSETS. ARE DOWN TOO?!
WE'VE BEEN CUT OFF FROM OUR ASSAULT TEAM...?
......
BUT THERE'S NO WAY THAT EVEN HE COULD'VE USED HIS LAPTOP TO HIJACK TRANSCEIVERS THAT COMMUNICATE VIA INDEPENDENT ANALOG SIGNALS...
--,...
D-DON'T TELL ME...!!
ONE WORD: BLUETOOTH.

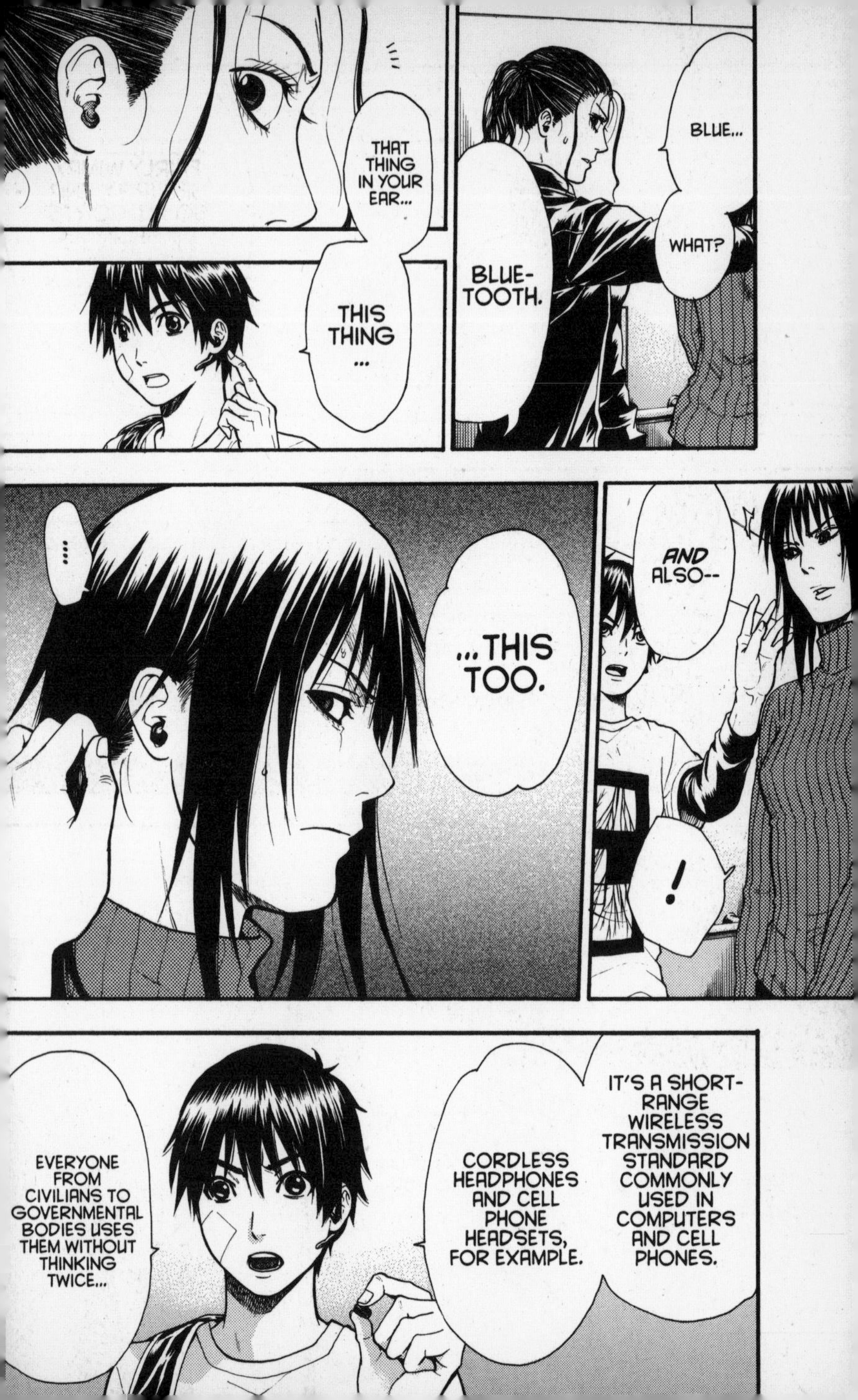
BLUE...
WHAT?
BLUE-TOOTH.
THAT THING IN YOUR EAR...
THIS THING ...
AND ALSO--
!
...THIS TOO.
....
IT'S A SHORT-RANGE WIRELESS TRANSMISSION STANDARD COMMONLY USED IN COMPUTERS AND CELL PHONES.
CORDLESS HEADPHONES AND CELL PHONE HEADSETS, FOR EXAMPLE.
EVERYONE FROM CIVILIANS TO GOVERNMENTAL BODIES USES THEM WITHOUT THINKING TWICE...

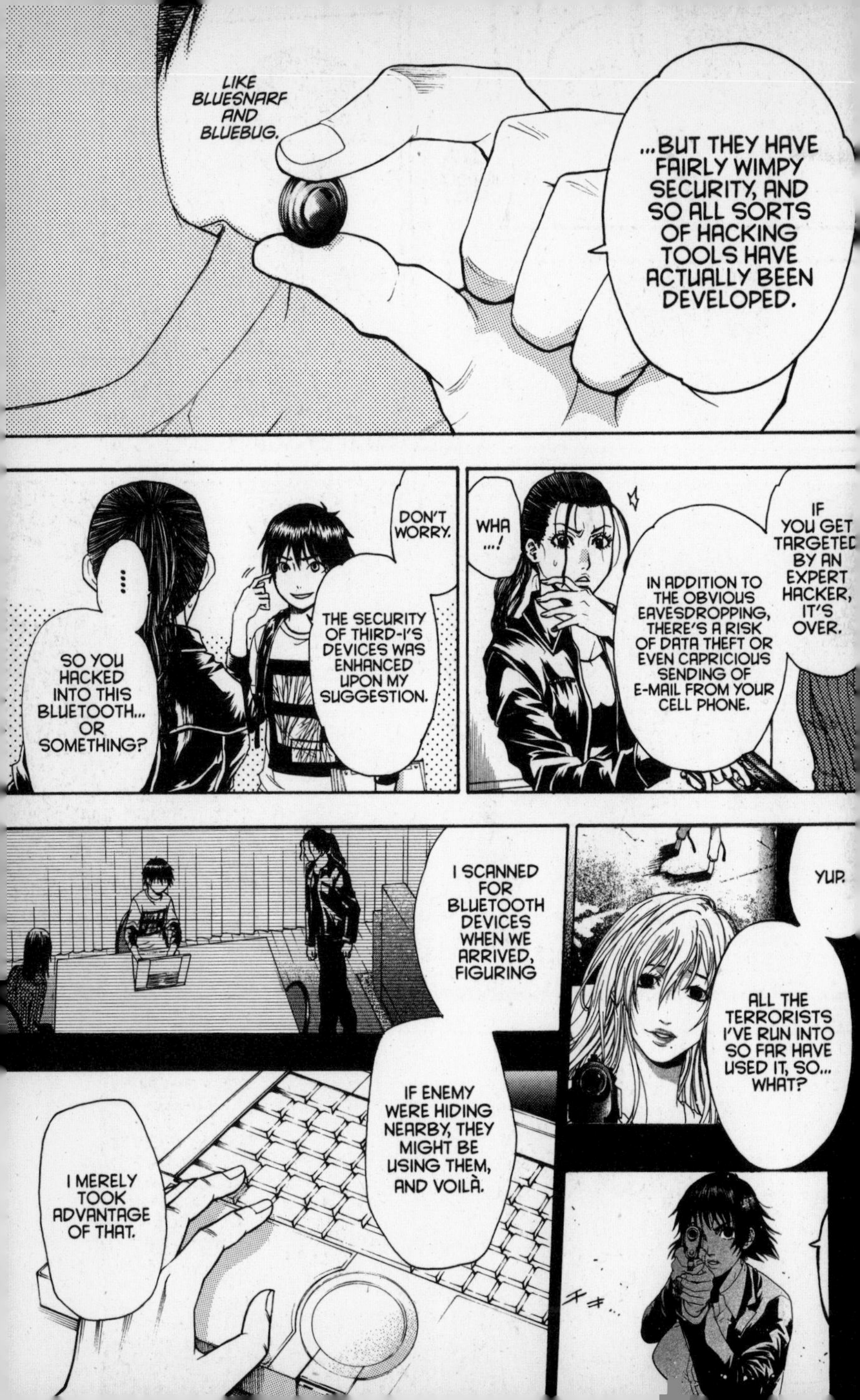
...BUT THEY HAVE FAIRLY WIMPY SECURITY, AND SO ALL SORTS OF HACKING TOOLS HAVE ACTUALLY BEEN DEVELOPED.
LIKE BLUESNARF AND BLUEBUG.
IF YOU GET TARGETED BY AN EXPERT HACKER, IT'S OVER.
IN ADDITION TO THE OBVIOUS EAVESDROPPING, THERE'S A RISK OF DATA THEFT OR EVEN CAPRICIOUS SENDING OF E-MAIL FROM YOUR CELL PHONE.
WHA ...!
DON'T WORRY.
THE SECURITY OF THIRD-I'S DEVICES WAS ENHANCED UPON MY SUGGESTION.
....
SO YOU HACKED INTO THIS BLUETOOTH... OR SOMETHING?
YUP.
ALL THE TERRORISTS I'VE RUN INTO SO FAR HAVE USED IT, SO... WHAT?
チキ…
I SCANNED FOR BLUETOOTH DEVICES WHEN WE ARRIVED, FIGURING
IF ENEMY WERE HIDING NEARBY, THEY MIGHT BE USING THEM, AND VOILÀ.
I MERELY TOOK ADVANTAGE OF THAT.

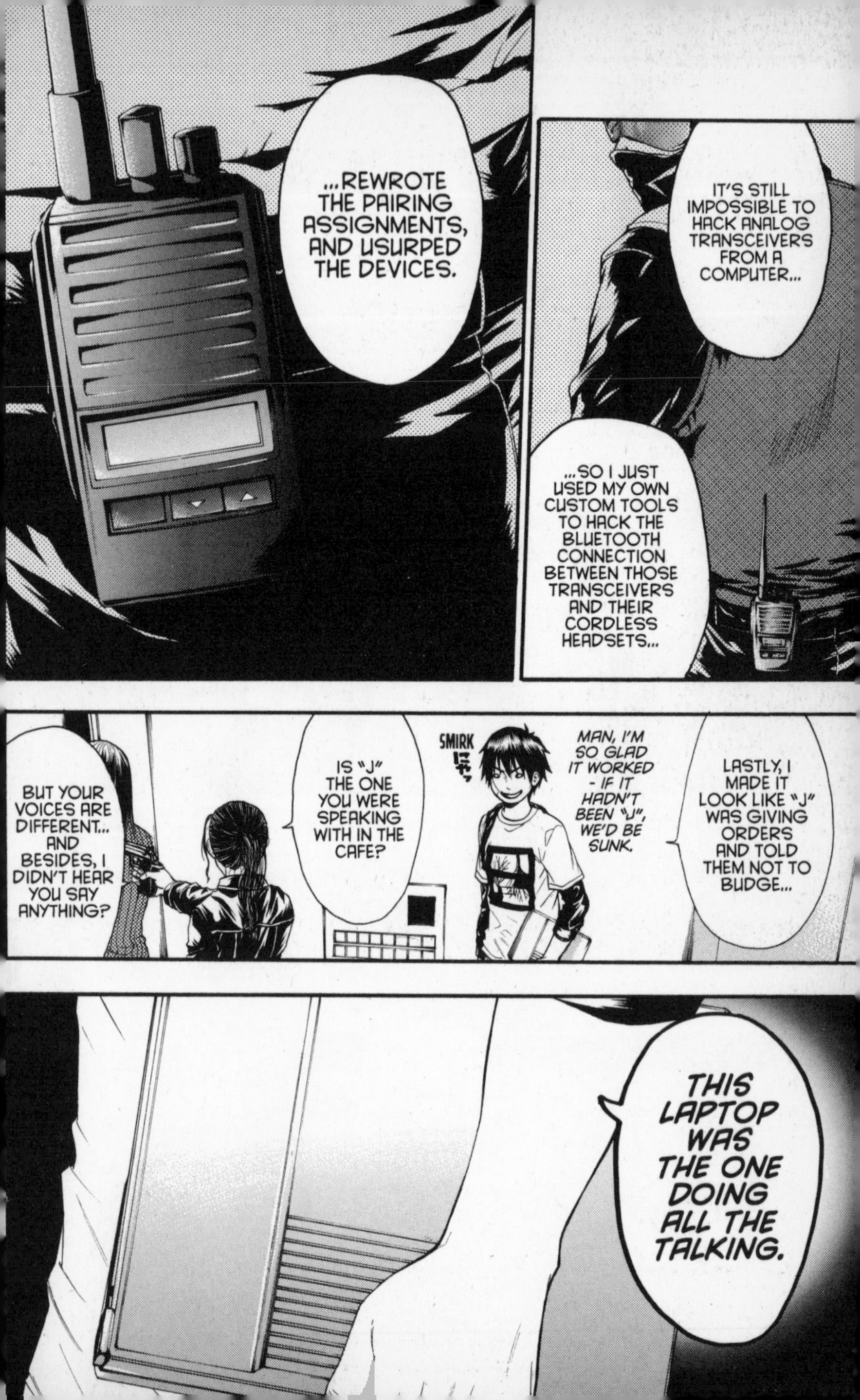
IT'S STILL IMPOSSIBLE TO HACK ANALOG TRANSCEIVERS FROM A COMPUTER...
...SO I JUST USED MY OWN CUSTOM TOOLS TO HACK THE BLUETOOTH CONNECTION BETWEEN THOSE TRANSCEIVERS AND THEIR CORDLESS HEADSETS...
...REWROTE THE PAIRING ASSIGNMENTS, AND USURPED THE DEVICES.
LASTLY, I MADE IT LOOK LIKE "J" WAS GIVING ORDERS AND TOLD THEM NOT TO BUDGE...
MAN, I'M SO GLAD IT WORKED - IF IT HADN'T BEEN "J", WE'D BE SUNK.
SMIRK
ニヤッ
IS "J" THE ONE YOU WERE SPEAKING WITH IN THE CAFE?
BUT YOUR VOICES ARE DIFFERENT... AND BESIDES, I DIDN'T HEAR YOU SAY ANYTHING?
THIS LAPTOP WAS THE ONE DOING ALL THE TALKING.

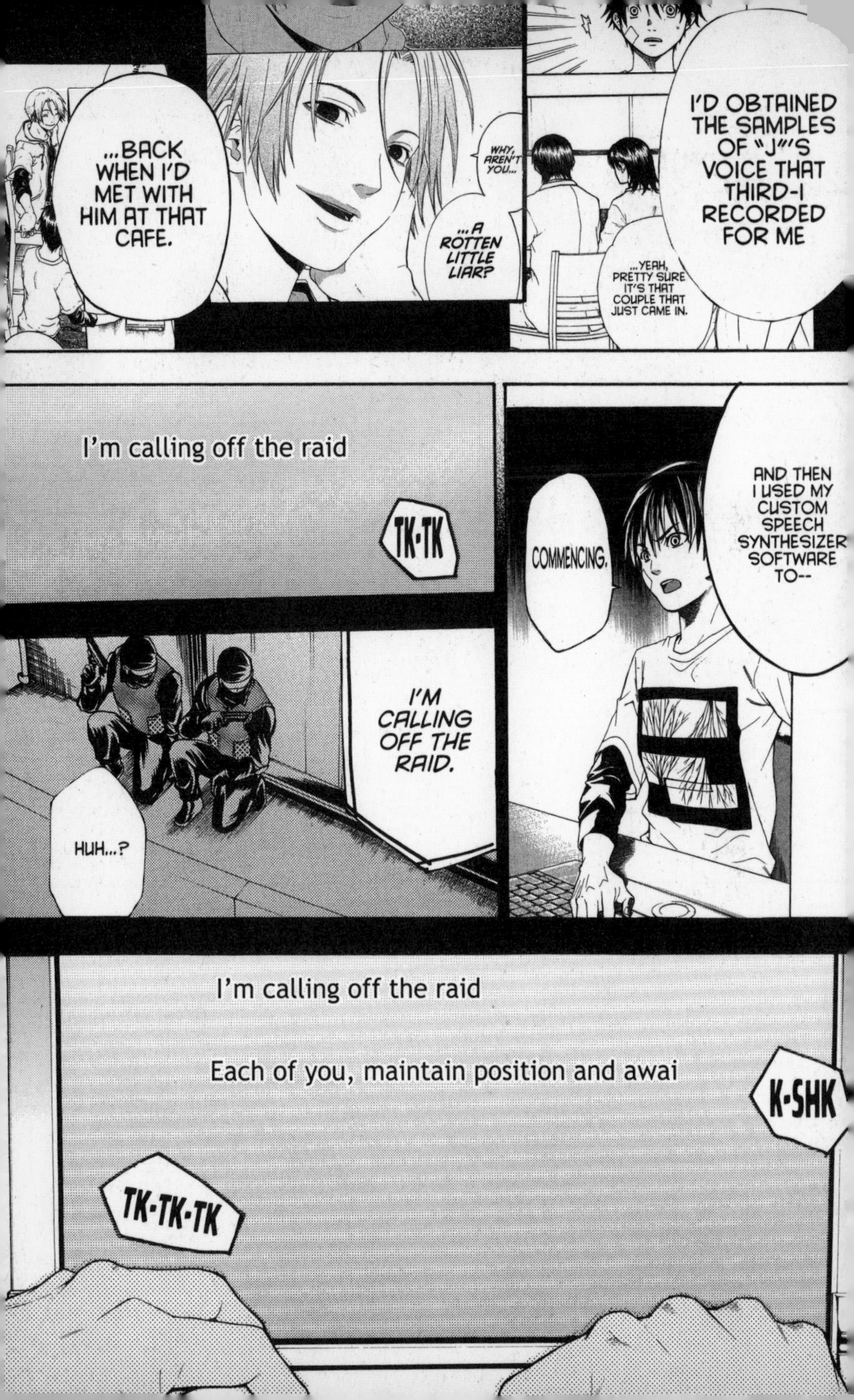

I'D OBTAINED THE SAMPLES OF "J"'S VOICE THAT THIRD-I RECORDED FOR ME
...YEAH, PRETTY SURE IT'S THAT COUPLE THAT JUST CAME IN.
WHY, AREN'T YOU...
...A ROTTEN LITTLE LIAR?
...BACK WHEN I'D MET WITH HIM AT THAT CAFE.
AND THEN I USED MY CUSTOM SPEECH SYNTHESIZER SOFTWARE TO--
COMMENCING.
I'm calling off the raid
TK-TK
I'M CALLING OFF THE RAID.
HUH...?
I'm calling off the raid
Each of you, maintain position and awai
K-SHK
TK-TK-TK

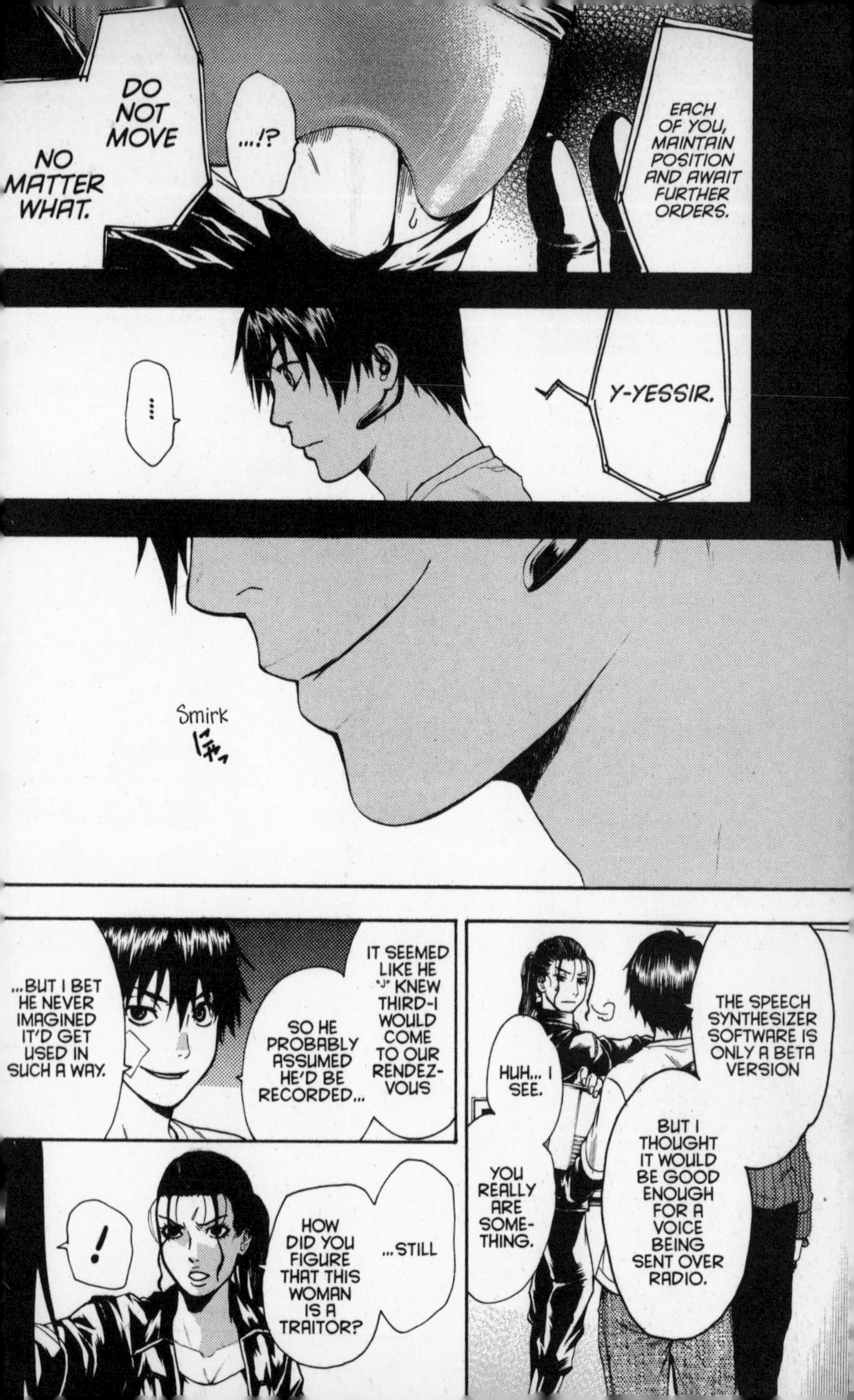
EACH OF YOU, MAINTAIN POSITION AND AWAIT FURTHER ORDERS.
...!?
DO NOT MOVE
NO MATTER WHAT.
Y-YESSIR.
......
Smirk
THE SPEECH SYNTHESIZER SOFTWARE IS ONLY A BETA VERSION
HUH... I SEE.
BUT I THOUGHT IT WOULD BE GOOD ENOUGH FOR A VOICE BEING SENT OVER RADIO.
YOU REALLY ARE SOME-THING.
IT SEEMED LIKE HE "J" KNEW THIRD-I WOULD COME TO OUR RENDEZ-VOUS
SO HE PROBABLY ASSUMED HE'D BE RECORDED...
...BUT I BET HE NEVER IMAGINED IT'D GET USED IN SUCH A WAY.
...STILL
HOW DID YOU FIGURE THAT THIS WOMAN IS A TRAITOR?
!

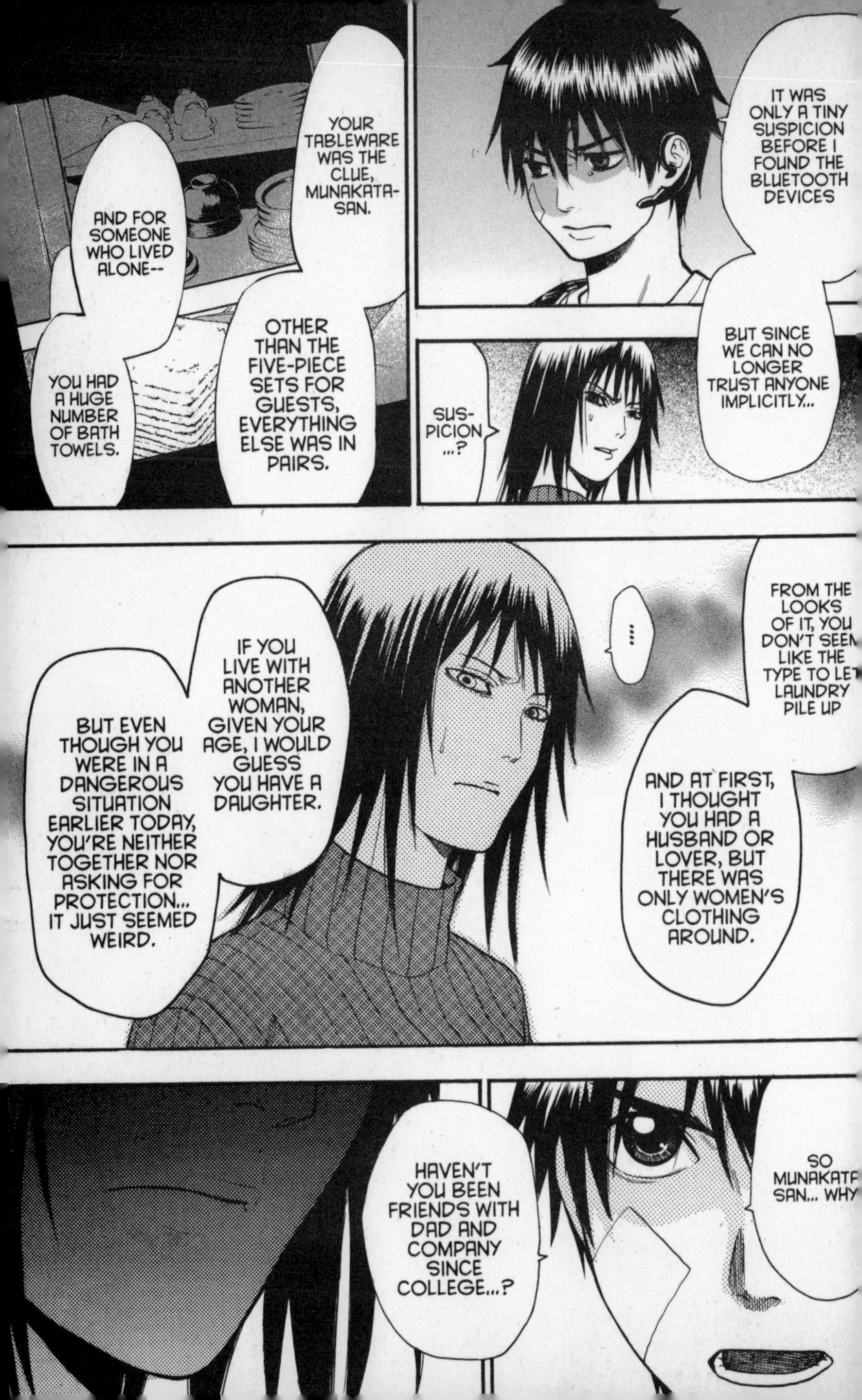
IT WAS ONLY A TINY SUSPICION BEFORE I FOUND THE BLUETOOTH DEVICES
BUT SINCE WE CAN NO LONGER TRUST ANYONE IMPLICITLY...
SUS-PICION ...?
YOUR TABLEWARE WAS THE CLUE, MUNAKATA-SAN.
OTHER THAN THE FIVE-PIECE SETS FOR GUESTS, EVERYTHING ELSE WAS IN PAIRS.
AND FOR SOMEONE WHO LIVED ALONE--
YOU HAD A HUGE NUMBER OF BATH TOWELS.
FROM THE LOOKS OF IT, YOU DON'T SEEM LIKE THE TYPE TO LET LAUNDRY PILE UP
....
AND AT FIRST, I THOUGHT YOU HAD A HUSBAND OR LOVER, BUT THERE WAS ONLY WOMEN'S CLOTHING AROUND.
IF YOU LIVE WITH ANOTHER WOMAN, GIVEN YOUR AGE, I WOULD GUESS YOU HAVE A DAUGHTER.
BUT EVEN THOUGH YOU WERE IN A DANGEROUS SITUATION EARLIER TODAY, YOU'RE NEITHER TOGETHER NOR ASKING FOR PROTECTION... IT JUST SEEMED WEIRD.
SO MUNAKATA SAN... WHY
HAVEN'T YOU BEEN FRIENDS WITH DAD AND COMPANY SINCE COLLEGE...?

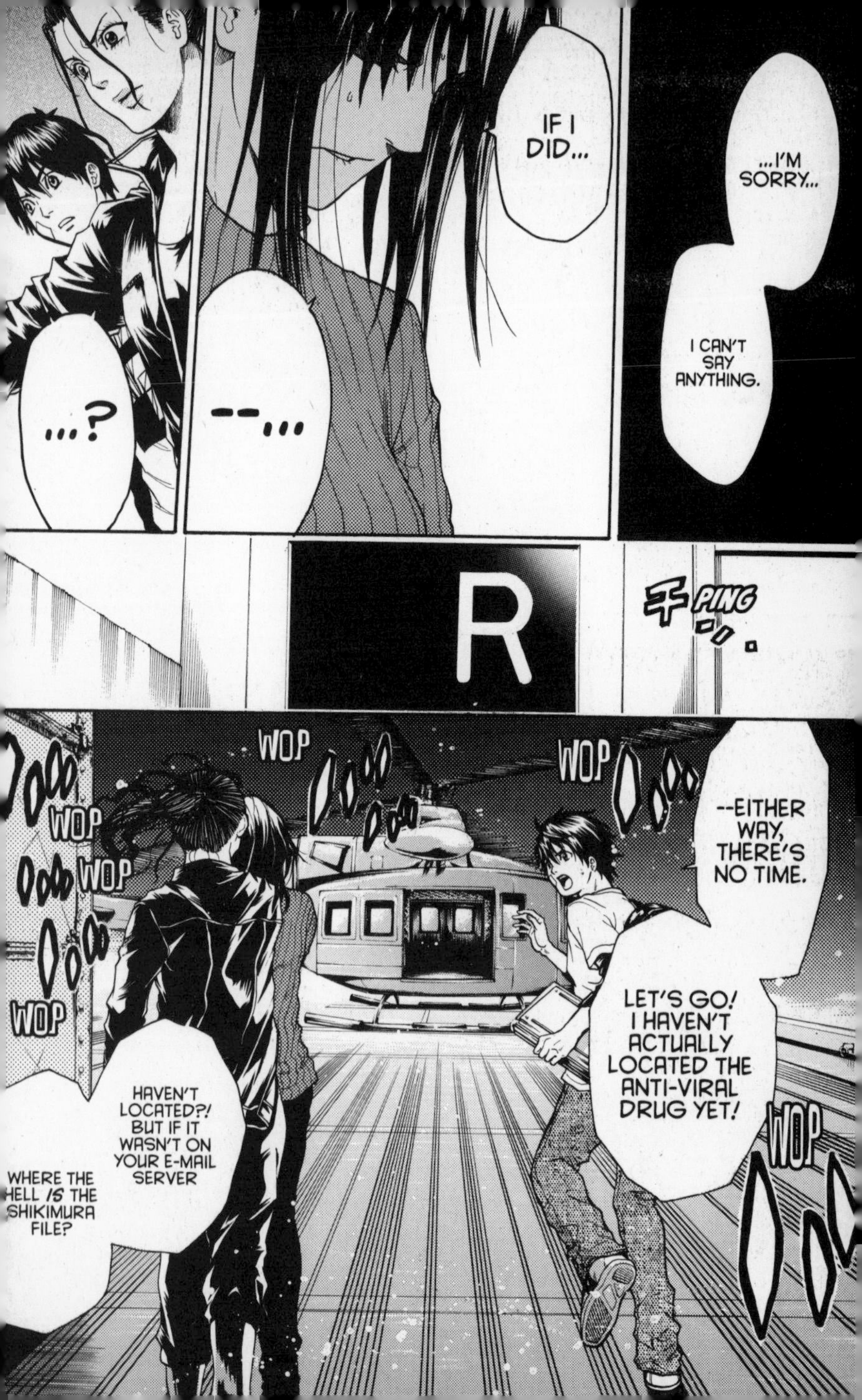

...I'M SORRY...
I CAN'T SAY ANYTHING.
IF I DID...
--...
...?
PING
R
WOP
WOP
--EITHER WAY, THERE'S NO TIME.
LET'S GO! I HAVEN'T ACTUALLY LOCATED THE ANTI-VIRAL DRUG YET!
WOP
WOP
WOP
WOP
HAVEN'T LOCATED?! BUT IF IT WASN'T ON YOUR E-MAIL SERVER
WHERE THE HELL *IS* THE SHIKIMURA FILE?

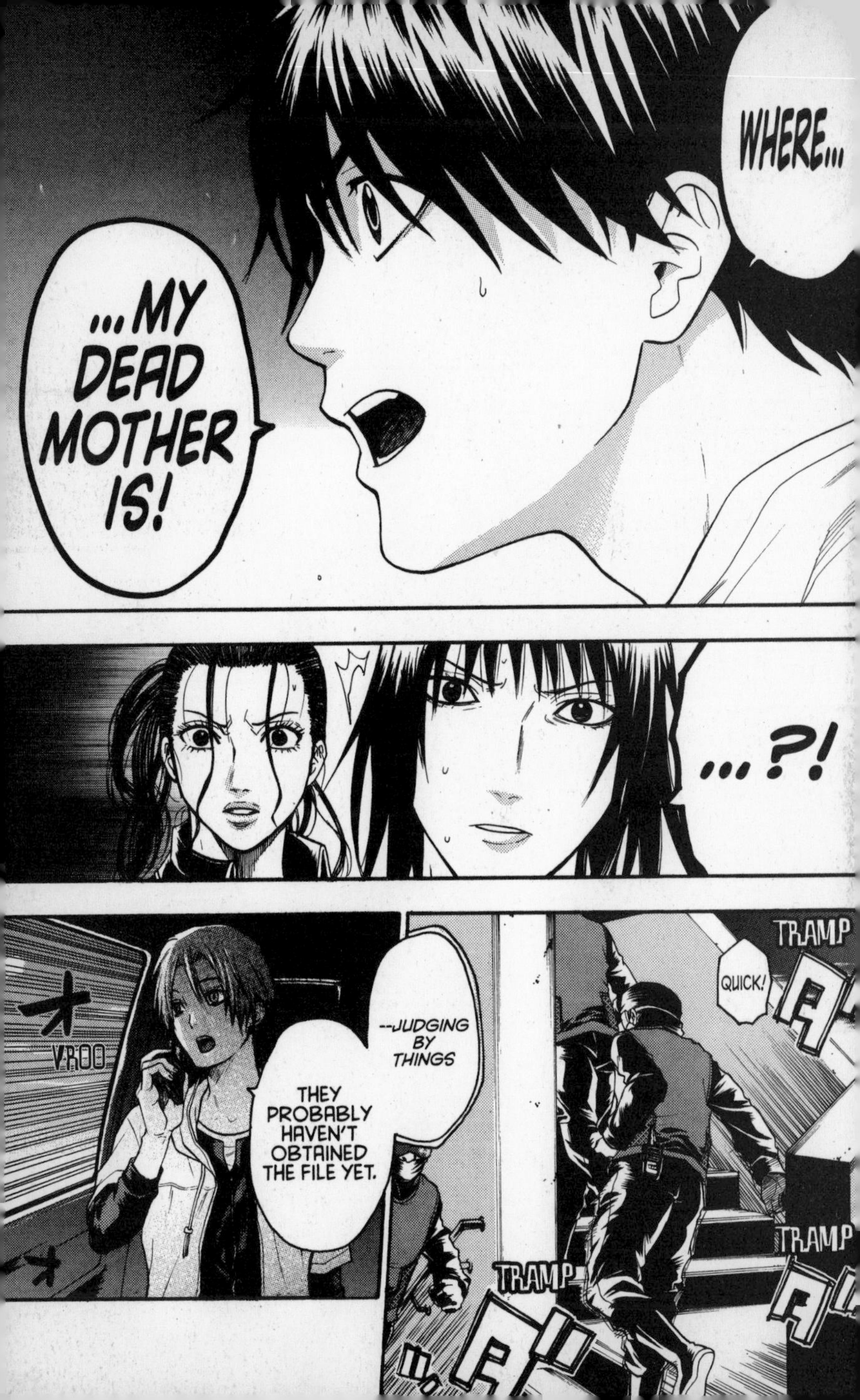
WHERE...
...MY DEAD MOTHER IS!
...?!
TRAMP
QUICK!
TRAMP
TRAMP
--JUDGING BY THINGS
THEY PROBABLY HAVEN'T OBTAINED THE FILE YET.
VROO

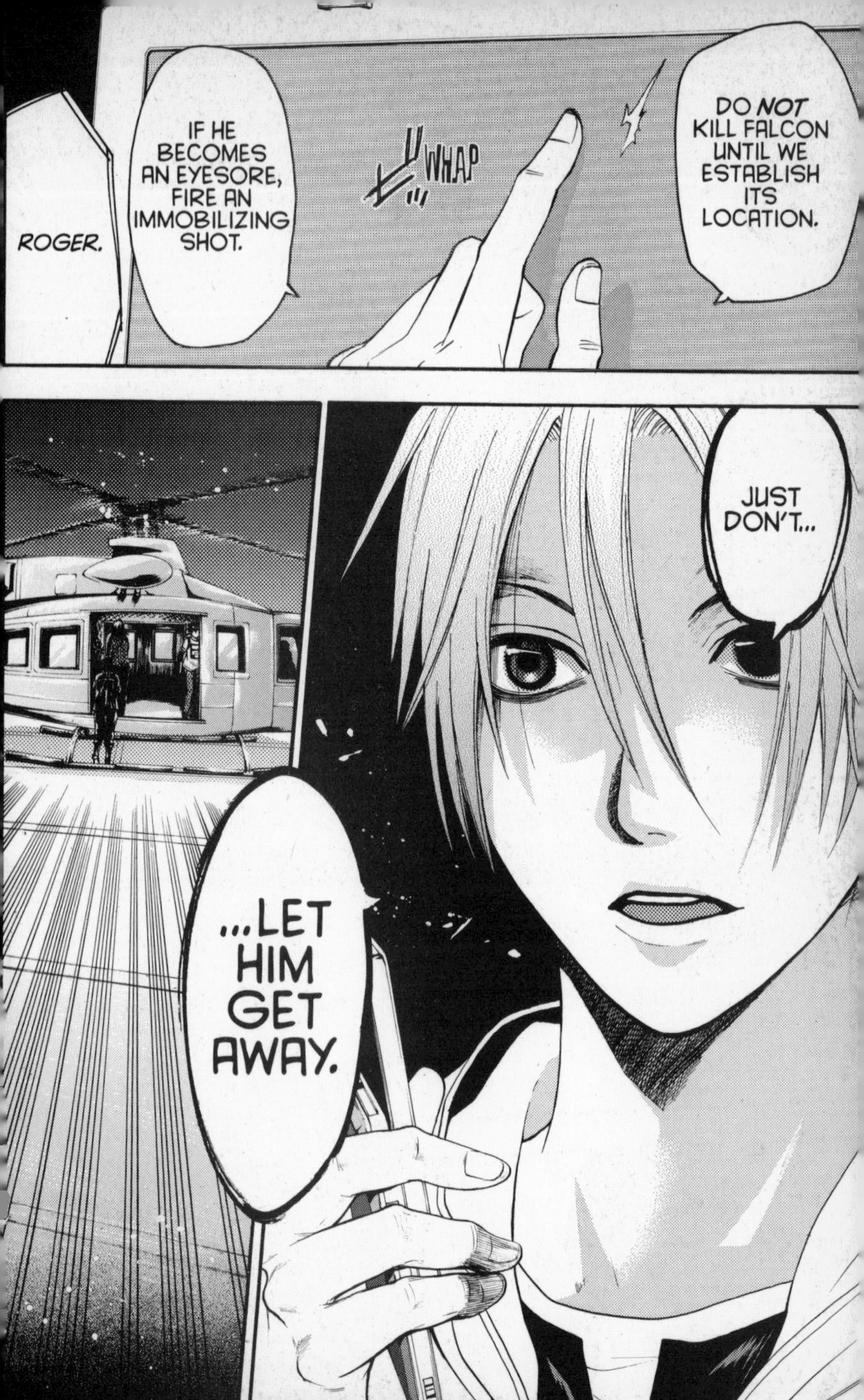
DO NOT KILL FALCON UNTIL WE ESTABLISH ITS LOCATION.
WHAP
IF HE BECOMES AN EYESORE, FIRE AN IMMOBILIZING SHOT.
ROGER.
JUST DON'T...
...LET HIM GET AWAY.

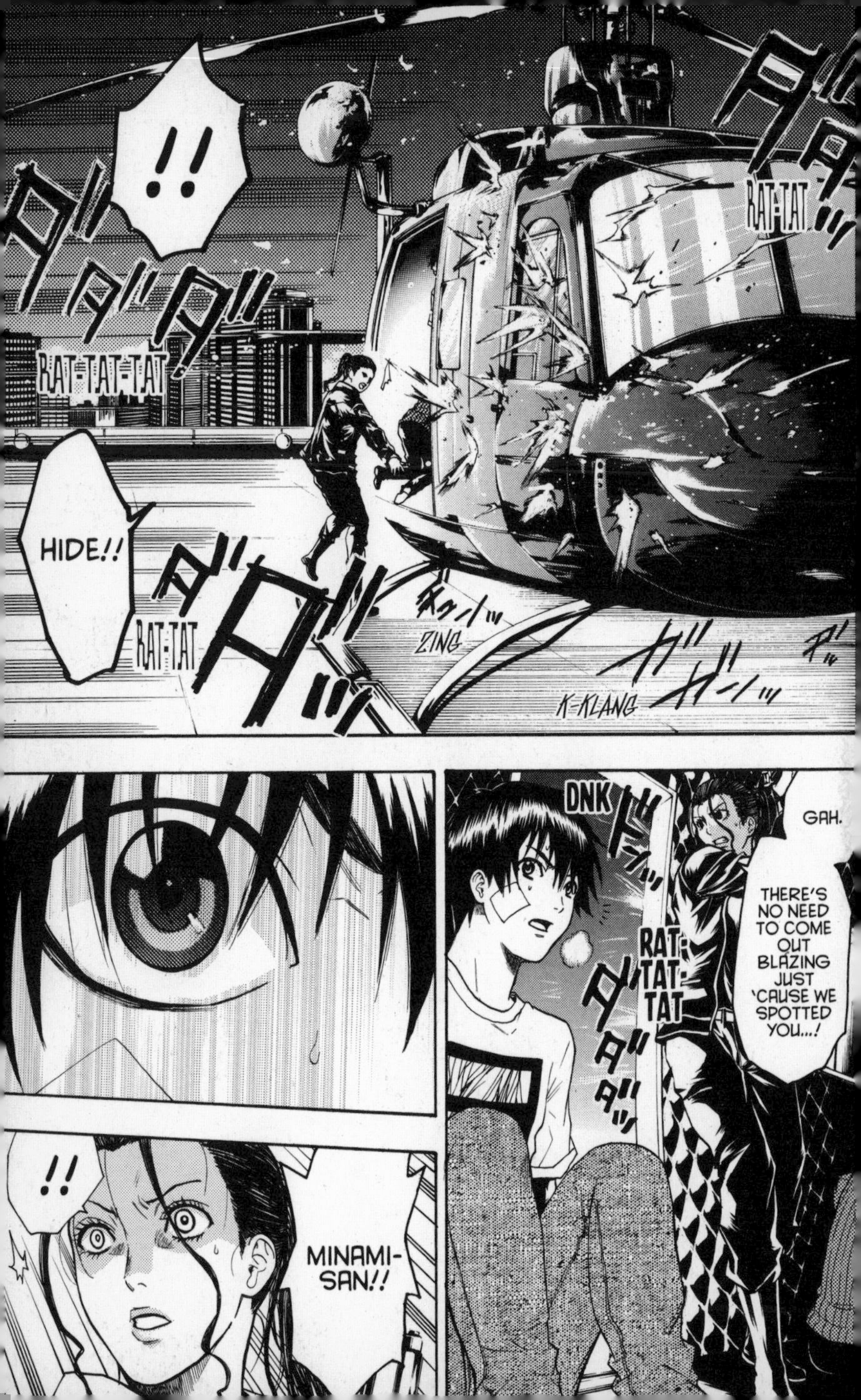
RAT-TAT
!!
RAT-TAT-TAT
K-KLANG
ZING
RAT-TAT
HIDE!!
GAH.
DNK
THERE'S NO NEED TO COME OUT BLAZING JUST 'CAUSE WE SPOTTED YOU...!
RAT-TAT-TAT
!!
MINAMI-SAN!!

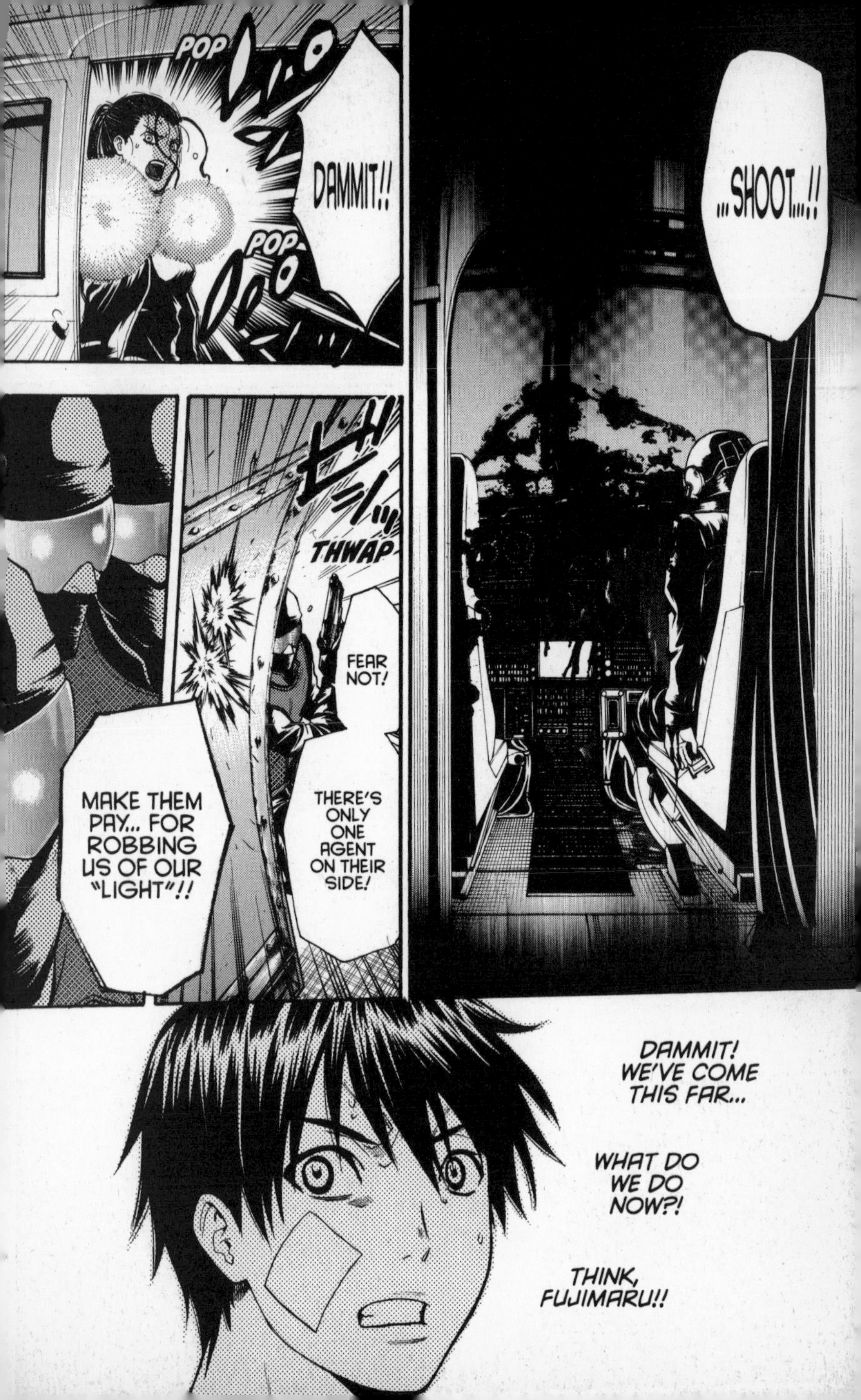
...SHOOT...!!
POP
DAMMIT!!
POP
THWAP
FEAR NOT!
THERE'S ONLY ONE AGENT ON THEIR SIDE!
MAKE THEM PAY... FOR ROBBING US OF OUR "LIGHT"!!
DAMMIT! WE'VE COME THIS FAR...
WHAT DO WE DO NOW?!
THINK, FUJIMARU!!

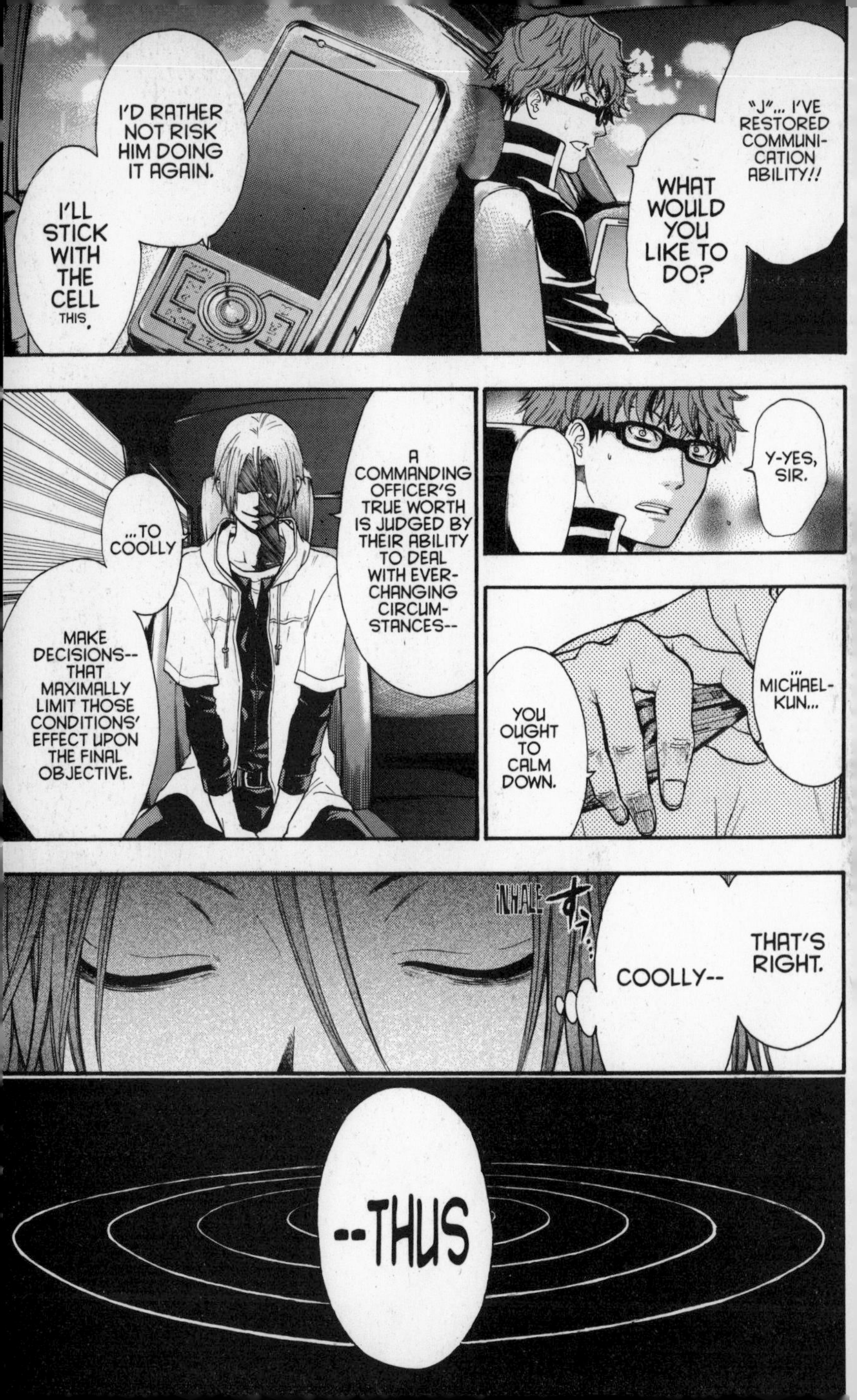
"J"... I'VE RESTORED COMMUNICATION ABILITY!!
WHAT WOULD YOU LIKE TO DO?
I'D RATHER NOT RISK HIM DOING IT AGAIN.
I'LL STICK WITH THE CELL THIS.
Y-YES, SIR.
...MICHAEL-KUN...
YOU OUGHT TO CALM DOWN.
A COMMANDING OFFICER'S TRUE WORTH IS JUDGED BY THEIR ABILITY TO DEAL WITH EVER-CHANGING CIRCUMSTANCES--
...TO COOLLY
MAKE DECISIONS--THAT MAXIMALLY LIMIT THOSE CONDITIONS' EFFECT UPON THE FINAL OBJECTIVE.
THAT'S RIGHT.
INHALE
COOLLY--
--THUS

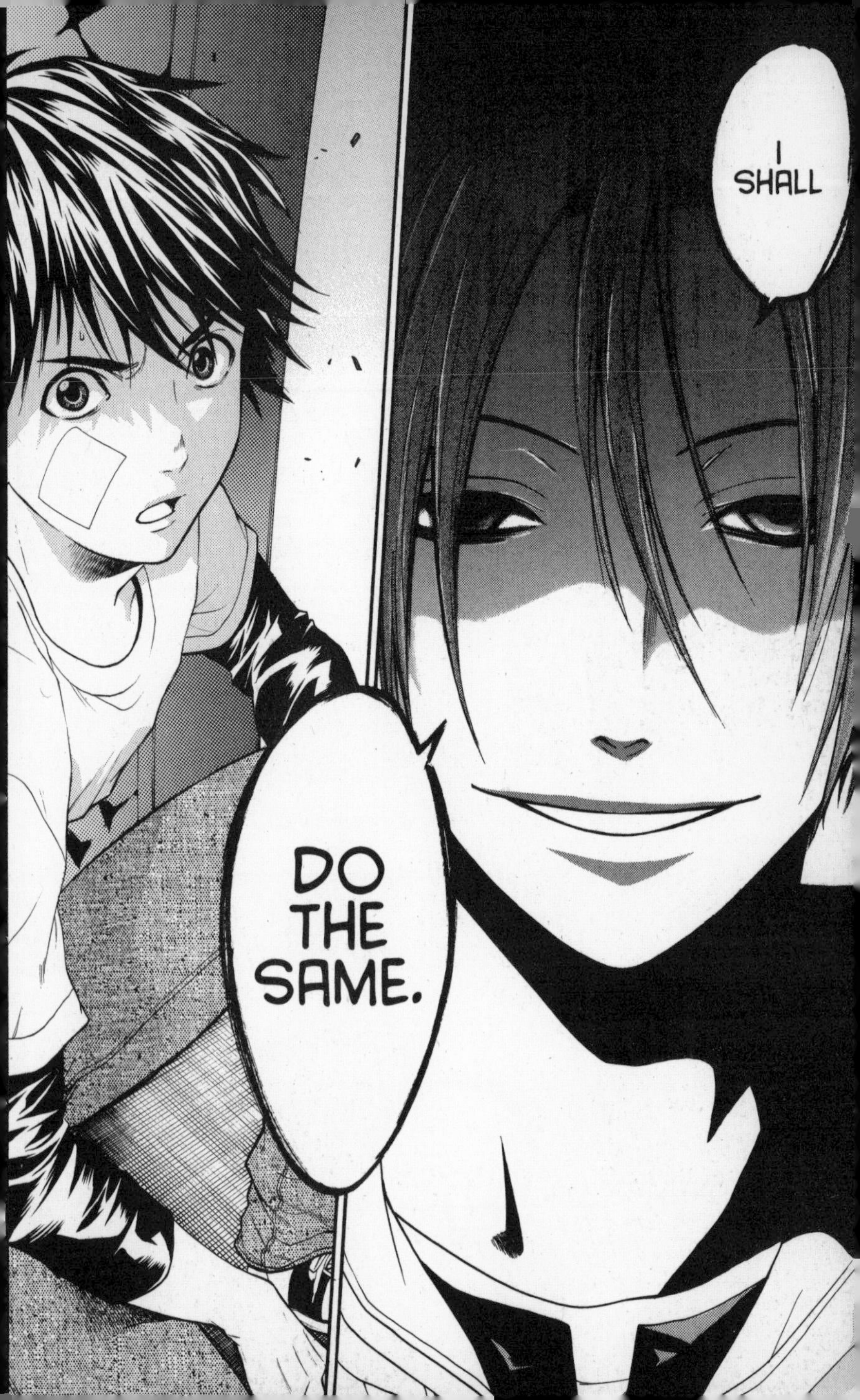
I SHALL
DO THE SAME.

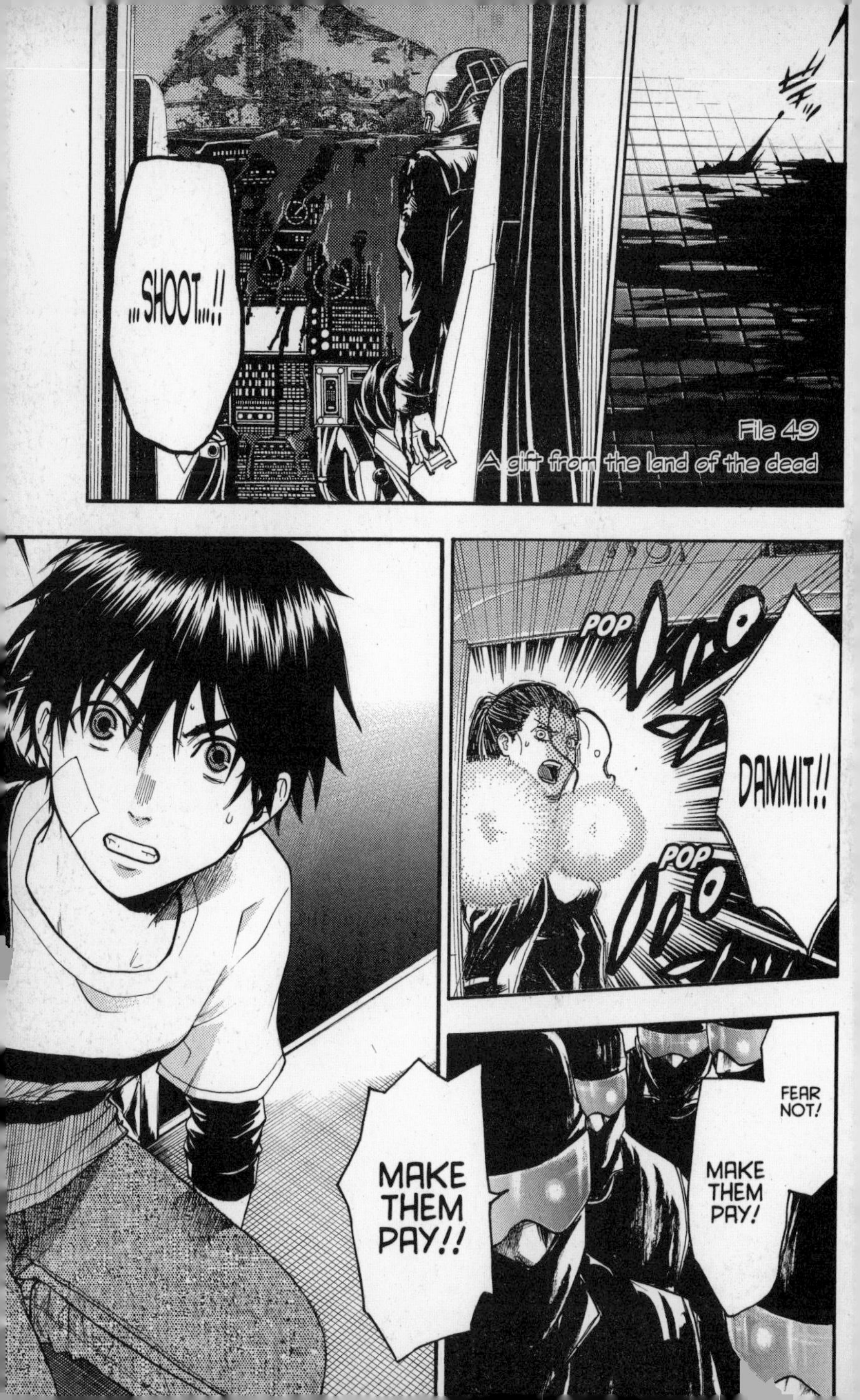
File 49
A gift from the land of the dead
...SHOOT...!!
POP
DAMMIT!!
POP
FEAR NOT!
MAKE THEM PAY!
MAKE THEM PAY!!

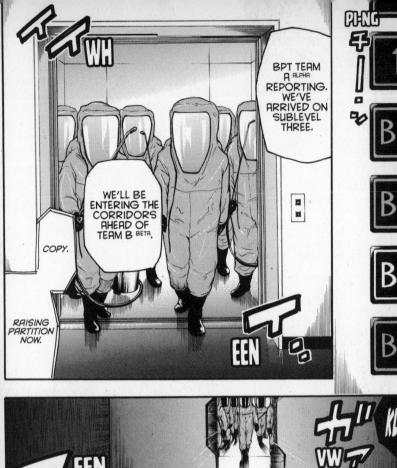

BPT TEAM A ALPHA REPORTING. WE'VE ARRIVED ON SUBLEVEL THREE.

WE'LL BE ENTERING THE CORRIDORS AHEAD OF TEAM B BETA.

COPY.

RAISING PARTITION NOW.

PI-NG

1
B1
B2
B3
B4

WH

EEN

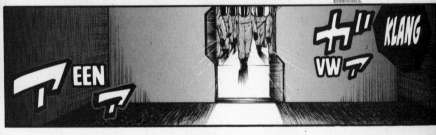

EEN

KLANG

VW

COMMENCING SPRAY OPERATION!!

SSH

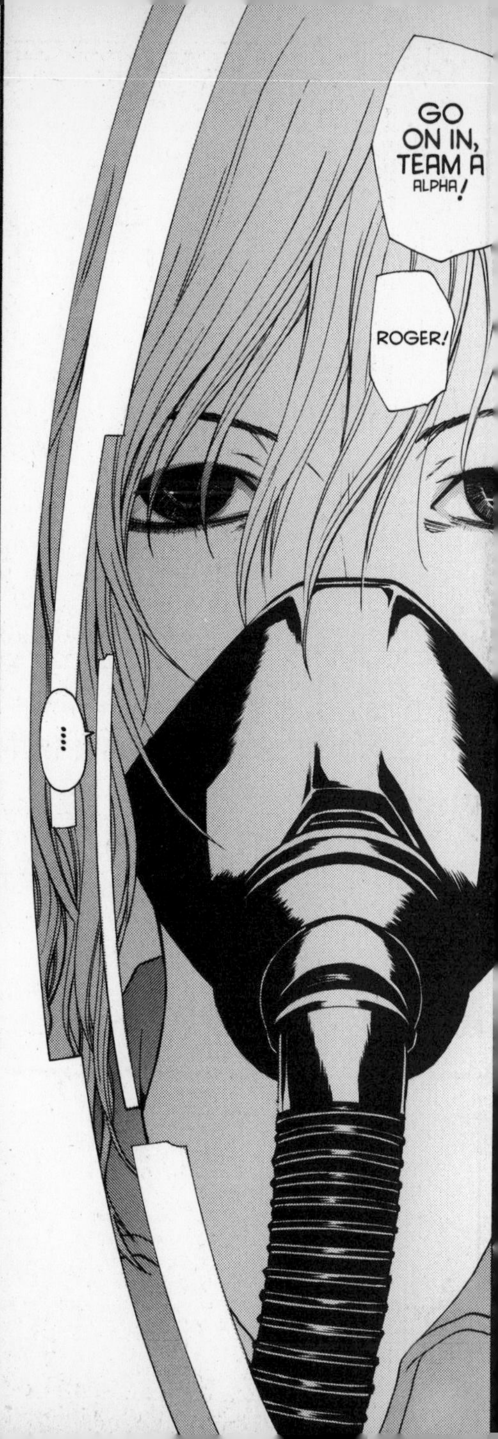
GO ON IN, TEAM A ALPHA!
ROGER!
....

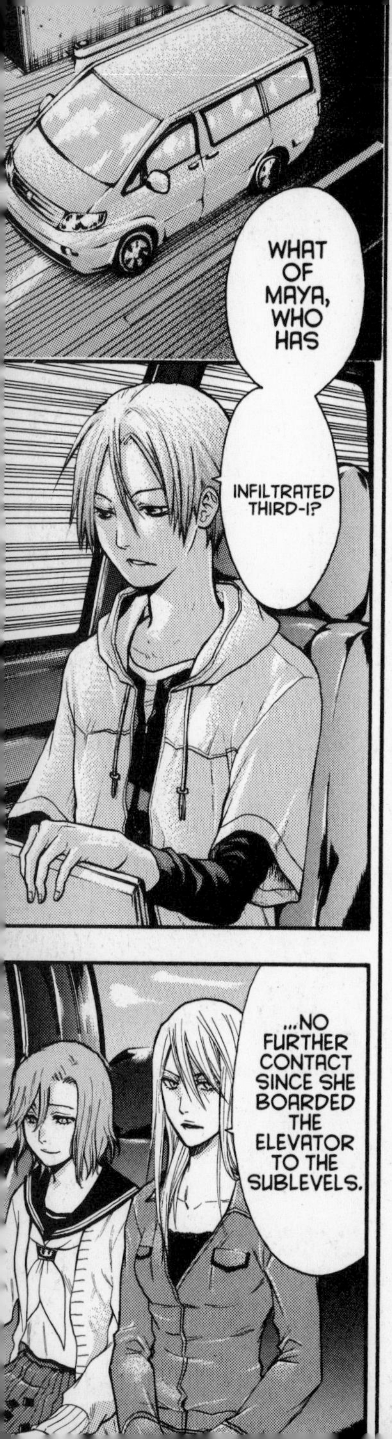
WHAT OF MAYA, WHO HAS
INFILTRATED THIRD-I?
...NO FURTHER CONTACT SINCE SHE BOARDED THE ELEVATOR TO THE SUBLEVELS.

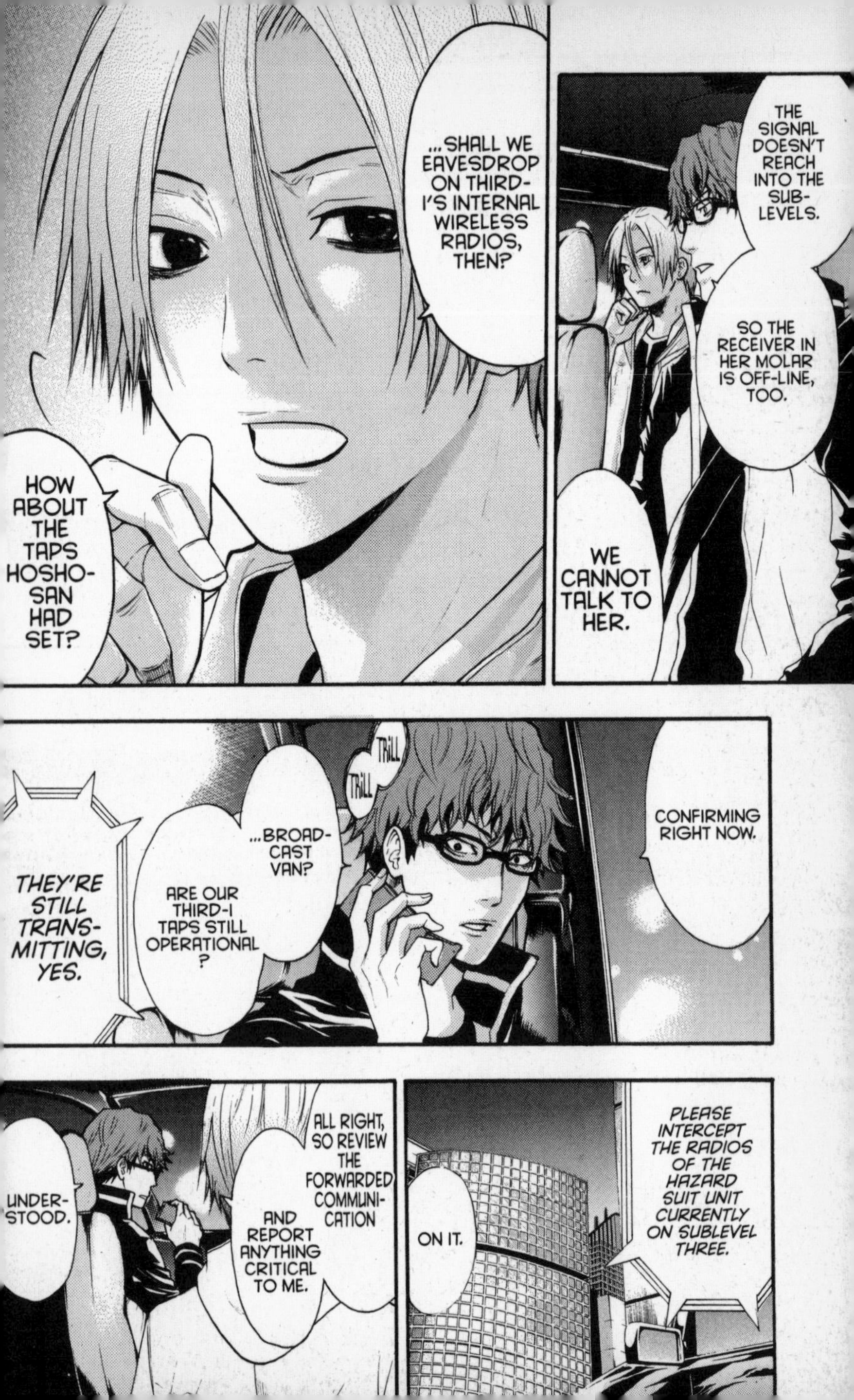
THE SIGNAL DOESN'T REACH INTO THE SUB-LEVELS.
SO THE RECEIVER IN HER MOLAR IS OFF-LINE, TOO.
WE CANNOT TALK TO HER.
...SHALL WE EAVESDROP ON THIRD-I'S INTERNAL WIRELESS RADIOS, THEN?
HOW ABOUT THE TAPS HOSHO-SAN HAD SET?
CONFIRMING RIGHT NOW.
TRILL
TRILL
...BROAD-CAST VAN?
ARE OUR THIRD-I TAPS STILL OPERATIONAL?
THEY'RE STILL TRANS-MITTING, YES.
PLEASE INTERCEPT THE RADIOS OF THE HAZARD SUIT UNIT CURRENTLY ON SUBLEVEL THREE.
ON IT.
ALL RIGHT, SO REVIEW THE FORWARDED COMMUNI-CATION
AND REPORT ANYTHING CRITICAL TO ME.
UNDER-STOOD.

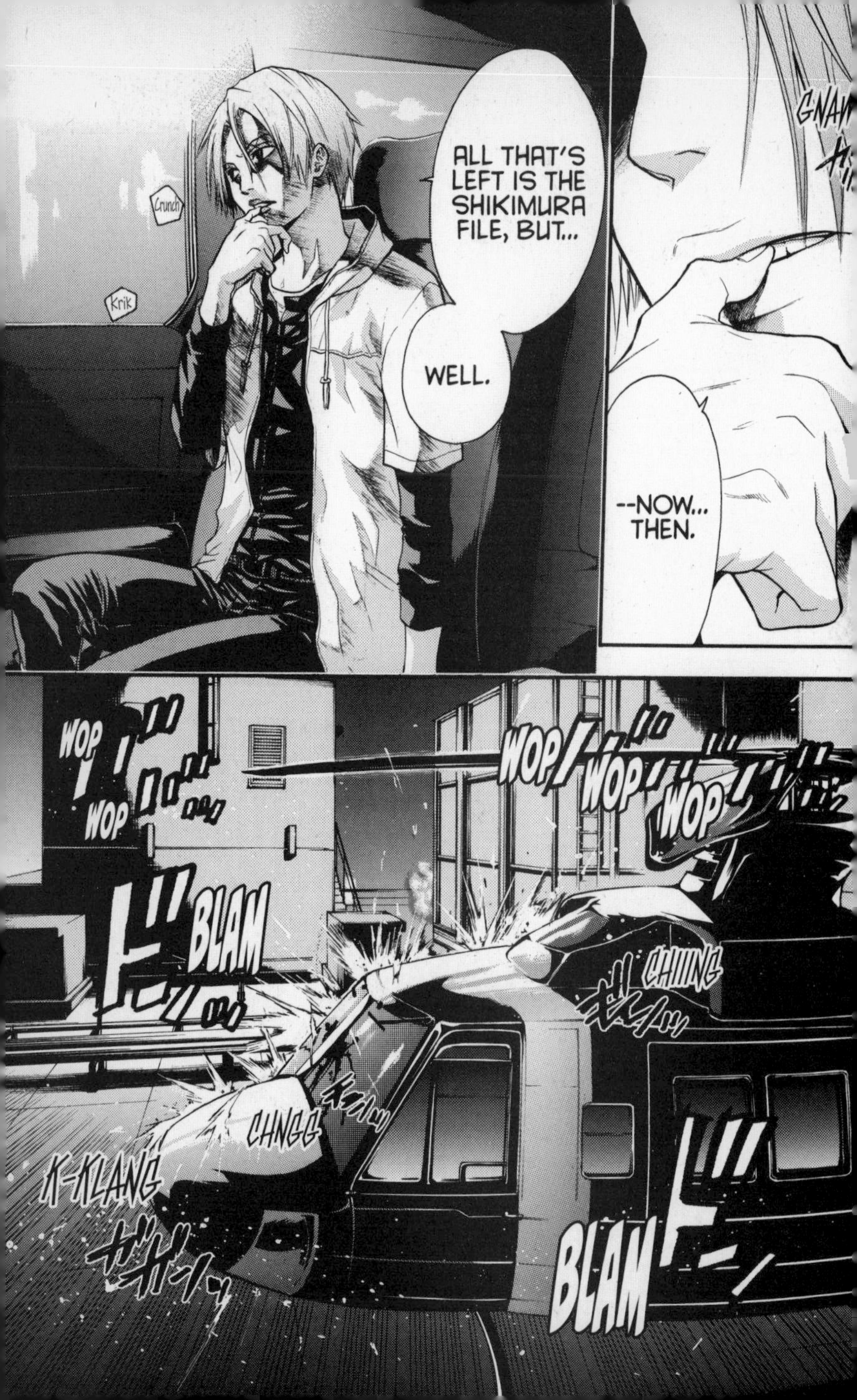

GNAW
--NOW... THEN.
Crunch
Krik
ALL THAT'S LEFT IS THE SHIKIMURA FILE, BUT...
WELL.
WOP
WOP
WOP
WOP
WOP
BLAM
CHIIING
CHNGG
K-KLANG
BLAM

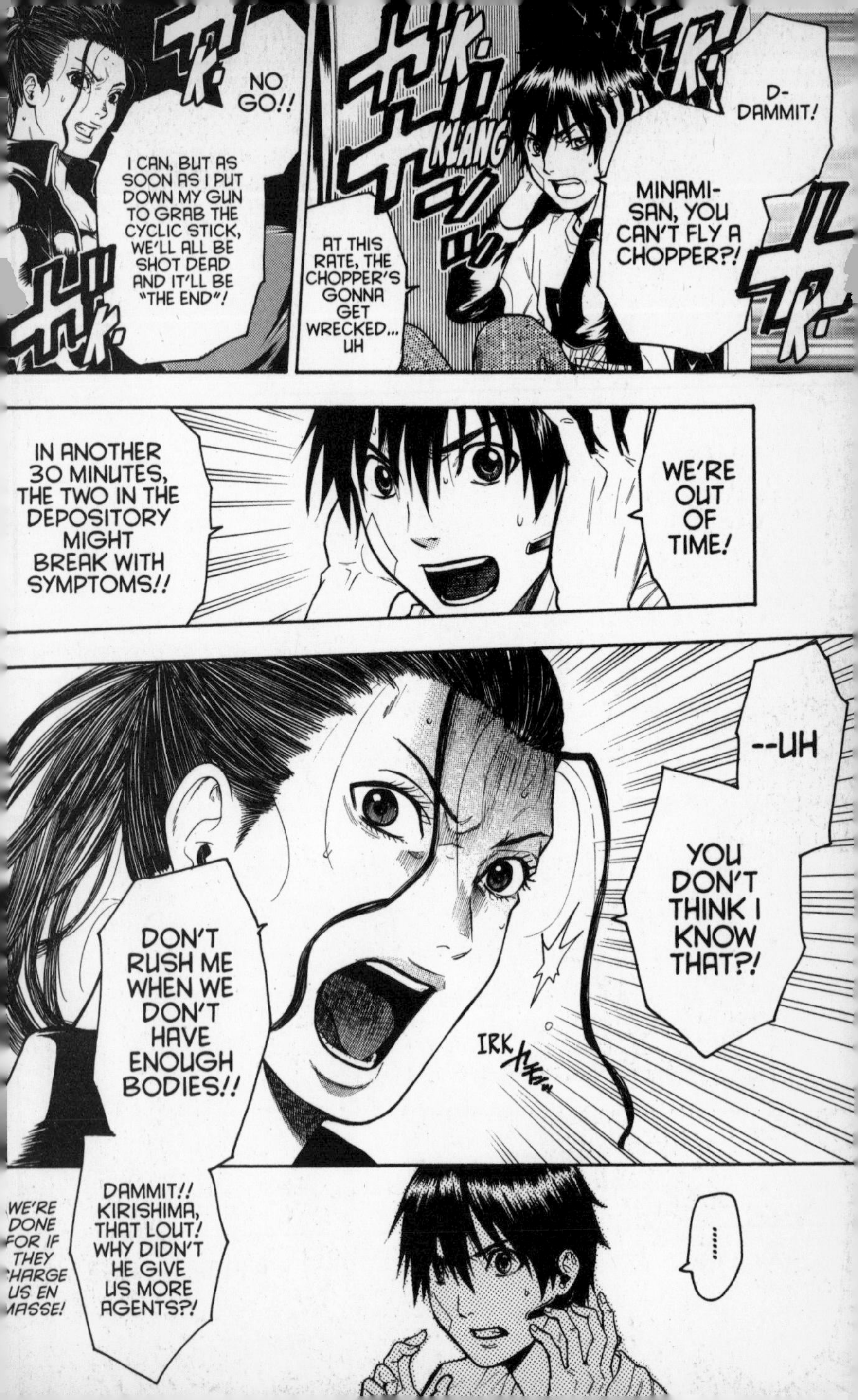
D-DAMMIT!
MINAMI-SAN, YOU CAN'T FLY A CHOPPER?!
KLANG
AT THIS RATE, THE CHOPPER'S GONNA GET WRECKED... UH
NO GO!!
I CAN, BUT AS SOON AS I PUT DOWN MY GUN TO GRAB THE CYCLIC STICK, WE'LL ALL BE SHOT DEAD AND IT'LL BE "THE END"!
WE'RE OUT OF TIME!
IN ANOTHER 30 MINUTES, THE TWO IN THE DEPOSITORY MIGHT BREAK WITH SYMPTOMS!!
--UH
YOU DON'T THINK I KNOW THAT?!
IRK
DON'T RUSH ME WHEN WE DON'T HAVE ENOUGH BODIES!!
......
DAMMIT!! KIRISHIMA, THAT LOUT! WHY DIDN'T HE GIVE US MORE AGENTS?!
WE'RE DONE FOR IF THEY CHARGE US EN MASSE!

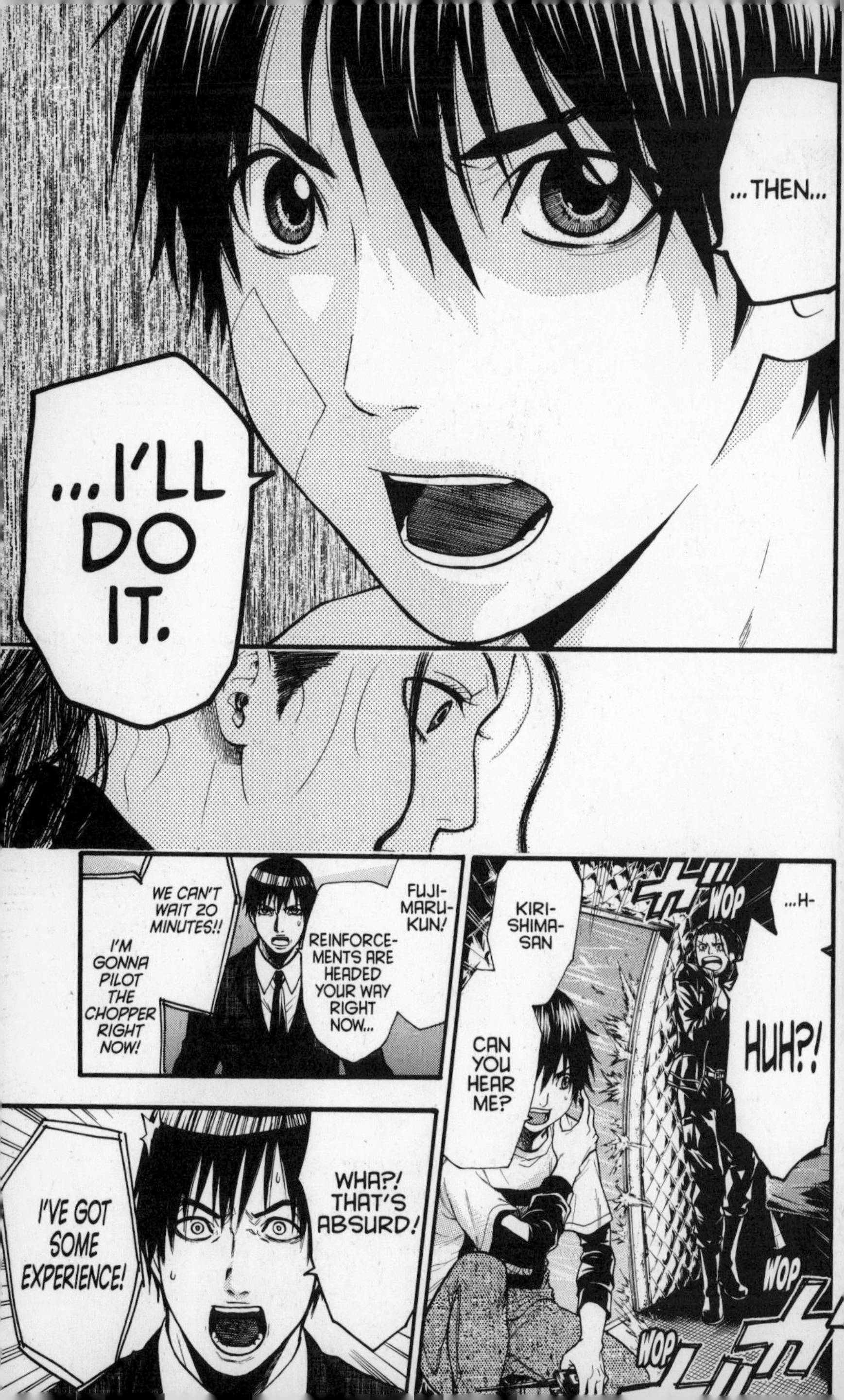
...THEN...
...I'LL DO IT.
WOP
...H-
KIRI-SHIMA-SAN
HUH?!
CAN YOU HEAR ME?
WOP
WOP
FUJI-MARU-KUN!
REINFORCE-MENTS ARE HEADED YOUR WAY RIGHT NOW...
WE CAN'T WAIT 20 MINUTES!!
I'M GONNA PILOT THE CHOPPER RIGHT NOW!
WHA?! THAT'S ABSURD!
I'VE GOT SOME EXPERIENCE!

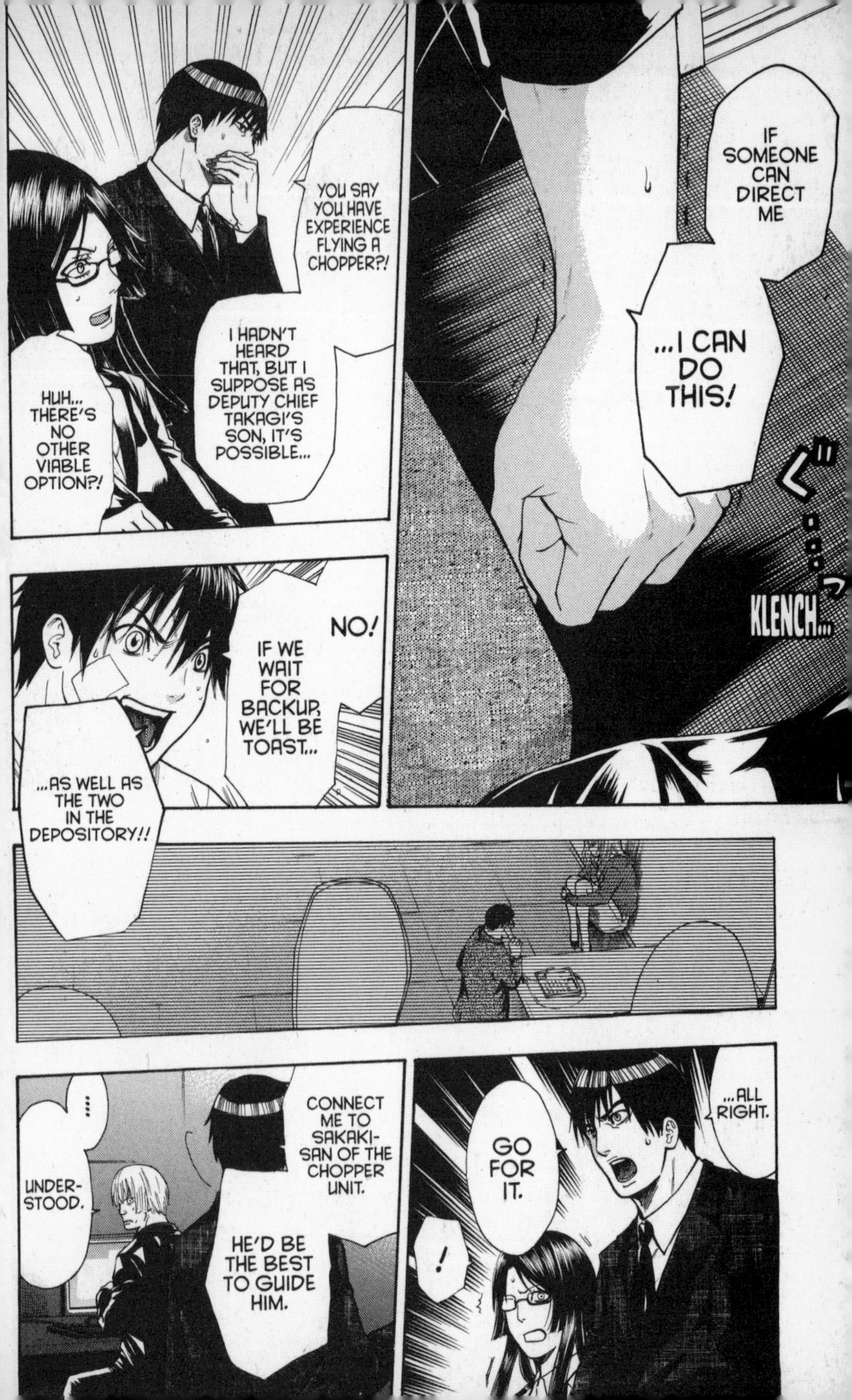
IF SOMEONE CAN DIRECT ME
...I CAN DO THIS!
KLENCH...
YOU SAY YOU HAVE EXPERIENCE FLYING A CHOPPER?!
I HADN'T HEARD THAT, BUT I SUPPOSE AS DEPUTY CHIEF TAKAGI'S SON, IT'S POSSIBLE...
HUH... THERE'S NO OTHER VIABLE OPTION?!
NO!
IF WE WAIT FOR BACKUP, WE'LL BE TOAST...
...AS WELL AS THE TWO IN THE DEPOSITORY!!
...ALL RIGHT.
GO FOR IT.
!
CONNECT ME TO SAKAKI-SAN OF THE CHOPPER UNIT.
...
UNDER-STOOD.
HE'D BE THE BEST TO GUIDE HIM.

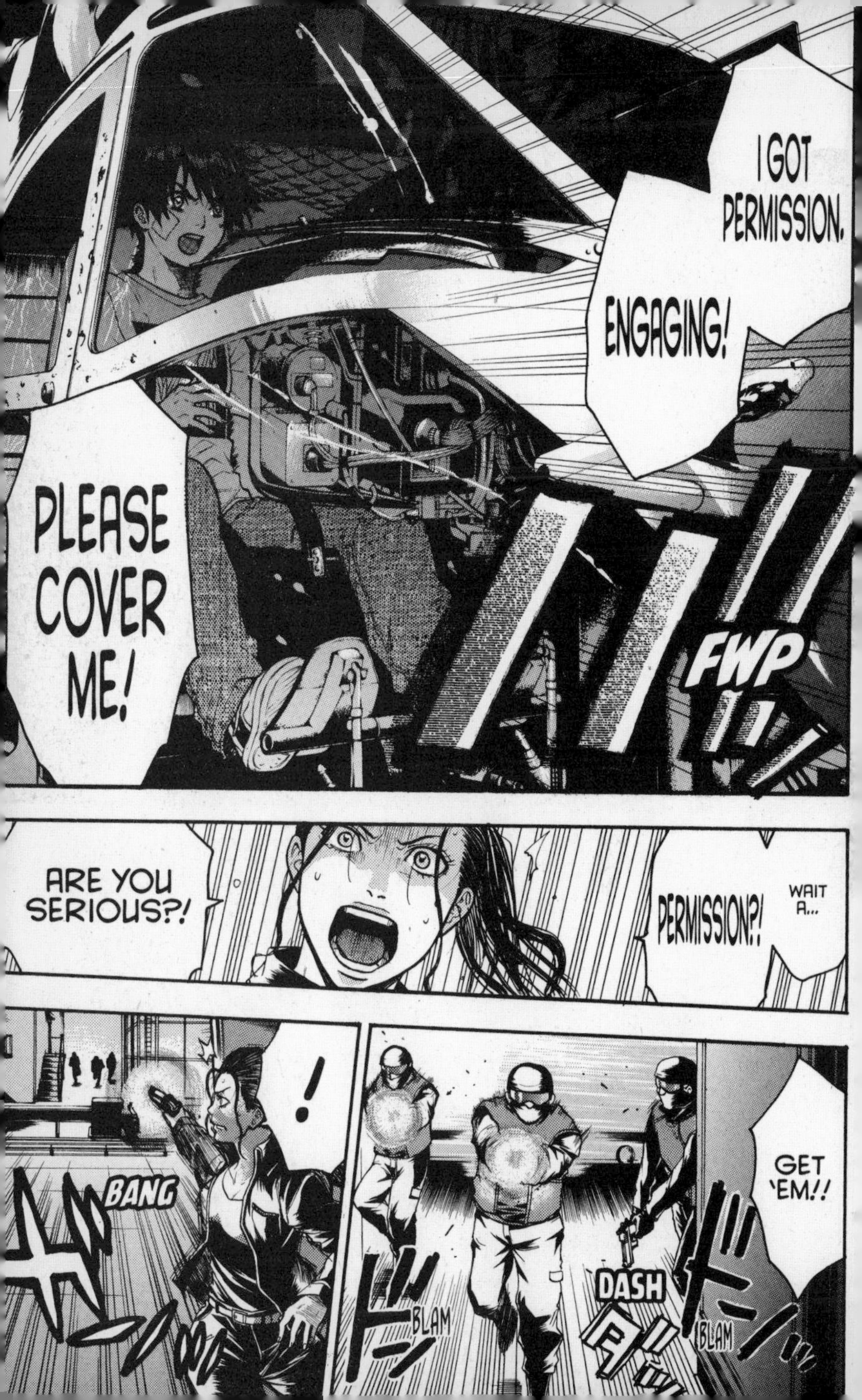

I GOT PERMISSION.
ENGAGING!
FWP
PLEASE COVER ME!
WAIT A...
PERMISSION?!
ARE YOU SERIOUS?!
GET 'EM!!
BLAM
DASH
BLAM
!
BANG

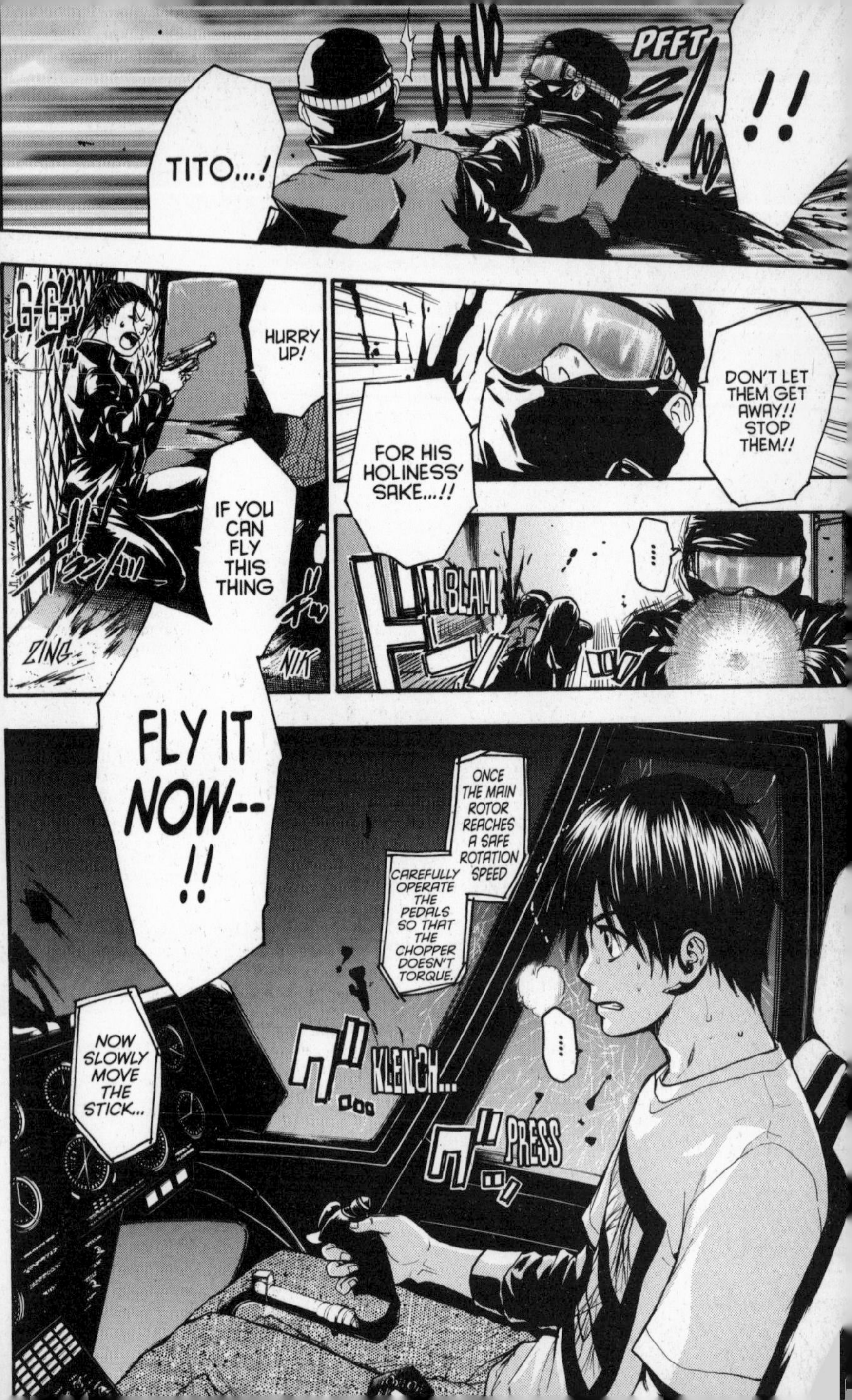
!!
PFFT
TITO...!
DON'T LET THEM GET AWAY!! STOP THEM!!
FOR HIS HOLINESS' SAKE...!!
...
BLAM
HURRY UP!
IF YOU CAN FLY THIS THING
G-G-
ZING
NIK
FLY IT NOW--!!
ONCE THE MAIN ROTOR REACHES A SAFE ROTATION SPEED
CAREFULLY OPERATE THE PEDALS SO THAT THE CHOPPER DOESN'T TORQUE.
...
KLENCH...
PRESS
NOW SLOWLY MOVE THE STICK...

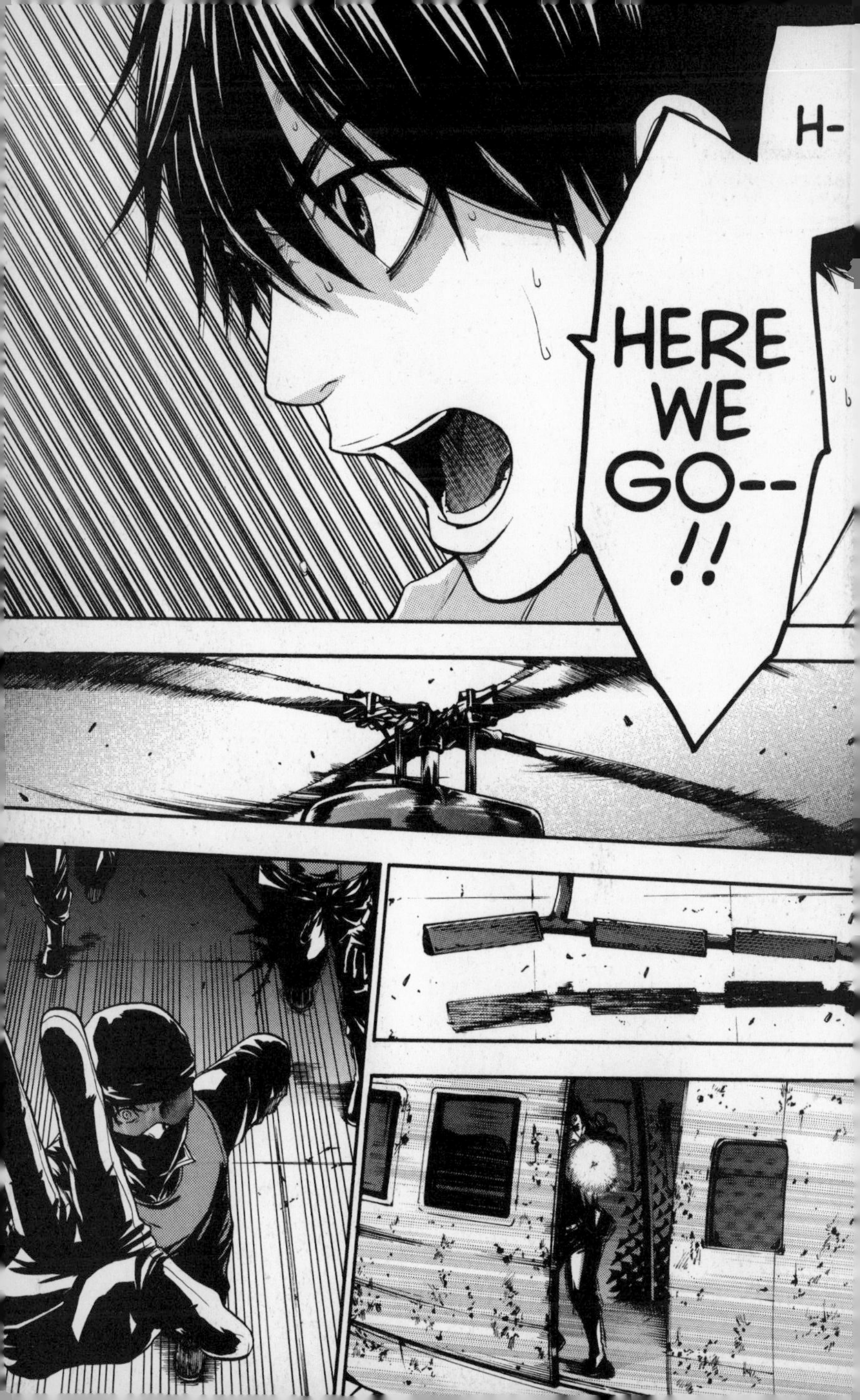
H-
HERE WE GO--!!

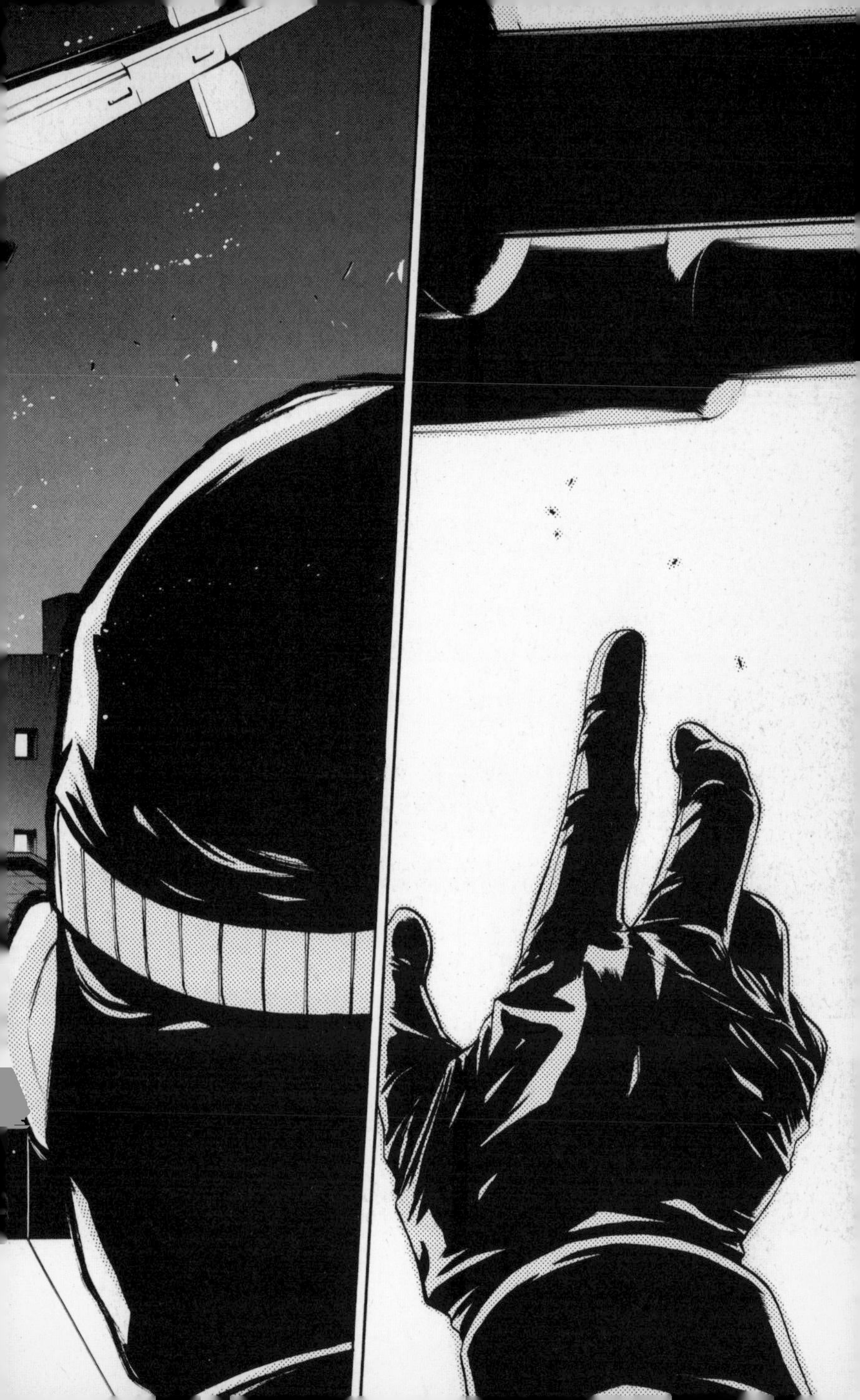

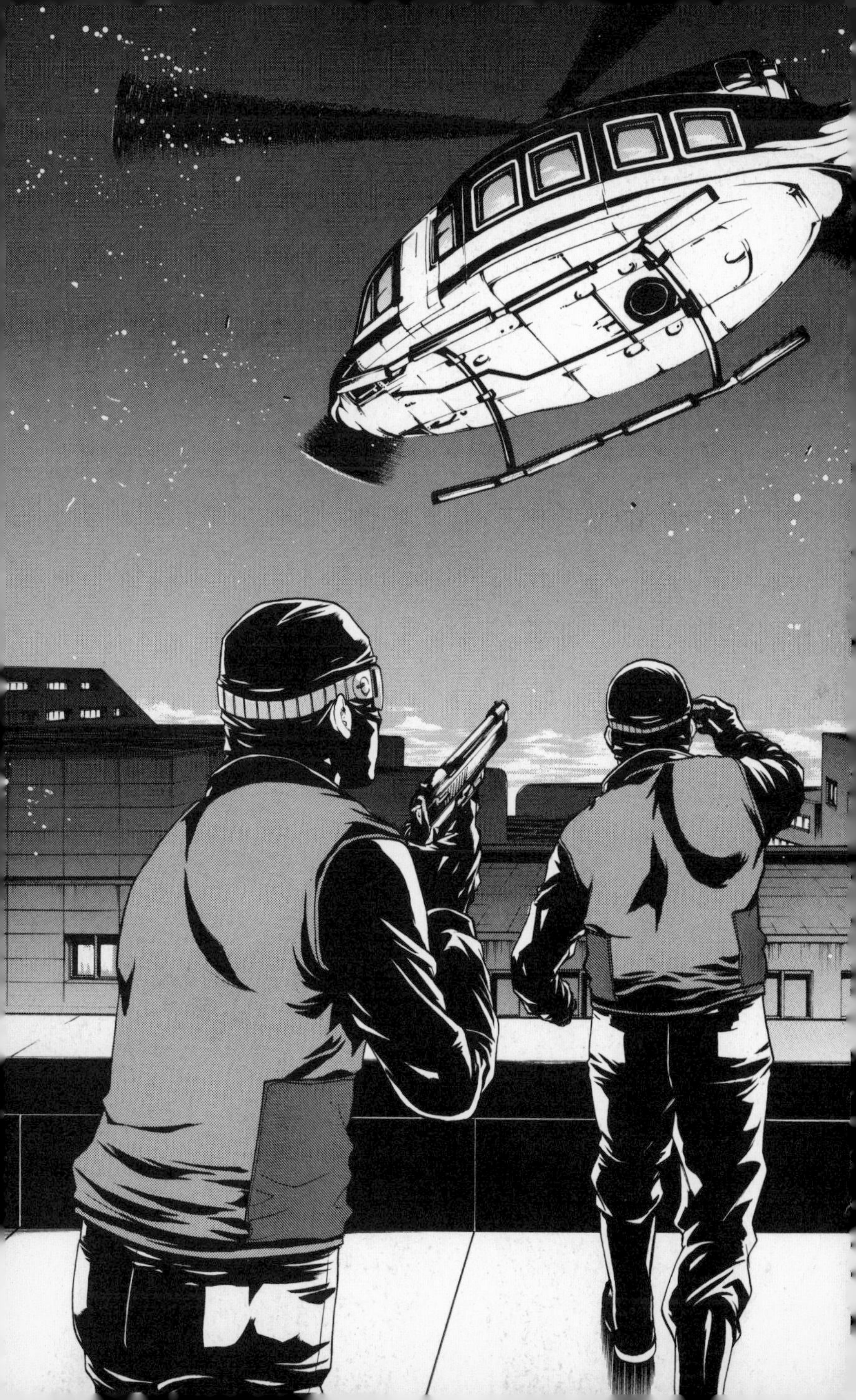

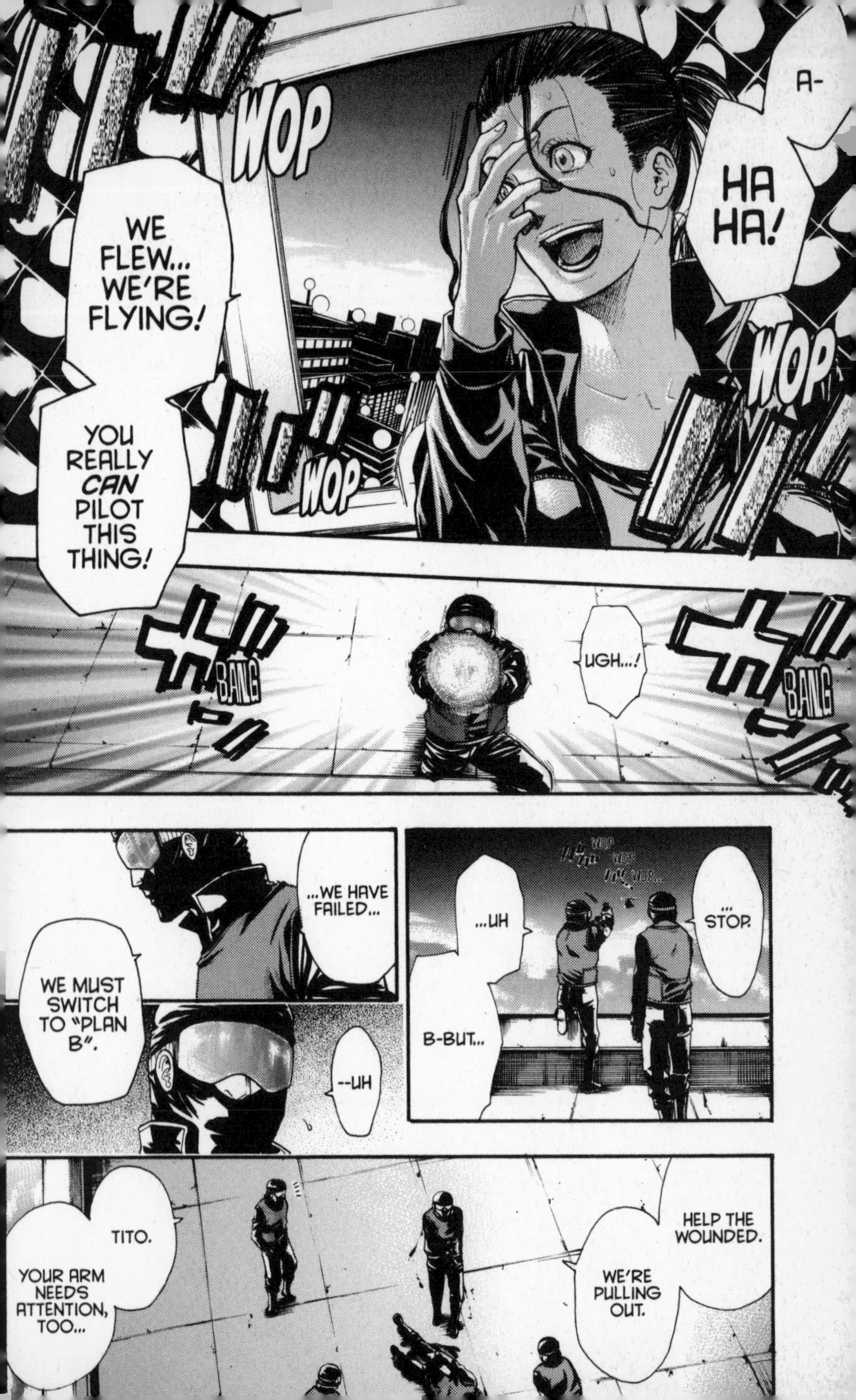
A-
HA HA!
WOP
WOP
WE FLEW... WE'RE FLYING!
YOU REALLY *CAN* PILOT THIS THING!
WOP
BANG
UGH...!
BANG
WOP WOP WOP...
... STOP.
...UH
B-BUT...
...WE HAVE FAILED...
WE MUST SWITCH TO "PLAN B".
--UH
HELP THE WOUNDED.
WE'RE PULLING OUT.
TITO.
YOUR ARM NEEDS ATTENTION, TOO...

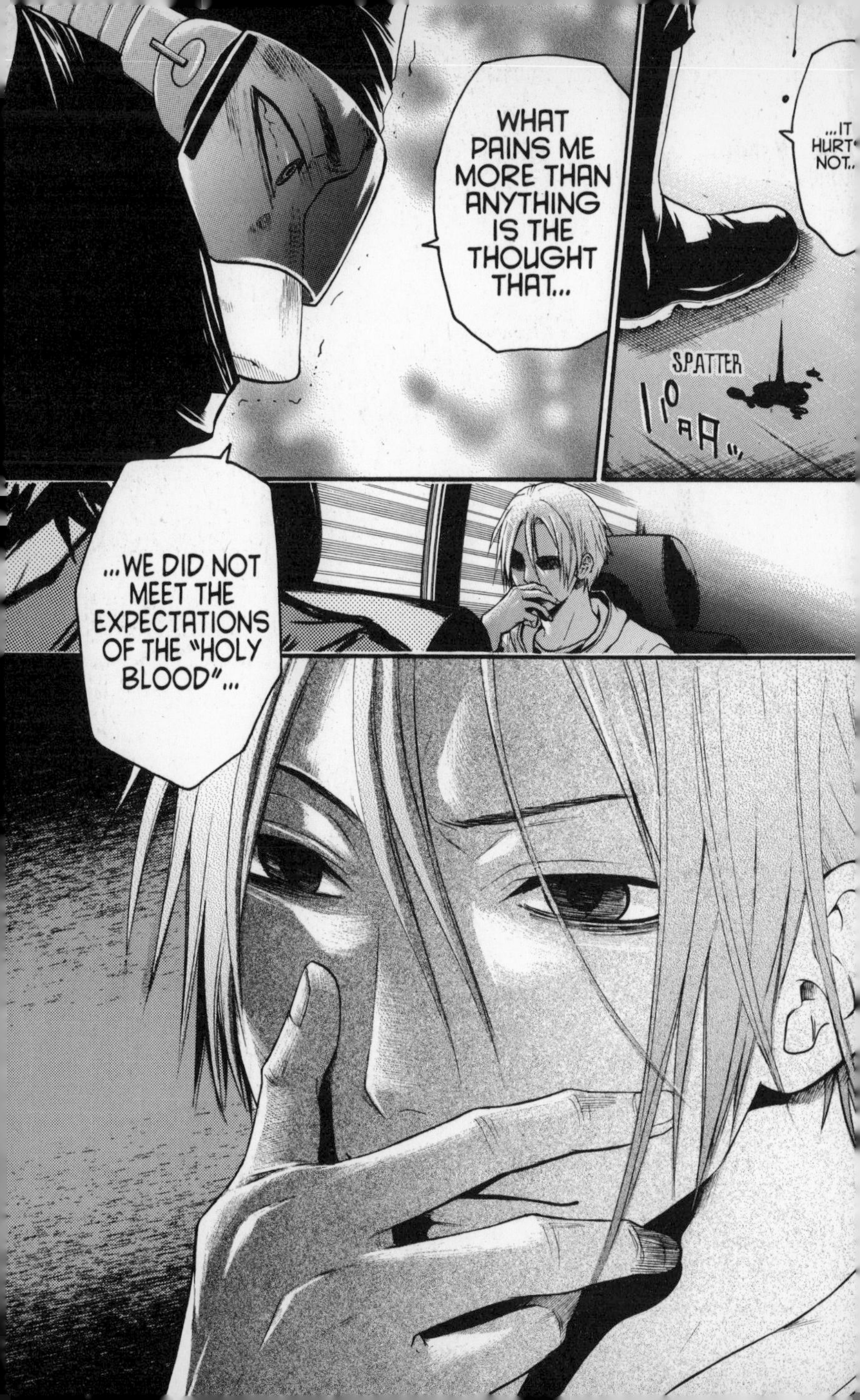
...IT HURT NOT...
SPATTER
WHAT PAINS ME MORE THAN ANYTHING IS THE THOUGHT THAT...
...WE DID NOT MEET THE EXPECTATIONS OF THE "HOLY BLOOD"...

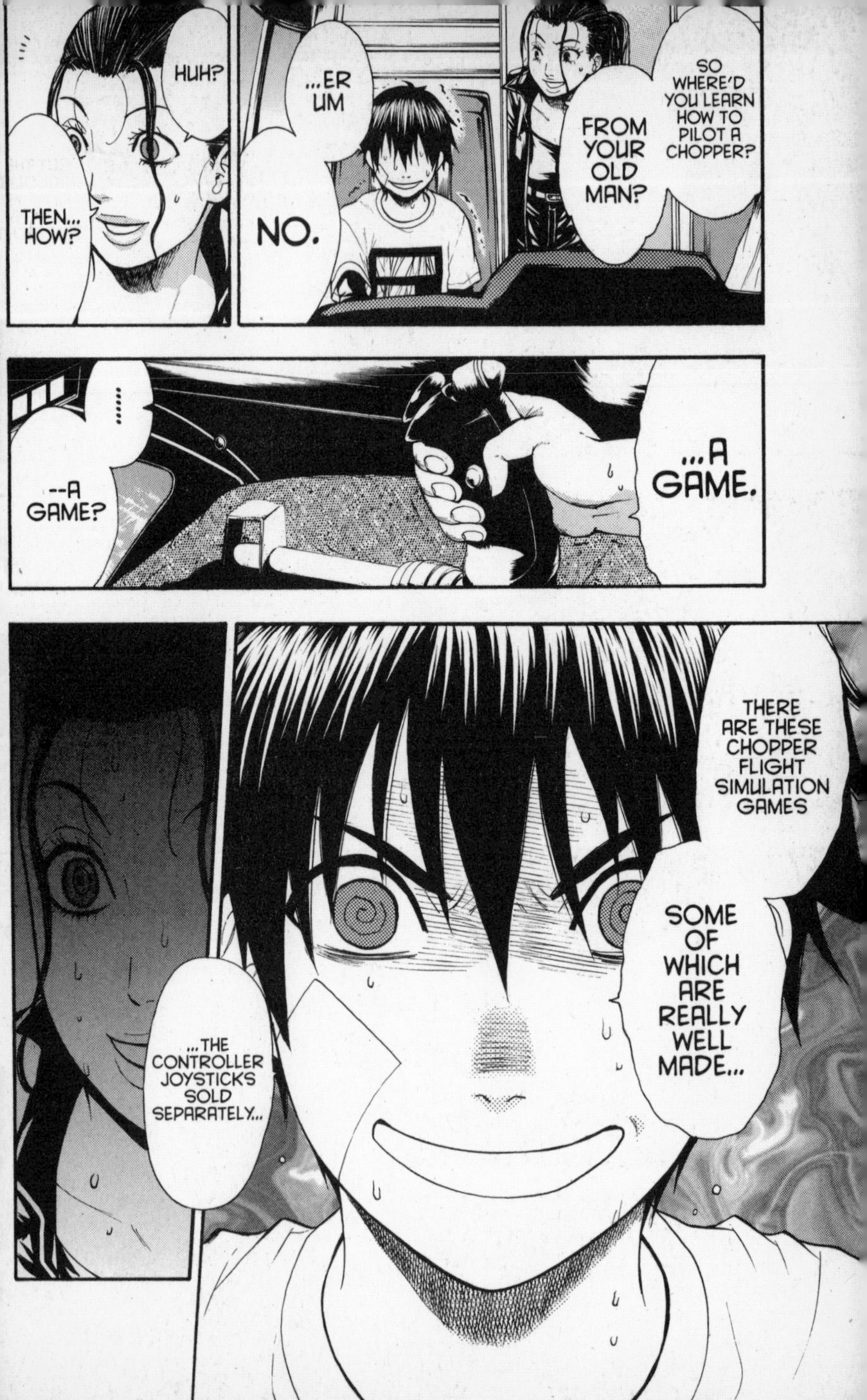
SO WHERE'D YOU LEARN HOW TO PILOT A CHOPPER?
FROM YOUR OLD MAN?
...ER UM
NO.
HUH?
THEN... HOW?
...A GAME.
......
--A GAME?
THERE ARE THESE CHOPPER FLIGHT SIMULATION GAMES
SOME OF WHICH ARE REALLY WELL MADE...
...THE CONTROLLER JOYSTICKS SOLD SEPARATELY...

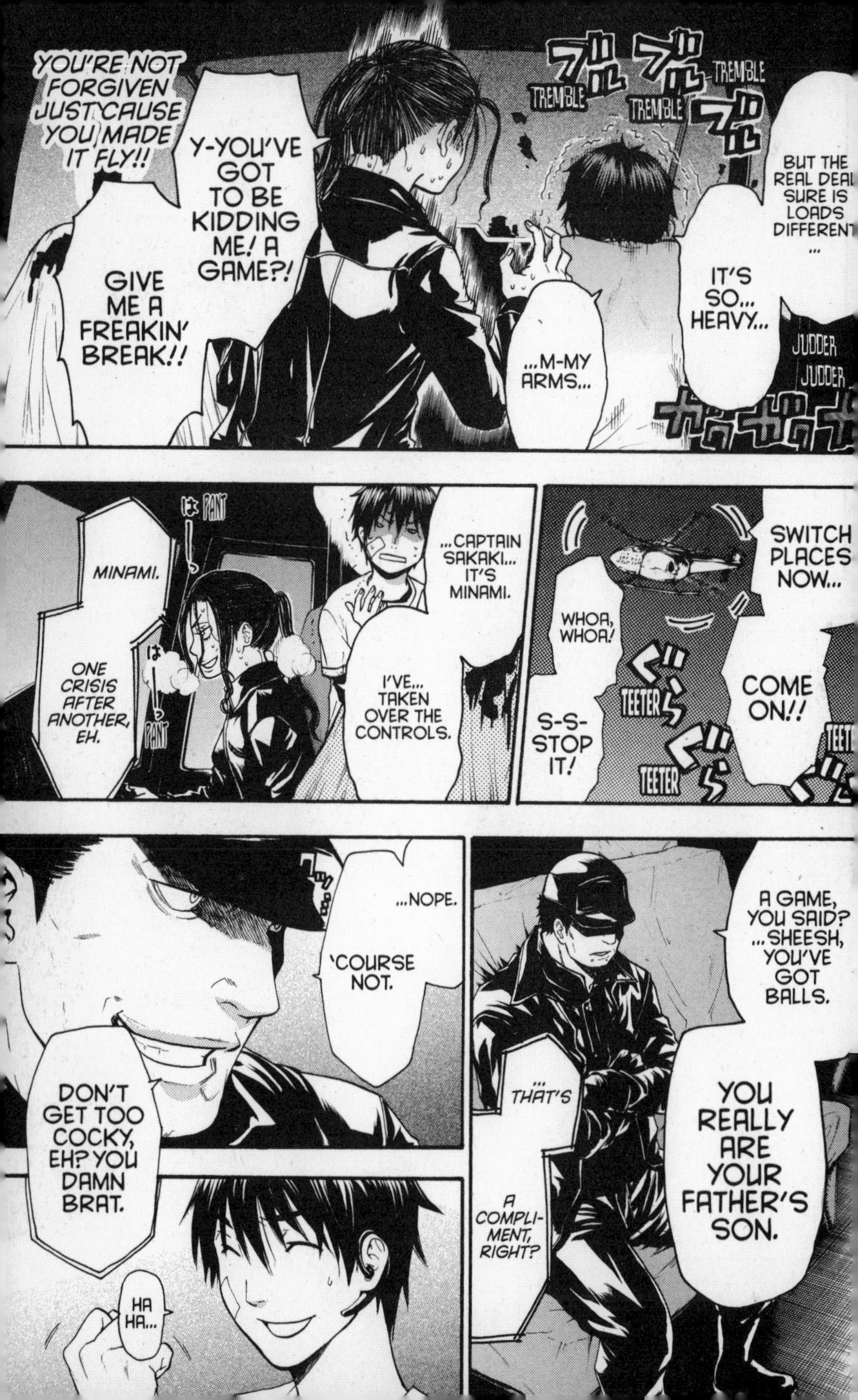
TREMBLE
TREMBLE
TREMBLE
BUT THE REAL DEAL SURE IS LOADS DIFFERENT...
IT'S SO... HEAVY...
JUDDER
JUDDER
...M-MY ARMS...
Y-YOU'VE GOT TO BE KIDDING ME! A GAME?!
YOU'RE NOT FORGIVEN JUST 'CAUSE YOU MADE IT FLY!!
GIVE ME A FREAKIN' BREAK!!
SWITCH PLACES NOW...
COME ON!!
WHOA, WHOA!
TEETER
TEETER
S-S-STOP IT!
...CAPTAIN SAKAKI... IT'S MINAMI.
I'VE... TAKEN OVER THE CONTROLS.
PANT
MINAMI.
ONE CRISIS AFTER ANOTHER, EH.
PANT
A GAME, YOU SAID? ...SHEESH, YOU'VE GOT BALLS.
YOU REALLY ARE YOUR FATHER'S SON.
...THAT'S
A COMPLIMENT, RIGHT?
...NOPE.
'COURSE NOT.
DON'T GET TOO COCKY, EH? YOU DAMN BRAT.
HA HA...

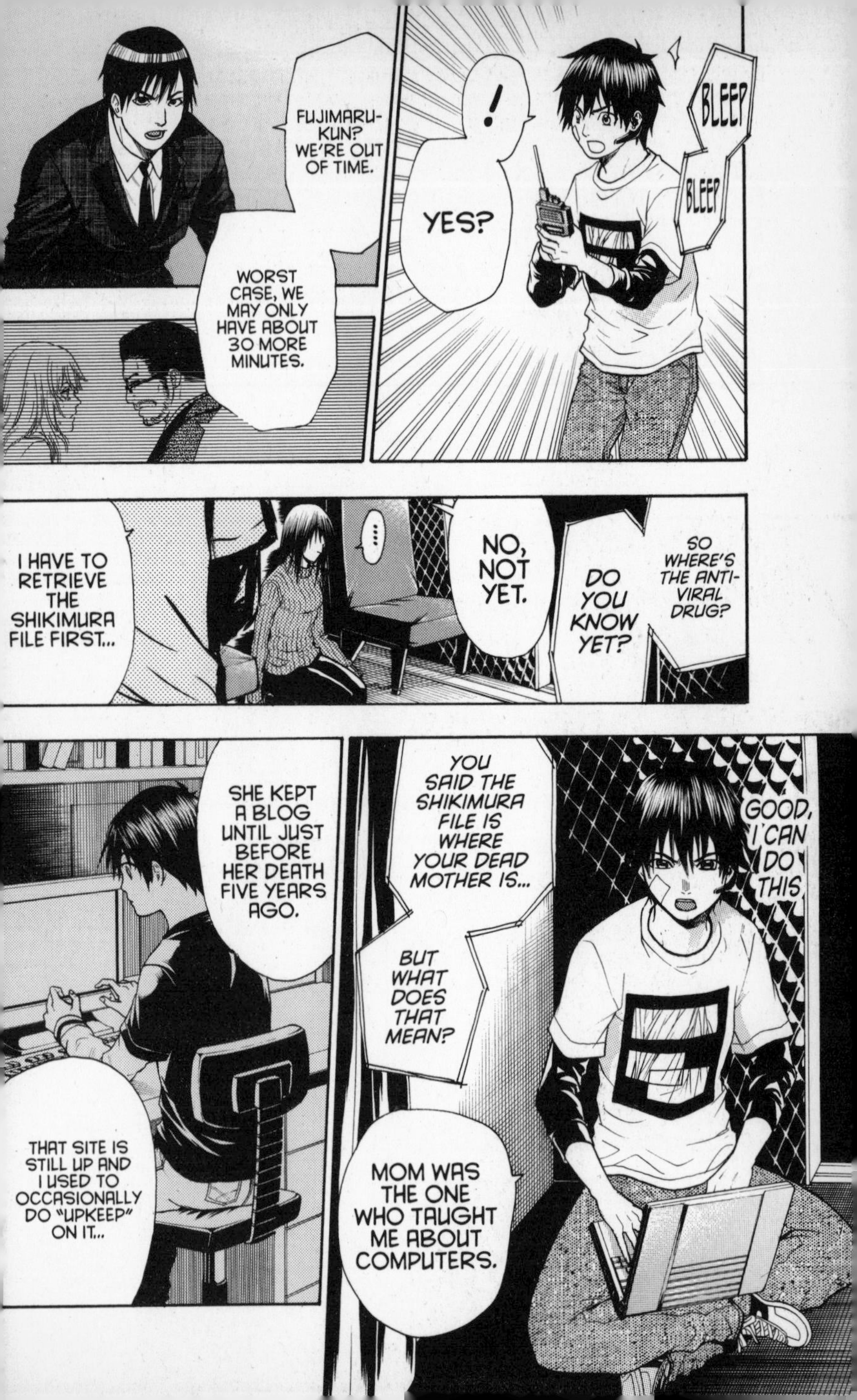
BLEEP
BLEEP
!
YES?
FUJIMARU-KUN? WE'RE OUT OF TIME.
WORST CASE, WE MAY ONLY HAVE ABOUT 30 MORE MINUTES.
SO WHERE'S THE ANTI-VIRAL DRUG?
DO YOU KNOW YET?
NO, NOT YET.
....
I HAVE TO RETRIEVE THE SHIKIMURA FILE FIRST...
GOOD, I CAN DO THIS.
YOU SAID THE SHIKIMURA FILE IS WHERE YOUR DEAD MOTHER IS...
BUT WHAT DOES THAT MEAN?
MOM WAS THE ONE WHO TAUGHT ME ABOUT COMPUTERS.
SHE KEPT A BLOG UNTIL JUST BEFORE HER DEATH FIVE YEARS AGO.
THAT SITE IS STILL UP AND I USED TO OCCASIONALLY DO "UPKEEP" ON IT...

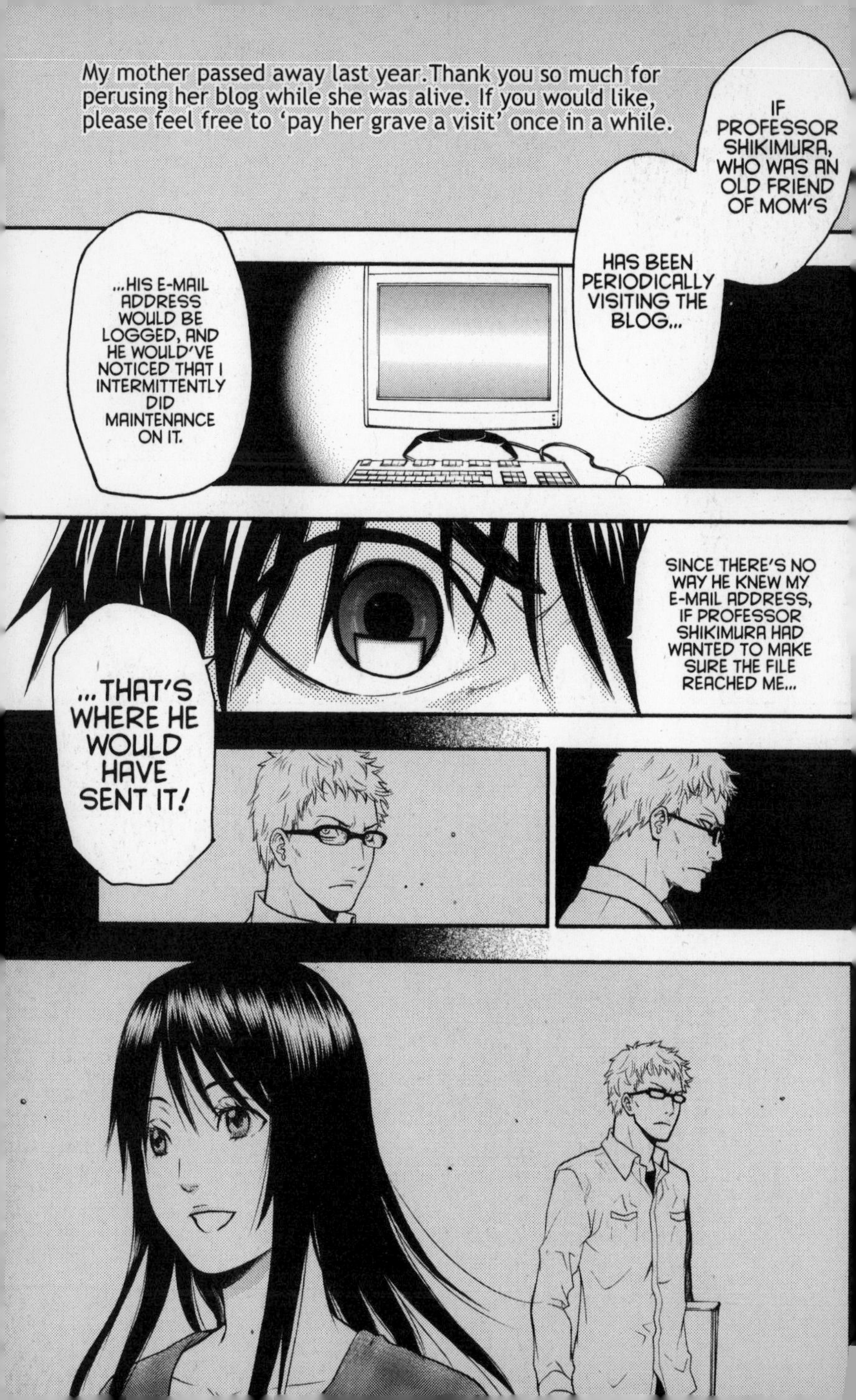
My mother passed away last year.Thank you so much for perusing her blog while she was alive. If you would like, please feel free to 'pay her grave a visit' once in a while.
IF PROFESSOR SHIKIMURA, WHO WAS AN OLD FRIEND OF MOM'S
HAS BEEN PERIODICALLY VISITING THE BLOG...
...HIS E-MAIL ADDRESS WOULD BE LOGGED, AND HE WOULD'VE NOTICED THAT I INTERMITTENTLY DID MAINTENANCE ON IT.
SINCE THERE'S NO WAY HE KNEW MY E-MAIL ADDRESS, IF PROFESSOR SHIKIMURA HAD WANTED TO MAKE SURE THE FILE REACHED ME...
...THAT'S WHERE HE WOULD HAVE SENT IT!

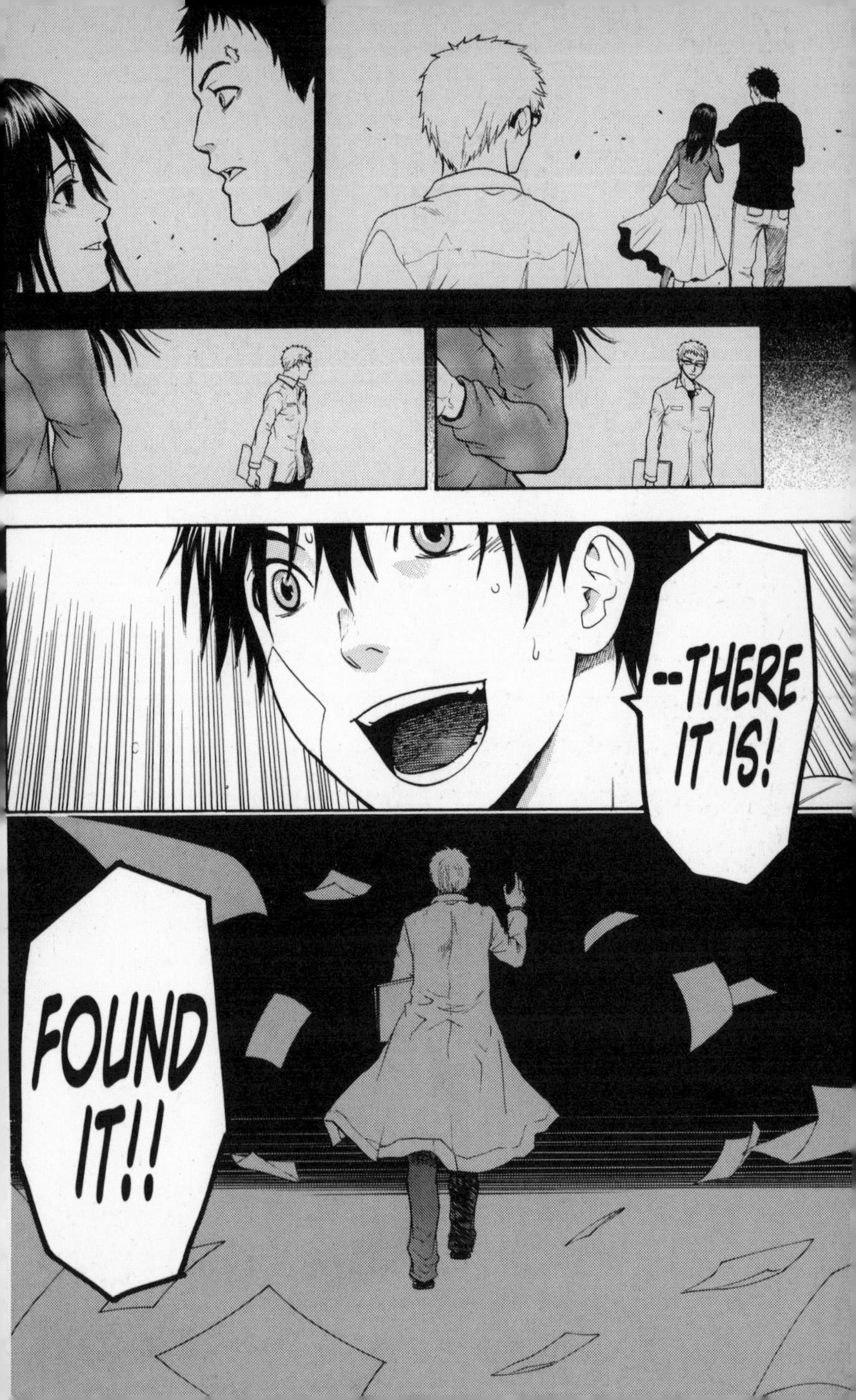
--THERE IT IS!
FOUND IT!!

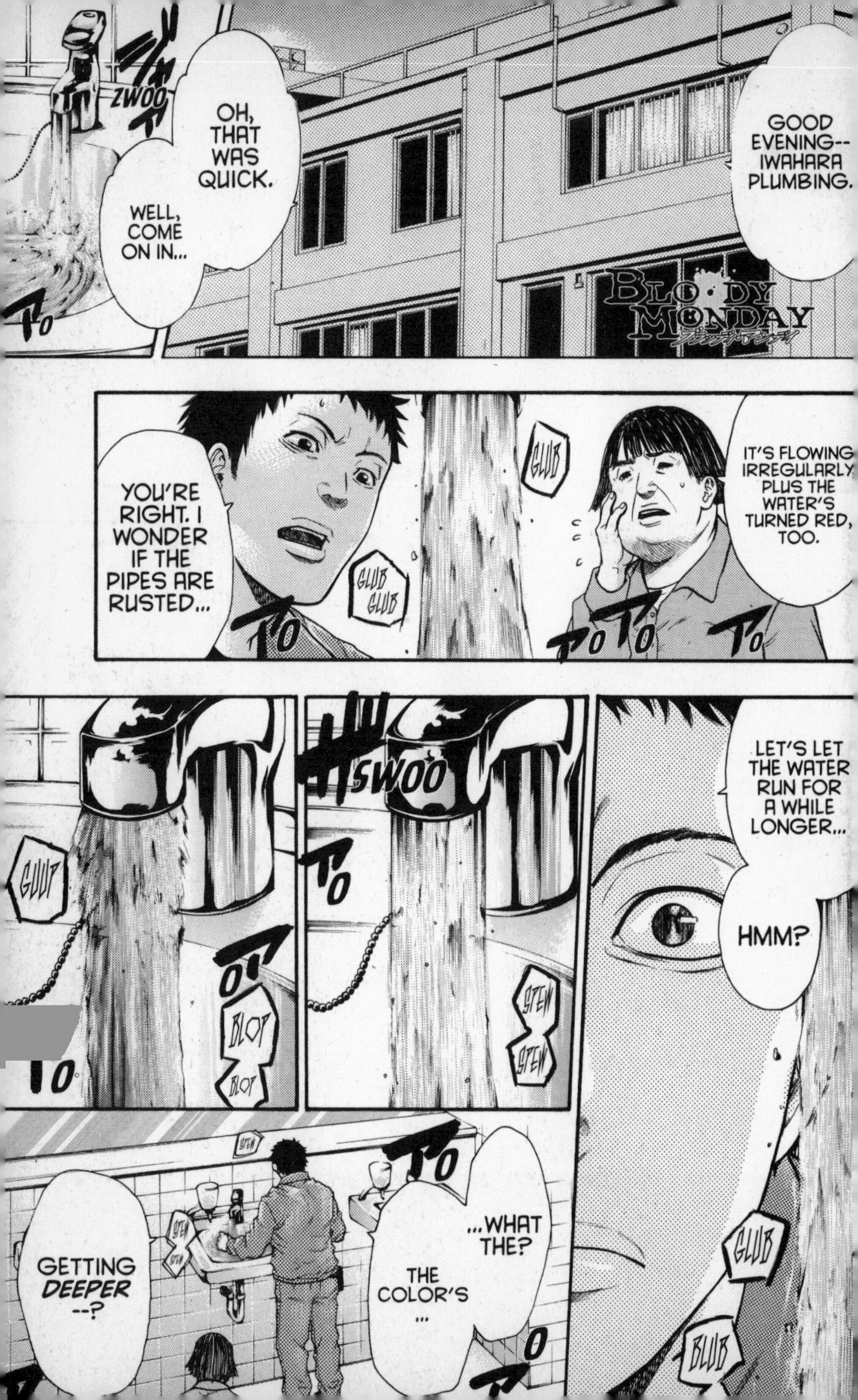
GOOD EVENING-- IWAHARA PLUMBING.
ZWOO
OH, THAT WAS QUICK.
WELL, COME ON IN...
BLOODY MONDAY
IT'S FLOWING IRREGULARLY, PLUS THE WATER'S TURNED RED, TOO.
GLUB
YOU'RE RIGHT. I WONDER IF THE PIPES ARE RUSTED...
GLUB GLUB
LET'S LET THE WATER RUN FOR A WHILE LONGER...
HMM?
GLUB
BLUB
SWOO
SPEW
SPEW
GLUP
BLOP
BLOP
...WHAT THE?
THE COLOR'S ...
SPEW
GETTING DEEPER --?

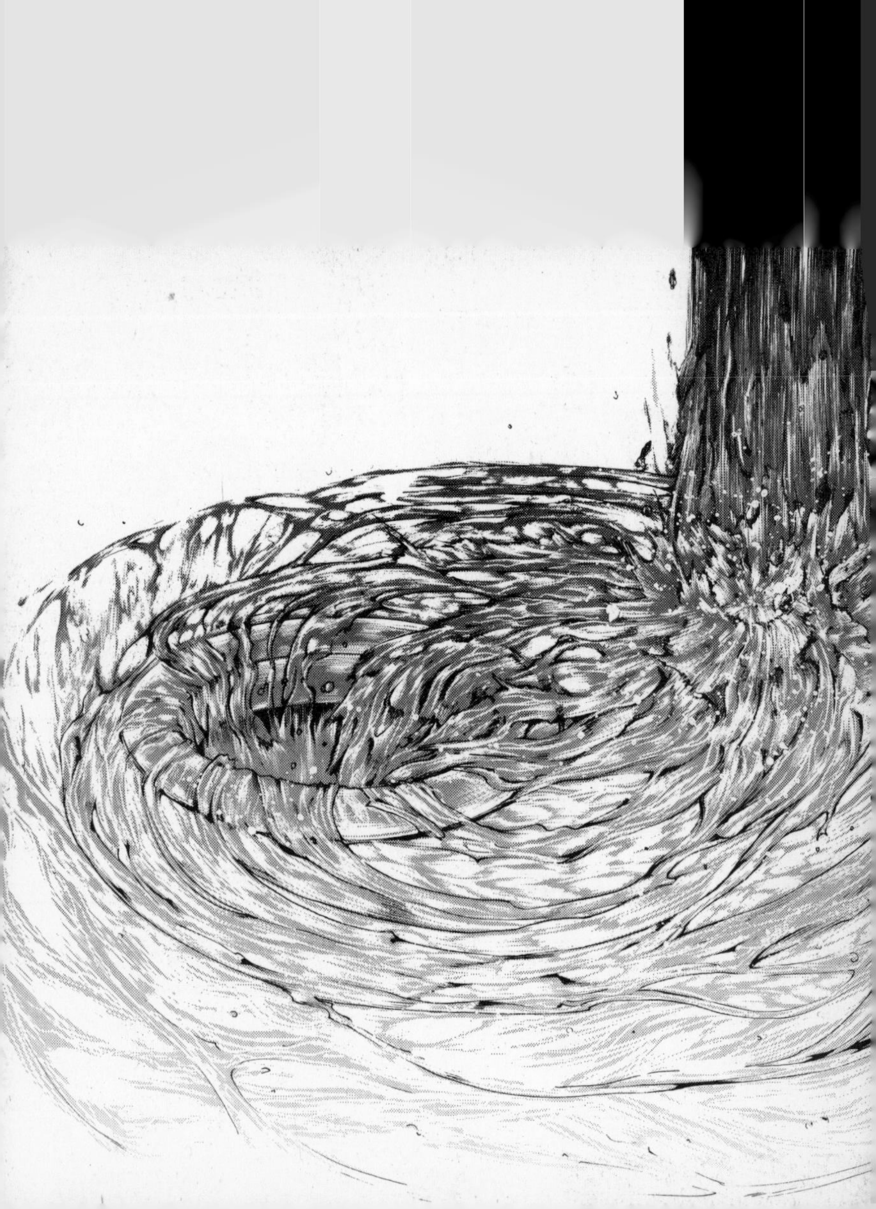

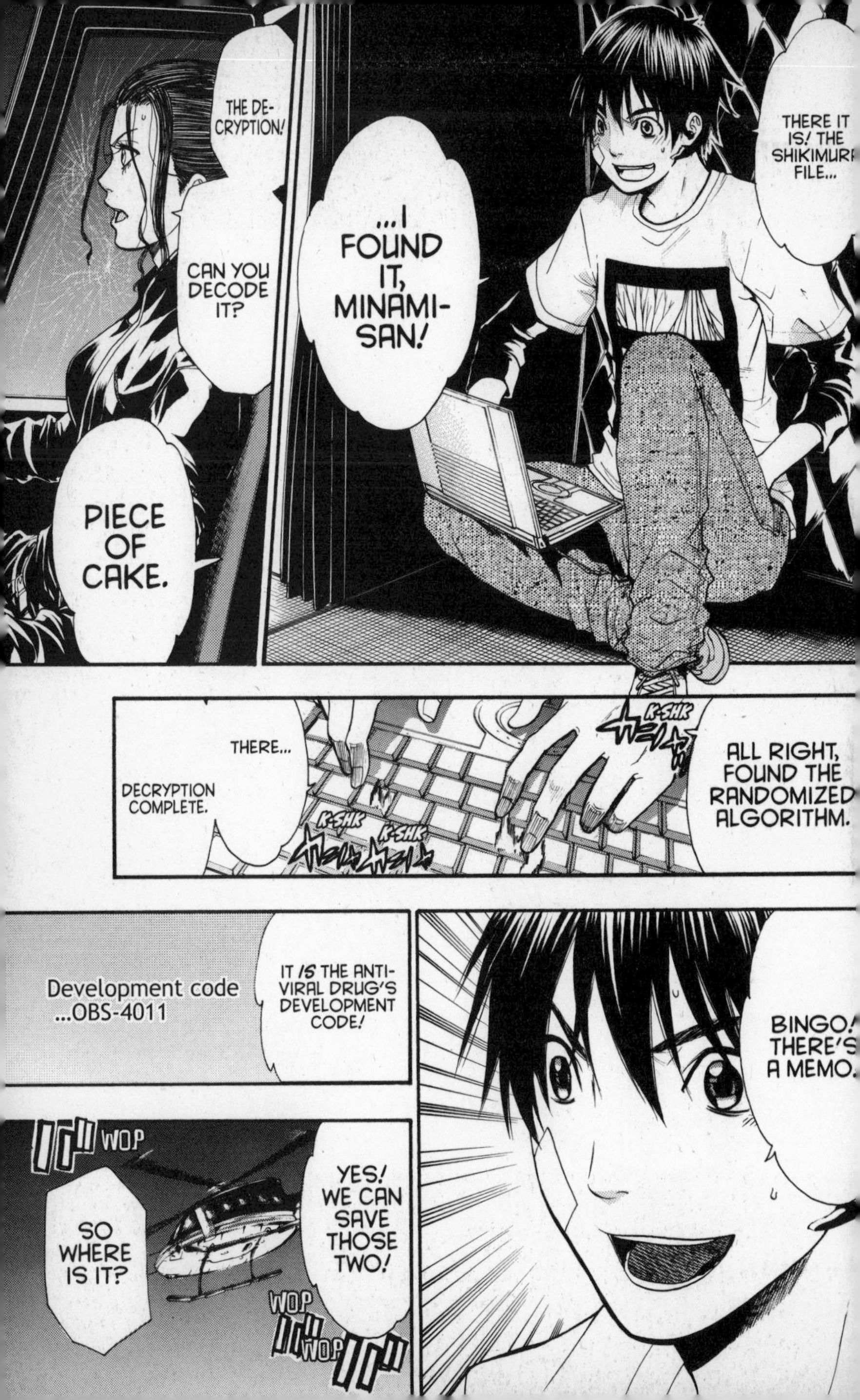
THERE IT IS! THE SHIKIMUR FILE...
...I FOUND IT, MINAMI-SAN!
THE DE-CRYPTION!
CAN YOU DECODE IT?
PIECE OF CAKE.
K-SHK
ALL RIGHT, FOUND THE RANDOMIZED ALGORITHM.
K-SHK
K-SHK
THERE...
DECRYPTION COMPLETE.
BINGO! THERE'S A MEMO.
IT IS THE ANTI-VIRAL DRUG'S DEVELOPMENT CODE!
Development code ...OBS-4011
WOP
YES! WE CAN SAVE THOSE TWO!
SO WHERE IS IT?
WOP
WOP

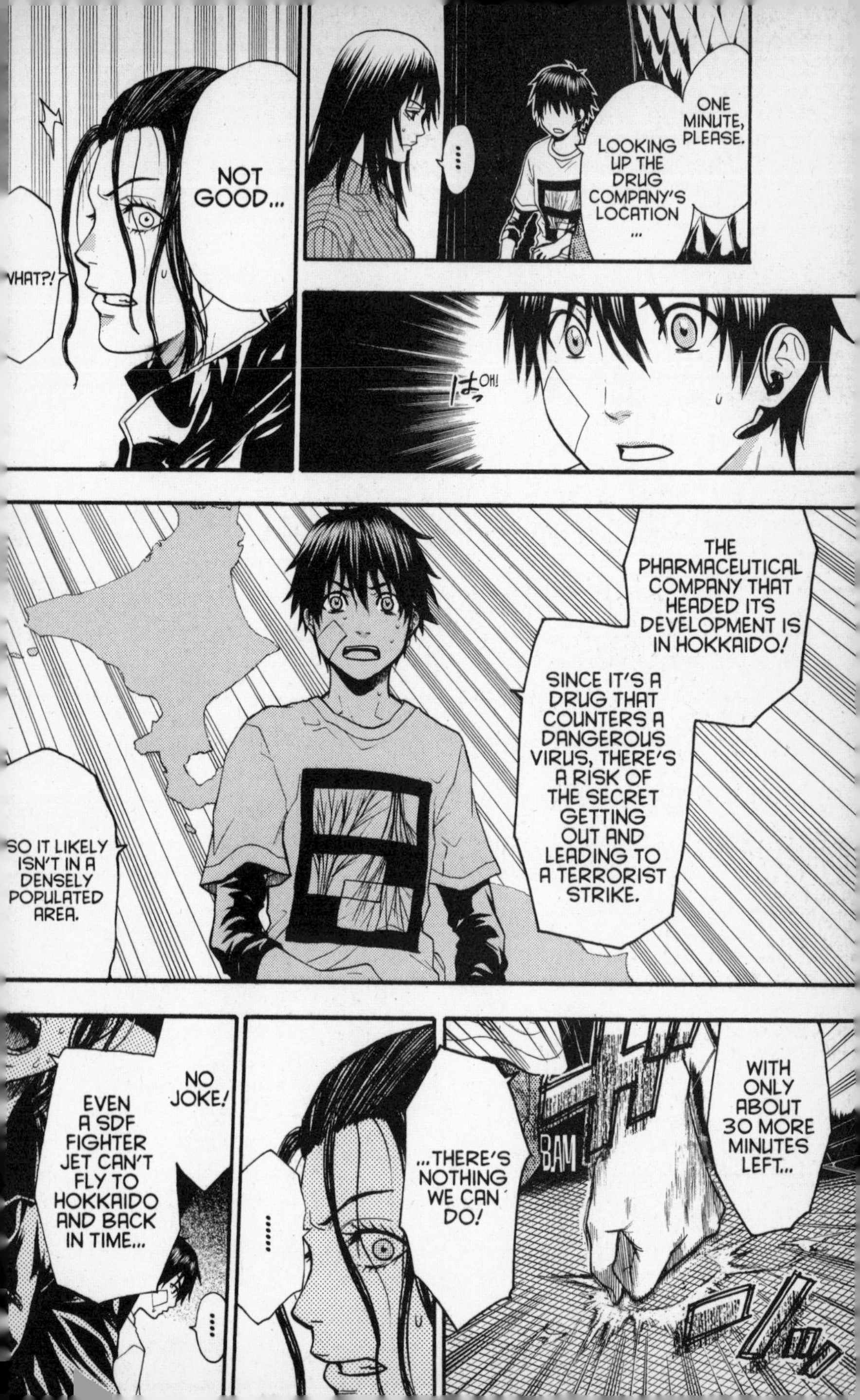
ONE MINUTE, PLEASE.
LOOKING UP THE DRUG COMPANY'S LOCATION ...
....
はっ OH!
NOT GOOD...
WHAT?!
THE PHARMACEUTICAL COMPANY THAT HEADED ITS DEVELOPMENT IS IN HOKKAIDO!
SINCE IT'S A DRUG THAT COUNTERS A DANGEROUS VIRUS, THERE'S A RISK OF THE SECRET GETTING OUT AND LEADING TO A TERRORIST STRIKE.
SO IT LIKELY ISN'T IN A DENSELY POPULATED AREA.
WITH ONLY ABOUT 30 MORE MINUTES LEFT...
BAM
...THERE'S NOTHING WE CAN DO!
......
NO JOKE!
EVEN A SDF FIGHTER JET CAN'T FLY TO HOKKAIDO AND BACK IN TIME...
....

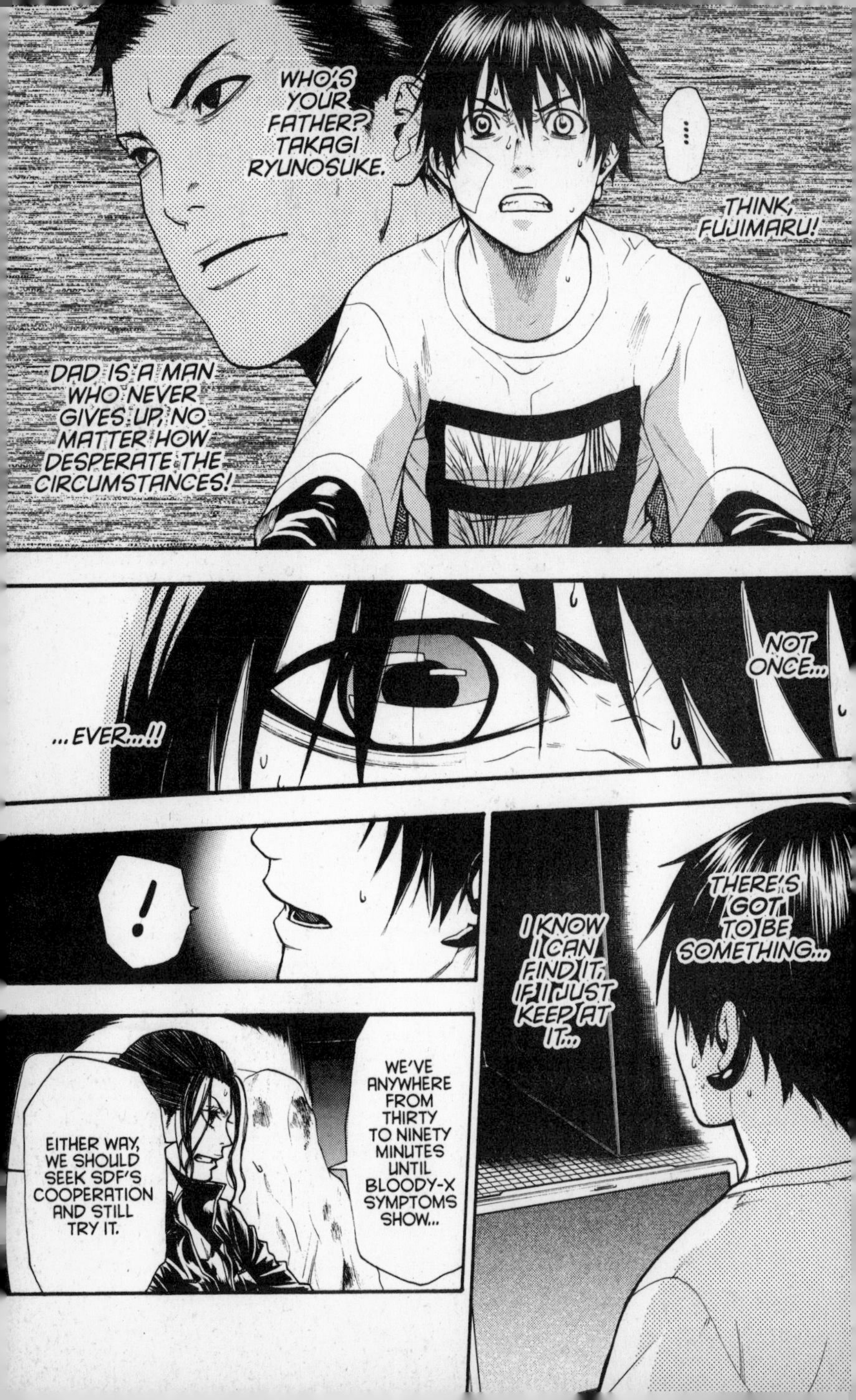
WHO'S YOUR FATHER? TAKAGI RYUNOSUKE.
...
THINK, FUJIMARU!
DAD IS A MAN WHO NEVER GIVES UP, NO MATTER HOW DESPERATE THE CIRCUMSTANCES!
NOT ONCE...
...EVER...!!
THERE'S GOT TO BE SOMETHING...
I KNOW I CAN FIND IT, IF I JUST KEEP AT IT...
!
WE'VE ANYWHERE FROM THIRTY TO NINETY MINUTES UNTIL BLOODY-X SYMPTOMS SHOW...
EITHER WAY, WE SHOULD SEEK SDF'S COOPERATION AND STILL TRY IT.

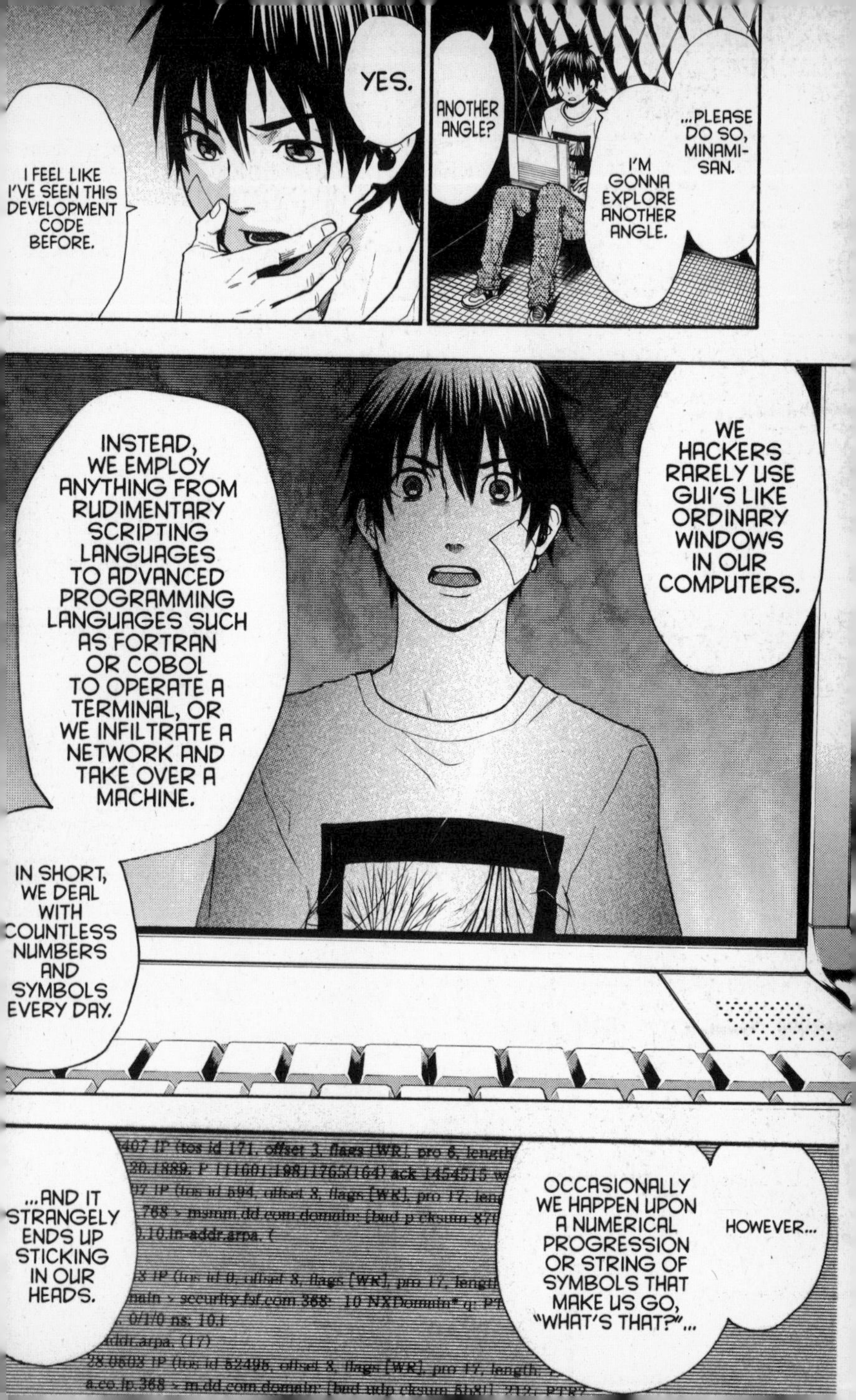
...PLEASE DO SO, MINAMI-SAN.
I'M GONNA EXPLORE ANOTHER ANGLE.
ANOTHER ANGLE?
YES.
I FEEL LIKE I'VE SEEN THIS DEVELOPMENT CODE BEFORE.
WE HACKERS RARELY USE GUI'S LIKE ORDINARY WINDOWS IN OUR COMPUTERS.
INSTEAD, WE EMPLOY ANYTHING FROM RUDIMENTARY SCRIPTING LANGUAGES TO ADVANCED PROGRAMMING LANGUAGES SUCH AS FORTRAN OR COBOL TO OPERATE A TERMINAL, OR WE INFILTRATE A NETWORK AND TAKE OVER A MACHINE.
IN SHORT, WE DEAL WITH COUNTLESS NUMBERS AND SYMBOLS EVERY DAY.
HOWEVER...
OCCASIONALLY WE HAPPEN UPON A NUMERICAL PROGRESSION OR STRING OF SYMBOLS THAT MAKE US GO, "WHAT'S THAT?"...
...AND IT STRANGELY ENDS UP STICKING IN OUR HEADS.

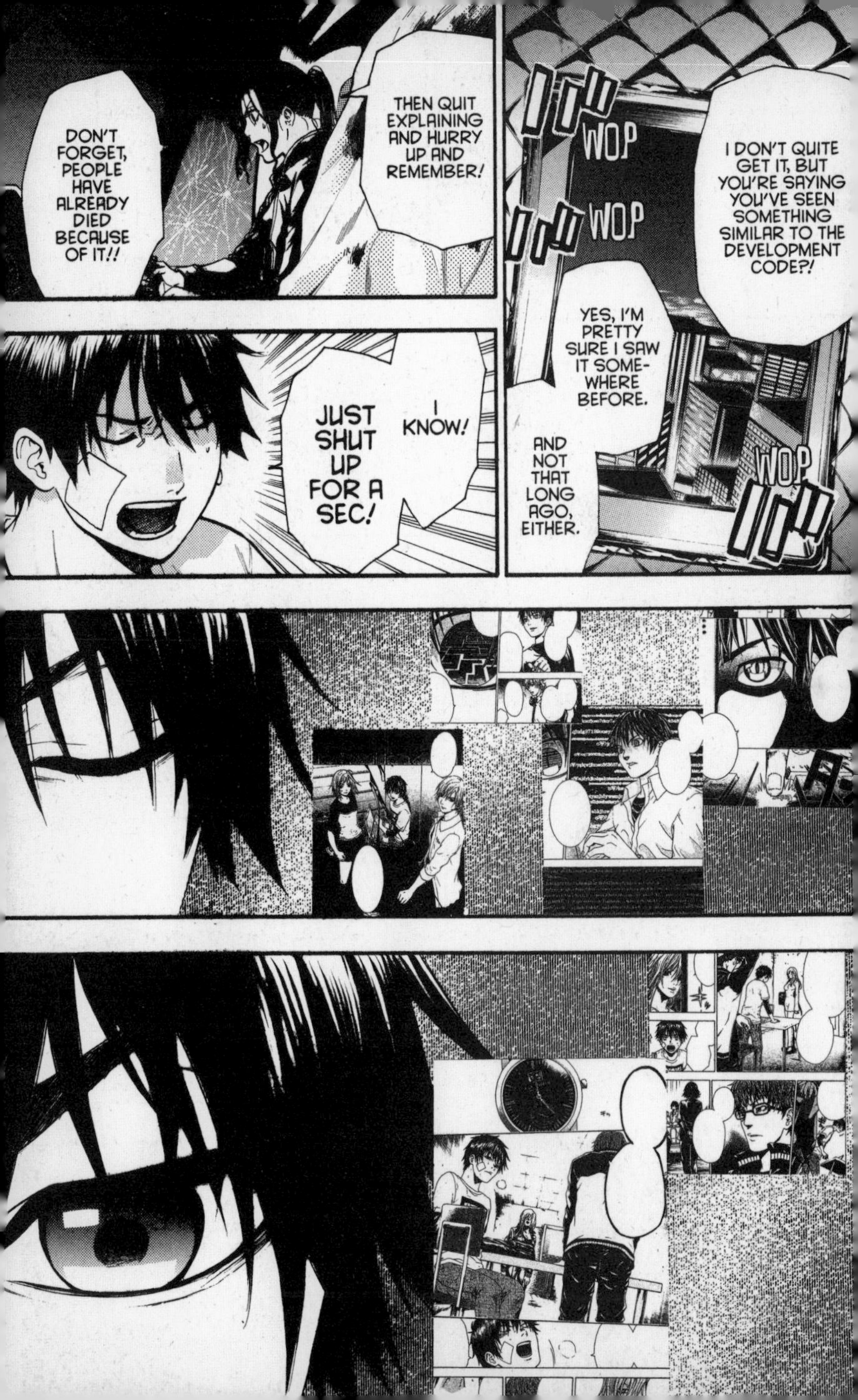
I DON'T QUITE GET IT, BUT YOU'RE SAYING YOU'VE SEEN SOMETHING SIMILAR TO THE DEVELOPMENT CODE?!
WOP
WOP
YES, I'M PRETTY SURE I SAW IT SOME-WHERE BEFORE.
AND NOT THAT LONG AGO, EITHER.
WOP
THEN QUIT EXPLAINING AND HURRY UP AND REMEMBER!
DON'T FORGET, PEOPLE HAVE ALREADY DIED BECAUSE OF IT!!
I KNOW!
JUST SHUT UP FOR A SEC!

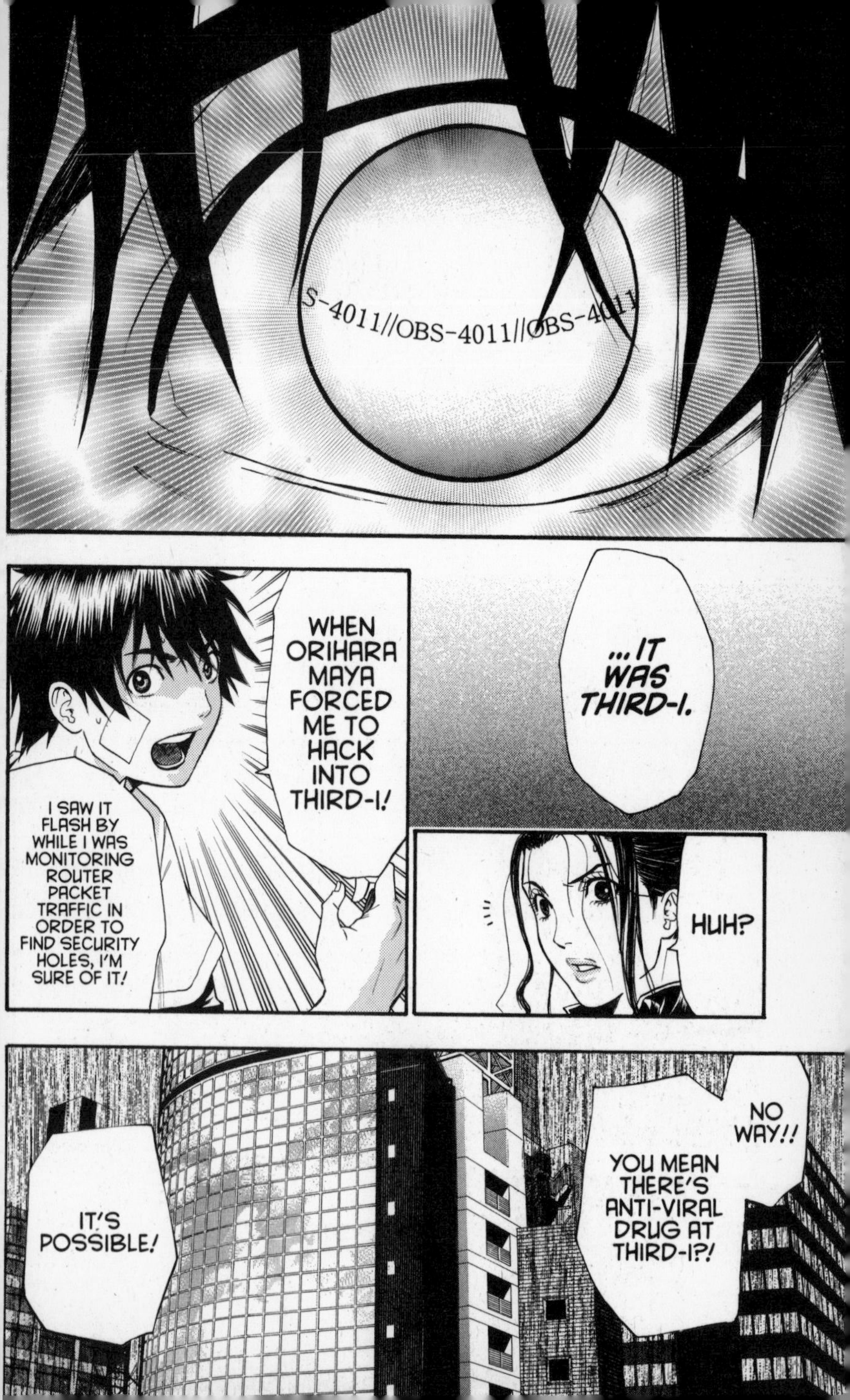
S-4011//OBS-4011//OBS-4011
...IT WAS THIRD-I.
HUH?
WHEN ORIHARA MAYA FORCED ME TO HACK INTO THIRD-I!
I SAW IT FLASH BY WHILE I WAS MONITORING ROUTER PACKET TRAFFIC IN ORDER TO FIND SECURITY HOLES, I'M SURE OF IT!
NO WAY!!
YOU MEAN THERE'S ANTI-VIRAL DRUG AT THIRD-I?!
IT'S POSSIBLE!

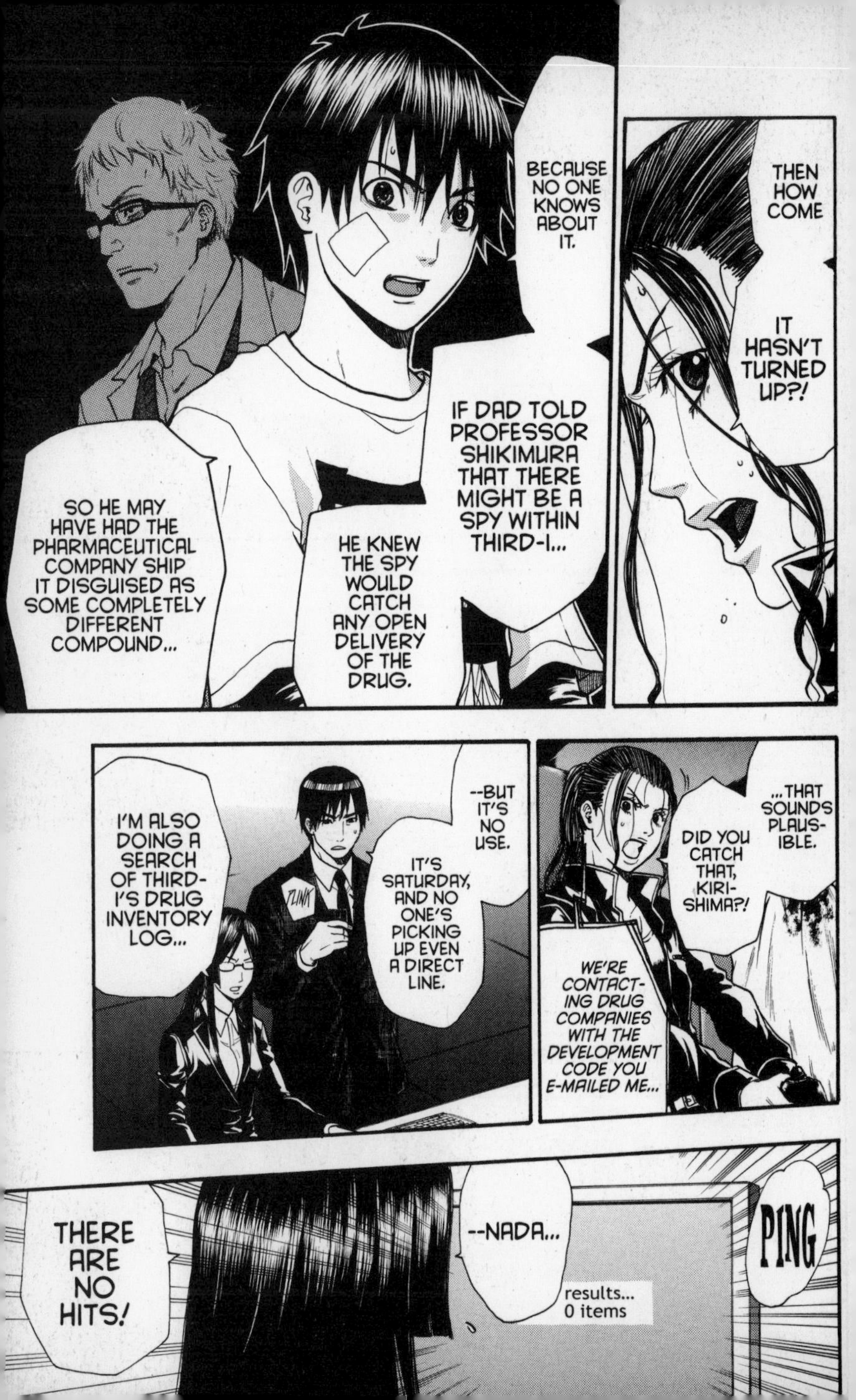

THEN HOW COME
IT HASN'T TURNED UP?!
BECAUSE NO ONE KNOWS ABOUT IT.
IF DAD TOLD PROFESSOR SHIKIMURA THAT THERE MIGHT BE A SPY WITHIN THIRD-I...
HE KNEW THE SPY WOULD CATCH ANY OPEN DELIVERY OF THE DRUG.
SO HE MAY HAVE HAD THE PHARMACEUTICAL COMPANY SHIP IT DISGUISED AS SOME COMPLETELY DIFFERENT COMPOUND...
...THAT SOUNDS PLAUS-IBLE.
DID YOU CATCH THAT, KIRI-SHIMA?!
WE'RE CONTACT-ING DRUG COMPANIES WITH THE DEVELOPMENT CODE YOU E-MAILED ME...
--BUT IT'S NO USE.
IT'S SATURDAY, AND NO ONE'S PICKING UP EVEN A DIRECT LINE.
PLINK
I'M ALSO DOING A SEARCH OF THIRD-I'S DRUG INVENTORY LOG...
PING
results... 0 items
--NADA...
THERE ARE NO HITS!

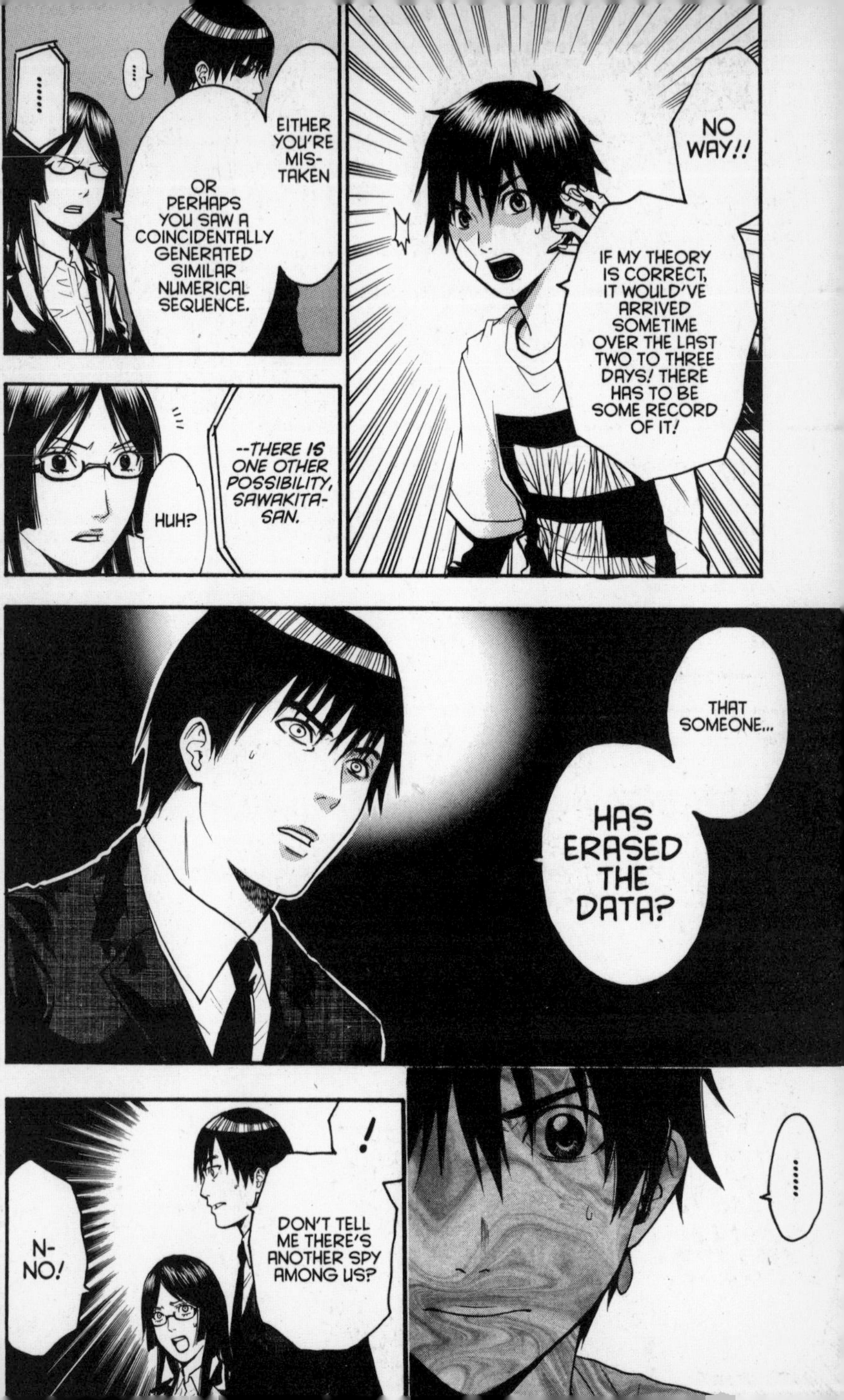

NO WAY!!
IF MY THEORY IS CORRECT, IT WOULD'VE ARRIVED SOMETIME OVER THE LAST TWO TO THREE DAYS! THERE HAS TO BE SOME RECORD OF IT!
EITHER YOU'RE MIS-TAKEN
OR PERHAPS YOU SAW A COINCIDENTALLY GENERATED SIMILAR NUMERICAL SEQUENCE.
...
......
--THERE IS ONE OTHER POSSIBILITY, SAWAKITA-SAN.
HUH?
THAT SOMEONE...
HAS ERASED THE DATA?
......
!
DON'T TELL ME THERE'S ANOTHER SPY AMONG US?
N-NO!

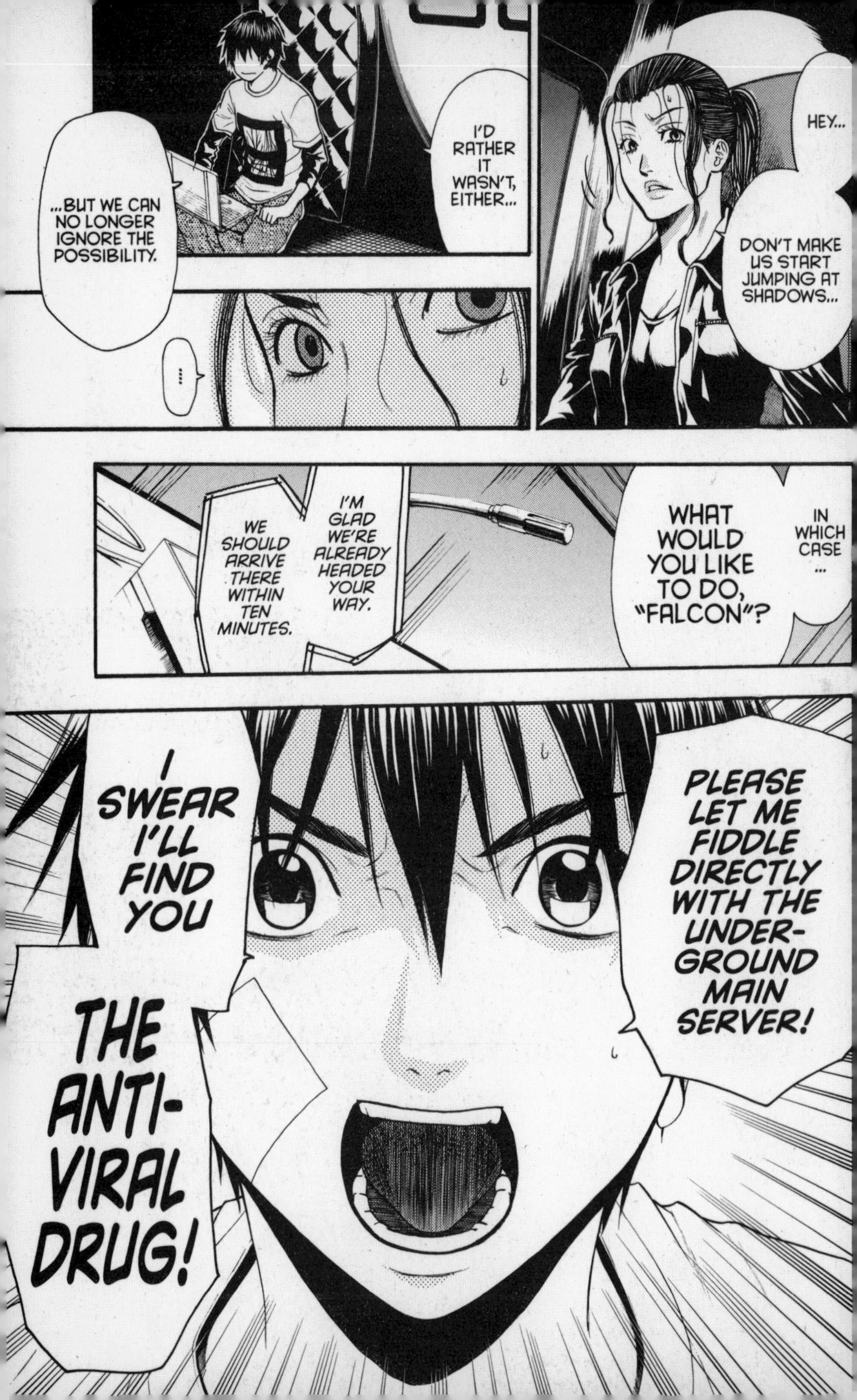
HEY...
DON'T MAKE US START JUMPING AT SHADOWS...
I'D RATHER IT WASN'T, EITHER...
...BUT WE CAN NO LONGER IGNORE THE POSSIBILITY.
.....
IN WHICH CASE...
WHAT WOULD YOU LIKE TO DO, "FALCON"?
I'M GLAD WE'RE ALREADY HEADED YOUR WAY.
WE SHOULD ARRIVE THERE WITHIN TEN MINUTES.
PLEASE LET ME FIDDLE DIRECTLY WITH THE UNDER-GROUND MAIN SERVER!
I SWEAR I'LL FIND YOU THE ANTI-VIRAL DRUG!

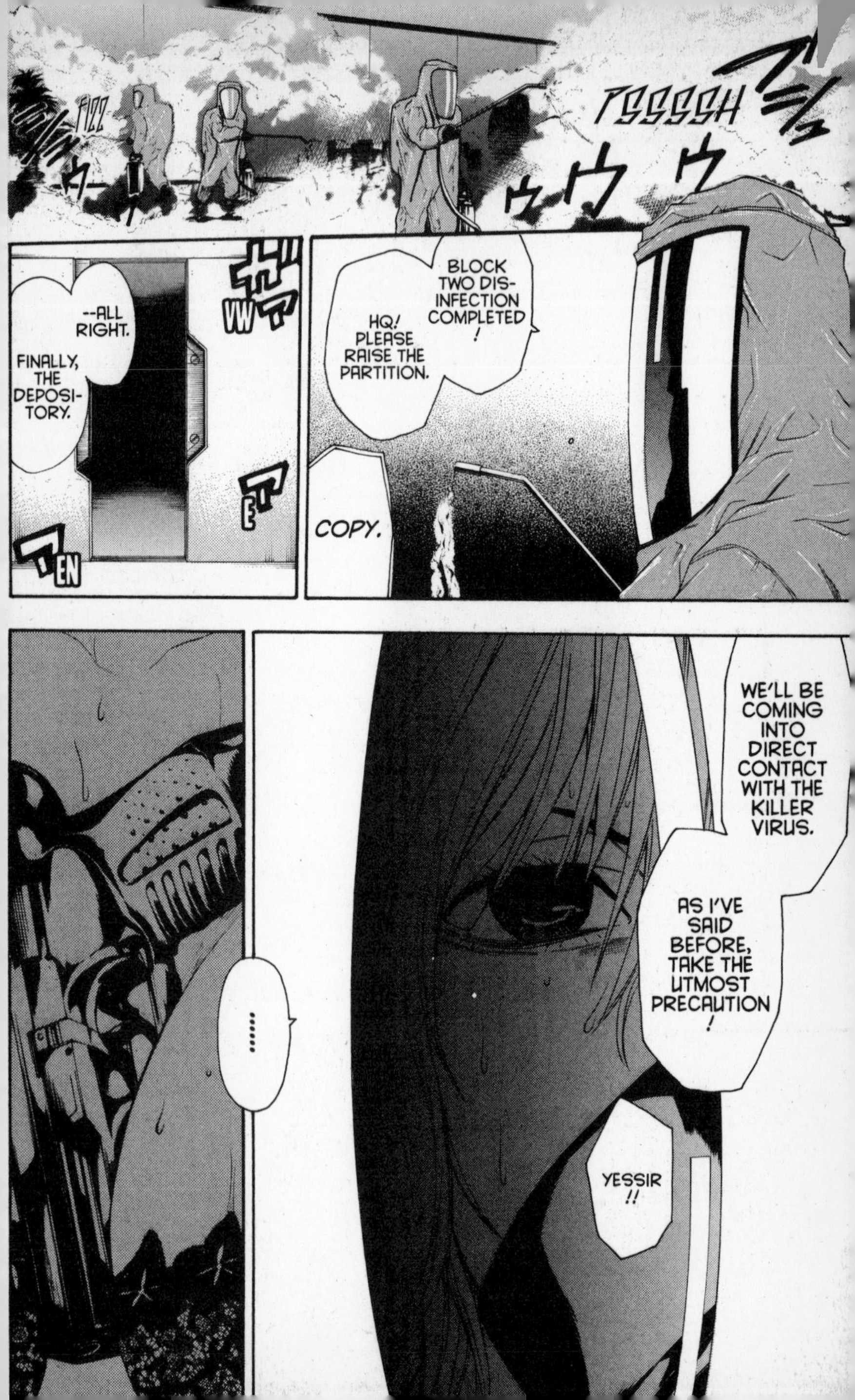
PSSSSH
FIZZ
BLOCK TWO DIS-INFECTION COMPLETED!
HQ! PLEASE RAISE THE PARTITION.
COPY.
VW
--ALL RIGHT.
FINALLY, THE DEPOSI-TORY.
EN
WE'LL BE COMING INTO DIRECT CONTACT WITH THE KILLER VIRUS.
AS I'VE SAID BEFORE, TAKE THE UTMOST PRECAUTION!
YESSIR!!
......

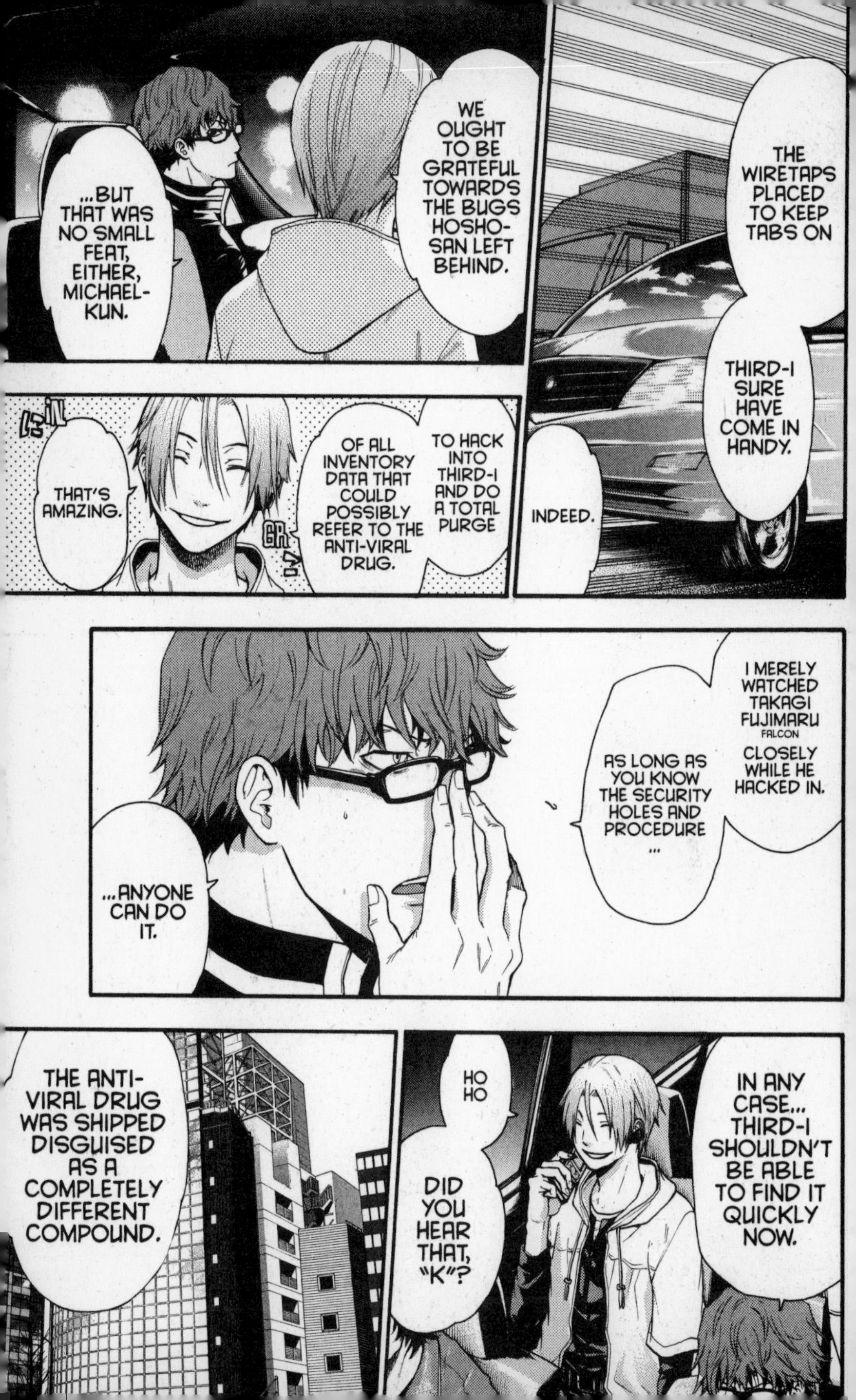
THE WIRETAPS PLACED TO KEEP TABS ON
THIRD-I SURE HAVE COME IN HANDY.
INDEED.
WE OUGHT TO BE GRATEFUL TOWARDS THE BUGS HOSHO-SAN LEFT BEHIND.
...BUT THAT WAS NO SMALL FEAT, EITHER, MICHAEL-KUN.
TO HACK INTO THIRD-I AND DO A TOTAL PURGE
OF ALL INVENTORY DATA THAT COULD POSSIBLY REFER TO THE ANTI-VIRAL DRUG.
THAT'S AMAZING.
I MERELY WATCHED TAKAGI FUJIMARU FALCON CLOSELY WHILE HE HACKED IN.
AS LONG AS YOU KNOW THE SECURITY HOLES AND PROCEDURE ...
...ANYONE CAN DO IT.
IN ANY CASE... THIRD-I SHOULDN'T BE ABLE TO FIND IT QUICKLY NOW.
HO HO
DID YOU HEAR THAT, "K"?
THE ANTI-VIRAL DRUG WAS SHIPPED DISGUISED AS A COMPLETELY DIFFERENT COMPOUND.

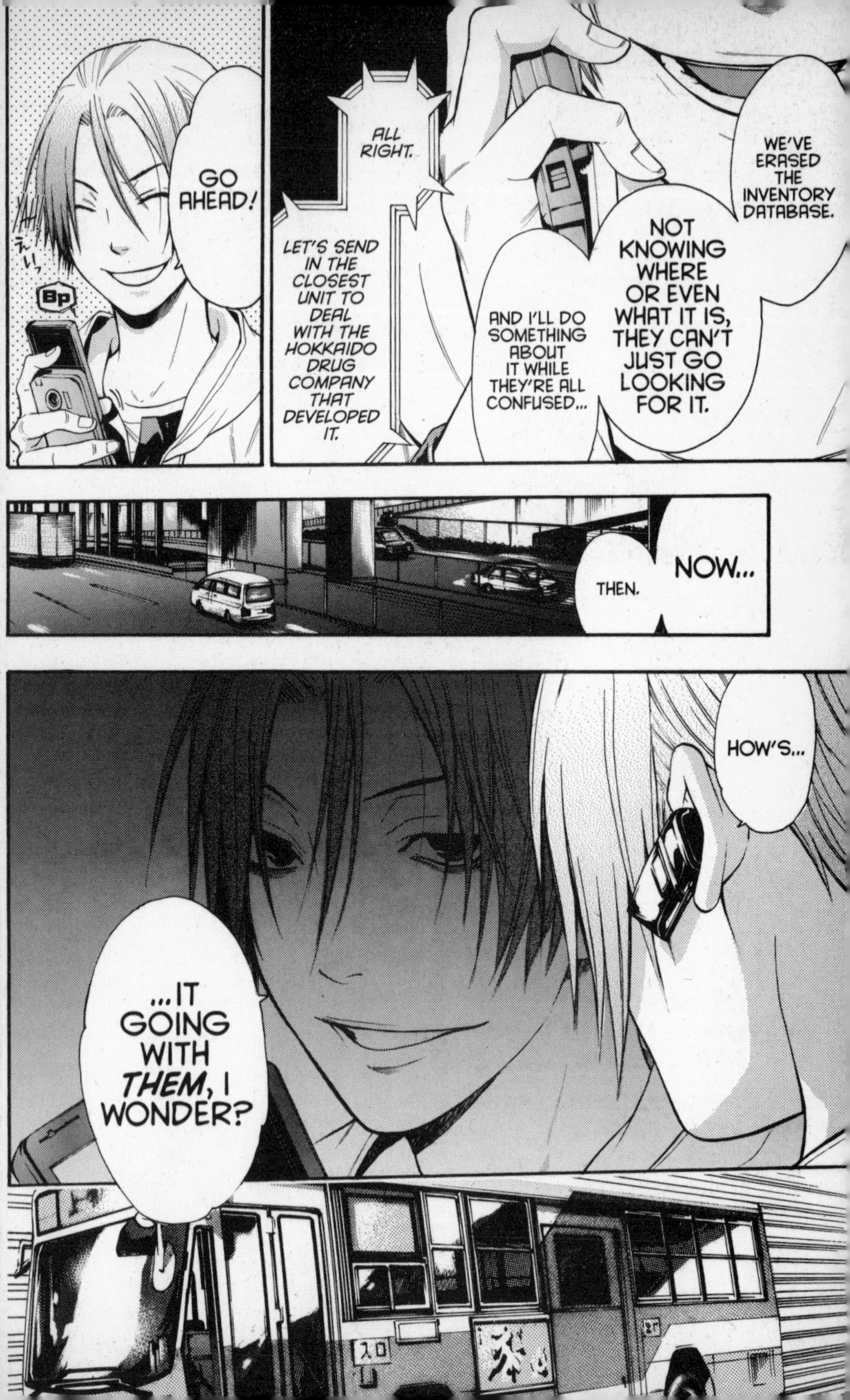
WE'VE ERASED THE INVENTORY DATABASE.
NOT KNOWING WHERE OR EVEN WHAT IT IS, THEY CAN'T JUST GO LOOKING FOR IT.
AND I'LL DO SOMETHING ABOUT IT WHILE THEY'RE ALL CONFUSED...
ALL RIGHT.
LET'S SEND IN THE CLOSEST UNIT TO DEAL WITH THE HOKKAIDO DRUG COMPANY THAT DEVELOPED IT.
GO AHEAD!
えいっ
Bp
NOW...
THEN.
HOW'S...
...IT GOING WITH *THEM*, I WONDER?

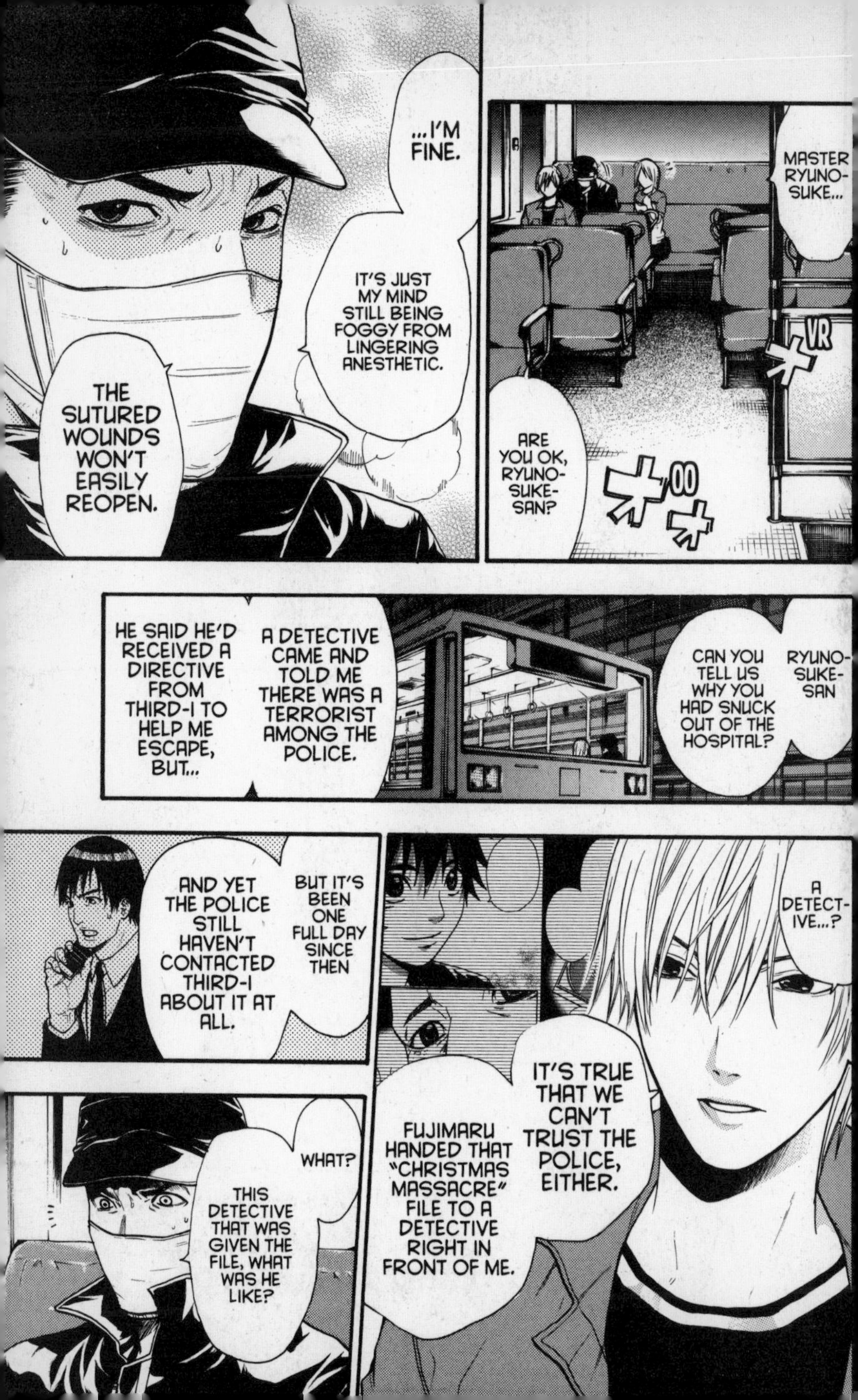

MASTER RYUNOSUKE...
VR
ARE YOU OK, RYUNOSUKE-SAN?
OO
...I'M FINE.
IT'S JUST MY MIND STILL BEING FOGGY FROM LINGERING ANESTHETIC.
THE SUTURED WOUNDS WON'T EASILY REOPEN.
RYUNOSUKE-SAN
CAN YOU TELL US WHY YOU HAD SNUCK OUT OF THE HOSPITAL?
A DETECTIVE CAME AND TOLD ME THERE WAS A TERRORIST AMONG THE POLICE.
HE SAID HE'D RECEIVED A DIRECTIVE FROM THIRD-I TO HELP ME ESCAPE, BUT...
A DETECTIVE...?
IT'S TRUE THAT WE CAN'T TRUST THE POLICE, EITHER.
FUJIMARU HANDED THAT "CHRISTMAS MASSACRE" FILE TO A DETECTIVE RIGHT IN FRONT OF ME.
BUT IT'S BEEN ONE FULL DAY SINCE THEN
AND YET THE POLICE STILL HAVEN'T CONTACTED THIRD-I ABOUT IT AT ALL.
WHAT?
THIS DETECTIVE THAT WAS GIVEN THE FILE, WHAT WAS HE LIKE?

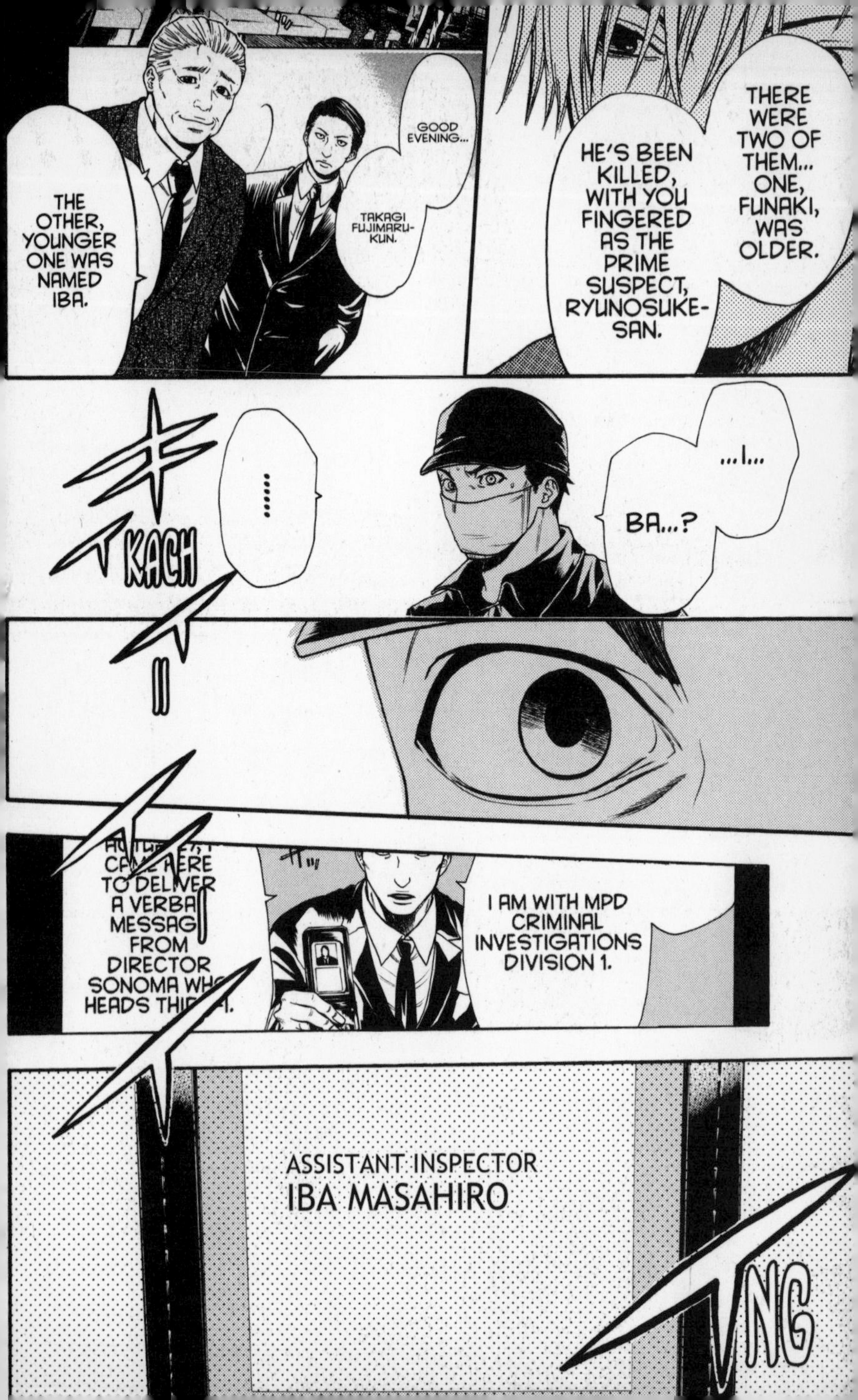
THERE WERE TWO OF THEM... ONE, FUNAKI, WAS OLDER.
HE'S BEEN KILLED, WITH YOU FINGERED AS THE PRIME SUSPECT, RYUNOSUKE-SAN.
GOOD EVENING...
TAKAGI FUJIMARU-KUN.
THE OTHER, YOUNGER ONE WAS NAMED IBA.
...I... BA...?
......
KACH
I AM WITH MPD CRIMINAL INVESTIGATIONS DIVISION 1.
TO DELIVER A VERBA MESSAG FROM DIRECTOR SONOMA WH HEADS THI
ASSISTANT INSPECTOR IBA MASAHIRO
NG

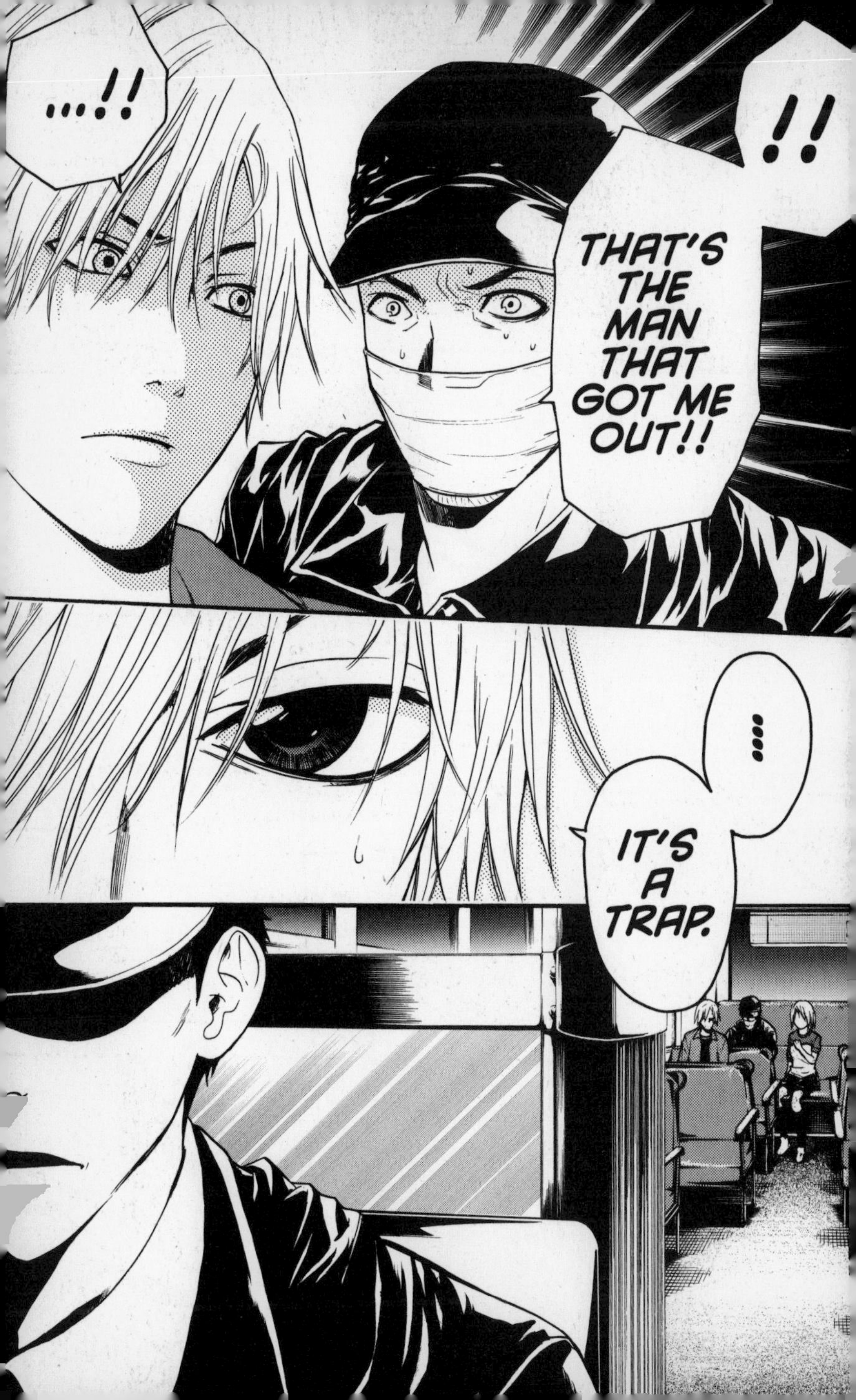
!!
THAT'S THE MAN THAT GOT ME OUT!!
...!!
....
IT'S A TRAP.

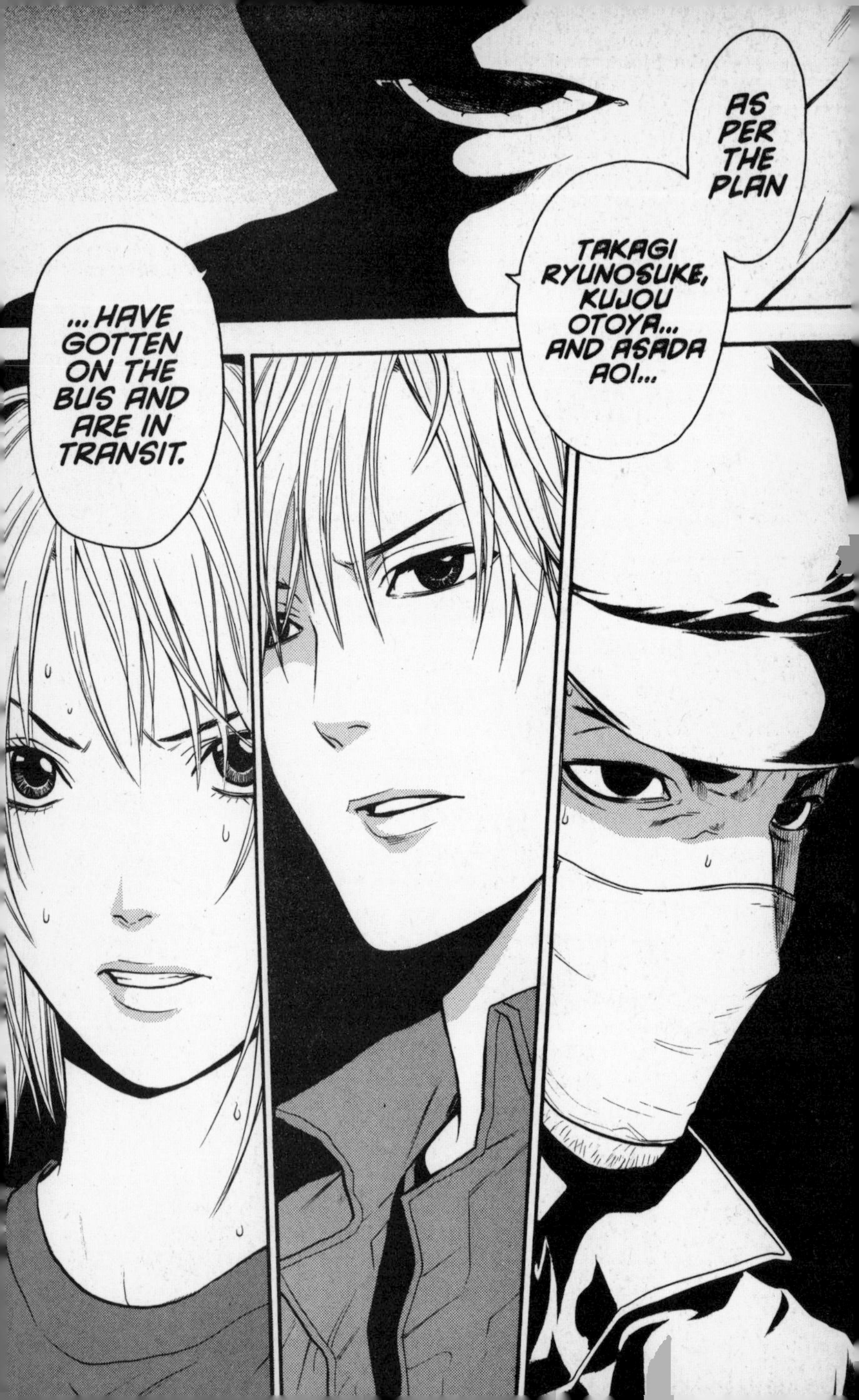
AS PER THE PLAN
TAKAGI RYUNOSUKE, KUJOU OTOYA... AND ASADA AOI...
...HAVE GOTTEN ON THE BUS AND ARE IN TRANSIT.

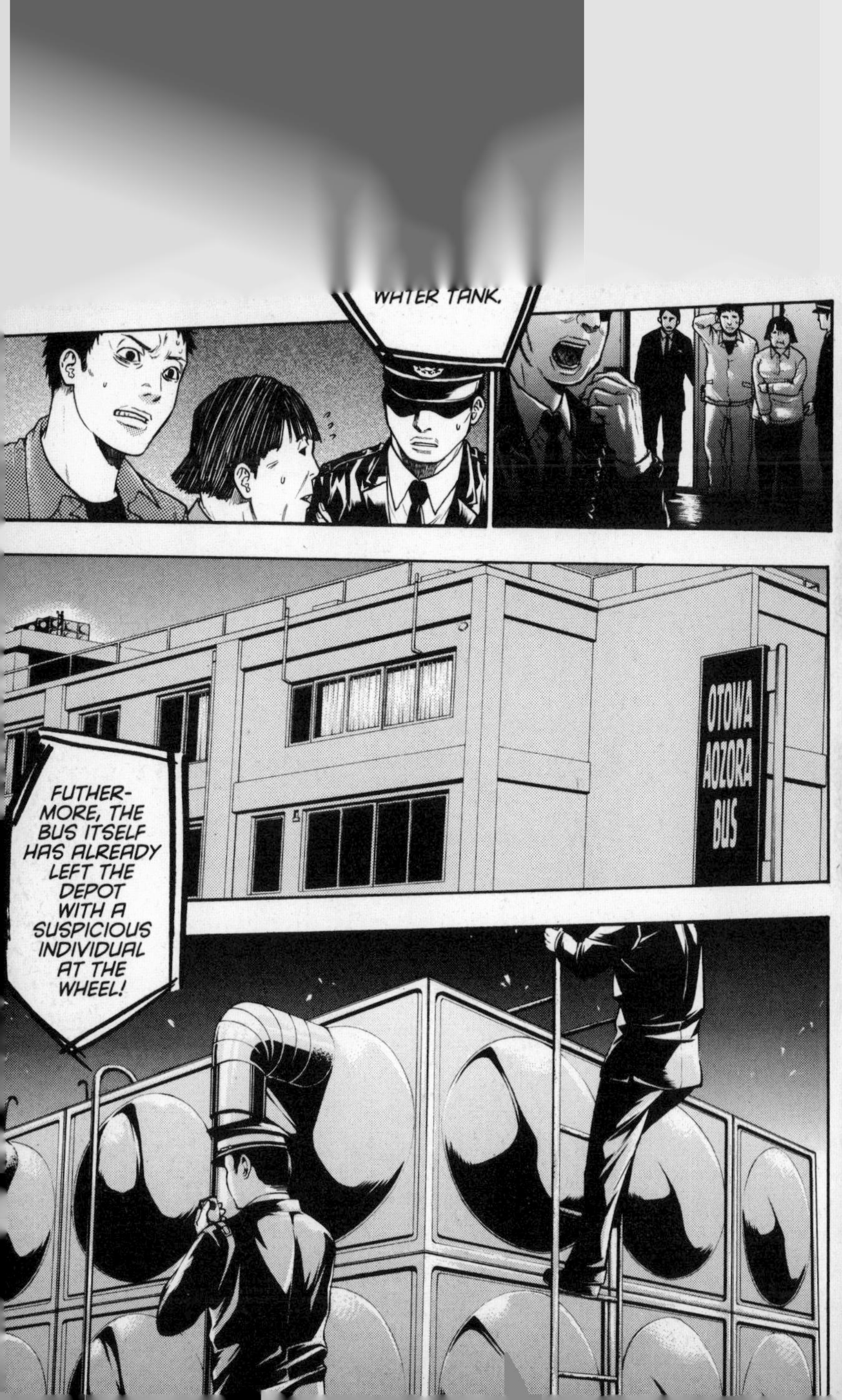
WATER TANK.
OTOWA AOZORA BUS
FUTHER-MORE, THE BUS ITSELF HAS ALREADY LEFT THE DEPOT WITH A SUSPICIOUS INDIVIDUAL AT THE WHEEL!

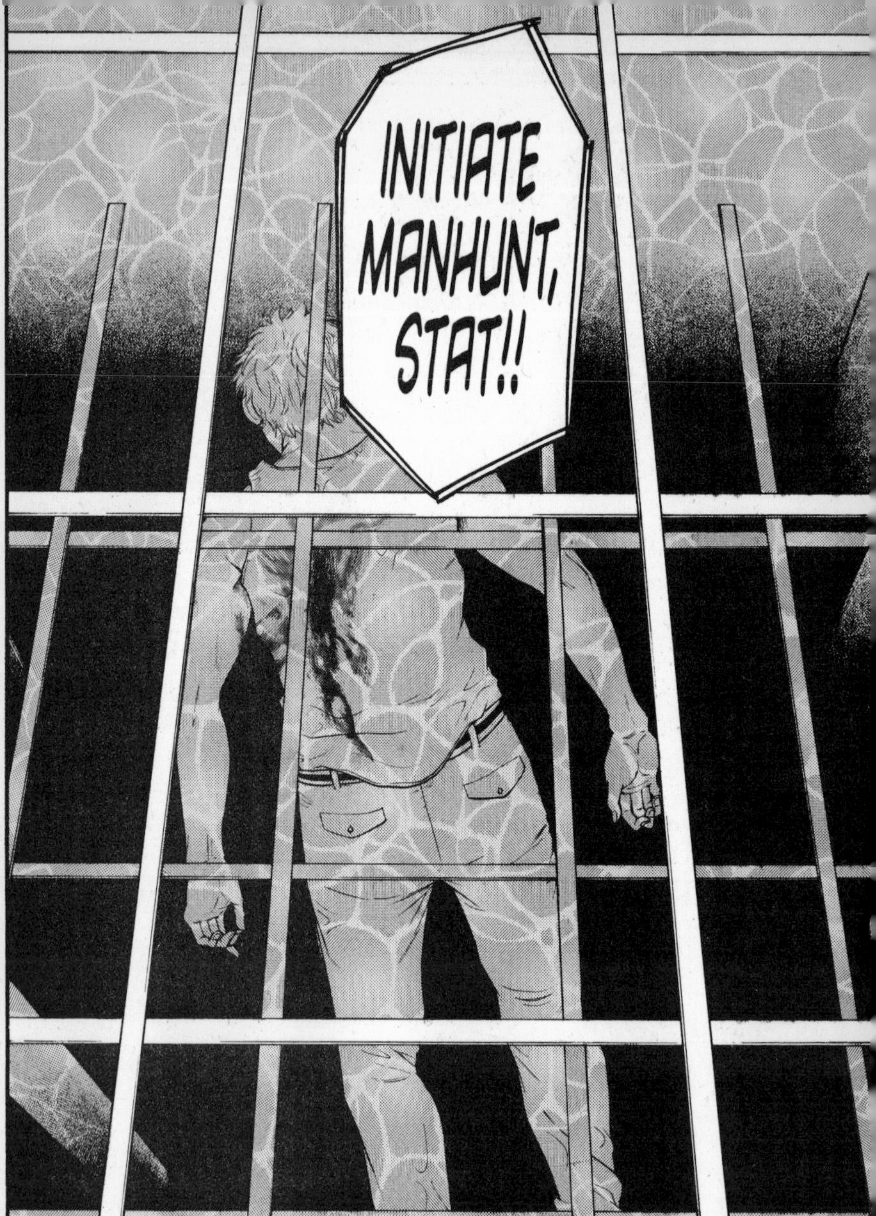
INITIATE MANHUNT, STAT!!

- **Many thanks**
  Daiwa Mitsu   Kawabata Kunihiro   Chûgun Kazushi
        Takada Hiroshi   Ôzaka Machiko

- **Editors**
  Sugawara-san   Sato-san   Kawakubo-san

- **Manga**
  Ryumon Ryou X Megumi Kouji

- **THANK YOU FOR READING!** •

TRANSLATION NOTES

Japanese is a tricky language for most Westerners, and translation is often more art than science. For your edification and reading pleasure, here are notes on some of the places where we could have gone in a different direction with our translation of the work, or where a Japanese cultural reference is used.

Land of the dead, chapter 49 title, page 151
The original term used by the author, "yomi", is the Japanese underworld that appears in Shinto mythology. It is somewhat comparable to the Greek Hades and is also sometimes likened to the Christian concept of hell, but it technically is neither a particularly sinister or beatific place, which is why I chose to use "land of the dead" in the chapter title.

MPD, page 5
MPD is short for Metropolitan Police Department, the police force that serves the entire city of Tokyo and is the largest municipal law enforcement agency in the world.

Michael, page 58
While the author has indicated the Romanized spelling "Michael" for this character, the katakana used spell out "Mi-ha-e-ru", indicating a pronunciation that renders the "c" silent.

Rear-loading bus, page 92
Many local buses in Japan are configured such that passengers board at the rear of the bus, taking a ticket, swiping a transit card, or tapping a RFIT chip, and then pay a distance-dependent fare as they exit the bus from the front, passing the driver on their way out.

"Falcon", page 95

Fujimaru's alter ego and hacker name. A phonetic pun, derived from the first part of his last name "Takagi"... it is only phonetic because his name uses a different kanji than that of the "taka" that means "hawk" or "falcon".

Cell phone e-mail, page 116

Cell phone e-mail is different from, and used much more frequently than, text messaging in Japan. As opposed to text messages, which are sent from a mobile number, every Japanese cell phone subscriber is assigned a unique e-mail address (where the subscriber chooses their own handle). However, it is also different from smart phone and other mobile e-mail in that one does not need to log in to a mail server, but can automatically receive and open messages on one's phone more similar to how text messages work.

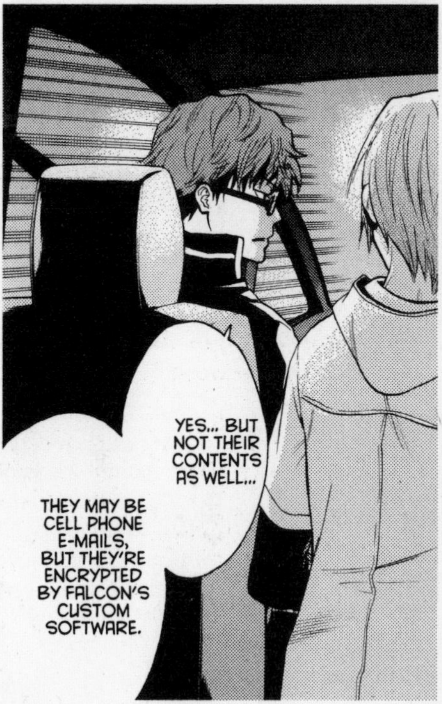
YES... BUT NOT THEIR CONTENTS AS WELL...
THEY MAY BE CELL PHONE E-MAILS, BUT THEY'RE ENCRYPTED BY FALCON'S CUSTOM SOFTWARE.

SDF (Japan Self-Defense Forces), page 174

The unified military forces of Japan established after the end of World War II and the post-war Allied Occupation. Following the ban of (offensive) rearmament as written into the post-war Japanese constitution, these military forces were originally restricted to defensive actions domestically only, although this has been relaxed in recent times to permit deployment abroad for peace-keeping and humanitarian operations.

Preview of

BLOODY MONDAY

VOLUME 7

We're pleased to present you a preview
from *Bloody Monday*, volume 7.
Please check our website
(www.kodanshacomics.com)
to see when this volume will be
available in English.

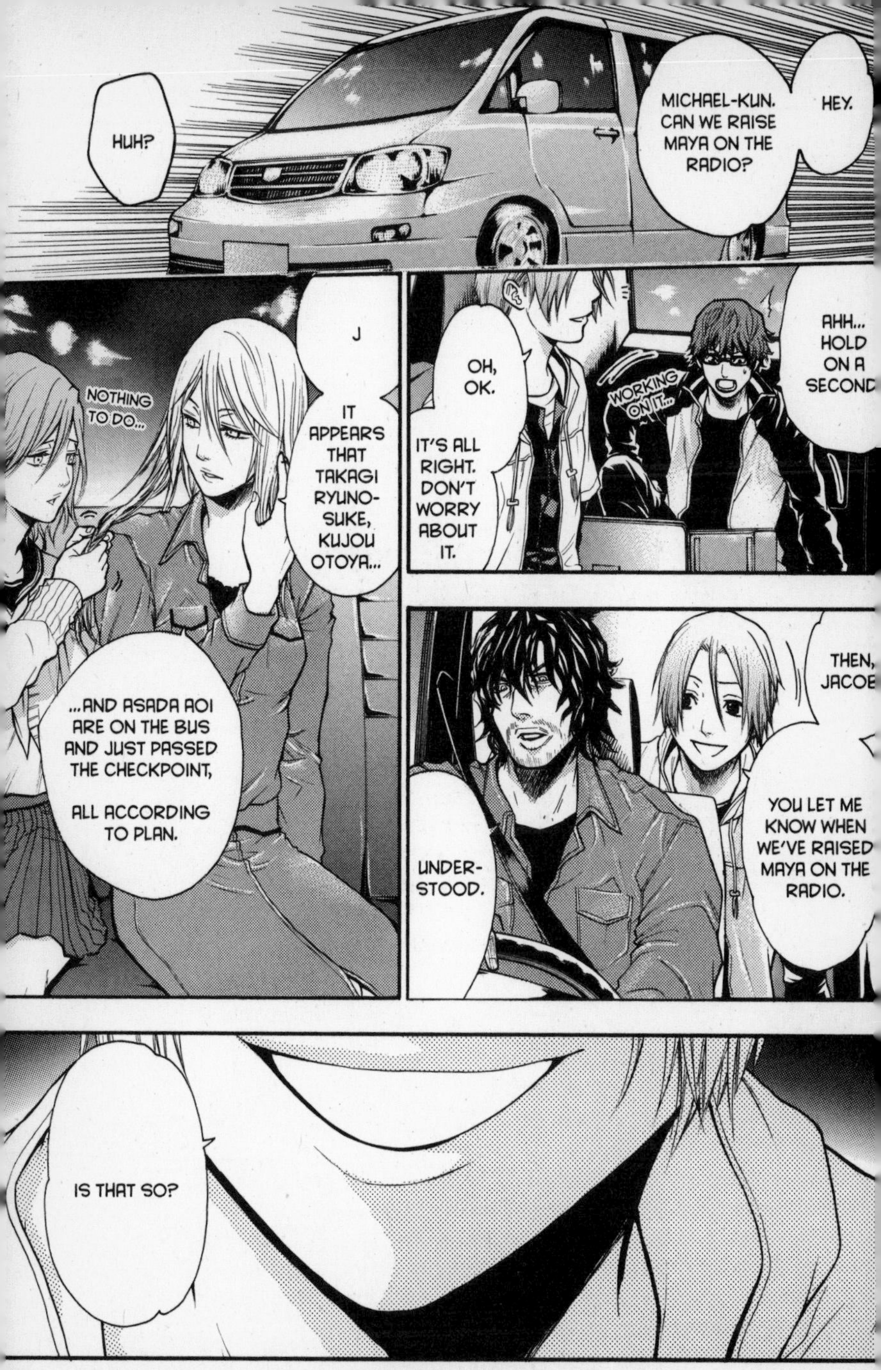
HEY.
MICHAEL-KUN. CAN WE RAISE MAYA ON THE RADIO?
HUH?
AHH... HOLD ON A SECOND
WORKING ON IT...
OH, OK.
IT'S ALL RIGHT. DON'T WORRY ABOUT IT.
THEN, JACOB
YOU LET ME KNOW WHEN WE'VE RAISED MAYA ON THE RADIO.
UNDER-STOOD.
J
IT APPEARS THAT TAKAGI RYUNO-SUKE, KUJOU OTOYA...
NOTHING TO DO...
...AND ASADA AOI ARE ON THE BUS AND JUST PASSED THE CHECKPOINT,
ALL ACCORDING TO PLAN.
IS THAT SO?

File 51 What we've been fighting to get.

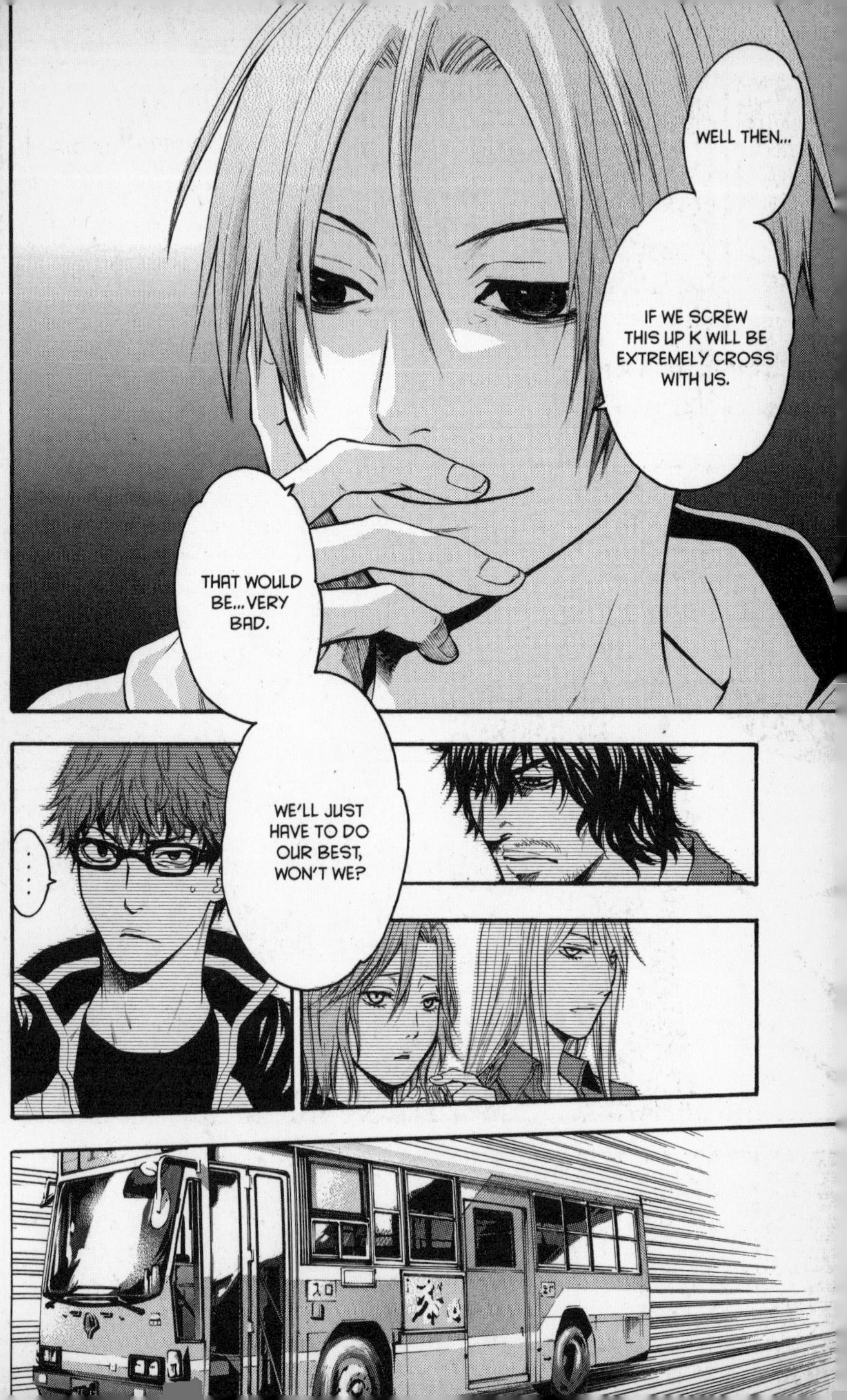
WELL THEN...
IF WE SCREW THIS UP K WILL BE EXTREMELY CROSS WITH US.
THAT WOULD BE...VERY BAD.
WE'LL JUST HAVE TO DO OUR BEST, WON'T WE?
....

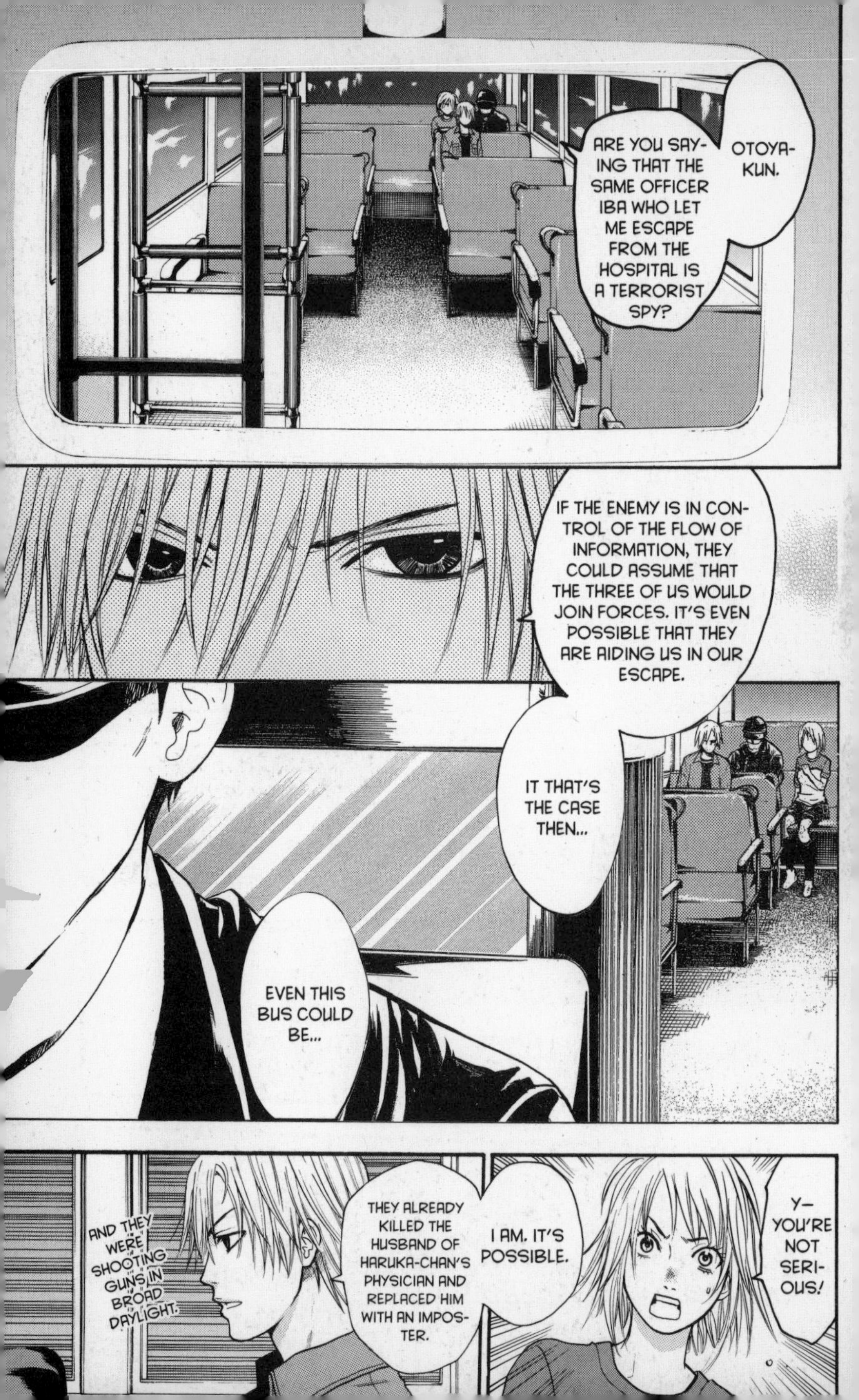
OTOYA-KUN.
ARE YOU SAY-ING THAT THE SAME OFFICER IBA WHO LET ME ESCAPE FROM THE HOSPITAL IS A TERRORIST SPY?
IF THE ENEMY IS IN CON-TROL OF THE FLOW OF INFORMATION, THEY COULD ASSUME THAT THE THREE OF US WOULD JOIN FORCES. IT'S EVEN POSSIBLE THAT THEY ARE AIDING US IN OUR ESCAPE.
IT THAT'S THE CASE THEN...
EVEN THIS BUS COULD BE...
Y— YOU'RE NOT SERI-OUS!
I AM. IT'S POSSIBLE.
THEY ALREADY KILLED THE HUSBAND OF HARUKA-CHAN'S PHYSICIAN AND REPLACED HIM WITH AN IMPOS-TER.
AND THEY WERE SHOOTING GUNS IN BROAD DAYLIGHT.

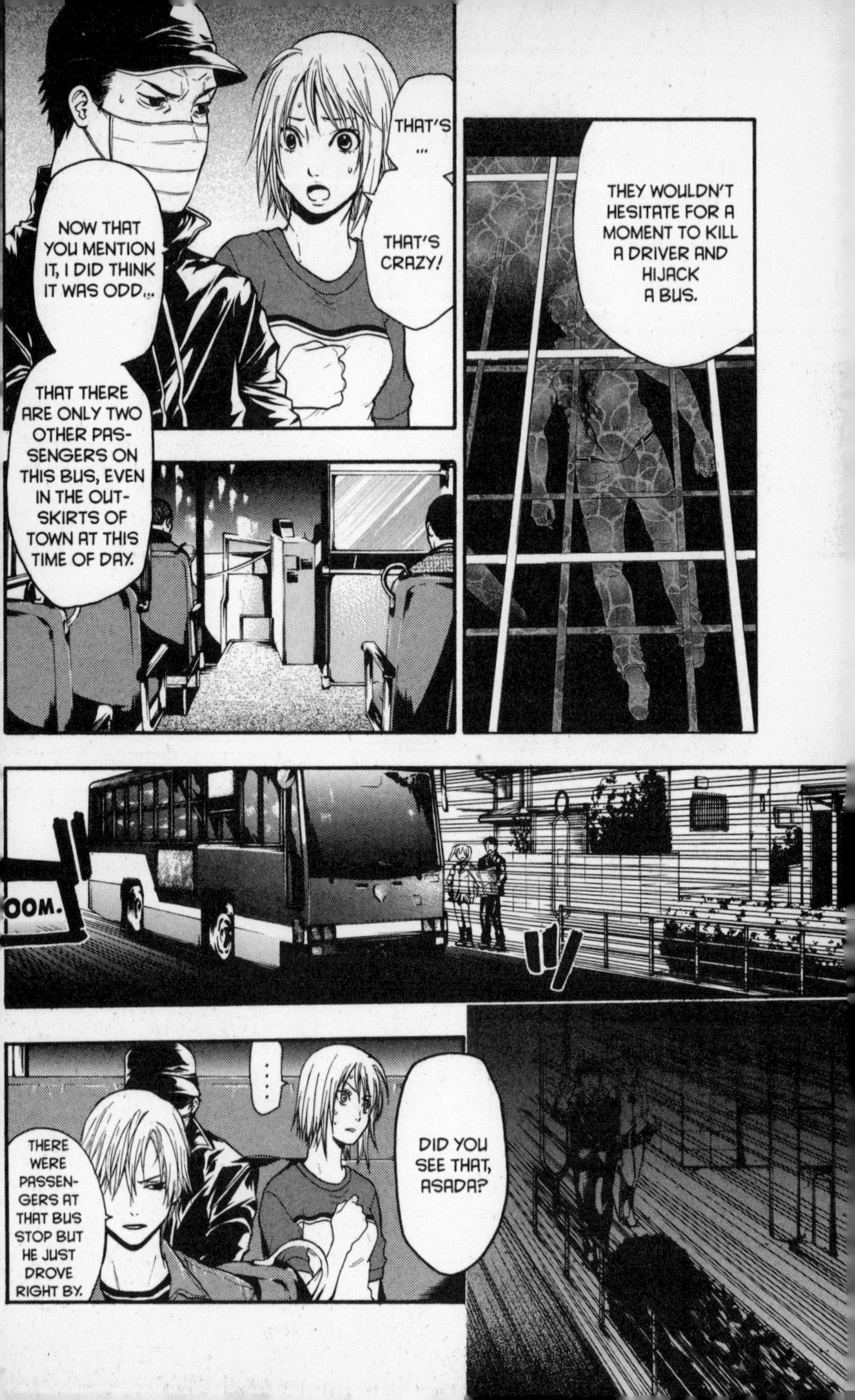
THEY WOULDN'T HESITATE FOR A MOMENT TO KILL A DRIVER AND HIJACK A BUS.
THAT'S ...
THAT'S CRAZY!
NOW THAT YOU MENTION IT, I DID THINK IT WAS ODD...
THAT THERE ARE ONLY TWO OTHER PAS-SENGERS ON THIS BUS, EVEN IN THE OUT-SKIRTS OF TOWN AT THIS TIME OF DAY.
OOM.
DID YOU SEE THAT, ASADA?
....
THERE WERE PASSEN-GERS AT THAT BUS STOP BUT HE JUST DROVE RIGHT BY.

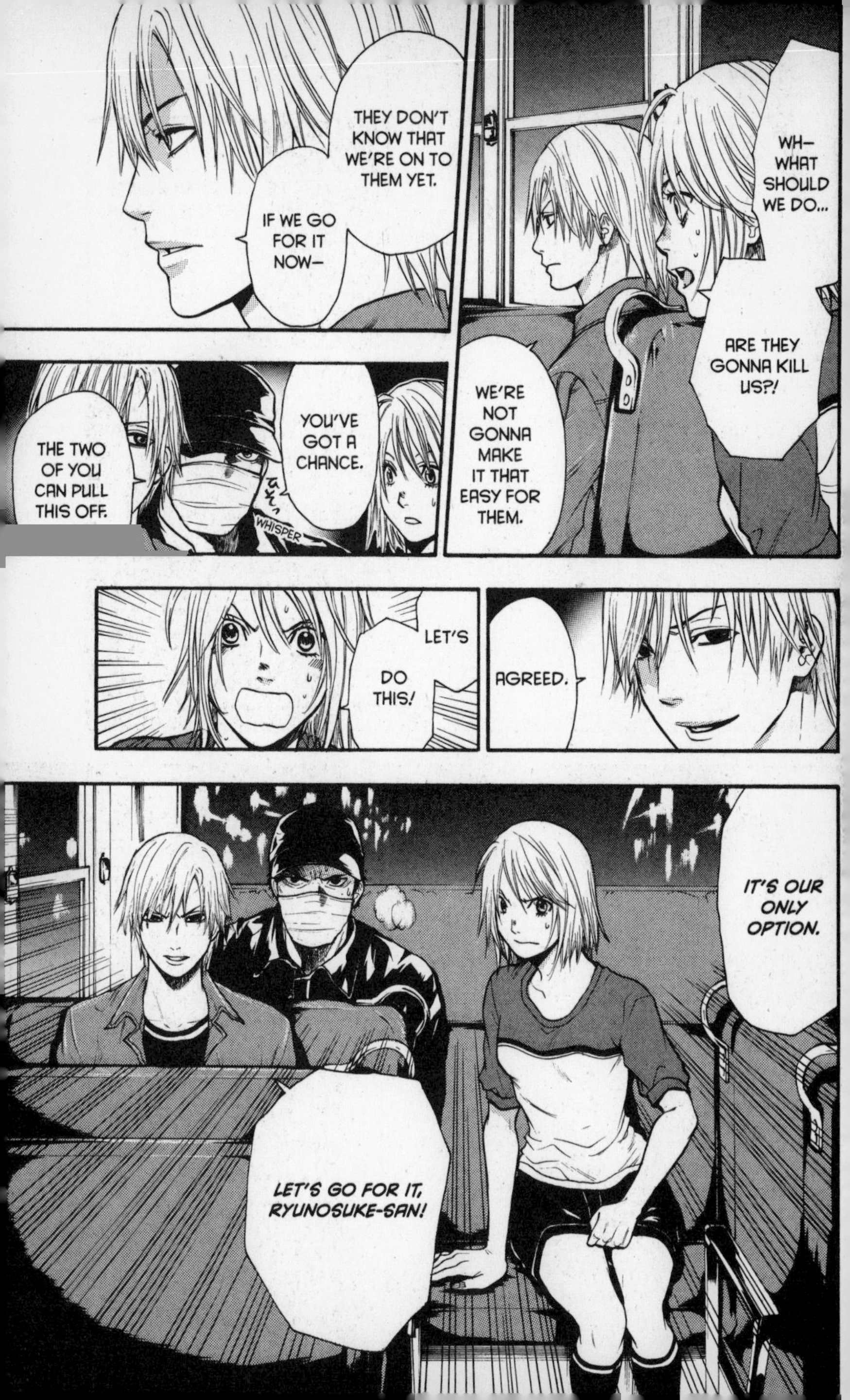
WH— WHAT SHOULD WE DO...
ARE THEY GONNA KILL US?!
WE'RE NOT GONNA MAKE IT THAT EASY FOR THEM.
THEY DON'T KNOW THAT WE'RE ON TO THEM YET.
IF WE GO FOR IT NOW—
YOU'VE GOT A CHANCE.
THE TWO OF YOU CAN PULL THIS OFF.
WHISPER
AGREED.
LET'S DO THIS!
IT'S OUR ONLY OPTION.
LET'S GO FOR IT, RYUNOSUKE-SAN!

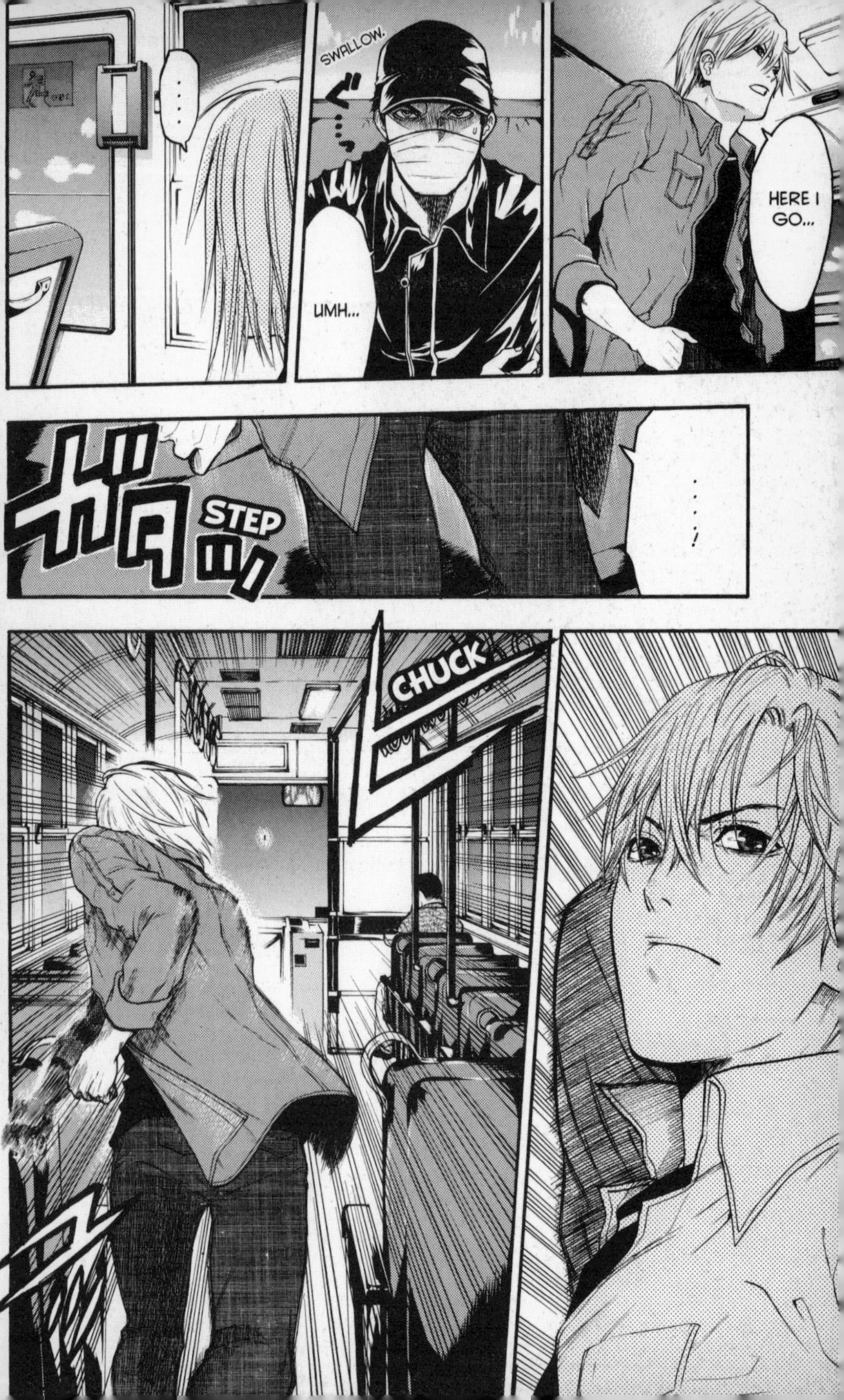
HERE I GO...
SWALLOW.
UMH...
...
...!
STEP
CHUCK

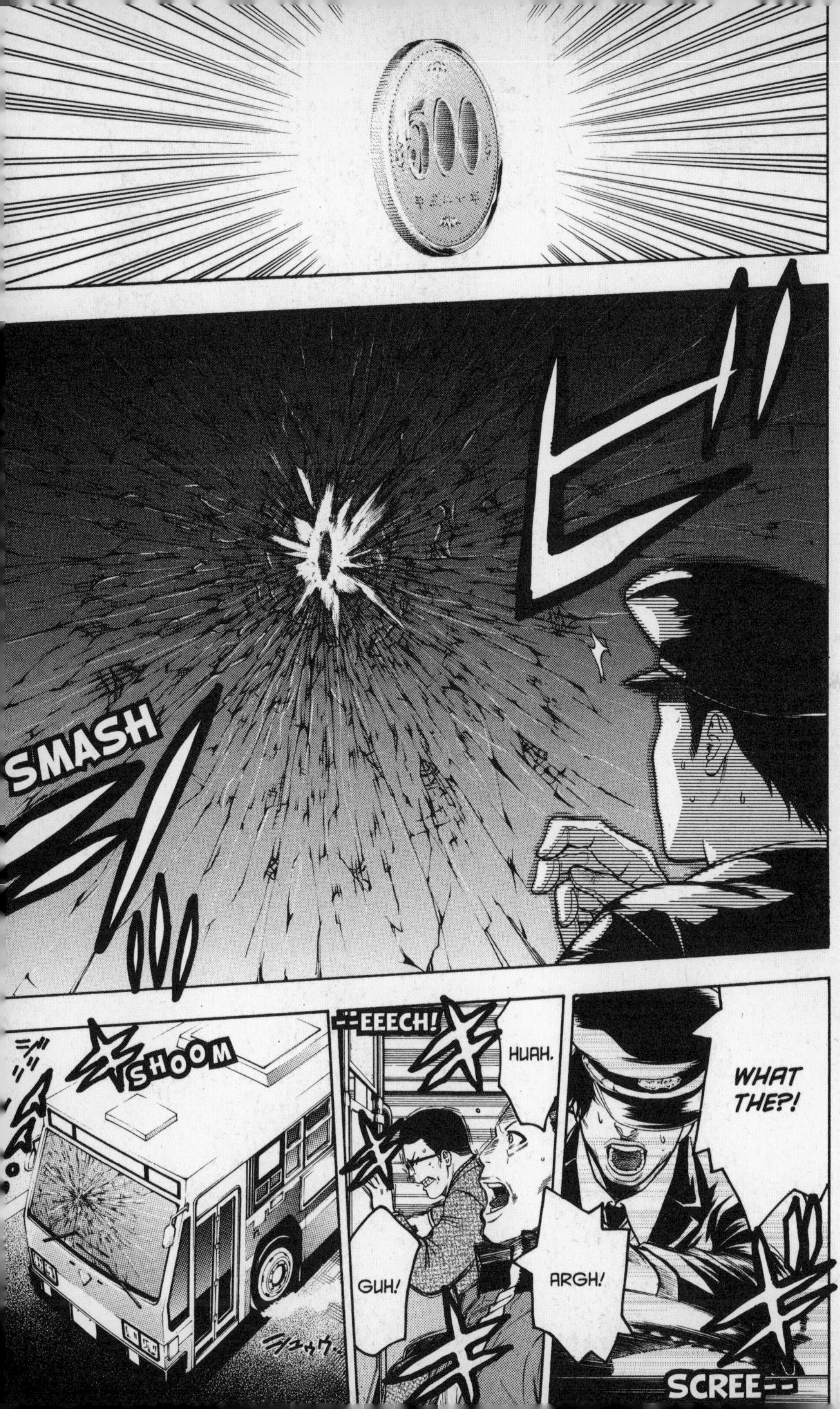
500
SMASH
WHAT THE?!
SCREE--
--EEECH!
HUAH.
ARGH!
GUH!
SHOOM

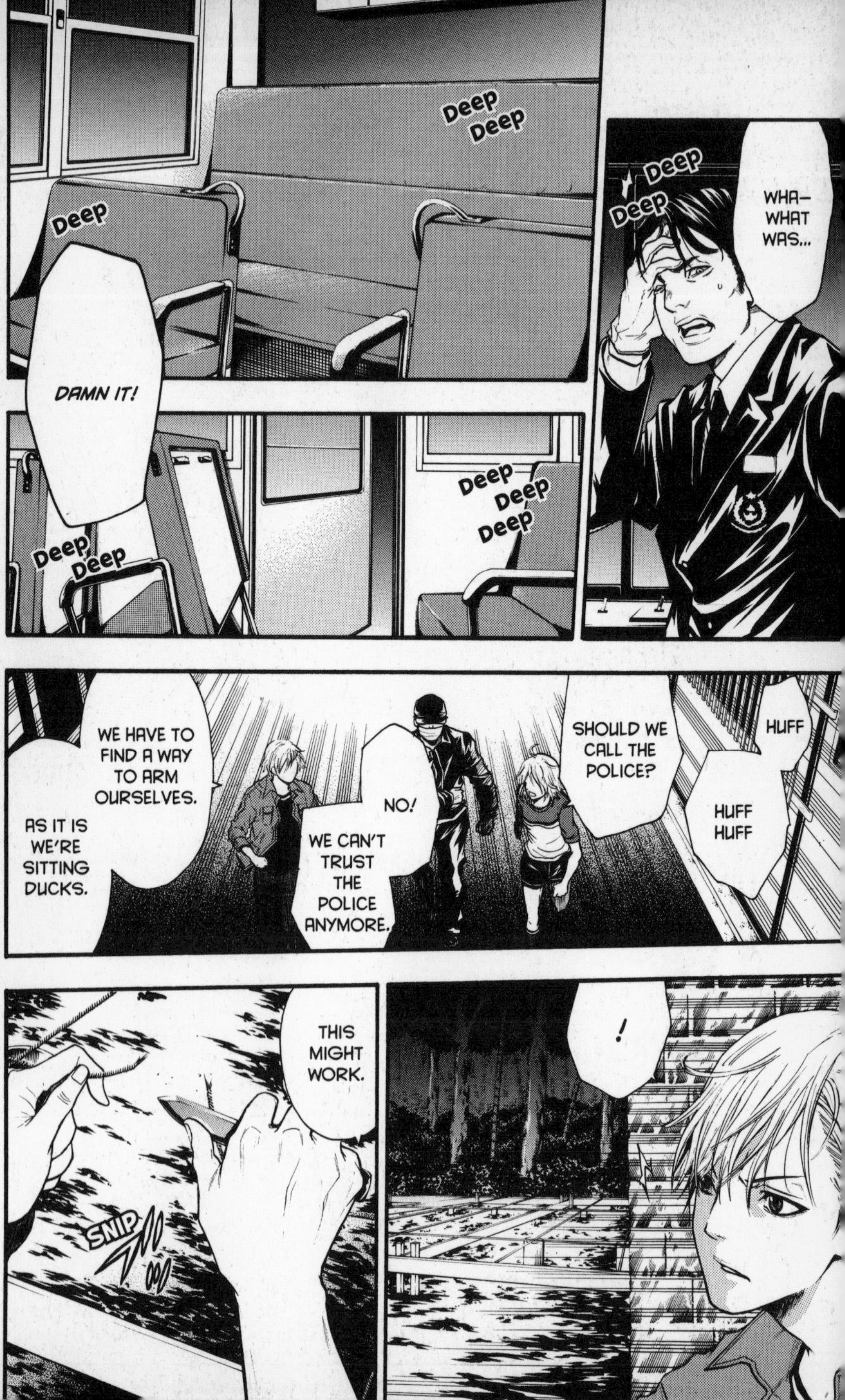
Deep
Deep
WHA— WHAT WAS...
Deep
Deep
Deep
DAMN IT!
Deep
Deep
Deep
Deep
Deep
HUFF
SHOULD WE CALL THE POLICE?
HUFF HUFF
NO!
WE CAN'T TRUST THE POLICE ANYMORE.
WE HAVE TO FIND A WAY TO ARM OURSELVES.
AS IT IS WE'RE SITTING DUCKS.
!
THIS MIGHT WORK.
SNIP

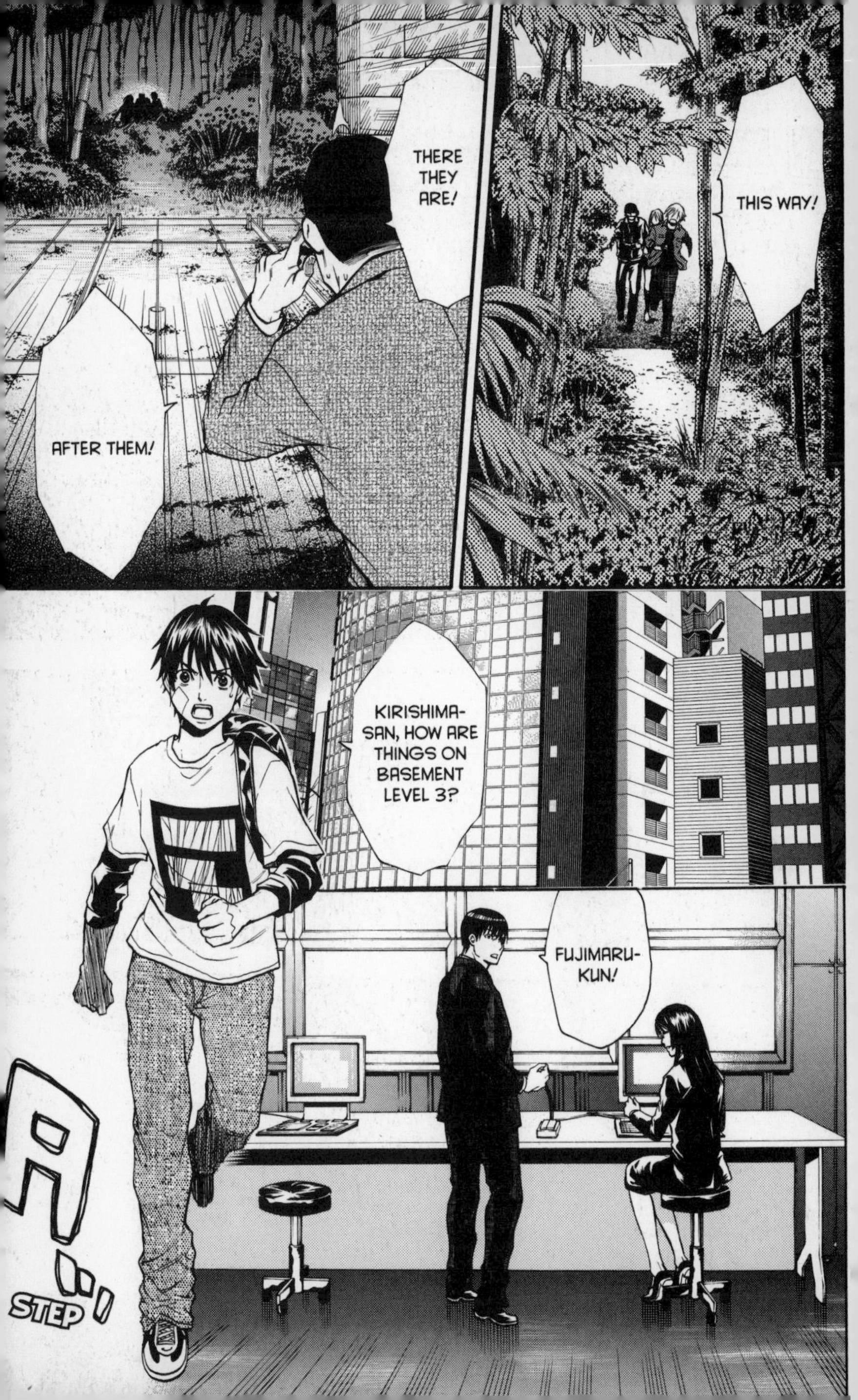
THIS WAY!
THERE THEY ARE!
AFTER THEM!
KIRISHIMA-SAN, HOW ARE THINGS ON BASEMENT LEVEL 3?
FUJIMARU-KUN!
STEP

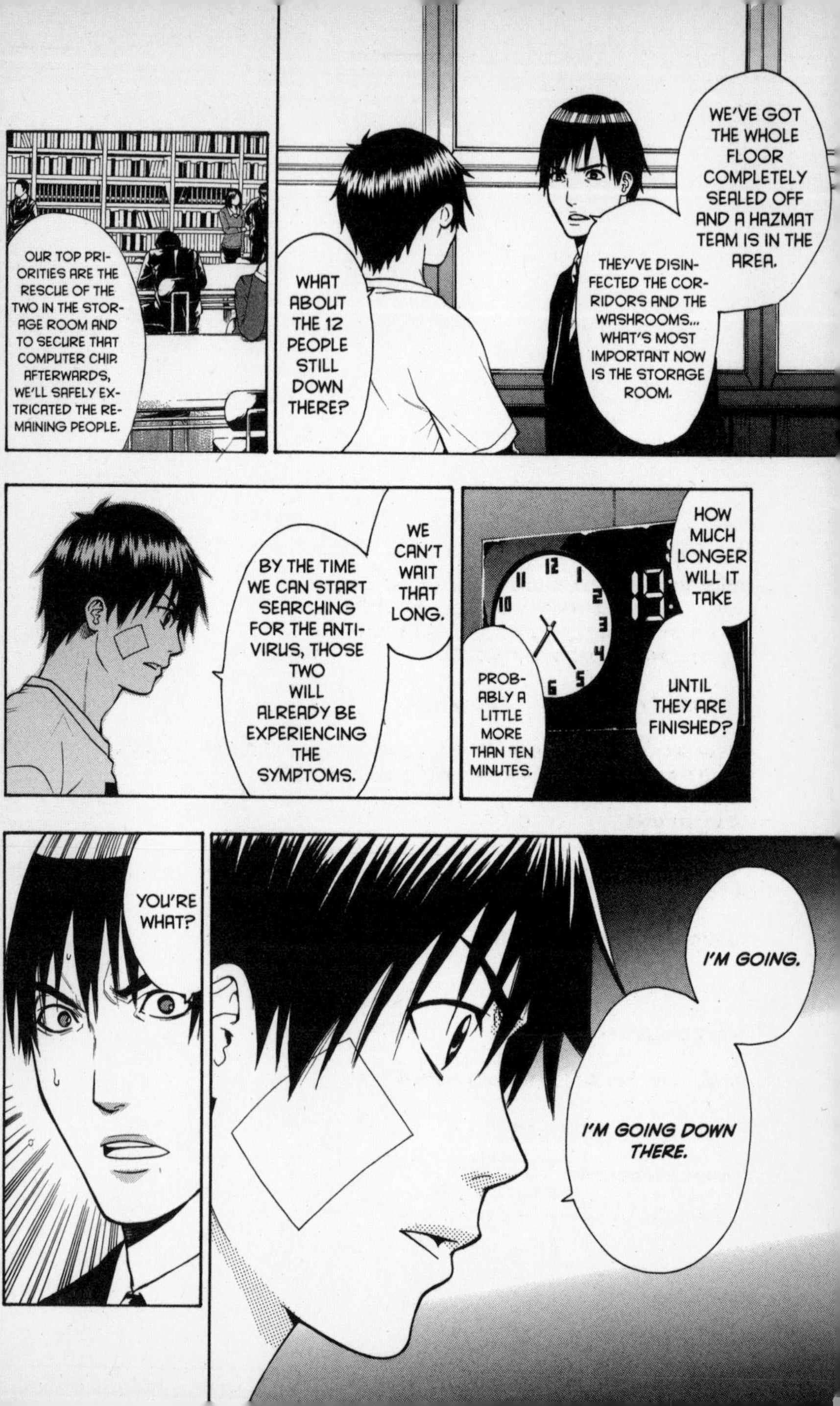
WE'VE GOT THE WHOLE FLOOR COMPLETELY SEALED OFF AND A HAZMAT TEAM IS IN THE AREA.
THEY'VE DISINFECTED THE CORRIDORS AND THE WASHROOMS... WHAT'S MOST IMPORTANT NOW IS THE STORAGE ROOM.
WHAT ABOUT THE 12 PEOPLE STILL DOWN THERE?
OUR TOP PRIORITIES ARE THE RESCUE OF THE TWO IN THE STORAGE ROOM AND TO SECURE THAT COMPUTER CHIP. AFTERWARDS, WE'LL SAFELY EXTRICATED THE REMAINING PEOPLE.
HOW MUCH LONGER WILL IT TAKE
UNTIL THEY ARE FINISHED?
PROBABLY A LITTLE MORE THAN TEN MINUTES.
WE CAN'T WAIT THAT LONG.
BY THE TIME WE CAN START SEARCHING FOR THE ANTIVIRUS, THOSE TWO WILL ALREADY BE EXPERIENCING THE SYMPTOMS.
I'M GOING.
I'M GOING DOWN THERE.
YOU'RE WHAT?

A Kodansha Comics Trade Paperback Original

Bloody Monday volume 6 copyright © 2008 Ryou Ryumon and Kouji Megumi
English translation copyright © 2012 Ryou Ryumon and Kouji Megumi

All rights reserved.

Published in the United States by Kodansha Comics,
an imprint of Kodansha USA Publishing, LLC, New York.

Publication rights for this English edition arranged through Kodansha Ltd, Tokyo.

First published in Japan in 2008 by Kodansha Ltd., Tokyo.

ISBN 978-1-61262-042-8

Original cover design by Takashi Shimoyama (Red Rooster)

Printed in the United States of America.

www.kodanshacomics.com

9 8 7 6 5 4 3 2 1

Translator: Mari Morimoto
Lettering: Karl Felton

TOMARE!

[STOP!]

You are going the wrong way!

Manga is a completely different type of reading experience.

To start at the *beginning*, go to the *end*!

That's right! Authentic manga is read the traditional Japanese way—from right to left, exactly the opposite of how American books are read. It's easy to follow: Just go to the other end of the book, and read each page—and each panel—from the right side to the left side, starting at the top right. Now you're experiencing manga as it was meant to be.